nev

J

M/

The Unspiked Rail

Books in the Lancehead Series

THE LANCEHEAD SERIES

NEVADA AND THE WEST

The Unspiked Rail

MEMOIR OF A NEVADA REBEL

by

**SALLY
SPRINGMEYER
ZANJANI**

UNIVERSITY OF
NEVADA PRESS
RENO, NEVADA
1981

University of Nevada Press, Reno, Nevada 89557 USA
Printed in the United States of America
Designed by William Snyder

Library of Congress Cataloging in Publication Data

Zanjani, Sally Springmeyer, 1937–
  The unspiked rail

  (Lancehead series: Nevada and the West)
  Bibliography: p.
  Includes index.
  1. Springmeyer, George, 1881–1966. 2. Nevada—
Politics and government. 3. Politicians—Nevada—
Biography. 4. Lawyers—Nevada—Biography. 5. Nevada—
Biography. I. Title.
F841.S67Z36   979.3′03′0924 [B]   80-39920
ISBN 0-87417-064-8

FOR MY FATHER AND MOTHER

Contents

Preface

MY FATHER WAS NOT given to looking back. When he had a stroke and, at seventy-nine, stopped going to the office for the first time in his life and began sitting still, I realized with a sudden shock that my father, who had always been so strong and vigorous, who had never seemed old, would not always be there, and I wrote down some of his stories as he told them to me sitting under the apple trees in his orchard or, after the days turned colder, on the sofa in front of the fire. But he told them only because I had asked. The present was where he lived, even when there was nothing in it but old age and illness and approaching death. The day he was in was the only place he ever wanted to be.

Even then I did not recognize those stories for the pioneer epic they were, nor did I see him as anything more than my father, and fathers were naturally presumed to be more or less a common breed. I still had not grown very far beyond the child who simply accepted him, living in the warmth of his affection, laughing at his funny stories, riding with him at our ranch, arguing politics over the dinner table, when he was just my father, significant only in his relationship to my own self-centered personage. I had to go away to a world filled with other people, unknot the tangled threads of my own life, then pause and look back, before I realized, many years later, that all the world was not the Springmeyers, and that their particular corner of it would have been a very different place without them.

Independent to a fault, incorruptible men in times of corruption, they risked the offices and honors of the political world in which they sought a place rather than gain all at the price demanded of them. If my father lost most of his political battles, if the Southern Pacific machine proved in the end too powerful to vanquish, still he made railroad domination the overriding issue of Nevada politics. He prodded and drove the hidebound state Republican party, which had remained frozen in the conservative posture assumed in decades past, to the forefront of reform, and did it almost singlehandedly, with none of the advantages conferred by powerful position, money, or influential friends. He whirled across Nevada politics like a human cyclone the way the newspaper cartoonists sketched him, and afterward the landscape was never quite the same. He was no ideologue, no man with a mission consciously setting forth to cleanse the political stables, but his refusals to compromise his ideals to serve the hour ended in making him something more than an officer of the law. He became Nevada's foremost reformer from the Progressive era through the Roaring Twenties, and may have been the strongest voice of reform she ever had.

As United States attorney in the Prohibition years, locked in battle with the united forces of crime and corrupted politicians and threatened with the loss of his position and even his life, he created a brief and shining Camelot of justice and honest legal administration. Time and again, in every public position he held, he made equality before the law a living reality to the weak and the oppressed—miners, railroad workers, Indians, Japanese who had no other champion. He made a difference. But I had much to learn before that era of Nevada history took shape before my eyes and I finally understood his place in it. Only after the sea of time had swept away my childhood land-

scape and nearly everyone in it did I know there was a tale to
tell and I alone, like Ishmael, was left alive to tell it. It was more
than the tale of an idealist fighting the good fight down to the
last bullet. It was the story of a Nevada life that couldn't have
happened just that way in any other place and of a Nevadan
who was as clearly a man of his time as the mountain man and
the Comstock king and left no lesser claim on remembrance.
Too late, long after my father's death, I went home, and at last
I really saw him.

His courage was one of the things I saw. It was visible in the
broad outlines of his life, the political campaigns fought alone
against the powerful Southern Pacific, the showdown on the
street with the ex-convict who had sworn to murder him. No
mental process of weighing or balancing or calculating was
involved. It was simply a natural part of the man.

Once when my father was United States attorney, he was
working in his office late at night. A woman telephoned. She
was connected to a bootlegging ring, she said, but she admired
him. That was why she wanted to warn him that if he walked
home that night along the dark road without police protection,
they would "pick him off." My father glanced at his watch and
said, "Well, I'll be going home at 12:30 tonight alone, and I'll
be ready for anyone." And I don't think he hesitated a minute.

He was also a man of rare honesty. If he told you something,
you knew it was true, and that was that, no deception, no
evasion, no half-truths, just pure, unadulterated reality. During
the 1910 Republican primary, he made an erroneous charge
against an opponent. Within days, he corrected it without ex-
cuses, evasions, or image-saving devices. Later on in the same
campaign, a critical moment arrived when it seemed that a few
smooth words about forthcoming cooperation with the Republican organization would guarantee my father's political future,
but it never occurred to him to say them. To cooperate would
have meant betraying his principles; to promise cooperation

and then renege after the election would have meant breaking his word. He would have been incapable of doing either.

If he was a good man, and those who knew him never doubted it, he was not the self-righteous kind. Like Mark Twain, whose stories his own often resembled, he laughed at the rogues around him and bore them no malice or ill will. To style himself "The Abe Lincoln of Nevada," as his opponent did in the 1910 primary, would have been a sort of conceit that was foreign to him. His recollections were far from a series of odes to his own triumphs. In fact, a good many of them were the sort he would term "a good joke on me."

Nor did he have a sense of his own importance. Some of his old friends saved everything, every letter, clipping, poster, picture, and brochure, and in old age, amid drawers, files, and stacks of memorabilia, could feel themselves turning into history. My father saved virtually nothing and unhesitatingly quashed the projects of Kay Boyle and other authors who wanted to write about him. The only meaning of life, he told me once when I was plying him with deep, philosophical questions, is in living it. "Look to this day," read the quotation from the Sanskrit I would find among his effects nearly twenty years later. "For it is life, the very life of life. In its brief course lie all the verities and realities of your existence." My father always looked to his days with total, joyous concentration, and there, if anywhere, the meaning lies. Telling how he lived his life is the real subject of this book, now that the time has come for the story he would not allow to be written while he was still alive.

An ebullient sense of adventure and a kind of pleasure in overcoming hardship flavored his life. Shades of Theodore Roosevelt, perhaps, for in some ways he was not unlike the Rough Rider he so greatly admired and so wholeheartedly fought for in the campaign of 1912. Going to Goldfield was probably the greatest adventure of all, and waking in the morning in your tent to find your blanket covered with snow was part of it. The campaign of 1910 was not only the lonely battle of a young man, not yet thirty, against the colossus of the Southern Pacific; it was also pretty damned exciting.

There was a touch of gallantry about my father. He may have been the last man in America who always tipped his hat to a woman and held her arm crossing the street, but he never shielded women and children from adventure or the hardship it entailed. When I was a very little girl, no more than four, our car ground to a halt in the snow on an untraveled road, and I went with my father to bring help. Being allowed to go stumping laboriously beside him over the hills through the heavy snow for over a mile was one of the most blissful days of my childhood. In the eastern suburb where I lived for a while, I used to think about that day sometimes, watching my smallest son, my father's namesake, standing at the school bus stop in the rain while cars went swishing past, filled with children whose parents didn't want them to get wet.

When I was older, I was allowed to ride with my father and his men on the all-day cattle drive in the autumn when we brought the cattle down from the summer range in the high Sierra to the home ranch. The drive was long, and sometimes the early snow had already fallen; once I fainted and slipped from my horse on the way. But even now when fall comes and I know the aspens are turning gold in the mountain canyons back home, I am glad I was there. As we passed close to the highway on one of these drives, some tourists emerged from a shiny, blue car and began taking pictures of us.

"What are they, Mommy?" asked the little girl, watching the bawling herd of Angus cattle amble past, followed by a dusty procession of riders—first my father, then in his seventies, followed by my Uncle Ed, a few years younger—slight, lean men with ruddy, sunburned faces and strong, roman noses, still as straight in the saddle as they had ever been.

"They're cowpokes, honey."

"Do they talk like us?"

"Sure they do. They talk like on TV."

If they were awaiting a mumbled commentary out of a television western on "gittin these here ornery leetle ole creeters down that thar trail," they were undoubtedly disappointed, though not so disappointed as they would have been if they had been able to overhear my father, who greatly admired the English language and rarely made an error in grammar, spelling, or pronunciation. Yet they were right to take his picture, more right than they knew. A cowpoke was only one of the things he was, and by no means the most important. But he was a true Westerner, more authentically Western than any of the plastic images they had seen on television. He was born there, lived there, died there; he belonged to Nevada, loved it in a way that is difficult to convey to a rootless generation that has been everywhere and belonged nowhere.

His whole family was that way. Westerners have often been described as a restless breed, always ready to move on, and this may have been true of the prospectors and native-born Americans who pushed steadily outward from the East. However, my family of immigrant ranchers were the very antithesis of restless. They moved just once from the Westphalian hamlet where their ancestors had lived time out of mind to the valley where many of their descendants are living still, and may yet remain, time out of mind. Of the ten children born to my grandparents, only one ever moved more than fifty miles away. When my father's sisters Ann and Clare were little girls, they used to daydream of running away and making sunbonnets for a living, but at heart they never really wanted to leave Nevada. My father's ventures into the world beyond were real at least, yet they never lasted long. Although he went to college at Stanford and Harvard, shot the rapids of the Colorado River, and served in Europe during the First World War, career opportunities

elsewhere were summarily rejected. Nevada was the only place
he ever wanted to be.

To him, the land was a recurrent wonder that he watched
with hardly less appreciation than the flawless profile of his
dark-haired wife and savored as other men taste wine. While
we rode or walked or drove, his keen, blue eyes were always
exploring the horizon with the questing, reflective gaze of the
outdoorsman. All around in the rocks and trees of this beloved
earth he found beauties that never ceased to give him pleasure:
the little, brown water ouzels that used to bob and sing on the
rocks in the Truckee River; the images in the thunderheads
sailing above in the bright, piercingly blue desert skies; the lane
of Lombardy poplar trees in Washoe Valley that he called "the
harp of the winds"; the howling of the coyotes, transmuted to
"the music of the desert" in his appreciative ear; the opaque
winter mornings when frost coated every twig and he would
speak of "pogonip," the white death, a word doubtless learned
from the Indian boy who was his first friend; the strong west
wind that blew down nearly every afternoon from the mountain peaks—"old weezer," my mother distastefully termed it,
for she disliked it, but to my father it recalled lines of poetry
about "the wind soughing in the trees." In the end, he said, he
wanted to be on the mountain overlooking the ranch that was
his and his father's before him. And that is where he is. One
spring day in May when the wild flowers were blooming, my
mother brought his ashes there, to the place where the lone,
lightning-struck tree stands, blackened and twisted, among the
windswept rocks at the top of Springmeyer Peak.

Acknowledgments

THIS BOOK IS PRIMARILY my father's. His reminiscences, dictated to me in 1960–1961, are the backbone of the narrative and the source of all the dialogue in the confrontations appearing in Chapters 9, 13, and 17. I corroborated and supplemented his recollections by extensive research in old newspapers and legal archives when I began this book in 1975, nine years after his death. He related some of his stories to me informally on various other occasions, and I have relied on my own far more imperfect memory only for small details and emotional coloration. My mother has contributed much to this book as well. My father's recollections extend no farther than Chapter 17; the next chapter is primarily drawn from her memory. I am also deeply indebted for valuable material to several other family members: to my cousin Duane Mack, for many contributions on our grandparents and the Carson Valley; to my uncle Edward Springmeyer, for boyhood memories shared with me before his death in 1978; to my cousins Arlene Rife and Aila Dale, for their contributions on our grandparents and on the Uber affair; to Ida Wennhold, granddaughter of my grandfather's half brother Karl, for useful and detailed information for Chapter 1 on the Springmeyer family in Germany and on her Westphalian homeland.

A number of friends and colleagues aided immeasurably in my research. Guy Rocha, Curator of Manuscripts at the Nevada

Historical Society, directed my attention to several important sources on the Prohibition era. He was also kind enough to read the entire manuscript and give me the benefit of his invaluable advice and suggestions. My debts to John Townley, former director of the Nevada Historical Society, and to Robert Nylen are also great. Through their generous assistance, much material I would not otherwise have been able to consult was made available to me from the Oddie Collection. Dr. Jerome Edwards, of the history department of the University of Nevada, Reno, furnished much-needed encouragement. Ellen Guerricagoitia, of Special Collections in the library at the University of Nevada, Reno, and Carrie Townley also provided much aid and many courtesies, as did Kay Murrow of the Esmeralda County Archives and staff members of the Federal Archives and Records Center at San Bruno, California, and the Nevada State Library. Judge Bruce Thompson, William Bailey, Ruth Shaw, and other family friends gave generously of their time and their memories.

Without the encouragement, patience, and support of my husband, Esmail, during years of writing and research, this book would never have been possible.

Westphalia

A CARRIAGE WITH a young couple inside clattered through the narrow streets of Bremerhaven toward the harbor. Although the young man no longer wore a uniform, the erect posture and the proud blue eyes suggested a soldier. As long as he lived, some would always think of him as "the Hussar." If his gaze remained hard, darkened still by memory of the fights and vengeful beatings that preceded his leaving, it would have softened whenever he looked down at the young woman beside him. She was a tiny woman, very simply dressed, who measured scarcely five feet tall beside his towering six-foot height and wore her long, brown hair knotted severely at the nape of her neck. The joyful spirit that animated her fresh, round-cheeked, little face made her seem prettier than she was, but no one had ever considered her a great beauty, and to his family, she was beneath consideration. He did not care; he had cursed them already for their refusal to accept her. He was defying them all, forsaking his village, and journeying halfway around the world to marry her.

Their passage toward an unknown frontier had begun at a farm near Halle, a Westphalian village of narrow, winding, cobblestoned streets and brick and stucco houses, crisscrossed with dark timbers and roofed with brown tiles, all clustered beneath the tall, red brick steeple of the Lutheran church. Not far away, on the banks of the Weser River, stood the larger town of Minden, hallowed ground where the heroic warrior General Herman once drove the Roman armies out of Germany. After Napoleon defeated the Prussian armies at Jena, however, no General Herman rose to challenge the conqueror. Prussia bowed, Austria had already submitted, and the Prussian province of Westphalia, combined with other fragments of Germany, became a kingdom for Napoleon's brother Jerome. When all of Europe lay at the French emperor's feet, the imperial gaze soon shifted eastward toward Russia. Vast numbers of conscripts were needed for the greatest invasion Napoleon had ever conceived. Even in the smallest hamlets of Westphalia, the young men were taken. One of them was my great-grandfather Johann Reelman, then just twenty-one.

Many years later Johann would speak to his small, blue-eyed, chestnut-haired son of the "bloodstained snows of Russia." He said his friends from Westphalia died there, all of them. Perhaps the boy was too small to remember much of what he said. Johann may have meant to wait until the boy was old enough to understand before he told him all he saw as he fought his way homeward on those bloodstained snows, but they would never speak as one man to another. They had only a little time together before Johann died in the cold of another winter when the child was only seven years old.

History amply describes the disastrous campaign of 1812, though no further details on Johann have come down to us. He may have served with Macdonald's Westphalian units, troops so disloyal to the French conqueror that Macdonald was unable to fight effectively. If he saw the snows, Johann must have endured through the Russian winter in the last stages of the retreat that saw the destruction of the Grand Army, as thou-

sands of men starved, froze to death, drowned while fording the
icy rivers, and were cut down by the avenging cossacks. No one
knows what he lived through on the road from Moscow. Survivors found it impossible to describe the horrors they had seen.[1]
We know only that he deserted and joined the Prussian army.
At the Battle of Waterloo in 1815, he is said to have fought with
such distinction against Napoleon's armies that he was decorated with the iron cross.

Johann then disappears from our view for the greater part of
his adult life. When next we see him in 1843, more than a
quarter century after Waterloo, he has returned to Westphalia
a widower and something of a war hero and married Katarina
Maria Springmeyer, a wealthy widow and the mistress of a fine
farm with a handsome fachwerk house of dark timbers set on
brick, adjoining a roomy stable behind a windbreak of tall oaks.
He was then fifty-two; she, twelve years his junior and the
mother of several sons. A married couple in that part of Germany customarily assumed the name of the wealthier spouse,
so the soldier took his wife's name, Springmeyer.

Behind that name was a story that may be true, or half true,
or unadulterated mythology woven around the moat-encircled
castle, the Tatenhausen, that adjoined the Springmeyer lands.[2]
As Katarina Maria told it, her first husband's ancestor of several
centuries ago, a man named Meyer, had belonged to a gang of
thieves who lived in a castle and preyed upon the surrounding
countryside. On one of these forays, the robbers were nearly
caught and fled with the avenging townsfolk after them. Ordered by the robber baron to hold the pursuers at bay while the
band made their escape, Meyer stayed behind. Too late he
reached the sanctuary of the castle. His comrades were already
safely within, and the drawbridge was rising in the air.

"Sprink [jump], Meyer! Sprink, Meyer!" they shouted to him.

Meyer sprang, caught the edge of the receding drawbridge,
and soared above the clamoring crowd to safety. From that day

forward, they called him "Sprinkmeyer," and all his family after him.

Thus Reelman became Springmeyer, and when the only child of this autumnal union was born in 1844, they named him Herman Henry in honor of General Herman. In school, where religion was a regular part of the curriculum, little Herman hated the harsh schoolmaster who tried to force him to accept the Lutheran doctrine of his family and his village and who beat him for denying the church. So I was told, yet understanding this child who was my grandfather is almost beyond the reach of my imagination. I can visualize a Puritan child in England or a Huguenot in France, sustained by family and friends and ready to endure persecution for their common faith. But not a child alone, standing up not in the sure and certain hope of heaven but in the name of nothingness. I can imagine a doubting child, but not a child so resolute that he could deny the church that was the center of all the lives in that tiny village, that he could say, "You're wrong, all of you, in this believing world," and close his ears to the commanding summons of the deep-toned bell, a child who knew he would be beaten for what he said and was still too stubborn to stop saying, "No, I will not say it. No."

I see that small, chestnut-haired boy as my father made me see him, and I guess at the thoughts in that young mind, fleeing for refuge in dreams of revenge and making the secret promise we know he kept. The blows rained down while this child stared stonily at the man, his teacher. He was young and thin, his father was dead, his half brothers would not protect him— but the time would come when he was no longer so helpless. "I will grow taller," he thought. "I will be as big and strong as you are, and then one day I will come back for you. I will not forget you, ever." He clenched his teeth against the pain and waited to grow up.

Rebelliousness still smouldered inside him when he was old enough to join the hussars and be a soldier as his father had been before him. During the 1860s, Prussia was waging the brief wars against Denmark and the Austrian empire that would finally unify Germany. Herman fought in both of these, but the battle he would remember most vividly was in the first war, against Denmark. Forward charged the hussars. Swords clashed. The captain under whom he served, a great, towering hulk of a man, sliced a Dane in half before the horrified young soldier's eyes. As Herman rode past on horseback, a Danish foot soldier's sword slashed him deeply in the calf of the leg, scarring him for life. He rode on, his hand clenched tightly on his sword.

When it was over, they brought the wounded in from the field. No doctors or nurses had accompanied the troops to care for them, and there were many wounded men. Was it a hundred or a thousand they had heaped together in the big barn? Herman no longer knew, but their sobbing and screaming was terrible to hear. With his pistol in hand, the big captain walked heavily into the barn. Shots were fired. The captain came out, and there was only silence in the barn behind him. In that battle, Herman must have seen the meaning in his dead father's words, spoken so long ago and never forgotten: *The bloodstained snows of Russia.*

Although in later years my grandfather took great pride in his time with the hussars, Prussian military discipline had actually suited him poorly. Perhaps that was why he served in three separate regiments, each uniformed in a different color. He loved the beautiful horses in the cavalry but hated the arrogant officers he was forced to obey. He would speak to his grandchildren sometimes of the rigid, mindless obedience of the Prussian hussar. Once told to advance, the hussar went forward, straight into a wall, a tree, a cannon; no matter what lay before him, he never deviated a jot from his course until he was ordered to do so. But Herman was a man with a course of his own to follow. Before long he left the hussars.

He had known many women while he rode with the army, yet only one remained in his memory for long, a girl he had first seen when they were schoolchildren together in Halle. He had helped her with her lessons sometimes, for she was three years younger than he. Perhaps her shining tenderness was a quality he had never seen among his own family, a harsh and pitiless household one and all—from his mother, who made her ailing daughter-in-law, heavy with child, dig potatoes, to his half brother, who mockingly threw their "pay" at his own daughters after he had worked them in the fields all day. Much of their iron fiber and their disdain for weakness ran in Herman also, but he had other qualities, invisible in them. He had the capacity not only to love but to cherish. When he came home from the wars, Wilhelmine Heidtman, the gentle schoolgirl he remembered, was still there, and she had taken no husband.

I have a photograph of her taken about then. For an age of ostentatious portraiture when the subjects, jaws set, eyes staring, and Sunday finery on display, were usually either stiffly posed in the parlor or arranged with proprietary pride before the front door, it is an oddly casual picture of a shy-looking girl in a white shirtwaist sitting with her two sisters in the grass of a sunny meadow behind the Springmeyer house. She probably owned nothing finer than the simple clothes she wore. The field conveys her place, for Wilhelmine was not welcome in the parlor or even on the threshold of the Springmeyer house. She is said to have been a woodcutter's daughter.

And that, in the universe of Halle, was a matter of no small importance. Neither ease nor refinement distinguished the inhabitants of the fachwerk house; indeed no woodsman in the beech forests worked harder than did the Springmeyers in their fields all day, the women side by side with the men. It was their house and their land that set them apart. The woodcutters and day laborers, who eked out an uneasy existence from one day to the next and lived, dependent on uncertain sufferance, in the huts on other peoples' farms, had neither. Herman harbored the rebel's hatred of the set orbits of church and village and army that fixed each German in his place and defined who he was and what he must do; his family, by contrast, clung to these encrusted traditions with an impassioned grip.

When Herman told his half brothers he intended to marry Wilhelmine Heidtman, they turned on him with the affronted fury of the rich peasant determined to guard his precious position and never, never to slip back among the landless toilers of the earth. The Heidtmans "own no land," they said contemptuously. Marriage to a woman so far beneath them was unthinkable. They ordered him to abandon this unworthy daughter of a lowly household and make a marriage becoming to a Springmeyer.

"She's a damn sight finer than I am!" Herman told them angrily. He was through with orders. He had been ordered to pray by the schoolmaster, ordered through his paces by the hussars, ordered to cast aside his chosen bride by his half brothers, and he would have no more of it. He would never give her up, he told them. Perhaps in the heat of that angry scene he also arrived at a decision toward which he had been moving for some time. He would take Wilhelmine Heidtman away with him, far, far away from Halle, from their fine fachwerk house, and from all of them. He was going to America.

Since he chose to ignore their wishes, they would make him pay for it, and dearly. When they divided their inheritance among themselves, Herman received much less money than his long-dead father had left for him. Perhaps they had always resented him, this youngest child, this son of the soldier who had moved in to take their father's place when he died suddenly of apoplexy at an early age; and now, since their mother's death while Herman was fighting in the Austro-Prussian War in 1866,

they no longer bothered to conceal it. Only Karl, the youngest
of his half brothers and the heir under German law of the house
and farm, remained on speaking terms with him. As for the rest,
Herman had nothing more to say to them; let them cheat him
as they would, the portion left to him was still enough for the
passage and a good beginning in America. None who remember
him ever doubted that he valued his Wilhelmine beyond all the
gold ever hidden in the stockings beneath the mattresses, secreted in the hearthstones, and buried in the dooryards of Halle.

* * *

To these two Westphalian peasants, America must have
seemed an idea less tangible than the moon, which could at least
be seen in the sky above the low-lying hills that were like
overturned saucers bordering the fields and forests of their village. Even when they had crossed the space on the map that
stood for weeks of voyaging by sea and reached the eastern
shore, they would not arrive, for Herman had chosen a farther
place, a new state called Nevada, way across the map of America and almost to the Pacific Ocean on the other side. Herman
had a friend whose brother had settled there and written back
that the Carson Valley had plenty of good land for the new
settlers coming in. He was going to join his brother, and two of
Herman's other friends were going too. All five would make the
journey together, yet Herman began to make preparations for
the time when their paths diverged again. He bought a massive
German medical book and a chest of homeopathic medicines.
To survive alone out there on that new frontier, they must have
the things they needed to take care of themselves.

Before leaving, there were certain farewells to be said. As the
years passed and the dutiful children came and went in the
village school, the master probably no longer remembered the
defiant chestnut-haired boy, but the boy had not forgotten him.
Once Herman had made a promise to himself and now he

meant to keep it. On his last night in Halle, he would seek out
his onetime schoolmaster, and they would see if he could fight
a man as well as he could beat a child. He could not. The boy
was now as tall as he, the little fists grown big and hard as
stones. Herman gave him blow for blow, knocked him down,
and left him to say those churchly prayers he set so much store
by.

There was another man, an arrogant officer of the hussars,
contemptuous of the soldiers in his command. This one also
Herman had promised himself he would meet again, not as the
soldier who hastened to obey the officer above him. They
would meet in the darkness as two men, one no better than the
other unless his fists could make him so, and then they would
see who was born to command and who was born to obey.
Herman beat him to the ground and left him to command the
dust.

Auf Wiedersehen then to the church with the steeple like the
blade of a sword, auf Wiedersehen to the narrow, steep-roofed
houses and the narrower souls within, auf Wiedersehen to
Halle and all it signified. Herman was ready to leave, and he
would never look back. The next morning he and Wilhelmine
got into the buggy, and Karl, with the reins in his hand, turned
the horses toward Bremerhaven.

* * * * *

Across the lowlands of Saxony from Bremerhaven lay another more famous harbor city where lived the family known
as "the merchant princes of Hamburg," the Rupertis. They had
been the first to open South America to German trade; the ships
of their line sailed the seas laden with goods; it was a Ruperti
who presented the keys of the city to Bismarck when Hamburg
was united with Prussia. Once, smarting with the lack of a title
to crown their wealth, the Rupertis quietly undertook some
genealogical research in the hope of finding at least a minor

princeling hidden among the leafy branches of the family tree. Instead they found that the earliest traceable members of their line belonged to the lowest order of medieval society, the grave-diggers. This well-kept secret was, however, a minor disap-pointment, for the Rupertis had been ascendant for many generations, and the present seemed firmly in hand. None could know how brief a time the favored world would last in which they took their ease among the rose trees in the shaded green of their country estate until two world wars had brought them to their knees. Had someone suggested that a Ruperti would one day marry the son of two Westphalian peasants, they would have dismissed the idea with disdainful amusement. When a Ruperti married, the union was always a suitable ar-rangement with another great German family like the Am-sincks, not with peasants. If the social distance between the hussar and the woodcutter's daughter was too wide to close, how broad, how unbridgeably far the chasm between those two and the merchant princes of Hamburg.

* * * * *

But America would be different. In this land of greater space, no distance would be too wide to close. As one proceeded westward from Europe, the strict imperatives of the unthink-able, the unacceptable, and the inconceivable would sound steadily fainter, fading to meaningless jargon, then to a low warning hum, and finally, somewhere west of the Mississippi, to complete inaudibility. On the way to the ship, Karl must have driven the buggy through the Bremen city square past the statue of a medieval knight, the words "I show you freedom" emblazoned on his shield. An auspicious beginning for their passage out of the old world and into the new.

They sailed to New York, then to Nicaragua, where they crossed the isthmus and continued by ship to San Francisco. It was "a hard journey," Wilhelmine later said, and coming as it did from a stoic young woman who never complained and rarely even took notice of adversity, that laconic phrase undoubtedly conveyed many difficult weeks of misery and hardship. When they journeyed across the Nicaragua route Commodore Vanderbilt had developed in 1851 as an alternative to the Panama crossing farther south, conditions were probably much as Mark Twain had described them two years earlier. A stern-wheel boat carried the passengers 120 miles up the San Juan River to Lake Nicaragua, where they changed to a steamer for the hundred-mile voyage across the lake. The last leg of the journey, a short road across the foothills, was traversed in a procession that Twain depicted as follows:

There were not a dozen good riders in the two hundred and fifty that went on horseback, but every man seemed to consider that inasmuch as the animals belonged to "the Company," it was a stern duty to ride them to death. . . . Such racing and yelling and beating and banging and spurring, and such bouncing of blanket bundles, and flapping and fluttering of coat-tails, and such frantic scampering of the multitude of mules, and bobbing up and down of the long column of men, and rearing and charging of struggling ambulances in their midst, I never saw before, and I never enjoyed anything so much.[3]

Then came the voyage to San Francisco from Nicaragua. We know the year of their arrival—1868—but not the season or the route they traveled inland. Perhaps they rode the newly completed Central Pacific across the lofty Sierra Nevada in early summer, stepped off the train at the Reno station, and saw the empty space on the map become, at last, a real place: a road thronged with coaches, wagons, and horsemen that led across the valley into an arid range of pink and gray mountains, devoid of any taller tree than the round, bushy pinon pine and speckled

Herman Springmeyer and Wilhelmine Heidtman Springmeyer, possibly photographed in Germany before their marriage.

with gray, pungent-smelling shrubs named sagebrush, a landscape surely alien and strange to eyes accustomed to the lush greens of the German countryside. No doubt they walked the crowded streets of Virginia City, a raucous boom town not yet ten years old, built high on the mountain slope above the myriad tunnels of the fabulous Comstock lode. Eastward lay a sea of desert, rippled by waves of purple mountains, on and on for hundreds of miles farther than they would ever see, for they had nearly reached the Carson Valley, now only one day's ride south. There they would work on the ranch belonging to H. F. Dangberg, the brother of Herman's friend, until Herman had learned the valley and decided where he would buy his own land.

Family tradition holds that Herman and Wilhelmine were married at a simple ceremony in Virginia City, where Herman slipped a plain, gold wedding band on Wilhelmine's finger. He believed the hands he held in his were one of the loveliest things about her. Nature, like Herman himself, was no respecter of German social distinctions and had endowed her with slender, graceful, smooth, long-fingered hands that could well have distinguished a queen. She, in her turn, placed a gold band on his finger. The passage from the Old World was complete: no longer was she the woodcutter's daughter and he the landowner's son. Here in the New World they were free to choose what they would become.

Settling In The
New World

ALTHOUGH THE GRASSY MEADOWS on the banks of Carson River had long served as a welcome stopping place for the immigrants en route to California and a few promising farms had already been established, the Carson Valley of the sixties was not yet "the garden spot of Nevada" it would be proclaimed in later years. A traveler in 1860 dragging himself painfully through the sand at the southern end of the valley after a "terribly severe" winter of heavy snow described it as "barren in the extreme." In the northern portion, "the soil was poor and sandy, producing little else than stunted sage bushes; and the few scattered farms had a thriftless and poverty-stricken look, as if the task of cultivation had proved entirely hopeless, and had long since been given up."[1]

The tillage of this desolate land was not easily accomplished. An early settler told of the terrible, spring windstorms of early years: trees were uprooted, roofs torn from buildings, and where the freshly cleared soil was loose in the western and southern reaches of the valley, the newly planted seeds were ripped from the earth in billowing clouds of brown dust. In some years, two or three reseedings were necessary.[2] Only by persistence through the terrible winters and raging winds and blistering droughts, only with infinite care, patience, and ingenuity, would the pioneers at last transform the wasteland beyond the meadows into an oasis of fragrant, green fields, poplar-lined lanes, commodious barns, and white, Victorian farmhouses.

Since 1848 immigrants en route to California had been stopping in the valley John C. Fremont had named after Kit Carson, the mountain man who guided his expedition through the region. The settlement at Genoa, originally named Mormon Station, probably dated from 1850. Seven years later many of the original Mormon settlers returned to Salt Lake City in response to Brigham Young's call to defend the faith. Their lands were quickly seized by new settlers, indifferent to the dreadful curses directed by the Mormons against thieving "Gentiles" who declined to make reparations. In 1859 the discovery of the Comstock lode some thirty miles to the northeast brought the sudden emergence of Virginia City, the wealthy industrial metropolis that would dominate Nevada political and economic life for thirty years, and the equally sudden emergence of the new state in 1864, a scant three years after gaining territorial status. When Nevada's original nine counties were organized in 1861, the valley region had been designated Douglas County in honor of President Lincoln's famous rival, Stephen A. Douglas.

As the Comstock sailed on the crest of the big bonanza and the dollars flowed like champagne, every city and hamlet from the Truckee Meadows to San Francisco prospered with it, and so did the Carson Valley, for Virginia City was ready to take all she could give, and more: her produce found eager buyers on the Comstock; her mountain slopes were stripped of their majestic pine forests to provide timber for the insatiable maw of the mines; her inns filled with travelers hastening to and from the Comstock, or journeying to the new mining "excitements" in Bodie and the Silver Mountains. At the same time, permanent settlers were arriving steadily. By 1870 the valley was a thriving agricultural community of some twelve hundred souls, roughly a third of them foreign born, including ninety-seven immigrants from Germany.[3]

When my grandparents arrived in 1868, less than a generation after the first cabin had been built at Genoa, it must have been pleasant to ride out of the desert into the natural meadowland beside the Carson River. To the west, the Sierra Nevada thrust straight up from the valley floor unsoftened by foothills. In the afternoons, the long, blue shadows and the west wind flowed down from their peaks, mottled with dark pines, and washed across the valley. On the eastern horizon, the planed surfaces of the Pine Nut Hills turned blue and mauve and purple as the sun sank. The phrase in the letter to Herman's friend that had brought them so many thousands of miles had not been wrong; it was a "good place," much of it still untouched but full of possibilities.

During the coming months, Herman would have to master an entirely different method of farming. In Westphalia there had been no need for irrigation because the crops were watered by the rain; in the arid Carson Valley the water must be channeled away from the riverside meadows into the desert beyond. Few ditches had yet been dug, but acre upon acre of land was fertile and ready to produce. Quick to learn, Herman was soon known as "a wonder" at the art of surveying a ditch with a level, a little sight box, and an unfailingly accurate eye (in an enterprise as time-consuming and laborious as these broad, deep, hand-shoveled ditches, no margin for error was allowed). The task was rarely an easy one, and someone was always on hand to say the slope was wrong or the drainage was poor and nothing could be done. Eyes narrowed with concentration, Herman would pace slowly over the ground. Then he would usually confound the skeptics by devising a plan that made the impossible more feasible than anyone would have believed.

Within two years of his arrival at the Dangberg Ranch in 1868, he had decided where he would buy his own land. However, he did not leave the Dangbergs until the spring of 1871, apparently because he had agreed to remain and keep an eye on the ranch while Dangberg was away serving in the state legislature. Herman combined some fine, level land bought from Dangberg and another rancher named Nesmith into a ranch of his own in the heart of the valley between the East Fork of the Carson River and the towns of Minden and Gardnerville. Then, of course, these towns did not exist. The churches, dry goods stores, hotels, smithies, courthouses, livery stables, houses, schools, and all the other components of a town were still in the future—save one. That indispensable edifice, the only one without which no town in Nevada could legitimately lay claim to existence, that essential foundation upon which all other social and community institutions must rest, had already been laid: the saloon was there; the rest of civilization would eventually follow.

That March, Wilhelmine began keeping house on their own ranch in a primitive cabin with uncurtained windows. She was there alone, her husband out working in the fields, when the Indians came. If such encounters were supposed to be conducted in a spirit of high tragedy replete with elements of mystery, awe at the white man and his mysterious inventions, and nuggets of unspoiled aboriginal wisdom, the Western novelists who excelled at this sort of storytelling had not as yet informed the Indians. As far as they were concerned, this was a comedy, and moreover, a comedy that was being played for their benefit. They appeared suddenly at the windows, clad only in rabbit skin blankets and breechcloths. Wilhelmine was frightened. They peered in at her, laughing uproariously at every move she made and lifting up their children to see the hilarious spectacle of a young housewife doing her domestic chores. Day after day, they came back to watch and giggle and terrify my grandmother. It is, perhaps, to be regretted that the white settlers proved to be less than comic in the long run, and the capacity of the Indians to laugh at their quaint customs and behavior has considerably diminished over the years.

As time passed, the Indians came to the ranch to work instead of to laugh and pitched their "campoodies," rabbit skin tents with willow poles, on an unused tract of land where the cotton-woods grew near the river. A grove of even larger cottonwoods, some as much as ten feet in circumference, grew across the lane from the orchard near the new bunkhouse. Herman's men con-structed a cook house, including a root cellar and spring house; a blacksmith's shop; and barns for cattle and horses, both as big and fine as the others that were going up in the valley. If monumental architecture is a clue to where the heart lies, the hearts of the Carson Valley did not reside in her dwellings, though these were handsome enough, nor in her little schools, nor in her courthouse, nor in the diminutive churches that arrived tardily on the scene. Rather, they lay in the generous sweep and cathedral hush of those roomy barns, built to last, as they have, a hundred years and more.

Herman and Wilhelmine's first cabin was replaced a few years later by a spacious, two-story, white frame house set in a yard shaded with apple trees, one named for every child that Wilhelmine bore. The fields filled with horses and the house with children, blue-eyed children with brown or red or chest-nut or golden hair. Once when the midwife was late, Herman delivered the baby himself with his trusted German medical book open on the bed beside his wife, looking from book to wife and wife to book like a cook with a recipe. My father, George, was the seventh child. After Edna, the youngest, was born, Herman named the tenth tree.

In addition to the family and the Indians, ten or twelve men usually worked at the ranch, and occasionally in the hay-ing season, the number swelled to twenty. Some were Prussians who had followed Herman over in the chain reaction typical of immigration. First came his wife's brother Pete, then young Fritz, not yet sixteen, the son of Herman's half brother Karl. And there were others. The local boys, who worked on the ranch six days of the week, walked home to Genoa across the valley late on Saturday night, and hurried back to the ranch in time for work on Monday morning. The itinerant workers, including a roving band of Civil War veterans who came tramping up the lane in spring when the season of heavy work began, stayed until early fall, then packed and left for California.

Wilhelmine, assisted by her daughters, spent most of her day cooking for the family and supervising the preparation of meals for the hired men in the cook house. Sometimes, when the perpetually unreliable cooks had left without notice, she had to cook for the men as well. In the old cabin she had done her cooking in a black iron kettle like a witch's cauldron that hung over the hearth. This was soon replaced by a modern stove, for Herman always quickly adopted the latest inventions (that same propensity later led him to install the first indoor plumbing in the valley). From the new stove or the old kettle, Wilhelmine's cooking was invariably delicious. In her small, capable hands the humble potato was transformed in so many different ways that her appreciative family lost count. She had a special touch with all the fresh garden vegetables, and grandchildren who ate the German-style stringbeans with bacon, fried onions, and vinegar that she was still preparing as an old lady nearly sixty years ago have not forgotten the taste even yet.

H.H., as Herman Henry Springmeyer soon became known, directed the men—and the sons. When they later looked back on those years, they remembered him as they most often saw him, walking across the fields to irrigate with a shovel tipped over his shoulder and wearing a suit. No one can recall ever seeing him less formally attired.

I like that image of the man with the shovel because it reflects the fundamental reality of ranching in the valley: water, the scarcity, channeling, rationing, and dispersion thereof. The easterners among whom I sojourn do not quite believe in this, or would rather not; it is not their idea of ranching. They want them dogies rounded up in rain or shine, sleet or snow, with a ki yii yippy yippy yay. They want range wars, or at least a gunfight at the OK corral, not the dam busting on the river and protracted litigation over water rights through which conflict in the valley was most commonly expressed. Nor do they care to hear about the shotguns conspicuously carried by the river as a warning to prospective water thieves, since no bleeding bodies ever littered the banks. They want a thundering stampede of longhorns turned aside at the edge of the cliff in the nick of time, not a herd of cattle driven slowly along at an ambling pace lest they grow thin from exertion. They want Ole Paint, that ornery leetle cayuse, galloping down that long, long trail awinding, not my grandfather's prized English shire stallion receiving his daily shampoo. Most of all, they want ten-gallon hats and six-guns, not suits and shovels. But that man with the shovel stands there anyway.

To be remembered working would probably have suited H.H. very well indeed. "Work is fun" was the maxim he was most fond of expounding to his family and his men. What they said in reply, I have never heard, but apparently his children learned it well. When the bell rang at 3:00 A.M., his sons used to rise with the men for milking. George never got beyond seven or eight cows, but his older brother Louis, short, fat, and "tough as a boot," was a phenomenal human milking machine who could squirt his way through twenty-five cows at a stretch. Like all the lessons acquired from their father, hard work was a habit they never set aside. After he grew up and left the ranch, George slacked off a bit and took to sleeping until 5:30 in the morning, but the day he spent working in court and in his law office often lasted until well after midnight. And it *was* fun. Vacations were an ordeal a man had to endure for the sake of his wife, but only as briefly as possible. George's brothers and sisters endured them not at all. There was hardly a day in their lives that work was not part of, even a wedding day. "In the morning I cooked breakfast for twenty men," my Aunt Clare used to say. "Then Maurice and I rode over to Genoa to get married."

The tragedy of growing old was tied up with working in H.H.'s mind too. As an old man, he sat in the pretty Jacobean house in Carson City where he had lived since his retirement with his daughter Ann and her husband. Small, polite great-grandsons were brought before him to receive his benediction from a respectful distance; his roses grew around him in glorious, fragrant profusion. But it was not enough. Every week until the October when he died, he insisted on going back out to the ranch of his making, prospering still in the good hands of his daughter Clare and her husband. It was not the knowledge that few days were left to taste the sun or the pains that came to a man after the eighty-fifth year of his life that he minded. It was sitting there, unable to decide, act, do, make, be. Then you were not a man anymore but a useless, forgotten object "on the back shelf."

"The German work complex," my mother used to call it, knowing that the need to work came from inside, not from economic necessity or the presence of a job to be finished. The Springmeyers, Germans to the core, took such pride and pleasure in working and seeing their work well done. One of the worst things my father could say about anyone was, "He's letting everything go."

When he was a boy, nothing like that ever happened on his father's ranch, where everything was done well. There were carefully tended fields of grain and alfalfa. During that first year on his new lands, H.H. had found some strange bushy plants with a strong, grassy scent and tiny, round, cloverlike leaves of dark, purplish green taking up fertile ground and precious water. He hooked one with his mattock, but the deep roots "as large as a man's arm" could resist even the powerful bent back of a hussar. Rooting them out took some time, and fortunately before the job was done, he noticed that the stock considered these troublesome weeds very tasty. The plants proved to be the first alfalfa in the state, planted by an earlier settler, abandoned and forgotten. When H.H. found out what it was, he baled it and, in 1875, became the first Nevada rancher to sell alfalfa hay commercially. In time, alfalfa, or "chili grass," as the old-timers called it, would become the principal crop in the valley and in the state.[4]

The petaluma hay press, an unwieldy contraption about eight feet high, compressed the alfalfa into two-by-three-foot bales. The men would push loose hay through a hole in the top, then fasten it down, and the two oxen, Roney and Jerry, would pull the long chain attached to the bottom out for fifty yards, raising the bottom and squeezing it against the top. As the bales came up, the men would force rope through the press to tie them. H.H. also built a dairy of seventy-five to a hundred cows and established the first creamery in the Carson Valley. Here the Springmeyers made their own butter and cheese with the aid of a donkey engine and shipped them to San Francisco and Virginia City by train from Carson City. Every week George's older brother Charlie set off for the Virginia and Truckee depot with a wagon filled with big, wheel-shaped cheeses, many of which would end up at the bars in Virginia City saloons. The dairy products were kept cool with ice sawed every winter in the Cottonwood Creek and packed in sawdust during the summer months.

Durhams had long been the only breed of cattle raised in the valley, but H.H. introduced Holsteins, bought from Sam Davis, the owner of the Cottonwood Ranch and editor for many years of the *Carson Daily Appeal.* Those he sold for beef were dispatched in bunches of seven or eight every two or three weeks with a lone rider on the two-day trek to the butcher he supplied in Virginia City. When he later decided to give up dairying, H.H. brought in the first Carson Valley Herefords, purchased from the registered herd on Governor John Sparks's Alamo Ranch south of Reno. After the two Hereford bulls arrived in Carson City on the railroad, they escaped and led the governor on a wild chase through the streets of the capital before they were captured and delivered to their new owner. If, as was noted in the press, it created "almost as much attention as a circus parade" when six of Sparks's Herefords were driven sedately through the Reno streets for delivery,[5] that stampede through Carson must have roused a sensation roughly equivalent to a state fair, two balloon ascensions, and a small Indian massacre.

H.H. took quiet pride in the innovations he introduced at the ranch, but he loved the horses best. Rarely were there less than fifty beauties grazing in his pasture; he bred them, raised them, boarded them, and unceasingly bought, sold, and traded them. He never missed the large annual meet at Carson City when the California circuit of trotting races convened there. Should the race horse owners find themselves short of cash, as they often did, and feel inclined to sell their horses, a tall, thin man with a cigar was always waiting in the crowd to buy the best ones. But only the best: strong, young, spirited, gentle, and well formed, and he could sometimes be very choosy about the color. Those piercing blue eyes could distinguish a flawed horse at a glance, and no amount of talking could change his mind. The hussars had taught H.H. to recognize and to care for fine horses.

His caravans of two and three wood- and iron-wheeled wagons hauled alfalfa hay and grain to Virginia City and sometimes to Bodie, the boisterous California mining town to the south.

Each team had a highly trained pointer horse on either side to keep the wagon from overturning on the sharp curves of the mountainous Virginia City road. The steep slope as well as the curves made these roads dangerous. Once the brake pin gave way on the descent to American Flat; the wagon slammed into the team, one horse had to be pulled out from beneath it with chains, and the teamster was seriously injured. Including pointers, each team had seven or eight spans of horses, all perfectly matched in color, on a jerk line. The number of jerks from the teamster on the single line hitched to the brake handle and extending straight to the bit of the lead horse told the horses which way to turn. Each morning before they were hitched up the teams were curried and brushed until they gleamed. In Carson City, near the site of the present-day Ormsby House, H.H. bought a piece of land where the teams could be rested and watered on their way to Virginia City.

Of all these fine horses, H.H. was proudest of Lord Ribblesdale, the great, black shire stallion he had imported from England around Cape Horn. In response to a large advertisement in the Douglas County newspaper announcing in language somewhat reminiscent of a debutante making her social debut that "Ribblesdale will make the season," mares from as far as a hundred miles away were brought to the ranch ($10 for single service). Every morning before his gleaming black coat was curried and brushed the black stallion was washed with castile soap by Billy Beggs, the runty, little Irish teamster whose principal job was caring for him.

Within the boundaries of my grandfather's ranch, nothing was let go; not so beyond the big stone gateposts he ordered quarried and set at the end of his lane because nothing less than stone was heavy enough to be sideswiped by his loaded wagons time and again without tumbling down. The roads and bridges his teams traveled over were in poor repair throughout the valley, and he wanted to do something about it. So he ran for county commissioner, although the nomination was not secured without one of the heated altercations that swirled around my grandfather's head as inevitably as the smoke from his imported Porto D'Oro cigars. At one point the president of the People's Mass Meeting, where county candidates were being selected, was obliged to remind those present that no one should vote who was not prepared to support the nominee and *"no gentleman* would attempt to vote who could not *take* and *keep this pledge.*"[6] H.H. emerged victorious and saw to it that those roads and bridges were fixed.

One thing leading, as it does, to another, he soon realized a good deal needed doing that was beyond the scope of a county commissioner, and someone was needed who would do it well. Politicians had been letting everything go for too long. He went to pay a call on H. F. Dangberg, who controlled the county Democratic convention.

Since the early days when H.H. and Wilhelmine had worked on the Dangberg Ranch, they had been on friendly terms with Old Dutch Fred, as Dangberg was generally known. They had talked together "like two brothers," H.H. later recalled, when Dangberg asked him to survey the ditches on his Upper Sagebrush Ranch, and my grandfather was rather proud of the successful plan he had worked out for watering a tract that had been thought impossible to irrigate. Friendship aside, asking Old Dutch Fred and respectfully accepting his curt pronouncements as the law of the land were the way things were usually done in the Carson Valley. Although he was not terribly old at fifty-seven and not at all Dutch—throughout the West the term was applied not only to Hollanders but also to Germans and sometimes to any north European whose native tongue was not English—he was indisputably Fred Dangberg, the owner of by far the biggest ranching operation in the county.[7] Where he had settled, the other Prussians from Westphalia had followed. But he had been *first,* and first he intended to remain—first in

ranching, first in politics, and first in the hearts of his country-
men. As they talked together, H.H. mentioned some of the
agricultural benefits he thought could be accomplished by state
legislation and explained that he wanted to run for Douglas
County's seat in the assembly.

"No, you haven't been here long enough," replied Old Dutch
Fred brusquely. My grandfather had been in the Carson Valley
for eighteen years then, five years longer than had Dangberg
himself when he first served in the legislature in 1869. "I have
someone else I want in there. He'll be elected. I'll see he gets the
Democratic nomination, since I control the convention."

"Alright," said H.H., "I'll be a Republican from now on, and
I'll get the Republican nomination."

He did just that. The former chairman of the Douglas County
Democratic Central Committee suddenly appeared as a Republican candidate for the assembly, no light reversal in a decade
when a Nevadan was somewhat more likely to announce his
conversion to Baptism or to divorce his wife than he was to
change his political party. He won. The partisan identity of the
Springmeyer clan, Republicans henceforth, was set and so was
an enduring coolness between the Springmeyers and the Dangbergs, which also affected the other valley families who ranged
themselves on one side or the other. Indeed the shadowy outlines of the estrangement that began that day in 1886, when my
grandfather refused to defer to the padrone of the Carson Valley and obediently wait his turn, are still visible in the present-
day alignments of Douglas County politics.

It may be inferred that the customary, mutual dam busting
on the river was afterward conducted with unusual relish by
both sides and that the race that ensued for the assembly in
1888 between H.H. and Dangberg proceeded in a more lively
spirit than most political contests in the valley. It is certain that
a number of stories, both factual and apocryphal, were related

about the two of them. Sam Davis's tale about the crossbreeding of a dollar mule is one of the better examples.

"The variety of mule I have referred to," Davis wrote in the *San Francisco Examiner*, "originated by an inbred cross between Fred Dangberg's mustangs and Herman Springmeyer's China jacks," an especially tough strain of mule originally mistaken for mountain sheep when they were first brought over the Sierra Nevada from Placerville over twenty years before.

"Dangberg knows nothing of mules and Springmeyer knows very little of horses," Davis continued, with heavy irony certain to elicit loud guffaws from his readers, "and so the two ranchers, whose land is contiguous, swap the worst stock they have with each other. When Springmeyer has a particularly hard mule or China jack, he goes over to Dangberg and, assuring him it is a thoroughbred with a recordable pedigree, offers it in trade, and Dangberg trots out an old calico bronco or registered Gardnerville plug which he has been carefully nursing for the occasion, and after considerable dickering, the trade is made. Each man has become so interested in doing up the other on stock that they have been for years breeding down the hardest strain they can find, purely for trading purposes. Each supposes that he is largely beating the other. For this reason, both these ranchers look happy and contented when they meet the other. Springmeyer is confidently expecting to be able to produce a dollar animal for the spring market, and I am disposed to think he will reach the goal of his ambition by next March.

"It had long been the idea of these breeders to eliminate the size and usefulness of the animal along with its pulling and carrying qualities and retain the stubbornness of disposition and hereditary hellishness of the original stock." This method of down and crossbreeding had been "very carefully and intelligently pursued with a result that landed the scrub mule upon the towering pedestal of infamy and unworth, but as a kicker and a bucker he left nothing to be desired, and as a bonebreaker and man-eater his record was without a blot." He was the kind of mule, in brief, that many have run across but few have stayed across. Davis declared that "stirring times" ensued when a United States government surveying party innocently purchased a string of these Springmeyer mules and the mules began "laying up" the surveyors.[8]

In loftiness and sheer grandeur of design, few ambitions could compare to the dollar mule. Yet it is clear that H.H. did have other, possibly lesser, aspirations. Though he was a novice at the state capitol and he scorned the underhanded manipulations of politics in the Gilded Age, conservation and reclamation advanced farther while he chaired the house committee on agriculture than in all the previous legislatures. His attempt to create a state forest commission foundered in the senate, but his bill establishing Arbor Day, important as a first step in conservation, was passed by the 1887 legislature. In the next session, while he continued to serve as chairman of the house committee on agriculture, Nevada's first reclamation act became law.

How much effect he had on its passage I don't know, but my guess would be not much, at least not in the sense that political influence is usually understood. When public interest in reclamation quickened with the decline of Nevada mining and the reclamation bill, which had first been proposed in 1883, was resurrected in 1889, he would have slapped no backs in the cloakroom, made no deals, offered no sweeteners to soften the recalcitrant. He would simply have stood, immobile as Grant at the siege of Fort Donelson, while the battle swirled around him. Still it is possible that his mere presence influenced the outcome. The doubtful would be assured that any funds appropriated for reclamation would not be misspent, if he were on the reclamation commission that spent them. His known integrity, his thoroughness, his reputation as a rancher who knew irriga-

The Springmeyers in front of their ranch house around 1882. The little ones on Wilhelmine and Herman's laps are Ann and George. Emma is wearing a white dress and Margaret a dark one.

tion from the ground up, would all have argued silently but powerfully on behalf of any enterprise he favored.

All the same, his efforts came to nothing in the end. Like John Wesley Powell and many another before and since, he would learn that the best of ideas are not necessarily the most politically feasible and that politics are altogether different from the natural world, where problems of engineering have direct and logical solutions. He knew how to move water from where it was to where he wanted it to go, but government funds did not work the same way. I doubt that he ever sensed the slope of political gravity intuitively the way he felt the slope of the earth. Probably he left that to his politician friends, only to find that they were unable to deal as effectively with their world as he did with his. When he was no longer serving in the assembly, the brittle majority of a drought year fractured once more into the old local rivalries that had brought session after session of legislative inaction, and the reclamation act was repealed. Arbor Day lapsed into desuetude, to my grandfather's deep regret.[9]

In later years the only legislative achievement he mentioned was Arbor Day; even this was less an achievement than an unfulfilled hope, the only visible dash of fantasy in a thoroughly tough and practical man. In other, greener countrysides, where ferns spread, fungi proliferate, grass grows easily, volunteer saplings are forever springing up in neglected corners of the garden, and where no one ever thought of counting the trees, Arbor Day seems redundant. It does not when you are crossing the arid wastes of Nevada and a grove of green trees is seen in the distance, a benediction to the eyes, to be watched with pleasure through miles of shimmering heat. You know few of these trees appeared by chance. Nearly every one was planted, cherished, and nurtured for years until at last its roots grew deep down where the ground water is. When the 1888 census of trees listed every shade tree and berry bush from the willows (5,841) to the gooseberries, there were pitifully few to count. Though never lush and verdant, it might have been a better, pleasanter place more like the shady forest landscapes in the paintings on the ranchhouse walls, if each man had gone forth each year to plant and tend a tree in the way my grandfather imagined. But it was too soon for the greening of Nevada; perhaps it still is.

A Carson Valley Childhood

WHEN MY FATHER was born in 1881, H.H. named him after his close friend George Ferris, a young engineer who belonged to another pioneer Carson Valley family. Later the big water-wheel turning near the Mexican mill on the Carson River would inspire Ferris to invent the Ferris wheel, which was the hit of the 1893 Columbian Exposition in Chicago, and of countless fairs, carnivals, and amusement parks ever since. Somehow it seems fitting that my father and that happy invention, both so full of laughter and sheer exhilaration, should be conjoined through his name.

Let it be understood that this George, born less than fourteen years after his parents arrived in America, was not the son of immigrants poised precariously between two cultures, one nostalgically remembered, the other imperfectly grasped. He was entirely an American, named for an American friend and unable to speak more than a few words of German picked up from the hired men on the ranch. Even his older brothers and sisters had not learned much. My mother, who spoke German fluently, used to tease him a bit about his poor command of the language. To this he would reply, with a reminiscent gleam in his eye, that during the First World War, years before he met my mother, "the girls in Germany understood me very well."

Mother was right about his German, but then, he had learned so little because he had not heard it at home. How his parents became so rapidly and thoroughly acclimatized in an isolated rural community with many other immigrants like themselves remains rather startling, yet that is what they did. The family used to laugh about my grandfather's sarcastic remarks concerning the "skriners" (Shriners), the lodge to which one of his sons-in-law belonged. Apparently that was funny because it was the only real mistake in English the old man made.

Today, when ethnicity has become the mode, immigrants who became Americanized like my grandparents are condemned as cultural social climbers, too eager to imitate WASP-ish ways and too irresolute to defend their national traditions. Let us remind ourselves that the choice they made was not unworthy of respect. That choice was America. The aims stated in the charter of the Douglas County Valhalla Society, an organization formed in 1885 in which my grandfather served as treasurer, included nothing at all about the preservation of German culture but rather devolved upon imparting "knowledge of our government and its laws." "Our government" meant America's, and none other. The Valhalla was clearly intended to help the new German immigrants still arriving in the valley to make the spiritual crossing my grandparents had already made.

In over sixty years in this country, they paid no nostalgic visits to the fatherland, nor even spoke of doing so. They hardly ever looked back. Perhaps, like my father, they lived only in the day they were in. They were not given to philosophizing about identity or anything else; searching for themselves in the external trappings of ethnicity, the old costumes, the old language, and the old customs, would probably have struck them as trivial and absurd. They knew who they were.

When my father went to school, he was not sent to one of the German language schools that Midwestern immigrant communities of that era were fighting so heatedly to preserve. His school was as American as his parents had become. A one-room structure built at the edge of his father's ranch and filled with a goodly number of his own brothers and sisters, it was named the Lincoln School (and that may have been just the school they needed in Douglas County in clear sight of Jeff Davis Peak).

Ever since the beautiful young teacher, Fanny Dorsey, came to visit at the ranch and took four-year-old George on her knee, he knew he was going to like school. And he did. Lessons were recited standing, though George was allowed to remain seated when one of his chronic asthma attacks left him struggling for breath. Nonetheless, he learned his own lessons and those of the older children as well, and the teachers were soon giving him special instruction. Pranks were punished by a sharp whacking on the hand with a black rubber ruler; George succumbed to that recurrent impulse to pull the long brown hair of Lottie Henningsen, who sat in front of him, only at his peril.

Recess was celebrated by running races along the eight-inch board that topped the school yard fence, or by walking down to the banks of the Carson to watch the logs floating downstream on their journey from Markleeville in the high Sierra to Mound House, where they would be hauled out for use in the Virginia City mines. The children were fascinated by the loggers, their poles and hooks in their hands, balancing on the logs as they drifted down to the next relief station, where new loggers would come out to take their places. Usually the timber slid smoothly down river and out of sight under the skilled prodding of the loggers, but the watching children felt a tingly sense of danger. More than once the logs had jammed and torn the river bank to pieces, and the river had flooded the countryside.

The favorite hobby of the boys in the Lincoln School was stealing birds' eggs, blowing them out, and lovingly hoarding them in boxes. The boy with the largest egg collection was an object of passionate envy. Although H.H. cautioned his children never to steal birds' eggs and often explained the valuable role of birds in eating weed seeds and killing mice, George had taken to spending a good deal of time looking up at the robin's nest in one of the apple trees in the front yard. One day temptation overcame him. He climbed the tree, filled his mouth with the precious blue eggs so his hands would be free for climbing, and began a cautious descent. He was so intent upon his mission that he did not notice his father waiting at the foot of the tree with a willow switch. Several stinging lashes from that switch knocked George out of the tree, and he fell so hard that the eggs broke in his mouth. They were full of baby birds, almost ready to hatch. The repugnant sensation of that mouthful of embryonic birds was more than sufficient to make George abandon egg collecting.

The chronic asthma that plagued my father throughout his childhood was worst in summertime. His younger brother, who slept in the same bed with him, later remembered being awakened at night by George's terrible, racking paroxysms of coughing and lying there for hours at a time, filled with pity and unable to help. One night when he seemed to be slowly choking to death before their eyes, the doctor was summoned. After the examination George arose from his bed and made his way unsteadily to the window of the second-story bedroom. He could hear the doctor talking to his parents on the porch below. His father was asking if there was any hope for him. No, said the doctor, there was none. There must be something they could do, said his mother, gentle and desperate for the slight, frail boy that of all the ten was her favorite child. Perhaps a hospital or a specialist in San Francisco. No, said the doctor kindly, it was no use. The best thing they could do was "leave the boy at home to die." The little boy listening at the window above looked out sightlessly at the dark sky and swore he would *not* die. Somehow he would make himself live.

And somehow, by luck, or by his mother's prayers, or by a shift in the wind that stirred the pollen in his father's fertile fields, or by sheer force of will, he did. The coughing subsided a bit, as he willed it to, he grew stronger, as he knew he must, and at last he was done with fighting to breathe and live. He could go out and play again with his beloved sister Clare.

She was his constant playmate, spirited, teasing, warm-hearted Clare, with her blue eyes and her beautiful chestnut locks. Born two years after George on the same September day as he, she was a soul mate in the truest sense, more like him in spirit than his other brothers and sisters and a little naughtier than any of them dared to be. So naughty, in fact, that she was the only child in the family who ever actually received ashes and a willow switch on Christmas. One of those days when Clare was being particularly naughty she and George later remembered very well indeed.

They were playing on the banks of the big ditch south of the house with Dick Springmeyer, a small Indian boy who, in accordance with the Indian custom of the period, had been given the surname of the owner of the ranch where he was born. Suddenly Clare uprooted a pretty plant with lacy, white flowers and thin, pointed leaves from the damp earth and began nibbling at the pithy, bulbous root.

"Bad! Bad! No eat!" shouted Dick with a kind of horror his playmates had never heard before, but Clare ignored him and took another bite.

"No, Clare, don't eat it! Throw it away!" cried George, convinced by the urgency in Dick's voice that his sister was somehow in danger.

Clare glanced at him with dancing eyes, licked her lips, and gnawed even more ravenously at the root, just to spite him.

George stared at her in mute frustration. She was a girl, so he never thought of wrenching it from her hand, and craft was alien to him, even then. But not to Dick.

"You say you want bite," he whispered in George's ear. Dick knew George must be the one to ask her.

"Give me a bite," George begged Clare. She looked at him uncertainly. They were so close, so dear to each other, that much as she loved to tease, she found it hard to refuse him.

"Oh, please, just one bite," he wheedled.

Hesitantly, she offered him the root. He sprang up and ran to the house with it. There they recognized it as "wild parsnip," a poisonous root the Indians used to commit suicide.[1] Wilhelmine hurried out to throw it in the privy, believing the little girl had not eaten enough to harm herself. George returned to his playmates, and the children wandered over to the temporary swing constructed on the frame ordinarily used to butcher beef. Two of George's older sisters, Ann and Emma, came out to join them. The incident seemed over, just another of Clare's naughty pranks.

But it was not. As Clare swung back and forth, foam began to bubble from her lips. Ann and Emma ran to fetch their father. One of George's older brothers rode off at a gallop to Genoa for the doctor. In the meantime, H.H. gave Clare a strong dose from the chest of homeopathic medicines he had brought from Germany so many years earlier for just such emergencies. That antiquated potion may have diminished considerably in potency during two decades of repose, but at least it remained sufficiently revolting to induce the intense vomiting that H.H. knew was necessary.

Later, when the doctor had examined the pale, crestfallen little girl, he chuckled and said, "Well, H.H., you gave her enough medicine for a horse, but it's the only thing that could have saved her life." H.H., as well, regarded the happy outcome

as a triumph for homeopathic medicine. George was scarcely
less relieved that she was safe than he was proud of having
helped to save her; yet it seems to me that the greater part of
the credit surely belonged not to her father, to her brother, nor
even to homeopathic medicine, but rather to a certain small and
canny Indian, just old enough to recognize the death plant of
his people and more than clever enough to know what to do
when he saw it.

* * *

The family lived almost as a self-contained unit, and the
children's world was the ranch. It was a world quite literally
created for them out of the raw elements of the desert by their
father, standing tall and powerful at the beginning of this world
as God stood at the parting of the waters. But he had not done
it in seven days, or even seven years; indeed he was never done
with making it. These broad fields, willow-lined ditches,
muddy sloughs, and sage country were their work, their suste-
nance, their pride, the source of most of the dangers which
assailed them—from wild parsnip to the pollen that so cruelly
aggravated George's asthma, a cause and effect not understood
until he left the valley years later for college and was suddenly,
almost magically, cured. The ranch was also the source of the
children's only pastimes.

George learned to fish. When he was very small, he caught
a beautiful sunfish and raced home in triumph to show it to his
parents, dragging the fish behind him. Then, reaching there, he
grieved to see that wondrous, shining, rainbow-colored fish, his
own, his very first, all covered with dust. He saw then that the
wild things were beautiful only in life—swimming in the
stream, soaring in the air, or bounding through the grass—not
limp and still in his hand. He knew his older brothers had to
shoot the vicious wildcats that came marauding on the ranch,

The Springmeyer children around 1890. From top left: Louis, Charles, and Leonard. Middle: Emma, Edna on Ann's knee, Margaret, and George. Front: Edward and Clare.

but he never went with them to hunt the ducks and geese that used to flock on the lower end of the pastures. He had no heart for killing.

George learned to swim when H.H., with characteristic directness and intolerance of fear in anyone, including small boys who could not swim, tossed him into deep water. George learned to ride, first on Lord Ribblesdale. H.H. would lift his youngest children up to the stallion's glistening black back, a back long enough to accommodate all the little Springmeyers at once with room to spare. Later came fine saddle horses, English riding habits for the girls, and riding of a riskier variety for some of the boys.

As George's younger brother Ed grew older, he began feeding a wild mule. The mule, in his turn, would bring a string of mustangs from the Pine Nut Hills into the corral where Ed waited to practice riding bucking broncos. The mustangs were wholeheartedly prepared to oblige him. When H.H., who had a low opinion of mustangs and of young men who squandered their time trying to stay aboard that kind of worthless horseflesh, inquired suspiciously what all those tracks in the corral might be, Ed ached from top to bottom—especially to bottom—but his large, blue eyes were innocence itself.

* * * * *

The merchant princes of Hamburg had also reached the New World. Justus Ruperti had arrived in New York as the American representative of the importing and exporting enterprises of the House of Ruperti, and soon, the society editors inform us, the slender young German with the resplendent handlebar mustache became "well known in the fashionable circles of this city." In the spring of 1893, in a milieu considerably removed in space and spirit from the bucking broncos and prowling mountain lions of the Carson Valley, a wedding considered quietly fashionable by the standards of New York society—the press described it as "simple but effective"—was held in New York's Church of the Heavenly Rest. Sallie Nicoll, Justus Ruperti's dark-haired bride, clad in a white satin wedding gown in the newly revived 1830s mode, her veil fastened by a diamond crescent entwined with orange blossoms, moved down the aisle to the strains of Lohengrin in a church bedecked for the occasion with palms and masses of hothouse roses and Easter lilies. Four hundred guests attended the reception that followed in the ballroom at Sherry's.

That day Justus Ruperti had married the glamorous daughter of an American family so aristocratic that his bride could, when she chose, trace her ancestry to the Plantagenets, to Eleanor of Aquitaine, and even to Charlemagne. The time when the paths of the Rupertis and the Springmeyers would intersect was still far in the future.

* * * * *

Weddings were a little plainer in the Carson Valley, and amusements too. On summer evenings when the air was fragrant with the sweet scent of alfalfa and the dusty golden beams of the sinking sun sifted through the canyons of the darkening Sierra Nevada, the men gathered on the benches in front of the bunkhouse to tell stories, sing, wrestle, and run foot races. The veterans sang songs remembered from the Civil War, always including H.H.'s favorite, "Tenting on the Old Campground." On Saturday nights, the men headed for the saloons. H.H. himself liked to lift a glass there, to indulge in a spirited argument on the Austro-Prussian War or Nevada politics, and perhaps to lay a small wager. A mahogany bar in Genoa still bears a deep dent where he slammed down the twenty-dollar gold piece he was betting on his future son-in-law in his race for the state senate in 1906 and said, "Spoil me that for Maurice Mack."

No one in the Springmeyer household ever went to church, and when the traveling missionaries H.H. commonly referred to as "those whiney, kiney guys" came calling at the ranch, they were bodily ejected by H.H. himself. But there was Sunday morning visiting. H.H. would take his wife, dressed up in her black, straw bonnet with the velvet ribbons, and his children in the spring wagon to call upon the neighbors.

On one of these visiting Sundays, George was left at home because his asthma had flared up again. At noon the nine-year-old boy and a dozen hired men sat down at the long, wooden table in the cookhouse for lunch. Charlie, the Chinese cook, brought in some chicken stew and George helped himself to a generous portion. As he was raising a mouthful to his lips, he noticed to his horror that the head and the feet of the chicken were floating around on his plate. He held them up and exclaimed, "Charlie, you son of a bitch, what do you mean by giving us this!"

Insulted, outraged, and indignant at this failure to appreciate his delicacies, Charlie started yammering in Chinese and dashed into the kitchen. Back he came, brandishing a butcher knife, and started over the table after George. The boy was so surprised that he fell over backward. Fortunately, the men were able to restrain—and calm—the raging Charlie before any damage was done.

Charlie's tenure as cook was particularly brief, but none of the cooks stayed long. Another that my father remembered more pleasantly than Charlie was a Frenchman who was a spellbinding storyteller. His stories, however, were of a far more Rabelaisian variety than the virtuous Wilhelmine ever realized when she used to smile fondly on seeing the children clustered around the cook. "Count me one," they would plead, because that, no doubt a mutation of the French verb *conter* (to tell), was invariably the introduction to one of his stories.

An even better storyteller was Tinker Pete, another French immigrant. Sooner or later each year, the shabby tinker with the stubbly salt and pepper beard would come walking up the lane carrying his tin sheets and his welding outfit, and the Springmeyer children would run to meet him. He would shed his coat, several sizes too large for him and turned back at the sleeves, light a fire in the can with the hole in the bottom, set his soldering irons in to heat, and warn the children to stay away from the muriatic acid as it began to boil. Then, while Pete repaired the pots and pans and kettles, the children would gather around to listen to his stories, related in English that was always heavily accented and sometimes unintelligible. The stories ranged from incidents he had seen as he worked his way from house to house in western Nevada and parts of California to yarns about French politics. And what was ever more melodramatic than French politics during the Third Republic, when anarchists had been terrorizing the country for a dozen years? Tinker Pete may well have told them of the fanatical Duval, who had killed a gendarme and proclaimed it a moral blow for anarchism, and the menacing Ravachol, who robbed graves for the cause. The most exciting story George remembered, and the children's favorite, was the assassination of President Carnot. Tinker Pete's voice rose to a dramatic crescendo as he related how the anarchist Vaillant had flung his bomb into the Chamber of Deputies, how Depuy had declared "the sitting will go on," how Vaillant had been condemned, and how, at last, the young Italian assassin Caserio, bent upon vengeance for Vaillant's execution, had approached the presidential carriage through the friendly crowd, waved a paper as though he wanted to present a petition, then leapt upon the carriage step and stabbed Carnot with the dagger he had carried concealed within a newspaper.

No wonder they were fascinated. Caserio and all the rest, with their bloody deeds and strange ideological incantations, must have seemed more bizarre than the giants, ogres, and witches of garden-variety fairy tales; this world of castles and communes and deputies in cutaways called the Third Republic must have sounded more exotic and remote than any once-upon-a-time kingdom. There certainly was nothing like it in the Carson Valley.

Long Valley

IN 1859 A WANDERING prospector named Pete Milich rode down from the Comstock toward Long Valley at the southeast corner of the Carson Valley. He turned his horse into the narrow canyon between low, sage-covered hills where the Indian Creek flowed to join with the East Fork of the Carson River as it emerged from the Pine Nut Hills. Along the rocky hillside he rode, past outcroppings of gray rock encrusted with yellow lichen, the water gurgling noisily below him in the stony creek bed. Farther on, the valley widened, sagebrush grew shoulder high in the fertile earth beneath a bluff capped with tawny stone, and the creek meandered along the eastern edge of the hills between earthen banks taller than a man on horseback. On the western side of the broadening valley lay a flattopped butte among smooth, gray hills that were like dunes; it was uncharacteristic of this region, an incongruous frieze from a southwestern landscape mistakenly transposed before the towering backdrop of the dark Sierra Nevada. Southward where the valley narrowed once more, an irregular hump of a mountain that would one day be known as Springmeyer Peak loomed over an arched bow of foothills. Across the canyon from the mountain,

Pete could see a barren, sunlit upland above a rocky cliff face and a slope of volcanic scree, blackened as though singed in the primeval fires.

Six years earlier the fleeing Indian marauders had halted in this canyon to fight the settlers. Terrorized by repeated Indian raids upon their livestock, a number of settlers had pulled up stakes and left the Carson Valley. The remainder determined to "clean out" the "hostiles" once and for all. The next time the Indians swept down on the Genoa settlement, a party of forty or fifty angry pioneers armed with rifles set out in pursuit. The Indians galloped hard to the south end of the valley, then veered northeast toward the Pine Nut Hills, heading through Diamond and Dutch valleys into the Long Valley canyon. Here they paused and fought. A number of Indians died before the battle shifted over the rocky lap of the hills to Horseshoe Bend. At this point, as it winds its way northward through canyons of pine nuts beneath lofty, stone precipices, the East Carson River curves smoothly around a little valley cupped by gentler hills. Again they fought. More Indians died, and the survivors fled into the trackless mountains. The stolen livestock was found by the river banks.[1]

With those last shots in Horseshoe Bend, Indian troubles in the area had ceased. Pete noticed that an unknown settler had built a cabin in Long Valley but the land was still unfenced. Carson Valley farmers used to go up in the summer to cut the grass hay that grew in the natural meadows in Long Valley and in Diamond Valley farther up the creek. Pete thought it was a good place for a homestead.

He turned his horse around the flank of the humped mountain and rode into the southern end of the canyon. The wind blew more mildly here; the narrow valley seemed sheltered, screened away by the low hills on either side from the raw grandeur of the Sierra and the sweeping space of the eastern desert. The hills beside him were thickly forested with blue-gray pine nut trees, sometimes interspersed with the bitter green of junipers spreading their shaggy-barked branches upward in uneven fans. These pine nuts were old and thick. They had been growing there when Pete Milich was still a boy in the Turkish-held region that today is Yugoslavia. The seasons that had passed while the triangular wound in his forehead healed to an angry, red scar and the broken bones where the bullets had smashed through his arm and his leg were mending had not added a penny's width to the pine nuts' narrow trunks. They would be growing there still, somewhat broader of crown, a trifle taller and more gnarled, slightly thicker and darker in the trunk perhaps, but very little changed when he had lived his life out to the end—and the end would not be soon in coming as long as Pete could keep on shooting straight. He rode on, following the creek steadily upstream, where he could see a small, conical peak of the distant blue Sierra framed between the hills at the end of the Long Valley canyon. He would remember this place.

When he came back in 1870, the unknown settler had gone. No one knows for certain who he was, nor probably ever will. Even this newest of new worlds was already crisscrossed by abandoned hopes, miscarried plans, empty cabins, and nameless graves. Nevada had a history, clearcut, written, and definite, a record of towns that endured, or at least made enough of a splash to be remembered, mines that flourished, settlers who stayed on. Flowing beside and beneath and between the interstices of this known past was a hidden past, invisible, like another dimension, an unwritten, untold history of small failures, unknown intentions, roads that led nowhere.

Pete took up squatter's rights and lived there on and off for nearly twenty years. He dug a ditch, raised a small dam that did not work out, kept a few pigs to eat the rattlesnakes that infested the homestead, and planted some cabbage and other crops. But somehow none of this made much difference. During those years, while Carson Valley became a fine community, Long Valley stayed half wild. It was a place where sage, juniper, squaw bush, pine nut, and wild peach outnumbered the cabbages; coyotes howled by night in the hills that circled the little valley; jack rabbits darted jerkily from beneath the sagebrush; flocks of hungry deer drifted down from the high country in the spring; and the wind blew harder than it ever blows in the Carson Valley. Nor has it greatly changed today.

H.H. first encountered Pete when he served on the jury during a case in which Pete was charged with stealing cattle, killing them on his Indian Creek Ranch, and selling the beef in Virginia City. The jury acquitted him on the ground that because Pete was a cattleman, although he had few cattle, the rancher from whom he had stolen cattle could get even by stealing his. Pete was inordinately grateful to the gentlemen of the jury for their wise and perceptive decision, and he became a frequent visitor at the Springmeyer Ranch. The Springmeyer children were always delighted to see him because they liked to hear the story about how Pete got the deep, triangular scar in the center of his forehead.

Speaking in a low, guttural voice that reminded people of a rumbling volcano, Pete would tell about the days when he was one of the early prospectors working the area that would later be the Comstock. He had staked out a mining claim there and built a small cabin nearby so he would be on hand to protect it from the gangs of claim jumpers that roamed the territory. Because claims were not yet regulated by federal law, gangs of seven or eight claim jumpers would often ride up to a claim and change the monument, throwing away the can containing the owner's name and the dates of his claims.

One day, having spent the previous night in a saloon as was his custom, Pete was sleeping the daylight hours away on the bunk in his cabin with six single-shot muzzle loader guns stacked in the corner. A gang of claim jumpers crept up to the window, peered inside, and saw Pete sound asleep. As he lay there, they shot an arm and a leg, breaking the bones; then, just to make sure, they shot him in the forehead. Understandably they left him for dead, but that was their mistake.

His wounds streaming blood, Pete dragged himself laboriously to the window. Outside he saw the claim jumpers busy moving his monument and smashing his can. Painfully, he balanced his guns on the window ledge and shot five of them. The others ran away. So he said, and there is no doubt that he was an extraordinary shot, as well as a born survivor. Some forty years later, he could still "maka da turkey go floppida" from a distance that few young men could match when he took part in a turkey shoot.

Pete dusted off his gun on a few other occasions besides turkey shoots, like the little disagreement with the Raycraft boys when Pete claimed his Indian Creek Ranch overlapped the Buckeye Mine on the Sage Ranch owned by the Raycrafts. Arthur Raycraft noticed Pete roaming around near the top of the hill behind his cabin and began shooting at him with his breech loader gun. Pete returned the shots. Suddenly Arthur's gun was silent. Thinking Arthur was playing possum, Pete "ringed" the cabin, shooting bullet holes a foot apart back and forth across the walls from floor to ceiling, but Arthur had already run away from the cabin unseen. He later said the gun battle got too hot for him when a bullet removed part of his mustache—a close shave. Pete had suffered one too, or at least a close rip, when one of Arthur's bullets tore a crease across the stomach of his jumper coat. But what was just one more bullet to indestructible old Pete Milich? He was a failure at everything he turned his hand to but a master at the art of survival.[2]

In 1889, an important gentleman named Francis Newlands made a well-timed and carefully planned move to Nevada. He was all that Pete Milich was not, although the scarred, old Yugoslav immigrant had been many things over the years—a murderer once, a miner for a time, a hotel keeper in Carson City, a wood dealer on Gold Hill, a homesteader who drifted into debt, a rustler sometimes, a wanderer first of all. Newlands, by contrast, did but one thing and did it well; he was a lawyer, educated at Yale and linked through his first wife to one of the great Comstock fortunes. He had arrived belatedly in Nevada, where a wealthy man with the right connections, whose political ambitions had been inexplicably frustrated in California, could be rapidly elected to Congress, as he was in 1892, and could ascend a decade later to his rightful place in the United States Senate. He knew how to manipulate a popular issue like free silver as well as any politician west of the Mississippi, but he was not merely a wealthy outsider using the rotten borough for his own purposes. In the final analysis, he became the closest thing to a statesman ever to emerge in the motley panorama of Nevada politics. Pete Milich had seen no farther than a ditch and a cabbage patch; Francis Newlands envisaged a statewide irrigation system to provide "the basis of an enduring civilization in Nevada."[3] A key part of it would be the Long Valley reservoir site he and his friend Herman Springmeyer had been discussing.

H.H. and Newlands rode out to look it over one day. Physically they must have been a somewhat unlikely pair: Newlands short, potbellied, and in all likelihood wearing one of the plaid suits that were his trademark; my grandfather tall, lean, and probably swathed in his beloved buffalo coat, if it was cold enough. But in the realm of ideas, Springmeyer's keen surveyor's eye, his practical understanding of irrigation, and his intimate knowledge of the Carson Valley region complemented Newlands's grandiose visions. Later, when Pete was told that H.H.'s friend was *the* Francis Newlands, wealthy investor, one time son-in-law of the fabulous Sharon, and rising star of Nevada politics, the old Yugoslav was unimpressed and muttered sourly, "I doan care. I only fedim cobboge." The next time

H.H. and Newlands went out to consider the Long Valley site, George watched with more amusement than dismay as Newlands's wagon overturned while crossing the narrow, rocky bed of the Indian Creek and the ladies in the Newlands party were upended in a bouquet of billowing skirts. In 1889 H.H. and Newlands bought the Milich homestead, three workhorses, one saddle horse, and three milch cows from Pete for $8,000.

The purchase was part of an ambitious plan for reclamation in the Carson Valley that H.H. and Newlands had developed together. An engineer named Lyman Bridges, engaged by the federal irrigation survey, reported to the U.S. Senate Committee on Irrigation that Reclamation Commissioner H. Springmeyer "accompanied me for four days to the head of the Carson Valley, going well up the head of the three branches of the Carson River." Bridges recommended a state-owned "grand receiving reservoir" in Long Valley, which he anticipated would irrigate more than 100,000 additional acres.[4] That was more than four times the number of acres under irrigation in Douglas County, enough to substantially improve the faltering state economy. Also, and by no means incidentally, it would ensure an adequate water supply farther downstream, where Comstock ores were processed in the Union Mills, an enterprise in which much of the Sharon fortune was invested and in which Newlands, as a Sharon trustee, was keenly interested. The Nevada Reclamation Commission, newly created by the legislature of 1889, asked Bridges to submit a plan and expressed the intention to proceed with construction.

In fact, H.H. and the other reclamation commissioners were hoping for the federal funds that Newlands was certain could be obtained. After posing the rhetorical question, "how shall this Great Work be done?" in their report to the Senate committee, the commissioners went on to plead for "a very small moiety" from the "national treasure house" to aid "this struggling people"; otherwise, they warned, "Nevada must remain as it is, poor in wealth and sparse in population."[5]

They well knew what they wrote: the grand receiving reservoir with its tunnel and canals was beyond Nevada's means. Since the mines had failed, the state had spiraled downward into the harshest depression Nevadans had ever known. The days now seemed immeasurably remote when Mark Twain could write of the Comstock, "Money was wonderfully plenty. The trouble was not how to get it but how to spend it, lavish it, get rid of it, squander it,"[6] and Sutro could actually construct his fanciful drainage tunnel four miles through the mountains.

Of course, money was still available in the proper places for the right projects. George Ferris's marvelous wheel, twenty-five stories high and big enough to carry 2,000 people at a time would presently be constructed in Chicago at a cost of $390,000. There was capital for such luxurious frivolities in Chicago; in Nevada, there was only desperation. People were leaving. During the eighties a quarter of the population departed. Every man, woman, and child still residing in Nevada in the nineties could have gone for a ride in less than two dozen turns of the Ferris wheel. The price of that wheel would have paid the entire expenses of the state of Nevada in the year 1890 with more than $50,000 left over in change.[7] Rudimentary as these expenses were, state revenues could barely be stretched to cover them, and the state was manifestly unable to appropriate sufficient funds for reclamation. In 1891 the Nevada Reclamation Act was repealed. Although Newlands was elected to Congress the following year, more confident than ever that federal money could be secured for the plan, nothing materialized.

My grandfather's faith in that small moiety from the national treasure house was obviously fading when he began extensive improvements on the Indian Creek Ranch, as the Milich place was known, and dispatched an Indian work crew under his foreman, Lyman Frisbie, to start clearing out sagebrush. At least, that was what H.H. hoped they were doing. It took a razor-tongued foreman to keep them at it. At pine nut time they always disappeared; sometimes they disappeared a good deal sooner, and they tended to be lackadaisical in between. They were still in the process of acculturation, used to another life, to the hunter's rhythms, and indifferent to purposes that were not their own. Their attitude toward ranch labor was well illustrated by the old Indian named Joe, whom my father encountered one spring day some years later when he went calling on pretty, young Lillian at the Fay Ranch. As he walked toward the house, George noticed Joe reclining by the side of the barn.

"Hello, Joe," he said, "how's the fishing these days?"

"No fish no more," said Joe mournfully. "Work all time."

"Is that so?" said George, looking at the recumbent Indian with some surprise. "Where are you working?"

"Maybe so pick potatoes for Pete Van Sickle next fall," said Joe in the tones of a man both overburdened and weary.

Well aware that the Indians did not fully subscribe to his firm conviction that "work is fun," H.H. made frequent trips to Long Valley to see how Lyman Frisbie and his crew were progressing. George was beside his father on the wagon one day when H.H. drove his team through the narrow, boulder-strewn canyon into the center of Long Valley. When they reached the crew, Frisbie was nowhere to be seen, but nonetheless the Indians were grubbing out sagebrush with astonishing industry. Mattocks swung vigorously, dust flew, the stacks of sagebrush heightened before George's eyes. They worked as though the devil himself were lashing their backs; in fact, as George soon learned, he was. Scarcely able to conceal his surprise, H.H. inquired where Frisbie had gone. One of the Indians grunted,

"Him catch fish in creek."

A little distance up the Indian Creek, H.H. and George came upon the truant foreman taking his ease on a grassy bank as he dangled his line in the stream. More curious than displeased, H.H. asked Frisbie how he could keep the Indians working so energetically without supervising them.

"Well, you know I have a glass eye," said Frisbie, "and they asked me what made it stand still. I told them, 'Debbil eye! Watch you all time.' Yesterday I thought I'd like to go fishing. I put the eye up on a bush and told the Indians the devil would watch them so they better work hard. You can see what they're doing."

H.H. roared with laughter. The devil made a hell of a good foreman. It was a shame he didn't last longer.

Some days later H.H. and George went out to Long Valley again. Frisbie was missing as before, but this time the mattocks were silent and the Indians were dozing lazily in the sun. When H.H. found Frisbie fishing upstream, he gave him a piece of his mind, and by no means the most amiable portion. The foreman was honestly puzzled. He protested that he couldn't understand what had gone wrong because that morning he had put "debbil eye" up on the bush just as usual. The three walked over to the bush and discovered that the Indians had found a way to beat the devil: a can had been neatly placed over "debbil eye."

From then on the trout could swim unmolested; Lyman Frisbie had to apply himself to his regular duties. The sagebrush clearing went on, but the grand plan never materialized. Small reservoirs were eventually built on the upper Carson: first the Alpine system in the nineties, planned and partially financed by H.H., Newlands, and Governor Sadler; later another system under the auspices of the Dangberg enterprises. Newlands, aided by the fortuitous accession of Theodore Roosevelt, did eventually father the Newlands Reclamation Act in 1902, and a large reclamation project using the surplus waters of the Carson and Truckee rivers was constructed with federal funds in Churchill County. But the grand receiving reservoir in Long Valley never existed outside the minds of the men who con-

ceived it. Like an empty cabin or a road overgrown with sagebrush and tumbleweed, it was another plan that miscarried,
another chapter of invisible history.

By 1897 H.H. was thoroughly disgusted. Newlands had
failed to obtain the needed federal money, and his proposals
had not even received serious congressional consideration. The
two grown sons to whom H.H. had planned to give the Indian
Creek Ranch and the nearby Falcke Ranch absolutely refused
to live out there in that wild place with the coyotes, the rattlesnakes, and the howling winds. The old man must have wondered sometimes how these sons would have endured the
windowless cabin where he and his young wife made their
beginning; we know he despised the weakness he saw in them.
In anger, he sold all his holdings in the area except the Indian
Creek Ranch, which he kept for a summer range. Clare and
George were watching when another Carson Valley rancher
walked into the living room and counted out the price in gold
for the Mud Lake reservoir H.H. had made from Pete Milich's
pond.

Newlands and H.H. remained friendly, and some may have
been surprised to note that whenever Newlands came to the
valley to make a speech for the Silverites, and after the demise
of the Silver party, for the Democrats, he later repaired to the
ranch of one of the community's leading Republicans to spend
the night. Most of those evenings were spent discussing politics, but Newlands also had a new investment in mind. He tried
to persuade H.H. to go into partnership with him to develop
some acreage he owned near Reno. At that time the two red-
wood houses that Newlands had built along the Truckee River
and the Lake House on the corner of Virginia and California
streets were the southwestern boundaries of Reno. The Newlands acreage extended southwest of the present courthouse
and was devoted solely to sagebrush.

When H.H. was thinking, he used to lie on the couch with his left arm crooked over his head to absentmindedly rub his right eyebrow. This time, however, there was no need for reflection. Newlands's idea was a smart investment, but somehow it was not my grandfather's kind of plan. It meant guessing where a city would go, buying land you cared nothing for and knew your sons would never work, and selling when the price was right. It was not the same as walking a new piece of land, scanning with your eyes and feeling the slope with your feet, laying the rods and figuring how you would channel the water to turn the gray to green, not the same as planting trees and watching them grow. You would expect him to say no and, in fact, that was what he said:

"Hell, no. I've got too much sagebrush land of my own."

Growing Up

A CARSON VALLEY NIGHT in 1897 at the Anderson's bar in Millerville. A scene so commonplace the imagination conjures it easily: the frosty November chill without and the warmth within; the clink of glasses; the scratch of brooms, as Henrietta Anderson, known to her family and friends as Yetta, and her sisters cleaned up after the Thanksgiving dance; the intermingling baritone of masculine voices, a little louder for the drink, from the men lingering on at the bar tended by Yetta's father. Yetta's young uncle Hans was still there. So was her red-haired sweetheart, Leo Springmeyer, waiting for her to finish her work. Though he was talking and laughing with the rest, his glance must frequently have strayed to the petite figure of the dark-haired young woman working so busily, and perhaps a little self-consciously, with her sisters.

The speed with which the events of the next few minutes unfolded was the only element on which everyone in the Millerville saloon could afterward agree. Hans Anderson was buying a round for the boys at the bar, but he had no intention of treating the itinerant young workman named Adam Uber, who had just walked in. Some said he knocked Uber to the floor and was kicking him when Uber pulled his gun; others claimed Anderson was just standing over Uber when he was shot.

Yetta Anderson saw none of these causes or justifications. It was all over in less time than it took to sweep the dust pile into her dust pan. What Yetta saw, frozen in her mind as a single, uninterrupted parabola of motion, was a strange man who simply walked into her father's bar and shot her uncle.

Before the day was out Anderson had died of his wound and Uber was in the county jail in Genoa. A few days later he nervously protested to a reporter that it was all over before he knew what had happened, that he was sorry, that his sister was a missionary, that his mother was a Methodist, that he had "very careful early religious training."[1] But trouble was coming all the same. Rumors were spreading. Men were meeting and talking of the agonies Anderson had suffered before he died. They despised Adam Uber for being the first to pull a gun, and nothing the frightened prisoner said made any difference.

On the night of December 7, young Ed Springmeyer refused to fetch the mail from the box at the end of the lane. Although the family reminded him that this nightly chore was his, he cowered fearfully on the floor murmuring something he had overheard about "bad men." My father was finally sent in Ed's place. His breath whitening in the cold air, George walked down the lane to the mailbox and pulled out the letters brought by stage from Genoa. He wondered why so many riders were out on the main road on an ordinary winter evening. A buckboard passed, followed by a group of horsemen, then another buckboard.

Yet this was no ordinary winter evening. When he later heard his father talking angrily with two of his older brothers, George understood that uncommon confluence of night riders on the road. H.H. had some reverence for the law and scant regard for any man with the dead Anderson's reputation for abusing horses. The agonies the teamster had suffered in the end were

slight compared to the pain he had long inflicted on the luckless
animals beneath his whip. This was the man, H.H. reminded his
sons, who had driven one of his horses until it was too exhausted to go on, then dragged it behind the wagon, injuring
the animal so badly it had to be shot. H.H. despised that kind
of senseless cruelty. As Hans Anderson had lived, so let him die.

Though my father made no mention of it, my guess is that
H.H. gave voice to a few more of the opinions we know he held.
He would have said the brutal Hans was just one of a bad lot,
a family of barkeeps and serving girls. Leo would do well to stay
away from those Andersons, including the girl he was so set on
marrying. Let the Andersons settle their own quarrels, no matter what Leo thought he had seen in the bar that night. He
would probably have added some pungent comments on the
Elgeses, who were so busy stirring things up. They were vicious
men most people were afraid to cross, but no Springmeyer
should be intimidated by them. I know the old man told Leo
and Charlie it was "a bad business" and forbade them to take
any part in it.

No one relates what Leo said in reply, although there is quite
a bit he might have said. That he thought the Andersons were
good people, not at all the kind that H.H. said they were. That
he had seen what happened with his own eyes and he was a
grown man now, able to make his own decisions. That Uber
deserved to swing because he was the first to pull a gun. That
the old man himself knew a little bit about revenge and about
making your own kind of justice.

But somehow I don't think he did. He was the kind who held
things inside and didn't talk much. I suspect he listened in
silent, sullen defiance, like a mule with his ears laid back under
the crack of the black snake whip. And Charlie stood with him,
either for reasons of his own or because he always went along
with Leo.

Then my father heard the sound of hooves like muffled drum beats as his two older brothers rode out to join the lynchers.

Sometime after midnight the mob, led by Henry and Fritz Elges, gathered at the Genoa jail. When the crowd of masked men armed with rifles and pistols demanded Uber, the sheriff handed him over without resistance. The helpless prisoner was stripped and dragged kicking and screaming for a quarter mile to the spot where the big cottonwood tree grew. As they looped the rope around his neck, Uber cursed the lynchers. Each one, he swore, would "lead a life of misery and come to a bad end." Five rifle bullets ripped into his body as it swung above Boyd's Lane. The sheriff and the constable, who had witnessed the scene under guard, were told to go home and "know nobody," and did.

No justice was forthcoming for Adam Uber at the hands of the law; the valley began to close ranks behind its own. The county commissioners pointedly abstained from offering a reward for the apprehension of the lynchers. When asked to explain this unusual omission, Commissioner Rodenbah observed that Uber had gained a bad reputation. Despite an order to leave town, he had hung around for several months selling whiskey to Indians. The roads around Gardnerville had lately been crowded with drunken Indians, who acted "very saucy and ugly." In the commissioner's opinion, Uber was "unfit to live." The governor finally posted the reward.[2] The local newspaper editor, reproved by friends and neighbors for his initial criticism of the affair, shifted into line. Replying to vehement attacks by other members of the Nevada press upon this "terrible offense against the laws of God and man," he warmly defended the Douglas County officials and advised his censorious colleague on the *Virginia Report* to "take a tablespoonful of Syrup of Figs in the solitude of your chamber every night before you say your prayers and leave the back door unlocked, and you'll come out alright when the season of green fruit comes again." Writing under the nom de plume of "Quelquefois" in an editorial column, Uber's former attorney argued that the prosecution of twenty-five to thirty men would be financially ruinous because it would bring a large increase in the tax rate.[3] So much for the laws of God and man.

Acting on a strong hint from the Ormsby County Sheriff, Charles Williams left town. He had been Uber's friend, perhaps his only friend. A ranch worker named Bill Jones who had been heard to remark that had he been present with his Winchester at the cottonwood tree "there would have been more dead men than Uber" received a letter in which he was "warned and notified to leave this valley and county never to return again before the end of this week or you will be treated in the same manner as Adam Uber." It was signed "Law Promoters." Jones, however, was made of sterner stuff than Williams. He announced that "I shall not leave this county until I get ready" and no doubt began oiling his Winchester. The letter was casually dismissed by the sheriff as a schoolchild's prank.[4]

Few men in the valley were fool enough to spit into the wind like Jones, and the gale was blowing strong. A petition signed by a lengthy roster of prominent local citizens accused the critics of "trying to encourage murderers." The petitioners stoutly asserted that "justice has been meted out for the first time to a murderer in Douglas County."[5] When the grand jury commenced deliberations on Uber's death, the judge found it necessary to instruct its members that the "social standing or financial worth of those who perpetrated the crime should not deter you in the least."[6] No indictments were returned.

The secret was sealed. Leo and Yetta married, the threat of indictment faded away, the years passed, but to the day he died, not one of their surviving children ever heard Leo mention the Uber lynching. Just before her death, Yetta told her daughter

Aila what happened that night in the Millerville saloon. She spoke of the curse. Though she did not say whether she believed in it, this was a woman superstitious enough to panic over a broken mirror or a glimpse of a black cat. The curse had probably festered for a long time. Yetta said she thought what the men had done was justified. But her silence over more than sixty years, broken only at the end by a single recounting, a kind of deathbed confession, suggests shame. Aila seems to have recognized this, for she told her sisters nothing.

"The Lord has saved me from all feeling against them," Uber's sister wrote to his former attorney. "I can pray for these fellows who murdered my brother."[7] Though they mocked her piety in the press, they had more need of her prayers than they cared to admit. Valley people knew how to shield their own from the laws of man. They knew how to keep a silence so complete it was as though that night had never been. But the curse remained.

Past midnight one Saturday, after a night of carousing in the saloons and dance halls of Genoa, Henry and Fritz Elges set out down Boyd's Lane toward home in their split cart. In the morning, so my father told me, their senseless bodies were found sprawled beneath the cottonwood tree, staring blindly at the sky. Several hours later, the doctor succeeded in restoring them to consciousness. The pair swore that Adam Uber's ghost, armed with a terrible strength the little man had never possessed in life, had swooped down from the branch that overhung the road as they drove beneath. They struck the ground; their fear-crazed horse raced away with the cart. When they tried to fight the ghost, their fists struck only emptiness. As helpless as the wretched Uber had been when the mob dragged him to that tree, they were pounded and beaten and pummeled until they knew no more. The branch was cut away, but the Elgeses were henceforth "peculiarly on the alert," as my father phrased it, when riding on Boyd's Lane after dark.

After that people started noticing things. Maybe it was the shared guilt that enveloped the valley like a family secret. Or perhaps the cruel accidents and soul-destroying hardships of Nevada ranching in those early days made it easy to believe in the malevolent presence of a vengeful spirit. Anyway, things happened and, quietly and privately, people began to talk. Two men who had been at the lynching were said to have drifted into insanity and died mysteriously. Another veered into madness after his son was shot in Goldfield. He could not get Uber off his mind, they said. He used to walk up and down murmuring about the way they had kicked and beaten Uber as they dragged him to the tree that night. The things that happened to the children were the hardest to bear—one child was crushed beneath the heavy wheels of a wagon, another tumbled into a boiling vat of ham and bacon, a small girl was caught and killed in the gears of a pump—and some said the stricken fathers who buried them had ridden with the mob.

If my father connected these tragedies with the lynching, he never said so, but he spoke soberly of his brothers: Charlie had died a suicide; Leo, once full of promise, had "never amounted to much" after the death of his only son from pneumonia. A miserable life, Uber had sworn when he cursed them, and the dying of the child had brought grief without end.[8]

I remember looking at the big old tree in Boyd's Lane and shivering a little as my father told me this story. I must have been about eight then. The light seemed suddenly grayer, the day colder than before. "It couldn't be true, could it?" I asked my father. "The dead stay in their graves. Ghosts don't swoop down from trees. And you don't believe in curses, do you?" I waited for him to say no. Surely he would, for he was a thoroughly rational man who could poke fun at superstition, walk through a graveyard at midnight without a qualm, demolish any miracle in the Bible with a hearty blast of logic, and gently tease my mother about what he liked to call "the mummery of popes." But he was slow to answer, and I knew he was remembering his dead brothers. The wind began to whisper, stirring up the pale undersides of the cottonwood leaves. It seemed a long time before he patted my shoulder and said what I was waiting to hear, "No, of course there's nothing in it."

* * *

During his growing up years my father was learning day by day, changing from the tiny unformed child the family had called "little papoosie" into the man he would be. The first memory of his life had been awakening to find himself sliding across the floor in his trundle bed as an earthquake jolted the house, then walking outside, his hand tightly clasped in that of his older sister, to see water boiling up from the innards of the earth through the cracks that had suddenly appeared in the lane. The water soon subsided, the cracks were filled and leveled, but even though neither the landscape nor the child had altered in any permanent way, remembrance began. In a sense, his childhood in the Carson Valley ended with another violent jolt, this time one that would have much to do with the future course of his life. It happened on the day in 1898 when Black Wallace came to call.

My father had never seen Black Wallace, but every man, woman, and child in Nevada must have known who he was. The Southern Pacific had ruled Nevada politics for nearly three decades, and Black Wallace, thus nicknamed for his dark hair and swarthy skin, had ascended from his original power base as the assessor of Eureka County in the barren deserts of the eastern part of the state to become the Southern Pacific boss for Nevada. Politicians might come or go, parties could win or lose, voters could enjoy some harmless diversion at the polls if it amused them, but Black Wallace reigned supreme, the lord of all he surveyed. County assessors valued property as he directed; legislatures obeyed; state conventions, as Sam Davis, who had attended many of them, later recalled, awaited his word as "the general order of a military commander to his troops."[9] It might be necessary at times to pack state central committees, arrange jobs for legislators, bribe voters, or set up a new political party when the citizenry grew particularly restive, but no one ever bucked Black Wallace, and few had ever tried.

H.H. had left the legislature after the 1889 session to concentrate on his work as reclamation commissioner; in 1892, after the reclamation act was repealed, he had campaigned for the assembly once again and had been swept aside, along with most Nevada Republican candidates in that year of political turmoil, by the onrushing tide of the victorious Silver party. In 1898 he was planning a campaign against Silverite incumbent Hank Martin for Douglas County's seat in the state senate. That year Black Wallace was running the Silver party as he had formerly run the Republican party, and running it with one supreme objective—the reelection of Senator William Stewart by the next legislature. His call upon the Republican candidate at a time when the Silverites already had an incumbent legislator on their slate remains a minor mystery, but it is clear enough that party labels were mere conveniences to Black Wallace.

Eager to see this infamous political boss, George waited unobtrusively in the living room and overheard the conversation that followed Wallace's arrival. First came a period of general pleasantries, for Wallace was always a courteous man. "Well, Herman, you've been in the assembly for two terms," the Southern Pacific boss at length remarked, referring to my grandfather's legislative service some years before, "and now you want to be state senator."

"Yes," said H.H., "and I hope to be elected."

Hope played no part in Black Wallace's calculations. It was too intangible, risky, uncertain, a word for men who did not know the outcomes. Black Wallace always knew. He dealt only in certainties, bought and paid for by the Southern Pacific. "The legislature will elect a United States senator next year," said Wallace, "and we want a man favorable to the Southern Pacific to be elected, and we want only laws which the Southern Pacific says are alright. So, Herman, the Southern Pacific will put up money to buy enough votes to elect you if you will vote the way I tell you."[10]

I can imagine how my grandfather looked at him. No man in Nevada had ever fought the Southern Pacific and won, but he did not care. He had battled the Danes, beaten his superior officer, defied his brothers, broken with the Dangbergs, and pushed back the desert itself; he had not journeyed halfway around the world to bend a servile knee before the Southern Pacific.

"There's no railroad collar around my neck," roared H.H.; "I'll vote as I damn please."

"Alright, Herman," said Black Wallace quietly as he stood up, "then you will lose. Hank Martin will be the senator. We'll buy the votes for him."

Black Wallace kept his word; he always did. H.H. lost the election. He never ran for the legislature again, but in time the son who listened that day would fight the Southern Pacific as he had fought, refuse the yoke as he had refused, and finally lose as he had lost. In 1898 the die was already cast.

* * *

H.H. turned his attention back toward his family and his ranch. The older children were growing up now. Margaret had married young Fritz, the son of H.H.'s half brother. Charlie had married Nasie Neddenriep in a fancy wedding that went on for two days at the Neddenriep ranch. The only trouble with the Neddenrieps was that they were Hanoverians, not Westphalians, and some years later when another Neddenriep started paying court to Clare, H.H. always left his shotgun conspicuously stationed near the front door. Emma had married a team-ster, divorced him, tied her two small children to a tree in her yard, and set out to become one of the first nurses in Nevada. Though I knew Emma well, this was the only glimpse she ever gave me of her past. My mother says it was a little different, that Clare took care of Emma's boys at least part of the time. But that is not the way Emma wanted to remember it. I recog-nize now that there was a dim personal triumph inside this heartless image: when her marriage turned out badly, she had not clung to it for fear of facing the world alone, she had not gone home to the ranch, ashamed and contrite for marrying against her father's wishes—she had learned a respectable pro-fession and made a life of her own. Probably she believed, as her father did, that the child thrown in deep water learns how to swim. So I will remember her the way she wanted me to, knotting the rope to a tree and turning her back on her children.

Louis had left the home ranch too. If Newlands was willing to oblige with a recommendation, H.H. wanted West Point for the boy after he finished his engineering studies at a California college. Then Louis met and married a woman named Snow, and that was the end of West Point. H.H. was furious, but he should have remembered, if no one had the courage to tell him, that he probably would not have let West Point stand between him and Wilhelmine either.

* * *

Life was easier for Wilhelmine now. The hard, early days in the cabin were past, the older children were grown, and she no longer carried a baby in her arms as she had done for twenty years of her life. But suddenly she, who had neither sickened nor faltered through all those years, became seriously ill with quinsy. H.H. learned that Dr. Black had gone visiting at the Ardery home in Carson City and took her there posthaste. When he had examined her tonsils, the doctor said tersely, "The only way to do it is cut them out right away."

Having no instruments with him, Dr. Black proceeded to sharpen his knife on a grindstone. Then, under the apple tree in Ardery's yard, he cut out the diseased tonsils without benefit of anesthesia. Although Wilhelmine had lost a good deal of blood and felt violently ill, she would never have thought of pausing to rest and recuperate in Carson City so far from the ranch. Herman, for his part, had seen her small, indomitable figure almost ceaselessly at work for nearly thirty years, cleaning, washing, sewing, and cooking for a family of twelve, and sometimes turning out three substantial meals a day for twenty men. Much as he cherished her, he was probably unable to conceive of anything she could not do if she set her mind to it.

Shaken but determined, she sat beside her husband in the open spring wagon so they could begin the drive of more than sixteen miles back to the ranch. The smooth, gray, sage-covered hill that separates Carson City from the Carson Valley must have swelled like a great barrier before her eyes; where the Sierra formed the western rim of the valley, the high, blue, pyramidal peaks of Job and Job's Sister, visible many miles away, must have glimmered as beacons do in the distance. Never before and never again would that road seem so long. When they crossed the alkali flats near the Cradlebaugh Bridge, the afternoon wind began to blow, and she, with the open wound in her throat, had to breathe the acrid, white dust that billowed around the wagon. Later, with her sons and daughters clustered quietly around her bed, she whispered, "I would rather give birth to ten more children than make another trip like that one."

It was one of the few remarks she made that anyone later remembered, though no one forgot her glowing sweetness and her many kindnesses. I have seen her only in photographs, most often in my father's favorite, where she stands in the chicken yard among her hens, a tiny, erect old lady in a high-necked, cotton dress, her once lovely hands as rough as pine bark. I have known her only by asking what she was like. The older members of the family, each in turn, always answer with the same story, unmistakably the one that each believes sums up her character entirely.

A few years before my grandmother's death in 1929, the old couple were discussing their burial arrangements at a large family gathering in the Carson City house where my grandparents had lived since their retirement with their daughter Ann and her husband, George Russell. H.H. said he favored cremation because "I don't want the pigs gnawing my bones," a strange anxiety which I suspect must have originated in some nightmare scene witnessed years before as a young hussar in the Austro-Prussian War. Seeing the utterly horrified expression the word *cremation* brought to his mother's face, George asked, "But what about you, Mother? What do *you* want?"

Wilhelmine composed her features, folded her hands, and said firmly, "If Papa wants it, that we do."

And this, they assure me, was the essence of my grandmother. H.H. subsequently left instructions for burial, not cremation, which may show more about him and her together than anyone seems to have noticed. H.H. could have told me more, perhaps told me things that no one else ever knew about the woman he always considered "a damn sight finer" than himself. He was a hard man, endowed with the original model of what has since become known around the valley as "the Springmeyer temper." He had exchanged angry words with all his brothers and his children. But no one ever heard him say a harsh word to her. And after she died, three years before him, he still lay down at night holding the place where she had been when he slept with his arms around her each night for sixty years.

After her death, his mood grew darker. He was harsh and impatient with the niece who drove him to Wilhelmine's grave each week. The car could not get there fast enough to suit him. He sat brooding by the hour in his high-backed, black leather rocker, no longer enveloped in the happy peace that emanated from her when she sat beside him with her rough, wrinkled, little hand in his. Supper time was spent vehemently arguing politics with his son-in-law, though both were staunch Republicans. Privately, and never so that Clare or George could hear, Russell used to call him "the old Bolshevik," a term that must have referred not to the substance of his ideas but to the revolutionary fervor with which he maintained them. Possibly his son-in-law never quite comprehended that the "old Bolshevik" enjoyed a rousing difference of opinion as much as he did a good cigar.

Aside from these animated nightly discussions, certain pleasures continued. The old man still rode horseback on his weekly visits to the ranch, even the week before he died at the age of eighty-seven. That is the last photograph we have of him, thin and spectral in a gray suit astride a black horse. With those he loved well, he remained observant, thoughtful, and humorous, still the gentleman of whom the others used to say "he was a cut above the rest." Every Saturday Leo's little daughters came to see him. They were cleaned up till they sparkled, warned not to bother grandfather with their chatter because he was hard of hearing, and brought into his presence to sit in total silence, awed and slightly fearful, before the fierce blue stare of the old man in the black leather chair. After about an hour, he would say, "You can go now," and give them each a dollar, which they thought a princely kind of largesse.

Perhaps he enjoyed these little girls as he did the fresh, pretty roses in his garden. Or looked in them for the shadow of a beloved face. Or thought of the great family tree with ever broadening branches that he and Wilhelmine had rooted in America. All their ten children save one had lived and thrived to grow up and to marry and to have children of their own. Edna, the youngest, blondest, brightest, prettiest child of them all had skipped across their lives like a little fairy and charmed even the gruff, hard-bitten teamsters who drove her father's wagons. No matter how many years passed, no one could ever remember her death without pain.

When I began writing this book three years before my Uncle Ed died, I went to ask him about his parents and the things he remembered. We talked for a time, but he seemed distracted. Something was wrong. He lapsed into silence, and tears came to his eyes. "There's something I have to tell you, but I can't say the words," he said finally.

He was past ninety then, so frail, so old, so easily broken. I could not bear his distress. "Don't tell me," I said. "Please. My father told me. I don't need to know more."

"It wasn't your fault," said his wife gently, as I think she had often done over the years. "She doesn't need to hear."

But all the same he felt he had to tell me. About the November day when his parents went visiting, about the older sister who neglected to watch the children, about the big brother who had been duck hunting and left his shotgun on the table by the creamery door, about the two little children who went running happily out of the house to play, about the little boy who picked up the shotgun and whirled it around, about the little girl who fell and lay so still.

My father had told me how they found Edna there on the brick floor of the creamery with her jaw shot away. They carried her tenderly into the house and laid her on the bed. Her wound was so terrible, her soundless agony so great, that none of her family—not her grief-stricken mother, nor her father with all his strength—could sit beside the dying child without breaking down except George, then just twelve years old. As he had willed himself to breathe when the asthma stifled and convulsed him, now he willed himself not to weep that he might comfort his sister, and the tears stayed inside. He sat beside her and held her hand. She never lost consciousness. All through the long night her blue eyes never left his face and when morning came, at last she died.

The good reverend who came to call in sympathy when it was over was not admitted. They had no use for the church in the days of their good fortune; they would have none of it now in their adversity. They would grieve alone. Even so, the whole valley came to stand beside them at the funeral. After they had buried Edna in the graveyard on the corner of the ranch, H.H. made a decision about George. "Anyone who could stand that ought to be a doctor," he said. So a few years later when George was sent away to college, everything was settled. He was going to be a doctor.

Leaving the Valley

WHEN MY FATHER set off on the fifty-mile journey from the ranch to the University of Nevada in 1898, he had never traveled so far before, nor had he seen so great a metropolis as Reno. He had visited Carson City, of course, but that was known as a "living cemetery," a town so dull that "men fall asleep in the middle of the street going from one groggery to another." Nevadans used to say if someone died on the courthouse steps in Carson City on a Saturday, he would not be found until Monday morning. Turn of the century Reno, by contrast, enjoyed the racy reputation of a "wide open town." By far the largest city in Nevada at that time, Reno was a busy commercial community of nearly 4,500 people clustered at the foot of the Sierra on the Southern Pacific line. New university students had to be warned about its "numerous temptations" and urged to the path of "systematic manhood."[1]

The University of Nevada my father saw was not the lovely campus of today with is fine tall trees, rolling green lawns, and spacious buildings. It was a tiny colony of eight brick buildings, a few skimpy new tree sprigs, and a corral fence situated on a barren hillside overlooking Reno. But in comparison to the one-room Lincoln School it must have seemed an awesome center of learning. Behind the mechanical engineering building was a new windmill. And there were real electric lights. A freshman was reported to have tried "long and earnestly" to light them with matches.[2]

This unenlightened freshman was not the only innocent among the university's students, then numbering about 300 and shepherded by a faculty of 25. Many students, newly transplanted from remote farming communities, must have been as naive as the rube described in a fable in the *Student Record,* their college newspaper. It began: "And it Happened that there came to the 'Varsity, from a Remote Corner of the Sagebrush, a Raw Rube. He Opined that he had Rind enough to Jar even the Dead Ones." He then met a blonde coed, but "when it came to the Great Circe Act she was a Lulu and a Wonder and the Way she Snared the Innocents was a Holy Fright." The smitten Rube spent his time writing poetry to her and soon began cutting lectures and failing exams. Suddenly his Circe went off with a "Wise Guy," giving the Rube the "Chilly Mit." "The Fellows passed him the Sympathetic Grin and told him he was Bug House. But in the course of time, the Rube got Next, and Worked off his Cons, and the Profs have him spotted for an Arc Light." Thus did the Rube learn wisdom in the girls' dormitory.[3]

Student romances were viewed far less indulgently by university president Joseph Stubbs, stern of eye and bristling of mustache. In the manner of the pre-Civil War college president, Stubbs considered himself as much a moral philosopher as an executive, and hence duty bound to mold the character of his students. He had grimly admonished his flock to "set our faces like flint against an undue interest in social life." This undue interest was one of the most insidious of the "perils" the watchful president saw lurking in coeducation, a dangerous innovation which he sought to forestall by directing women students

toward courses "suitable to a young woman's calling in life."[4]
In fact, moral perils beyond President Stubbs's darkest suspicions were already tunneling through the student body. At
election time no small number of college boys could be observed at Dolph Shane's Reno butcher shop, where tidy sums
could be collected by collegians and other unscrupulous individuals willing to vote, and vote repeatedly, for the machine
candidates Dolph had been ordered to swing into office.

At the time, his friends' business at the butcher shop amused
George, though when he was fighting the Southern Pacific in
1910, he would find the machine politics Dolph Shane represented considerably less amusing. But that battle was still more
than a decade in the future. In 1898 exciting new vistas were
opening before him as he left the closed world of the home
ranch behind for the first time. The asthma that had plagued
him all his days was gone with the alfalfa fields of home, except
for an occasional mild bout. The nights of coughing and choking, the terrible paroxysms, the days when he had huddled in
his chair at school, gasping for breath and too weak to stand,
were in the past. He began to feel healthy and strong, and even
to think of sports. Too small for football, he had to content
himself with turning out for track and cheering loudly from the
sidelines when the University of Nevada football team won
their astonishing victory over Stanford. He studied hard. What
had seemed brilliance in the Lincoln school shone no less
brightly among the accumulated arc lights of the University of
Nevada. Nonetheless the vigilant eye of President Stubbs could
no doubt have detected the telltale signs of an undue interest
in social life.

George's friends teased him about turning into a ladies' man
and taking a different girl out for ice cream sodas each day.
Unlike the weary editor of the college newspaper, who found
the waltzes and two-steps of a weekly dance increasingly burdensome, George was discovering he loved to dance. Other

distractions kept turning up—picnics, candy pulls, or skating parties. And the "most triumphant social and dramatic event of the year," at least in the eyes of the society editor of the *Student Record,* was a Darktown Promenade given by the coeds. "The room was tastefully decorated with palm leaves and the various flora of Equatorial Africa." Guests were regaled with "My Ragtime Girl" to the accompaniment of a tom-tom, served steam lemonade and pretzels, and treated to a series of tableaux, including "Cupid in Georgia," the "Dusky Sirens," and "Venus Shelling Hot Tamales."[5]

"Venus Shelling Hot Tamales" was not, however, the tableau my father remembered most vividly from his college years. It paled by comparison to the scene he viewed on the evening when his new college friends took him along to what they said was a party, although it seemed to him a bit gayer and more informal than most parties. Presently one of the ladies graciously accepted his invitation to dance. As he whirled her enthusiastically around the floor, he suddenly realized with astonishment that she was *not wearing any corset.* He stopped abruptly in his tracks. His startled blue eyes circled over the buxom, dancing figures in the room while dreadful supposition swelled to certainty. Not a single woman in the room was wearing a corset, and that could mean but one thing: this was a house of ill fame. He was so shocked that he dashed out the door and ran all the way back to the dormitory.

University of Nevada ghosts were easier to handle, although students in the Lincoln Hall dormitory had goaded each other into a titillating state of terror. At night a mysterious light gleamed in the hillside cemetery outside their windows. It was a ghost, they said, perhaps even a monstrous oriental specter from the Chinese graveyard, and no one dared to walk in the cemetery after dark. It was easy enough to be brave by day, striding along the campus with one's cadet coat jauntily unbuttoned and risking a frown from President Stubbs, but another matter entirely when the sun sank behind the Sierra. Night after night they crowded to the windows to watch and shiver. There it was again. "That's silly," said George. "Ghosts don't exist."

"No?" asked the others. "Then why don't you go see what it is?" So of course he had to show he had rind enough to jar the dead ones, even if he was less certain than he said. Later, when he was at Harvard, he read every book on religion he could find, concluded that "Jesus Christ was a very smart man," became an atheist, and totally rejected all things supernatural. But that was later. On this night he had to pick his way through the headstones in the darkness while his friends watched from the windows of the dormitory. When he reached the mysterious light, no troubled spirits rose from the grave to confront him, and he picked up the piece of glass the moon had been shining on. A triumph for the forces of rationalism. Still everyone except George was a little disappointed.

He made the University of Nevada debating team, but although he would later become an outstanding trial lawyer and a fiery political campaigner, his early oratorical efforts were inauspicious. In a debate with a team from another university, George, who was always slight and was barely five feet six inches tall, nervously made his speech with one hand tucked in his vest over his stomach. The opposing debater began his remarks with a devastating reference to "the little boy who has just said his piece." George blushed, the audience roared with laughter, and the rival university easily won the debate.

After this unlikely beginning, he went on to become a fine debater. Others listened, he learned how to sway them, and, as he put it, "I began to like talking more and more, so I decided to become a lawyer." Many of his qualities—the keen, logical mind, the encyclopedic memory, the capacity for hard work, and the warm sympathy—would have served him well as either doctor or lawyer. But medicine would not tap the magnetism, the verbal powers of expression and reasoning, and the rare ability to think and act instantly, to ride the swift current in court as deftly as the loggers he used to watch from the school-yard had stepped from log to bobbing log on the river, always nudging, probing, shoving, and finally guiding the heaving multitude in the direction they desired. His mind was as quick and nimble as their feet, and he was made to move not logs but men.

Debating was already showing him what he could do, and law was a happy choice in ways he could not have foreseen—it was bound to freedom, justice, and democracy as medicine was not. If atheism had left a doctrinal void, the law would fill it. (In retrospect, it amuses me that instead of reproving me when I brought home my first four-letter words as a little girl, my father said, "We never use those words in a court of law," and I, who had absorbed through my very pores his unspoken conviction that law was a golden rule for all of life, never thought to protest that we were standing at the time not in a court of law but in a corral, where bad language might not have been entirely inappropriate.)

Law also suited his combative, optimistic temperament in a way that medicine could not. He loved winning. His victories tended to fade away in a halcyon golden haze, but his few defeats were indelibly graven on his heart. In an age when the principal function of medical men like Doctor Black was to place the benediction of science upon the inevitability of death, those who battled the grim reaper were often destined to lose. Better that he should take law and win.

George's science professor, who had begun to take a proprie-tary interest in his career, was very angry over the change, and George must have anticipated a similar, and far worse, reaction from his father. However, H.H. proved unexpectedly amiable and agreed to law. Although George had entered college under conditions as a result of his limited early schooling, his academic performance had been outstanding, and he expected to graduate on schedule and go on to law school. As it turned out, his leadership in a student rebellion would compel him to hastily depart from the university at a much earlier date than he had anticipated.

When he became editor of the student newspaper in 1901, the editorial page assumed a more aggressive tone: the Faculty Committee on Student Affairs was criticized for refusing to meet with student committees; the football manager was hotly defended in a controversy with the Reno newspapers; and these same papers were angrily lambasted for their "yellow journalism" in an article on hazing at the university, where freshmen had reportedly been paddled in a "lonely rendezvous." They had it all wrong, George insisted; this was but "the folly of some forlorn scribe." In fact, the upperclassmen had done no more than mildly reprimand the freshmen by administering "such slight chastisement as to vividly revive the memories of childhood," and their aim was, of course, the loftiest: to avoid the decadence that befell the Romans when they abandoned war.[6] If this was the most farfetched excuse for hazing ever devised by the senior mind, George would have been reluctant to admit it.

Apart from these early warning signals, the *Student Record* continued much as it had under previous editors. Students were exhorted to form a glee club, to join the debating team, and to study diligently ("then will our vacation be pleasanter and our return to work fraught with more joyous anticipation"). Student literary efforts were published (The Fallen Waysider's Story, A Christmas Waif, The Soul of the Rajah), as were student jokes ("'Ha, I will fool the bloodhounds yet,' cried the fugitive hoarsely, and slipping on a pair of rubbers, he erased his tracks").[7]

When a smallpox epidemic broke out in Reno about February 8, 1902, a protest was soon brewing at the University of

Nevada. City schools were closed, and quarantine measures were imposed by the State Board of Health. Readers of the *Nevada State Journal* were advised of a never failing cure: one ounce of cream of tartar, dissolved in boiling water and drunk at intervals.[8] A week after the breakout of smallpox, few cases had been reported. The disease was mild, and the quarantine measures were arousing marked resentment. "The silly hysteria caused by excessive and uncalled for quarantine measures" was sharply criticized in the *Journal.* The six patients confined to the pest house were reported to be "knocking over the hills at their own sweet will" and spending their time "prospecting instead of saying their prayers and making their wills."[9]

At the university, students objected to the unreasonable "semi-quarantine" measures imposed upon them. Resident students were confined to campus under the threat of suspension, but students living in town were allowed to come and go as they pleased. As George later explained in the *Student Record,* a semi-quarantine means "when you're There, you can come Here, but when you're Here, you can't go There." President Stubbs refused to endorse the more stringent quarantine measures resident students requested in the belief that restrictions should either be applied to the entire student body or revoked. The college men living on campus in Lincoln Hall then held a meeting and voted unanimously to visit Reno whenever they pleased, as the nonresident students were permitted to do. Led by George, about thirty students marched defiantly into town; the following day eight were suspended. At another meeting held that evening, the students voted to demonstrate their support for the suspended eight by going downtown. Mass suspensions followed: all resident male students were suspended until February 24 and fined. Seniors might be readmitted only by application after that date. More than seventy students, roughly a third of the total student body, had been dismissed.[10]

Public support for these punitive measures was only luke-

warm. At the request of the students, a committee of prominent
Reno citizens attempted unsuccessfully to dissuade President
Stubbs from issuing the blanket expulsion order. The *Nevada
State Journal* termed the whole affair "A Regrettable Occur-
rence." The adverse effects upon university athletics were de-
plored, and the *Journal* observed that "one can not help but
admire the unanimity with which they [the students] stood by
their convictions."[11]

How their parents reacted, I can only guess. The uncommon
privilege of a prestigious college education was not lightly
treated in those days. Boats had been rocked, careers hung in
jeopardy, and all for the sake of a student protest. It was the sort
of situation to evoke stern parental reprimands, but not, apparently, from H.H. Perhaps rebellion against unjust authority had
aroused an echo of approval in the man who had suffered from
it as a boy and as a young hussar. One thing is certain: if H.H.
had expressed displeasure with his son that February, I would
have heard about it. When the old man was angry, no one
forgot his remarks.

After February 24 many students were permitted to return,
but my father's detente with the university authorities was
short-lived. Although university officials had succeeded in sup-
pressing the February 15 issue of the *Student Record* (they had
perceived "too much truth in most of the articles, " the editor
explained), they could not long stifle George's determination to
uphold his original promise to "give voice to student senti-
ments" in the *Record*. When the March 1 issue appeared against
all odds, the pages fairly crackled. President Stubbs was furious,
and my father was permanently expelled from the university.

It is not difficult to see why. The witty article in which
George described the advantages of suspension, including an
occasional holiday for the students during which "places like
the Tivoli, the Oberon, and others of classic name, and Bacdric
interior will prove more potent as educators of youth than all

the assembly sermons of a generation," might have been considered acceptable. So, perhaps, might the poem by "G" about the student protest, which ended with a hint of more rebellion, "But of all bold words of tongue or pen/ The boldest are these: 'They'll do it again.' "

But in an age hardly noted for student power or youthful insurrection, an age when parental and institutional authority was universally accepted, the rest was clearly beyond the pale. President Stubbs appeared in "A Quarantine Fable" as the chancellor of a "Far Eastern Plant for the Diffusion of the Highest Culture," an authority who "Yearned to be the Whole Banana, but he was Wise, that to many he seemed only the Peelings." The faculty ("Guaranteed to be without Convictions and Yielding Readily to Pressure") hardly came off any better. The sarcastic moral of the fable was "Young men, come West to escape the Pressure of Paternal Government."

President Stubbs's alleged aspirations for a seat in the U.S. Senate were also ridiculed. He was depicted as Shylock, gloating over the fines imposed on suspended students, ("I'll have my bond! I'll have my bond! Though the noble towers of this institution fall to rise no more. Avaunt! ye spirits of justice! I say I'll have my bond. After all these long days of suspension, schemes and sleepless nights, to lose the sweet revenge, the sight of student tears, the savor of human flesh! Justice be hanged! They worsted me and all my hopes, long cherished, of a senatorial chair now lie dying in the dust. My twenty-dollar bond! I'll have my bond!").[12] That clinched my father's enforced departure from the university.

The April 1 issue of the *Student Record* appeared under a new editor, announced that George had gone to another university, and eulogized him as an outstanding student whose moral character was the admiration of all who knew him. "He fell in the discharge of his duty, in expressing the sentiment of students who, by virtue of his position, he represented," the new editor somberly declared. "Few, if any, of those who have been cut off from their student work in this University have left with so much sympathy from the student body.... When he was or believed he was right, fear of results was to him a thing unknown." That much was evident even then, when he was not yet twenty-one. In the June 1 issue of the college newspaper, his picture appeared with the caption, "I'll speak, though hell itself should gape and bid me hold my peace."

It is too bad he was barred from the commencement ceremonies, in which the band, with singular appropriateness, played "The Ultimatum March." He missed seeing those classmates who used to frequent Dolph Shane's on election day listening with beatific innocence to Edward S. Farrington's scholarship address: college men were urged to set aside their "disgust for the polls" and get into politics, where their "pure, strong motives" would "raise the moral tone" of the entire political system.[13] He would have enjoyed that. Instead his diploma arrived in the mail, probably as a concession by President Stubbs to a very angry father and a tacit admission that the penalty imposed had been an excessively harsh one.

Next came summer school at the University of California, then Stanford, where his shift from medicine to law required him to earn an A.B., in addition to the B.S. he had already received from the University of Nevada, before entering Stanford law school.

Little more than a decade had passed since Stanford admitted its first students. David Starr Jordan was the president, as he had been since the beginning, and his official style bore little resemblance to the modern czars of university empires, enshrouded in protective layers of secretaries and appointments. He did not consider himself too important to be bothered with students, and he and my father had many long talks. Good-humored arguments would, perhaps, be a better term, because my father warmly disagreed with Jordan's rather conservative views on class and race.

By 1902 the difficult years when the faculty had sometimes gone unpaid and it had seemed uncertain whether Jane Stanford would really be able to finance this ambitious memorial to her dead son were in the past, and the university had become a rather special place of scholastic eminence, combined with a faintly aristocratic aura. A few years later, when George was running in the Republican primary for Nevada attorney general and charging that his opponent was a corporation lawyer, he was condemned for his mudslinging campaign. A rather pompous telegram from a fellow graduate accusing him of conduct unbecoming to a Stanford man was widely publicized in the opposition press.[14] That Stanford men were a superior breed bound by a different code of conduct than anyone else would never have occurred to my father, a wholehearted egalitarian who was as ready to talk to a miner on the streets of Goldfield or a stranger encountered on the stagecoach as he was to an Italian prince or a Rockefeller and, what is more important, to listen to them. But that was the way other people regarded it. They thought the Stanford man was entitled to put on airs; he was one who had received "great advantages."[15]

Some of these advantages were not precisely the sort the newspaper editors had in mind. Freshmen had the advantage of being "tubbed" till they were out of breath. Juniors and seniors had the advantage of the "plug ugly," a no holds barred free-for-all in which seniors strove to destroy the juniors' class plugs, while juniors fought to halt the advance of seniors to the Inner Quad. And every drinking man who chose to ignore Dr. Jordan's "unceasing call to the clean life" had the advantage of a Stanford weekend of beer busts, frat banquets, uproarious parades of revelers from one frat house to the next, and pranks upon the teetotalers who failed to join in.[16] These included

George, a lifelong teetotaler because he disliked the taste of liquor. One night he climbed into a bed full of dead chickens, thoughtfully tucked there by Charlie Norris, the younger brother of the famed novelist, but it would have taken more than a bunch of dead chickens to change George's mind.

After receiving his law degree at Stanford, George applied for admission to the California bar. In those days, when law was often apprenticed through clerking or studied in solitude as well as transmitted in law school, candidates for the bar were a mixed group of all ages and degrees of literacy. The motley collection gathered together in the room where George took his oral examination included an old man who answered every question incorrectly.

At length, the examining justice inquired sternly, "Have you read these books?" He indicated the stack of law books beside him.

"Oh, yes, I read them all through once," said the old man with the proud air of the mountaineer who had daringly and laboriously ascended the dizzying heights to plant his flag upon the topmost peak and was now prepared to receive the accolades of an admiring world.

"Once?" exclaimed the justice with astonishment. "You mean you read them only once?"

"Once was enough!" said the old man vehemently, with a baleful glare at the wall of massive tomes forbiddingly ranged before him. "I wouldn't want to look at those books again."

My father did better in his bar exams than that candid old man, and he had high hopes for his first case. His fraternity of incipient lawyers, the "Figis," chose him, as the most gifted of their group, to represent them in a suit brought by their landlord over the payment of back rent. George's argument was carefully prepared according to principles that had received the highest commendation during years of study before the leading lights of the Stanford law faculty. He was primed to be elo-

quent, his verbal powers honed to the razor's edge in readiness
for this moment. He arrived determined to bring triumphant
vindication home to the Figis, henceforth to be recognized
throughout California as a body of invincibles no rascally landlord would dare to tangle with. He stepped forward, very ner-
vous, but ready to take his place with John Marshall, Daniel
Webster, and Oliver Wendell Holmes, only to return to his
fraternity brothers in short order with an ignominious defeat.
The judge had ruled in favor of the landlord; not only that, but
George personally, not the fraternity he represented, was declared responsible for the payment. His legal career could
hardly have begun more disastrously.

* * * * *

After Stanford George went to Harvard for a year of post-
graduate "polishing up." The Westerners in Boston in those
days were regarded as interesting and faintly exotic creatures,
not unlike the foreign students two generations later. They
were lodged together in a special house and, on one occasion,
were royally wined and dined, like the visiting ambassadors of
another country, by the wealthy members of the Hasty Pudding Club.

If my father was intimidated by this wealth, or by the other
students from powerful and distinguished families, if, like his
classmate Felix Frankfurter, he arrived at Harvard "scared
stiff,"[17] he never gave an indication of it. If he thought the
colonial city on the harbor, already generations old when Kit
Carson first rode into the Carson Valley, impressive or charming, he never said so. Looking back, nearly sixty years later, he
spoke only of tossing coins to the organ grinders with their
prancing monkeys in the Boston streets. There were no such
creatures at home on the ranch.

There were no mines on the ranch either, but Westerners
were supposed to know all about them. In class Felix Frank-

furter, whose brilliance and intellectual curiosity my father admired, used to ask detailed questions about Nevada mining operations that my father was embarrassingly ill-equipped to answer. He had never seen the mines. Within a year he would learn the answers.

H.H. wanted to send his most gifted son to Europe for further study at Heidelberg, but George had heard about Goldfield, the incrediby rich mines, the city of thousands that had sprung up in the southern Nevada desert overnight, a city of boundless opportunity, where fortunes were made and lost every day and the air was electric with excitement. Europe, the medieval university town, and further study sounded dull by comparison. Though he did not say so, I suspect there was another reason. He had been away at Stanford and Harvard the better part of four years, the longest exile from Nevada he ever endured, and I think he wanted to go home.

> Mornin' on the desert, and the wind is blowin' free,
> And it's ours jest for the breathin', so let's fill up, you and
>   me.
> No more stuffy cities, where you have to pay to breathe,
> Where the helpless human creatures move and throng and
>   strive and seethe.
> Mornin' on the desert, and the air is like a wine
> And it seems like all creation has been made for me and
>   mine.

Not a quotation from Swinburne or Millay or any of the other poets he read so often and appreciatively, only the beginning of an anonymous verse found on an adobe hut in the Nevada desert. But that was the poem that hung framed on his wall when I was a child, so I know how he felt when he took the train from Boston in 1906. *No more stuffy cities, where you have to pay to breathe, where the helpless human creatures move and throng and strive and seethe.* The train would rumble steadily westward through Indiana and Illinois. Red barns, black, fertile earth, and green fields. The cities were left behind. But such small farms, so close together, and all laid out in neat, meticulous, checkerboard squares. Still a crowded, lilliputian landscape to eyes homesick for desert space. Westward through the plains. The farms are growing farther apart, and there is a starting sense of broader sky. But the land is so drab, so drearily flat, a uniform expanse of brown and green, unbroken by anything save the box of a farmhouse or the tiny cylinder of a water tower.

Then come the Rockies, first of the great western mountain chains that will be repeated again and again for more than a thousand miles to the sea. From now on, the panorama of the mountains will never be out of sight. The train whistles past the Utah-Nevada border. Less than five hundred miles to go. At the open window, the sky is brilliantly blue, and the ceaseless pulse of the wind seems to bring the familiar dry, pungent smell of sage and dust. *Mornin' on the desert and the air is like a wine, and it seems like all creation has been made for me and mine.* There is a sense of boundless space. Whole cities could be lifted from the East and set down in the declivity between one peak and the next, only to diminish to the proportions of anthills in this infinitude. But there are no cities, just a few towns, scarcely glimpsed before they pass. Men have not stayed long nor mattered much. This desert has scarcely altered in a thousand years, yet it constantly changes with the shifting play of color and light. Cloud shadows meet and part on the gray sand like fish swimming in a transparent sea. As the sun slips down from the meridian, the western mountains darken from gentian to slate to a velvety indigo blue, while the eastern range warms from gray to mauve to mulberry. Pools of dark shadow fade to gauze, rocks turn luminous, and the sharply cut canyons dissolve in a rosy mist. The blue eyes at the window, always scanning the horizon, would watch and rest content.

The valley drew nearer, and so did the faces, affectionately remembered for so long. He would change from the Southern Pacific in Reno for the trip to Carson City on the Virginia and Truckee line. His sister Clare would meet him in Carson with the buckboard, as she did each summer since he had gone away to college.

She was a beautiful woman now, with her glorious chestnut hair piled high on her head beneath a fashionable hat. She had not, after all, run away from the ranch to make sunbonnets for a living as she had once vowed to do. She had not really wanted to go, and, as it turned out, she would never leave the ranch as long as she lived. Helping her mother at home each day, Clare had mastered all the feminine arts. Her sponge cakes were a marvel of fragrant, golden-brown perfection. The poppies and peonies she tended in the garden responded with a riot of bloom. And her accomplishments didn't stop at the garden border. Clad in the English riding habit her father insisted was the only suitable garment for a lady on horseback, she could ride as well as any chapped and booted cowpuncher, if not better, and no man drove a team more smartly. Not every young lady of 1906, even in the Carson Valley, would drive a buckboard alone for sixteen miles to the train depot; not a few would collapse with the vapors at the prospect. But Clare wouldn't hear of letting anyone else go to meet George.

The buckboard would turn toward home. There would be so much to tell—Harvard, the Hasty Pudding Club, even the divine Sarah Bernhardt. George had seen her perform on her farewell tour of the United States, and he thought she really was as marvelous as she was supposed to be. And Clare had a very serious beau now, a young storekeeper named Maurice Mack. Even H.H., who cast a very cold eye on all his daughter's suitors, approved of him.

There would be a good deal of teasing too, for Clare's blue eyes under the curved hat brim still danced with the mischie-

vous gleam of the little girl who had nibbled wild parsnip.
George's apple tree, the one named for him in the yard, was
doing very poorly this year, she would say. Such a shame that
George's tree was leaning so and had scarcely produced an
apple, while hers was so much taller and simply laden with
fruit. George would doubt that; he always insisted his tree
stood "straight and firm" and bore as plentifully as Clare's.

Laughing, they would pass the gray, sage-covered hump of
a hill that lies south of Carson City, and George's heart would
lift. Before him lay the smiling, sunlit valley of his childhood,
the dark Sierra towering to his right, leftward the Pine Nut
Hills, and to the southeast, the bowed arch of Springmeyer
Peak, barely visible against the jagged, blue outline of the Silver
Mountains. Though he and Clare were too far to see the eagles
in the distance, he knew the rhythm of their flight. They soared
up, beating their powerful wings until they rose above the
peaks, arching toward the sun. They floated lazily down, their
wings widespread and nearly motionless, sailing ever lower,
letting the wind carry them down to their nests on the rocky
hills near Springmeyer Peak. George too had flown far, and
would again, but for now he could rest back and let the current
carry him home.

* * * * *

Three years before George rode the buckboard into the valley, turning his back with aversion on the East and all it represented and knowing he had come home to Nevada to stay, a
baby named Sallie Maria was born to Sallie and Justus Ruperti
in their New York City brownstone mansion. This daughter
bore the stamp of their features, especially her mother's pi-
quant, upturned nose. Yet, as she outgrew her babyish chubbi-
ness and became a little girl, she looked distinctly unlike her
brother and her sisters. They were brown haired and rather
stolid and blunt featured; she had black hair and golden skin

and proud carriage, and she moved among them like a black swan among brown ducks. "Where did this little one come from?" family friends would laughingly inquire, seeing the tinge of exoticism that had given her mother the nickname "Gypsy" in girlhood magnified beyond their recognition in this child. In truth she seemed to resemble the Spanish flamenco dancers whose fiery performances her shy, withdrawn father loved to watch. It was almost as though she were the child of dreams.

* * * * *

Only one shadow marred George's return to the ranch—his father's inescapable displeasure over Heidelberg. George was not a man prone to apprehensions any more than he was to regrets. Such emotions were always firmly set aside as useless indulgences. Nevertheless, as the buckboard turned up the familiar lane, he must have felt tensions not easily suppressed. Until the day H.H. died, George always treated him with the greatest deference and respect. Now, for the first time in his life, he was defying his father, and he knew "a big row" was on the way.

He never told me what they said in that interview, only how angry his father was. It would not have lasted long, for Herman Springmeyer's words could slash as quickly as a sword and wound as deeply. In the same way he pruned off an ill-grown branch from an apple tree, so too he could amputate his own children from his mind and heart if they displeased him. Leo, Charlie, Louis and Emma—all had crossed his will and remained in the outer darkness, unforgiven. He never mellowed; he never forgot. He had been that way from the very beginning. When we first saw him as a child, hating the brutal teacher he will finally batter to the earth years later on his last night in Germany, we knew there was something irrevocable about him.

Understanding this, I find that interview remarkable not in its

angry beginning but in the amicable ending that came when
H.H. reluctantly agreed to George's wish to set up law practice
in Goldfield. Was George forgiven because he was the favorite
son? He knew he was his mother's favorite, and other sons, less
loved, believed he was also his father's. If that was so, why was
he favored? He was the seventh child and the fourth son, easily
obscured, one would think, in a crowd of ten children. Perhaps
it began with the asthma. Watching the flame of that small,
fragile life flicker low as a guttering candle, his parents may
have come to cherish him beyond the others. Perhaps forgiveness was granted because he achieved more than the rest, came
closest to satisfying Herman's hopes—so his brothers believed
and bore him no rancor, so far as I can tell. They too were proud
of him and accepted the favor bestowed on him as just. Perhaps
there was another reason as well. Much of Wilhelmine's
warmth and glow and tender gaiety were reflected in George.
To say he had charm would be false because it suggests a
manner purposely and consciously assumed. All the same, he
had a quality, natural and unintentional, which could disarm
even his unforgiving father.

It was a happy homecoming after all, and George made plans
to leave for Goldfield in September. In the meantime, H.H. had
recently purchased the Douglas County *Record Courier,* and
George settled down to edit the paper for his father, observing
in his first editorial that "the more carefully the writer investi-
gates the party system of politics, the more fallacies and evils
does he find in its theory and practice. However, conditions are
such that one must make a choice."[18] Only by this roundabout
route, only with obvious reluctance and distaste, did the new
editor arrive at a declaration of his "fixed fealty"to the Republicans. Such musings fell considerably short of an enthusiastic
endorsement of the Republican loyalties he had inherited from
his father. Party regulars might well have noted that the ardent
faith and glad hosannas of an incipient Republican politician,

or even the customary flatteries of the party press in an election year, were markedly absent here. Even so, less than three weeks later, George found himself the Republican nominee for attorney general of Nevada.

Since Black Wallace's death in 1901, the Nevada Republican party was less tightly disciplined than in the past. Leadership had been assumed by Senator George Nixon, a man whose friendly relationship with the Southern Pacific political bureau in California suggested that connections formed early in life when he was a station agent on the railroad had never really been severed. Nonetheless, Nixon, as the holder of a high national office and as a wealthy banker and partner in the Wingfield mining enterprises, was less the party professional than Wallace had been, less autocratic, and less determined to control Nevada politics. And he was less capable of controlling them. The Silver party episode had shattered traditional party discipline during the nineties; new Democratic voters had poured into Goldfield and other boom towns after 1902; and the Republicans, who had dominated Nevada politics from the Civil War until 1890, declined to a minority party position. No longer did party conventions await the orders of the commander; instead nominations involved a degree of infighting that would have been inconceivable under Wallace's regime.

In this fluid situation a mining millionaire named Woodbury persuaded H.H. that George should oppose Ed Roberts, an experienced lawyer who had served as Ormsby County district attorney, for the nomination. Although Roberts made a brisk fight in the convention, H.H. and Woodbury prevailed. The assemblage of Republicans turned a blind eye to Ed Roberts's superior legal experience and nominated the old hussar's son— a slight youth, with straight, sandy hair combed smoothly back; bushy eyebrows; candid, blue eyes; and a strong, roman nose, deeply indented at the bridge (perhaps General Herman had not expelled the Roman armies from Germany quite speedily enough). George was then twenty-four years old, a youthful candidate even by the standards of Nevada, where no major party nominee for the office in that decade was past thirty.[19] He had never practiced law, and no one was more astonished at his nomination than he was.

When he set off to tour the state with the other candidates on his first campaign, he met O. R. Morgan, the powerful editor of the *Reno Evening Gazette,* who, he later recalled, "took me for a wealthy man's son ripe for the plucking"and "endeavored to hold me up in return for the *Gazette's* support."[20] Few Nevada politicians would have been shocked by such a proposition. The politically subsidized press was a long and dishonorable tradition,[21] but my father wanted no part of it. Paying a newspaperman to praise you was almost as bad as paying a voter to vote for you. It was wrong. He told Morgan so, making an enemy who would seize many opportunities to revile him in future campaigns.

If that seemed uncompromising or impolitic, H.H. could be even more so. Forcefully suggesting to the delegates at the Republican convention that Douglas County deserved some consideration at nomination time in return for staunch Republicanism was fair enough. But that was about as far as Herman Springmeyer was prepared to go. The new editor who succeeded George at the *Record Courier* later recalled that when he diplomatically suggested a slight shift in editorial policy to H.H. in the interests of garnering some additional Democratic votes for George, the owner responded, "To hell with George. It's the truth, and if we had more truth in politics, the state and the nation would be better off."

The campaign wore on. There were rallies with bonfires and brass bands, sometimes even with skyrockets and red fire, where my father, billed as "the native son of the sagebrush" and looking very boyish, expounded Republican principles, protested that he was not really too young for the job, and defended President Theodore Roosevelt on the trusts. Jim Mitchell, the Republican nominee for governor, described his rise up "life's ladder" from toiling newsboy to successful mine operator and spoke vaguely of a "square deal." John Sparks, the incumbent Democratic governor who would call in federal troops a little more than a year later to smash the Industrial Workers of the World in Goldfield, was billed as "the Peacemaker and the Peacekeeper." Provided he was reelected, Sparks vowed, "the reign of musketry is not required." Republican editors inquired when Sparks had demonstrated this "marvelous capacity for pacification" in labor disputes and took note of his inefficiency and absenteeism. Democrats countercharged that Republicans, when last in office, combined "WASTEFUL EXTRAVAGANCE in administration with FOOLISH PARSIMONY in dealing with the schools." Mitchell, they suggested, had nothing to offer but "good fellowship."[22]

It was, in short, a thoroughly dull campaign by the standards of the period, and its most memorable moment had nothing whatever to do with politics. When the Republican campaigners arrived in Goldfield, the town was in a fever of excitement. A battle of cosmic importance had just taken place. It had been billed as "the battle of the century," and the contestants were still at hand—few men in Goldfield had spoken or thought of anything else for weeks. It was not the election; hardly anyone in Goldfield had noticed that there was one. It was the famous Gans-Nelson fight. My father saw it, all forty-two rounds, but what he remembered most graphically was not the fight itself but "Battling" Nelson's hideous appearance when he encountered the fighter and his manager on the train a few days later. George was shocked to see that Nelson's battered head appeared to have swollen to twice its normal size, the flesh had split in several places, and his skin had turned horrible shades of green, yellow, and purple.

For sheer torpor, none of the campaign stops could compare to Las Vegas, then a small handful of houses that had only recently been included in the railroad network. George and his friend Gib Douglass, who was seeking reelection as secretary of state, went quail hunting in the meadows that now lie cemented beneath the city of pulsating neon erected to service the fantasies of southern Californians. In 1906, before the invention of air conditioning made summer temperatures tolerable, this tourist mecca was beyond the outer reaches of the imagination. Gib thought the autumn meadows were pretty and wondered if they should buy some land there; George was certain it would never be worth anything.

Riding one of the first trains on the new line to Ely, where copper mines had recently been discovered, the Republican candidates were seated together in a pullman in the company of Judge George Brown and his wife. When the judge passed through the vestibule on his way to the men's room, a crazed drunken brakeman rushed up, seized the judge by the throat, and wrestled him to the floor. Before the ensuing fracas was over, the conductor had beaten up the brakeman, and the brakeman had chewed off the conductor's thumb. Several passengers had to hit him in the face before he would cease gnawing on the conductor. The train halted, and the brakeman was shoved out into the desert, at least twenty-five miles from any habitation. Outraged at this unseemly attempt to chew a conductor up instead of out, every man on the train except George gave the brakeman a kick or a punch as they pushed him off.[23] All things considered, it was probably the most noteworthy event of the 1906 campaign.

When the election returns were in, George, together with most of his Republican comrades in arms, was soundly defeated. It was his own fault too, said one of his friends, because —and here, having failed to record the joking that accompanied

Maurice Mack and Clare Springmeyer on their wedding day in 1908. (Courtesy of Duane Mack)

his advice, I'm filling in from dim recollections—the kid still had a lot to learn about politics. He'd gone and gotten things all turned around somehow and started taking all that talk about the president and the trusts so seriously that when he was told in confidence how elections really were won, he didn't pay proper attention to it, even started laughing like it was all a big joke. Goodness knows, they'd tried to educate George, given him the best advice in the world, but he'd gone ahead and ignored it, just like a greenhorn. Any real politician knew for a fact that winning had nothing to do with speeches and rallies and brass bands and such—and no one knew it better than George's good friend and adviser, because he had personally put the matter to the test. If a man had just signed up to while away the time between haying season and Thanksgiving by taking a long scenic train tour of the state and buying some rounds for the thirsty citizens in every bar from Winnemucca to Caliente, why he was entitled to his preferences. But if he really meant to see his name in the winners' column, no bones about it, there was only one thing to do: spend the night before the election with a black whore "for luck." That was how he himself had won.

With the campaign rapidly dwindling in memory to the dimensions of the conductor's thumb, my father went on to where he had originally meant to go before accidentally tumbling into politics—Goldfield. He had made some friends, some enemies too, and it seems he had acquired a lasting taste for politics.

7

Goldfield

WHEN MY FATHER ARRIVED at Goldfield in late November, just four years had passed since a Shoshone Indian prospector named Tom Fisherman brought some gold samples into Tonopah. Learning of this discovery, two eager prospectors ventured forth in a raging windstorm to the Rabbit Springs area where Fisherman had been spending his time, east of the Montezuma range and a few miles south of the natural boundary demarcating the taller sagebrush of the Great Basin Desert to the north from the ground-hugging bud sage, the creosote, and the shaggy, creaking Joshua trees of the Mojave. The Indian had called the region "Gran Pah," a Shoshone phrase meaning "land of much water." If the name was not a bitter joke, it must have signified that to a thirsty, wind-scoured, sun-weary prospector in that arid waste, where dust devils danced, even the smallest spring was welcomed as "much water." Northeast of a long, rock-capped mesa, gray as driftwood, where the low triangle of Columbia Mountain rose in isolation from the desert floor, they found the gold and christened the camp they envisaged rising on the empty desert sands with the word they had heard Fisherman use, "Grandpa." Although they cared little for Shoshone names, they liked that word because they believed a strike there would be the grandfather of all the gold strikes. They were not far wrong.

Prospectors are not given to niggardly visions of the future, but within a few years, the new claim had outstripped their most extravagant predictions. By 1904 Grandpa had been rechristened Goldfield, and a full-scale boom was on. Perhaps 20,000 people were living there in 1906, housed in a random jumble of hastily erected frame buildings, bottle houses, cabins, tents, and cave dwellings dug out of the hillside. George estimated the population at even more than 20,000. No one really knew, and thousands more were streaming in every month. The rutted streets, broad as they were, grew so crowded with people and burros that a man had to give up any idea of walking freely and resign himself to pushing along at a slow shuffle. One night as George was inching slowly forward with the crowd, he saw two miners brawling in the street. Finally one knocked the other down and jumped on his face with his mining boots on while the crowd pushed slowly past. No one but my father seemed shocked by this brutal trampling, or even mildly interested in it. The others were old hands in Goldfield.

At first George stayed at the Esmeralda Hotel, a three-story structure where guests slept in six-hour shifts with blankets only, no changes of bedding, and no fancy frills and services like bed making. After a week at the Esmeralda, he moved to the relative comfort of a canvas-topped cabin, shared with two other men. Accommodations were so precious that every prime square of Goldfield dirt was worth a fight. Once on disputed turf, twenty-five armed men battled with newly arrived squatters who had usurped their places, and the losers were cast out of their tents into the snow. Those who could find no better abode rolled their blankets on the frozen ground.

The winter was unusually hard that year, and little warmth or shelter could be gleaned from the barren desert. At one point, the shivering Goldfielders even stole the telephone poles and chopped them into firewood. The number of deaths, attributed by the *Goldfield Daily Tribune* to "pneumonia and alcoholism," soared to more than five times the level recorded during the preceding and following winters.[1] On many mornings my father woke to find his blanket heavily laden with snow blown in through the canvas roof by the howling winds.

George's first office was located in a long, narrow, wooden building behind Lou Finnegan's brokerage office and diagonally across the street from a similar building which housed the famous Northern Saloon. The Northern had been so named because its two proprietors, Tex Rickard and Kid Highley, had come from Alaska. Rickard, who had launched the Gans-Nelson fight with a spectacular bombardment of publicity, would later gain a reputation as a fight promoter; Highley's dark-eyed, voluptuous wife was celebrated already as the heroine of one of Robert Service's Alaskan yarns. At the Northern's sixty-foot bar, more like a tunnel than a gathering place, a dozen bartenders poured drinks around the clock. Roulette, faro, poker, craps, twenty-one, and other diversions were continually in progress in the gambling hall, and violence could be anticipated at least once a day. One afternoon when George and Will Virgin, an old friend from the Carson Valley, were in the brokerage office, shots suddenly rang out at the Northern. George hurried to the window in time to see a man, clutching his hat in his hand, tumble out of the saloon, glance fearfully up and down the street, and start running. Another man dashed out of the saloon behind him, shooting wildly. By this time, George was hanging out the window with excitement. Will Virgin yanked him hastily inside and hauled him behind Finnegan's heaviest safe, shouting, "Get back here, kid! I promised your mother and father I'd take care of you."

The famous bad man known as "Diamondfield Jack" Davis, employed as a guard by the owners of the Goldfield Consolidated Mines, patronized the same restaurant where George ate supper. Every evening Davis and *his* two bodyguards would enter through the swinging doors, choose seats facing the entrance, and lay their guns beside their plates. Diamondfield Jack had named the section adjoining Goldfield where he claimed to have a fabulous mine "Diamondfield." The treasure it produced appeared somewhat less than fabulous, but no one was disposed to argue with Diamondfield Jack. He had earned his reputation as a bad man in eastern Nevada some years before. John Sparks, the wealthy cattleman Nevadans later elected governor in 1902, had hired him to intimidate the sheepmen who were encroaching on the open range, and it was rumored that Diamondfield Jack had shot two Mormon sheepherders in the course of his activities.

At the restaurant, apart from those guns beside his plate and the wary eyes that scrutinized each newcomer in the doorway, Diamondfield Jack's unobtrusive demeanor contradicted his murderous reputation. He was a man of medium build with a slight mustache, and a generally mild and unassuming appearance. No longer did he behave like the swaggering young gunslinger who had succeeded in talking his way behind bars in 1897 by boasting that he was "shooting sheepherders for a living." Five years of repose in an Idaho jail for a crime he did not commit and a hair's breadth reprieve from the gallows had toned him down considerably.[2] But when my father later saw Diamondfield Jack speeding over the desert at fifty miles an hour in his car as he picked off every jack rabbit in sight with a pistol of deadly accuracy, George realized Diamondfield Jack could shoot just as well as they said—and he liked to practice. Down underneath the stories clustered around his name and the lies he used to tell about himself, perhaps there really was a killer.

In the final analysis, however, Diamondfield Jack was only a hired gun, less powerful and dangerous than the man who employed him. That man was George Wingfield, known only a few years before as "the Peely Kid" because the skin was perpetually flaking off his sunburned nose. By the time my father and Wingfield became friends in Goldfield, no one any longer spoke of the Peely Kid. Wingfield's titles now tended to the royal ("the King of Nevada"), or even the imperial ("the Napoleon of Nevada finance"). Like kings and presidents, his most trivial pronouncement, indeed his mere presence, was front-page news, and the shape of his consort's hat was a matter of public concern. He was an Arkansas-born cowboy turned gambler who had made some money in Tonopah a few years before and gone on, in partnership with George Nixon, to realize a fortune in Goldfield's Great Mohawk Mine before he turned thirty. Then he created Goldfield Consolidated, a masterful combination of mining enterprises in a single, powerful unit and by far the largest producer of gold bullion in the district. As was the Parthenon on the hill to Athens below, so became Wingfield's Goldfield Consolidated plant on Columbia Mountain to Goldfield. The editor of the *Goldfield Daily Tribune* confessed to emotions akin to those of Francis Scott Key beholding the Star-Spangled Banner when, after a small fire, the flames "subsided in sullen impotence and the moonlight disclosed the immaculate white asbestos walls of the Consolidated Mill in stately grandeur and perfect form filling the air with a thunderous diapason."[3]

Goldfield Con may have been overcapitalized, and Wingfield may have run it with cavalier disdain for customary business methods. Yet only a fool would dismiss him as a lucky gambler. "Among stud poker players," observed a man who had run afoul of Wingfield, "he was famed for a half-cunning expression of countenance which deceived his opponents into believing he was bluffing when he wasn't; in card games he was usually a consistent winner."[4] He had a competence and a steely nerve that few men could match. Many had gained sudden fortunes in Nevada mining strikes and lost them just as fast in wildcat investments and high living. Not George Wingfield. He knew exactly what he wanted, exactly how to get it, and exactly how to keep it.

When the miners' union went on strike in March 1907, my father saw Wingfield in action. Restaurant owner John Silva was shot by a union man in a picketing dispute. As the air prickled with tension, George Wingfield began to muster his troops. Company guards were dispatched to patrol the streets; a vigilance committee was organized as a counterweight to the union; 150 additional gunfighters were sworn in as deputies; and Diamondfield Jack sped out of town on an urgent mission, returning with the tonneau of his auto stacked high with guns. Union men were packing guns too. When union men temporarily boycotted the *Goldfield Chronicle* and threatened physical injury to anyone who bought a copy, Wingfield wanted to see the men back down. He was not yet ready for a full-scale showdown with the union radicals, but there were certain things in which he took a peculiar personal pleasure. Tucking a bunch of newspapers under his arm, he walked over to a group of strikers, whipped out the gun he always carried, and told each man to buy a ten-cent paper for a dollar apiece. They bought the papers.[5] Late in April the miners' strike was settled, and the city returned to normal for the time being, if normal was a word that ever applied to Goldfield.

When it came to mining investments, my father was no George Wingfield. Like most Goldfield investors, he was not exactly a will be, nor a has been either, but more of a might have been. The streets were full of might have beens; indeed they kept Goldfield's mining-stock exchange busy every day. "Outside of the exchange the stridulous, whooping, screeching, detonating voices of the brokers that kept carrying the market up at each session could be heard half a block away," wrote one observer. "Later, did you find your way into the crowded board-room, the half-crazed manner in which notebooks, arms, fists, index fingers, hats and heads tossed and swayed approached in frenzy a scene of violence to which madness might at once be the consummation and the curse."[6]

All had discovered the "*real* secret" of mining as elucidated by Mark Twain many years before: it was *not* to mine ourselves "by the sweat of our brows and the labor of our hands, but to *sell* the ledges to the dull slaves of toil and let them do the mining."[7] Accordingly Goldfield teemed with brokers' offices doing business at a furious pace. Mining as they conducted it was a genteel occupation that, as Twain had rightly noted, had no immediate connection with delving, chipping, blasting, and burrowing in the rock. It required a piece of property (almost any would do); the organization of a company (with a respectable sounding name); and the issue of stock (handsomely printed). Not least it required the selection of a name for the mine, often a glamorous name evoking a treasure trove of royal dimensions (the King Midas or the Pride of Gold Mountain, never the Modest Hope of Greasewood Flat).

Above all, it required an ability to talk. And once they had mastered the lingo, men who did not know latite from dacite and could not tell an automatic grizzly from a churn drill held forth knowledgeably about breaks in the cross cut, hanging drifts to the foot wall, shafts, blind leads, stopes, ledges, placer gulches, gold bearing zones with fissures and dikes in fractured porphyry. They discoursed about contact veins, gumbo dikes, mill headings, and highly decomposed audacite, both silicified and friable. They talked most of all about gold—free gold, gold in nuggets and pay dirt, gold beyond a man's most extravagant imaginings in rich stringers and picture rock, gold in rich float and pay shoot, gold in ribbons and splashes and globules in bonanza ore, gold in boundless profusion in high-grade seams and glory holes.

For the more fraudulently inclined might have beens, the name and the lingo were bolstered with mine salting and false advertising. Few of these gentlemen were inclined to write their memoirs, at least before the statute of limitations had run out, but one of those who did, Jacob Herzog, alias George G. Rice, widely known as the man behind the L. M. Sullivan Trust Company, an organization in which no investor would have been well advised to place his trust, aptly entitled his recollections *My Adventures with Your Money* and dedicated them to "The American Damphool Speculator, surnamed the American Sucker." Rice himself was memorialized as "John Skinum Binks" in an ode which went in part,

> Binks engaged in promoting; "mines" was the line he was
> in.
> Assays were German to Skinum; he essayed to "get the tin
> . . ."
> When he launched a "mine" on the market, the gudgeons
> jumped at the bait,
> Binks' mines were never developed but their prospects
> were always "great."[8]

In the feverish atmosphere of Goldfield, shifty souls became grand swindlers and honest men grew temporarily deranged. As Twain had noted of the Humboldt craze nearly half a century before, "I would have been more or less than human if I had not gone mad like the rest."[9] So too with my father. Although he earned just enough to live, with no surplus for investment, he had plenty of legal talent to offer. Pretty soon he joined up with one of the saner and more trustworthy of these Goldfield might have beens, an entrepreneur named Ralph Bailey who had raised $50,000 for mining purposes. Together they organized the Mountain Crown Mining Company, with George handling the legal work and Bailey the finances, and hired George's close friend Harry Taylor and two other engineers to examine the Mountain Crown Mine. Following his reconnaissance, Taylor told them no gold would be found because a fault had broken off the rich vein passing through the nearby Florence before it reached the Mountain Crown. With tears in his eyes, Taylor begged Bailey and George to go in with him and his fellow engineers on the lease they had obtained on the Florence and offered large shares to both of them. George was certain Taylor was right and said so, but Bailey was not to be persuaded. He remained convinced there was gold in the Mountain Crown, and neither George nor Taylor could dent his impassioned certitude. Because he controlled the company's funds, the decision was his.

Lower, ever lower, they sank the timbered shaft, to a final depth of 400 feet, but just as Taylor had predicted, never a sign of gold appeared. All George ever got out of the Mountain Crown was a touch of claustrophobia, acquired when he and a friend, having climbed 150 feet down a ladder in the shaft, were continuing their descent in a bucket powered by a Fairbanks-Morse engine. In keeping with the general spirit of the Mountain Crown, the engine broke down, and the two men were left swinging in the bucket, unable to go up or down for a period of hours that seemed to encompass several lifetimes. Perhaps it was a pity that Felix Frankfurter was not in that bucket too. It would have been an appropriate time for George to explain all he had learned since Harvard about how the mines worked. And how they failed.

In the meantime Taylor had found a backer, and during the three-month period of his lease, $1,850,000 worth of ore was brought up from the Florence, reportedly one of the richest leases in Goldfield history. Now it was Bailey's turn. Recalling that incredible tale of the broken vein and those earnest, heartfelt pleas, so firmly brushed aside because an investor could not risk his capital on the mere word of an impecunious young engineer, was more than enough to bring tears to Bailey's eyes.

When the financial panic of 1907 struck, the streets of Goldfield seethed with rumors. George quickly realized banks were going to fail. It had often happened before. His thoughts raced home to the Carson Valley. Fortunately, most of his father's assets were in ranchland and in the Carson City property. However, in the Nye and Ormsby County Bank, H.H. had an account, the accumulated savings of a lifetime of hard work and careful planning. If that were lost, it could never be replaced. The old man was past sixty now and preparing to retire from the ranch to Carson City. There were not enough years left in him to begin again. George immediately wired his father that the panic was serious and all his deposits should be immediately withdrawn.

At home in the valley H.H read the telegram and started out for the bank to reclaim his money, only to turn back after encountering a friend who dissuaded him. Fifteen thousand dollars, all the old man possessed, was lost in the crash of the Nye and Ormsby County Bank. Meanwhile, in Goldfield, Ralph Bailey and George hastened out to withdraw the Mountain Crown's dwindling capital. They found the bank overflowing with crowds of people milling nervously around and trying to reclaim their money.

George asked Will Virgin, the cashier, for the Mountain Crown's deposits, and Virgin said derisively, "What's the matter, kid? Are you scared? You take all that money and someone will rob you."

"No," said George firmly, "but we want it."

Virgin reluctantly counted out $8,000 in gold, as Bailey and George stuffed it into their overcoat pockets. Bent over by the weight, they toiled home to the stone, dirt-floored hut they were sharing with two other men. While the gold was hidden in the hut, someone kept watch at all times, and they slept with loaded pistols beside their beds. Bailey was very touchy about it: money destined to be poured down the shaft of the Mountain Crown was not to be appropriated and lightly squandered by feckless thieves. If there was any appropriating and squandering to be done, he would do it himself, and he would call it "investment."

His anxieties were infectious. One night when George was on guard, he dropped off to sleep. Bailey came in, and George wakened with a start, automatically pointing his pistol at the dark figure in the doorway. He lowered the gun a moment later with the hollow realization that if Bailey had waited a second longer to speak, he would have shot him. Even my father was succumbing to Goldfield fever.

* * *

In a way the Mountain Crown was Bailey's personal mirage, but Goldfield had real mirages too—real, at least, in the sense that they were identifiable visual phenomena perceived by everyone at the same time. There was something about the place, both atmospherically and psychologically, that lent itself to illusion. Indeed the only mirage I have ever seen in many hot and dusty forays in the Nevada desert materialized near Goldfield. That vivid, quivering scene of green hills, a lake, and white pavilions akin to the Italian lake country seemed extraordinary at the time. But all the same, it was nothing like the mirages of the boom town years. My father remembered a day when a city, complete in every detail down to the last saloon and the blacksmith's shop, swam before the eyes of the Goldfielders, and miners who had worked in Alaska recognized it from the Klondike. The most extraordinary mirage of all was the twenty-mule team that magically appeared in the sky over a range of mountains not far away.

That was Goldfield as they knew it, a place where realities and mirages were hopelessly entangled in an atmosphere where even nature played hallucinatory tricks. Why should men strive to be practical, reasonable, or sensible in their affairs? Such goals were outworn, cast aside; they had no meaning in Goldfield. When a phantom city flickered on the horizon just beyond the stone and wooden huts of this one, why should a man prefer the known world? When twenty-mule teams emerged from the skies, why should fortunes not issue from the earth? All things were possible—if not today, then surely tomorrow. Once seized with this unreasoning certainty, no matter how old a man became, how far he traveled, or how much he learned, he never really stopped believing it. At an isolated way station in the desert not far from Goldfield, my father once met one of the most venerable of these visionary men. This was Senator William Stewart. Some bystanders asked George, as he paused in his journey, if he would like to see the senator. George found the old man lying down and resting in the back of a shack. William Stewart was then past seventy-five. His tall, lanky frame had thickened in age, and his long, wispy beard had whitened; but the piercing, gray eyes that had always looked black except in the brightest sunlight were still the eyes of a young man. Stewart inquired courteously after H.H., whom he said he had known well.

Indeed there probably were few pioneers in Nevada whom Stewart had not known well in a career extending over half a century since he arrived in the territory, made a vociferous appearance at the first Nevada constitutional convention in 1863, and became a primary cause for the constitution's defeat by Nevada voters who feared that he intended to deliver the fledgling state government over to his clients, the large mining corporations. Undaunted, Stewart then helped write the second constitution; voters, alarmed by a serious depression on the

Comstock, were by then prepared to accept it as an antidote to hard times. They accepted Stewart too, and would see both their best hopes and their worst fears realized in him, simultaneously.

William Stewart had known them all, from the killer desperado Sam Brown to the Comstock millionaires. This was a man who could win over a mob of eight hundred miners when they gathered to lynch him and could lend his services to the Southern Pacific for a price. "I know he must live," wrote Collis Huntington to one of his partners on the railroad's board of directors, "and we must fix it so he can make one or two hundred thousand dollars."[10] Stewart may have been the closest thing to a founding father Nevada had; certainly he was the founding father Nevada deserved.

He had served five terms in the United States Senate, but after his last election in 1899, won only by the astute machinations of Black Wallace and the blatant bribery and even kidnapping of Nevada legislators, he had fallen from grace. Once described by Mark Twain as he who "does bestride our narrow range like a colossus," Stewart was attacked in the Democratic state platform of 1902 as a "charlatan" and a "renegade" whose "insensate and insincere ravings" had harmed the sacred cause of free silver.[11] The people, who had liked him for his cleverness and his nerve and tolerated his roguery for nearly forty years, had finally turned against him.

But on this day in the shack somewhere in the Nevada desert, he was not thinking of the political power that once was his nor the faces long since gone, but of the fortunes he had lost. For two or three hours, he stroked his beard and ruminated on the thousands that had slipped like sand through his hands. He was going to make another fortune, he said. He had done it before, and he could do it again, just the way he always had. It wasn't too late. He just needed a little more rest, a few more minutes or so. As soon as he got up, he was going to "get on my mule

George Springmeyer
as he appeared on a
1914 campaign card.

and ride out and make another fortune." That would be soon
now, very soon. He was nearly finished resting. He had been
down in borrasca more than once before, and people had
thought he was finished. Maybe he was a little older now, but
he wasn't finished, not by any means. He didn't know where
that fortune would be, but he knew another one was out there
somewhere waiting for him. That was how it had always been.
When he got on his mule, he would find the way.

For a long time my father listened to this waking dream, then
finally said good-bye and continued on his way. He still had far
to go. But William Stewart would never ride out on his mule
to make another fortune. Not long after that meeting, my father
read the notice of the old man's death in the papers.[12]

* * *

Some, like Stewart, never ceased to hope. Others, faced with ugly realities painfully at odds with the golden dream that had drawn them to Goldfield, foundered in silent misery. Reading through the pages of the Goldfield newspapers, one is struck by the recurrent reports of suicides, and struck even more by the juxtaposition of this act of irredeemable despair and the extravagant hopes that rose and arched skyward each day anew as punctually as the desert sun. Too many examples come to mind. A nameless stranger walked into a mine tunnel on the Atlanta Boom one January night and drank poison from a whiskey bottle. The same day headlines proclaimed a wide body of rich ore newly uncovered in a drift going southward in the Red Top lease. Ed Meyers, another victim of despair, stood before the mirror in his room in the Esmeralda Hotel and fired a six-shooter into his head. He had been in charge of mining properties in Gold Crater and was said to be "financially embarrassed." That day the newspapers announced two distinct ore shoots just unearthed in the Hart-Jumbo that would "probably eclipse anything before discovered in the southwest." Uncle Jimmy Clark drank potassium cyanide in the back room of a saloon and slumped unnoticed over the table. He had been asking about "the best stuff to take a man off with, quick." People said he had been a brilliant linguist educated in Germany. No one seemed to know how he had ended up in Goldfield dishing out chili and noodles behind the lunch counter in the Hermitage Saloon. That same week Goldfield hailed a record high in ore production, $332,000 in seven days.

In the tenderloin the dark, slender beauty who called herself Juanita Dean (it was not her real name) drank potassium cyanide late one Saturday night. She had left Grass Valley, the simple community that was her home, telling her mother she wanted to see the American fleet sail into San Francisco on its tour around the world and believing her beauty would bring her an easy fortune in Goldfield. She never returned. Goldfield had not turned out the way she imagined. In less than a year she was a penniless prostitute, deeply in debt, and all of nineteen years old. Grass Valley was only a short journey away, but Juanita Dean had traveled too far to turn back. That week the press jubilantly reported "what promises to be the biggest strike of the district" in the Reagan lease on the Mazuma.

The fabulous wealth of Goldfield would not fill the pockets of Tom Fisherman, the prospector who started it all, nor would Fisherman gain much wealth from the Stimler district that was his second great discovery. Yet, if his hopes were disappointed, he did not turn to potassium cyanide or a six-shooter. He would live on, not much better off than he had begun, for more than twenty years after he brought in those first gold samples from Gran Pah. Then, stumbling drunkenly through the streets of Tonopah on a January morning, he fell eighty-seven feet to his death through the open stope of the Silver Top Mine. Ironically, Jim Butler, the discoverer of Tonopah, had died not long before him and was being widely eulogized in the legislature and the press, but few took note of Tom Fisherman's passing. After all, he was only an Indian.[13]

Men like Tom Fisherman were born in this world and moved through it with the shadowy, unhurried sureness of the coyote. Yet this was desert, inhospitable to man and all his works. The tree planted by man to shade his rest died swiftly, the water sucked away in the sand without moistening its parched roots. The boards of his shanty bleached and shrank and cracked in the harsh sun; the shingles curled. His crops shriveled away in the hot wind—none grew here, nor anywhere for many miles. All that Goldfielders ate or wore or used was shipped in from far away.

Inhospitable is too mild a word for this northern fringe of the Mojave. Instead, one should call it *deadly*. It had not changed in the half century since the bones of the immigrant pioneers were buried in Death Valley, not far south. Other valleys in these parts were given different names, but Death Valley would do for all of them. In this vast sea of sand and mountain waves, Goldfield floated like a life raft, from which novices blithely set forth only to learn in agony and desperation how the desert could destroy.

Stories about these desert neophytes appeared in the newspapers from time to time. The man who died of sunstroke had lost his way while walking from Tonopah to Goldfield, a well-traveled distance of only thirty miles. The English girl who set out to prospect and went mad from heat and exposure. The lost tenderfoot who stumbled into town demented—he had found his way back only because he happened upon a railroad track in his wanderings. When a rescue party finally located his partner, they had given up any hope of finding him alive after five days in the desert—but he had subsisted by chewing cactus and eating lizards. And there was the inexperienced traveler who lost his way on a journey between Tonopah and Ellendale. He had drunk all his water, expecting to replenish it at a well on the way, but where the well was, he no longer knew. As he struggled thirstily onward, he thought he heard trickling water. An elusive pool appeared and disappeared and reappeared before his eyes, the legendary mirage that comes before death. At times it seemed "the mountains were chasing round me like the rim of a gigantic flywheel." But he succeeded in making his way back by following the North Star.

Even for seasoned prospectors who had worked the desert for years, a single mistake or a turn of bad luck could be fatal. When Malapai Mike reached Goldfield, the boys couldn't make sense of his delirious ravings at first. Gradually they figured it out. Mike and his partner had been prospecting for a power site in Death Valley. One of their burros collapsed. That meant only one man could ride out of Death Valley and live. They flipped a coin and his partner crawled to the spot where it lay buried in the hot sand to call the toss. He turned to say Malapai Mike had won, and stayed behind to die.

* * *

Goldfield never slept. Neither night nor day existed in the black tunnels of her mines. Although her days seethed with activity, she came fully alive only after sundown. To know her as she really was, to learn the secrets never told on the nearer side of midnight, you had to walk her by night, to watch and pause and talk, and, most of all, to listen. George was becoming a vigorous walker (Alf Doten and he later claimed they clocked the record time for the hike of over twenty miles from Truckee to Reno), and soon he knew every board and rut of these Goldfield streets by heart.

He would stroll past the stock exchange, another long, low, barracks-shaped, one-story building like the Northern, but fronted with windows from floor to ceiling so spectators could view the pandemonium within. At the same crossroad stood the offices of Goldfield Con, a corniced three-story structure of stone blocks done in the Wingfield monumental style. He would take in the Tex Rickard residence, brick with white trim, tiny and cramped, but styled in sharp geometric angles with two bay windows topped with stained glass in startling lapis lazuli blues, deeper than desert twilight. He would walk past the stores and the Palace baths beside the Lyric motion picture theater and make his way to the first Presbyterian church, simplicity itself, with painted boards and a simple spike turret, its fine stained-glass window the only touch of splendor.

He would walk north on Fifth Avenue past small, unembellished one- or two-room houses squatting in the treeless, grassless, flowerless dirt. One of the tiniest of these exhibited a sign declaring it "The Epicurean Cafe." The most luxurious was painted white and sported the refinements of a tiny fence and a window with lace curtains. Reaching the flank of Columbia Mountain, he could reverse his steps, pausing to talk to the men in the street, as he made his way back toward the rock-crested mesa of the Malapai.

This was his Goldfield, the magnet to his metal, the city he had sought without fully understanding why he sought it. Now he had found the excitement that had drawn him irresistibly as a magnetized filing across intervening space in the faces that converged from far and wide in these streets. Their stories and their varied lives endlessly fascinated him, and on his midnight wanderings among them, they became his friends.

I don't think Goldfield had made him the complete egalitarian I remember in the days when he held a black army veteran and a Jewish haberdasher in as affectionate esteem as his friends of wealth and distinction (he would have claimed they were, in their different ways, all equally distinguished and would not have found his own attitude in any way remarkable). His way of looking at the world probably went back much farther. To be the son of a wealthy rancher, as well as a lawyer with a distinguished education and good connections, was often enough to inflate a rather oversized frog in a rather small puddle with a gaseous sense of his own importance and superiority. But this young man had watched his father defy the Dangbergs and the system of domination and deference they represented. He was the son of the stubborn hussar and the woodcutter's daughter. The ringing denial of inborn social distinctions that had joined them was the source of his own beginnings, and he could not see the world in any other way.

He moved with natural ease between the world of the local elite and the world of the streets. It was during his nocturnal wanderings that he came to know the miners and the "high graders" (illegal assayers). The ore in the Goldfield mines was so unusually rich that the miners would steal some whenever possible, hiding it in their pockets, their specially constructed double crown hats, or even in their mouths. In this way the mines lost perhaps $25 to $100 worth of ore per shift (the mine owners, of course, made much higher estimates, but my father did not find them plausible). The miners would take the stolen ore to a high grader. Although the number of high graders has been variously estimated at 50, or 60, or even 106, my father remembered no more than three of any consequence.[14] Using their own smelting machines, they converted the contraband ore into gold bars to be sent to the San Francisco mint.

After the legislature passed a stringent law making it an offense to reduce stolen ore, a high grader named Mike Smith was arrested and promptly hired his friend George Springmeyer to defend him. Although my father knew a Goldfield jury would probably sympathize with any high grader, he did not share Smith's confidence. He was still smarting from his disastrous legal debut in the landlord's suit against the Figis, and he had never tried a criminal case. Doubting that he could possibly carry it off alone, he persuaded a more experienced lawyer to associate with him, and together they won the case. Later, when Smith was once more arrested for the same offense, they again secured his acquittal. A few victories later, George's early doubts and anxieties about his skill in court were permanently ended. He had found he could do it, and was doing it better every time. His clear, logical, incisive style of argument began to take shape, and he developed a zest for his work and a solid confidence in his own ability that he would never lose.

By the late fall of 1907, trouble was again stirring in Goldfield. Efforts by the mine operators to halt high grading by installing change rooms were resented by the miners, who regarded stealing ore as a fringe benefit to which they were morally entitled. Ostensibly, the immediate cause of the strike which set off the events of that winter was scrip, which the miners had been compelled to accept as payment during the cash shortage that followed the October bank panic. Actually the issue was the Industrial Workers of the World (IWW) and its affiliated miners' union, the Western Federation of Miners (WFM). Formed in Chicago in 1905, the IWW, familiarly known as the Wobblies, had united the most radical union men in the nation. The Goldfield branch was associated with two revolutionary concepts, both anathema to the mine owners. One was socialism, a doctrine new to the United States, where many feared its potential popular appeal and none could know how scant a following it would achieve at the polls; the other was a comprehensive mass union including every wage earner in the community from the waitress to the miner. That kind of union could match the mighty Goldfield Con in muscle, perhaps even wrestle it to the floor. Still more disturbing to the mine owners, these union radicals were not dismissed as windy philosophers by their more practical coworkers and relegated to the street-corner soap boxes where they belonged. So rapidly had their power increased that even goals as visionary as theirs seemed almost within reach. George Wingfield made up his mind to eradicate union radicalism from Goldfield.

By November 27 the miners' union was on strike over the scrip issue. The ultimate weapon in the union arsenal was supposed to be the strike. However, if union leaders, in their innocence, supposed that the strike was unwelcome to the mine operators, they were sadly deluded. A WFM strike at this juncture was, in fact, an essential item on Wingfield's agenda. In the first week of December, Wingfield, in conjunction with the other mine operators, prevailed on Governor Sparks to call in federal troops to protect life and property in Goldfield. Suddenly, ungainly young soldiers in broad-brimmed hats and long, double-breasted overcoats that hung down below their knees appeared in the streets, and odd, squatty tents like Mongol yurts mushroomed on the outskirts of the city.

The peace of Goldfield had not been visibly disturbed during the strike, but the troops provided a useful cover beneath which Wingfield could proceed with the extermination of the WFM and IWW. When members of a commission appointed by President Theodore Roosevelt arrived to investigate the carnage that had provoked these drastic measures, they were shown two dead dynamite caps in an electric power pole. To suggest that the Goldfield miners were unable to blow up a pole if they were so minded was much like saying they did not know how to swing a pick or man a drill. Indeed it put considerable strain upon the credulity of the Roosevelt Commission; as they phrased it in the measured language of their report, "the circumstances in the case and the clumsy way in which the work was done at least raises a reasonable doubt as to the genuineness of the attempt."[15] Since there were no additional calamities to view, the commission then listened to testimony by various citizens who expressed fears that violence might erupt should the union commence to resist the reduction in wages, the importation of strikebreakers, and the card system that had been instituted by the mine operators.

These anxieties were needless; by spring Wingfield and his scabs had completed the quiet, bloodless, efficient destruction of the union. Once the mad Wobblies, those "anarchistic slumgullions from foreign climes," as they were sometimes termed in the press, had terrified every right-thinking citizen with their wild, revolutionary talk. Only a year before they had shocked Nevadans with their "Bloody Sunday" parade to commemorate the massacre of their Russian brothers in St. Petersburg and to protest the jailing of their leader, Big Bill Haywood, in Idaho on assassination charges. A reckless gesture, a reach beyond grasp, defiant of all convention, but stamped with Goldfield's brand of bravura. They belonged here, if they belonged anywhere at all, and unlike their careful, conservative rivals in the AFL, edging cautiously step by step toward small incremental goals, they had flourished in this place. But even here, in this city of moonstruck men, none had conceived so grand a dream as theirs, a dream of Goldfield as the industrial Eden of the new working class. The dream ended that winter. They had held their own with Goldfield Con, but they were not prepared to fight the United States government. The union men drifted silently away.

At first my father thought the mine operators were justified. But he began to spend time talking with the men as they stood idle in the street during the long nights of bitter cold. The scene as he might have known it takes shape in my imagination. I see that street as Remington would draw it in pen and ink, only darker. The moon is shrouded in clouds; there are no street lamps, only the faint wash of light from windows or the brief opening of a door. The stars themselves seem windblown and very small, tiny sparks from the tip of a cigar spilling away in the darkness. The winter wind lashes through the city, then retreats and draws its breath only to rage once more with redoubled fury, as though determined to obliterate this obstruction of a city which bars its passage across the empty desert. Wearing shabby suits and overcoats, hats pulled low over their ears, heads bent down against the wind, the men stand in a knot, waiting.

A slight figure moves toward the group. He is not immediately accepted. The shadows speak. One suggests with weary bitterness that he belongs down at the Montezuma Club with his pal George Wingfield. But there are others who know him, one who remembers he defended the high grader Mike Smith. Maybe he is a lawyer and one of Wingfield's bunch, but if he wants to stand out here in the street with us on a night like this, we ought to make room for him. The group shifts a little to admit him.

"You're a brave man staying on in Goldfield, what with life and property being in danger. Or ain't you heard about them two dead dynamite caps George Wingfield stuck in the power pole?" It is the voice of "Mr. John D. Rockefeller," or possibly of "Mr. Andrew Carnegie," the names two of the IWW men will give when the judge, commenting upon their eloquence, sentences them to jail for vagrancy a few years later in another Nevada town. And John D. has a lot to say.

"You think there might have been violence here? And you call to mind the time Silva got shot last spring when we was trying to unionize his restaurant? Well, let's look at Silva, let's look at him real good. Come out of that restaurant waving a gun at Morrie Preston, didn't he? And when a man's waving a gun, you draw. Sometimes you draw a little too soon. Happened more than once in the Northern. Do them flunky politicians call in the troops to save us all from violence every time some trigger-happy fool gets hisself shot up in a saloon? Not unless they see the chance to bust a union man."

"And what about the trial? Preston convicted on the sworn lies of a gunman from Butch Cassidy's Wild Bunch. Now there's a real fine, upstanding witness for you. And Preston's buddy Smith convicted of voluntary manslaughter and sent up for ten years. Smith was just sitting home eating dinner when Silva got hisself shot. He's the only man in these United States ever got convicted on a charge like that. You call it justice? That's Wingfield's kind of justice."

A match flares and momentarily illumines the thin, unshaven face of Mr. Andrew Carnegie, frowning with concentration, before the wind snuffs out the flame. Another match sputters and dies. The shadows lean toward one another, joined by the spark. The smouldering tip of a cigar lights the cigarette sheltered by carefully cupped hands, and the voice resumes. "This strike's been run peaceful. Ain't even one of the boys got out of hand. And we got to strike. Wingfield's going to walk over us with both feet if we don't show him some muscle."

"You say the strike ain't right and high grading ain't nothing but another word for stealing? It's stealing alright, but ain't got nothing to do with the union. Miners was high grading here long before there was any Wobblies in Goldfield, and they'd still be high grading if there wasn't no union here but them tame rabbits in the AFL. Miners always has and always will, anywhere there's ore rich enough to be worth taking." A muffled laugh from someone is swallowed by the wind.

"So you think we been trying to make those other unions join us when they got no mind to? Well, we did order them carpenters to join last March. But only after our WFM carpenters got kicked off the job and the toadies in the AFL quit construction on the union hospital. Wouldn't be no hospital yet, if you was waiting on them. Maybe the boys do cut up a little rough sometimes, but union organizing ain't exactly a testimonial banquet. We got to fight them scabs Wingfield keeps bringing in and them lackey unions he's always raising up to cut us out. A lot of the boys been blacklisted since last spring, before this strike ever started."

The wind is dying to a low mutter as the night wanes. Not many hours now until dawn. The knot of men grows smaller, as some of the shadows melt away in the surrounding darkness. "You read in the papers where we been talking revolution against the government? Don't they teach you lawyer fellas nothing in school? Ain't this a free country where a man can say anything he wants? Or maybe this ain't the U.S. of A. out here no more but some other country with a king by the name of George Wingfield who's got the courts and all the politicians under his thumb. Wouldn't you talk revolution if you was us?

"We got our constitutional rights, same as anybody else. Well, if you see that, maybe there's hope for you yet, even if you are a lawyer. We ain't saying all lawyers is running dogs for the corporations. One or two are alright. Old Harry Morehouse. Gus Tilden, who's defending us now in that injunction suit Wingfield slapped on us for being a conspiracy and a criminal society. Maybe you make three."

The voice of Mr. John D. Rockefeller subsides in long, racking coughs, which echo like blows in the street. When it resumes, it is hoarse and weary. "You say Wingfield don't run every man in Goldfield and there's going to be justice when the right ones get elected? Justice here in Goldfield? Well, maybe so, but we ain't yet seen the day. And won't see it this side of socialism neither, I don't believe. You got an awful lot of faith in politics."

I am just imagining. No one knows what they said. The shadows are gone, the voices are scattered like dust, and all that remains of that winter are the night, the wind, and the desert. I know for certain only that my father talked with the union men night after night in the street, that he listened to them, and that in the end he came to believe they were right.

The District Attorney's Office

THE REPUBLICAN STATE convention of 1906 had been an education; the Esmeralda County convention of 1908 was a free-for-all. Of course, in Goldfield, where occasions of every sort tended toward the riotous, an orderly political gathering was hardly to be expected. George had persuaded Fred Balzar, a friendly easygoing railroad conductor he had met during the campaign of 1906, to run for state senator, but the convention battle in which George and his friends helped Balzar win the Republican nomination was bitter. No doubt a faint ideological division was already perceptible between the machine politicians and the courthouse crowd on the one hand and the outsiders and the progressive Republicans on the other. And when the convention was finished, Arthur Barnes and the rest of the courthouse crowd were not. One day shortly afterward, the irascible Barnes encountered George on the sidewalk in front of the Goldfield Consolidated Mines Building.

"I'm going to lick the hell out of you," said Barnes. "Wait till I take off my glasses." He proceeded to arrange his glasses and coat on the windowsill of the building.

"I don't believe you can," said George. "Wait while I take off my coat." Barnes was a much taller and heavier man, but had he been as formidable as Battling Nelson himself, my father's sense of honor would never permit him to decline a challenge.

When George was halfway out of his coat, Barnes began battering him in the face, blinding his eyes. Finally George got an arm free, and with one lucky sightless punch he struck Barnes on the chin, knocking him off the wooden sidewalk down to the recently graded street some two and a half feet below. At this point George Wingfield and some friends stopped the fight.

George applied steaks to his face, even tried leeches, but for three months, he was a conspicuous sight in court. Goldfield had lawyers tall, short, fat, and thin; balding, bearded, and mustachioed; inebriated and sober; juvenile and senile—but only one lawyer in town sported two blooming black eyes.

To his Republican comrades in arms, at least, those black eyes were as war wounds honorably acquired on the field of battle. Arthur Barnes and the courthouse crowd to the contrary notwithstanding, Balzar was victorious, a major step in a long political career that would finally culminate with the governorship in 1926; Augustus Tilden was elected district attorney for Goldfield on the same ticket. He appointed George as his chief assistant.

"Vice flourished luxuriantly during the heyday of our 'flush times.' The saloons were overburdened with custom; so were the police courts, the gambling dens, the brothels, and the jails —unfailing signs of high prosperity in a mining region."[1] Mark Twain had written these words about Virginia City in its prime some forty years before, but they applied equally well to Goldfield, where vice and crime blossomed as the rose did not and none considered these conditions particularly alarming. No clarion calls for reform were sounded. No one, with the possible exception of a few visionary socialists, proposed to eradicate crime by abolishing social injustice. No commissions were appointed to ponder, weigh, and study the causes of crime in Nevada mining towns; perhaps it was considered that these had already been sufficiently elucidated by Myron Angel in 1881 when he wrote in his *History of Nevada*: "The expectation of gaining sudden wealth fires the hearts of a restless class. . . . Defeat of expectation begets a restless disposition; recklessness is followed by dissipation, gambling and other attendant vices . . .[man] becomes a very demon from plans miscarried, hopes deferred, ambitions thwarted, and body and brain stimulated with strong waters produced by the subtle art of the distiller. The greater proportion of homicides result from reckless bravado. Persons meet in saloons, bagnios and gambling places with deadly weapons upon their persons; they drink, gamble, dispute when half intoxicated, banter each other, and at last draw out their weapons and for fancied causes alone slay each other."[2]

Goldfield did not lack for a restless class fired by expectations of sudden wealth, and if overburdened courts were an unfailing sign of high prosperity, the city had sound reasons for self-congratulation. A small staff of law enforcement officials was nonetheless expected to cope with all eventualities. In the main they did it by working harder and longer than their modern counterparts. The district attorney and his assistants, ranging in number from one to three, were constantly present in Goldfield's two district courts trying criminal cases. Because the docket was so crowded, jurors were allowed time off only for supper before returning for hearings that often lasted as late as 11:00 at night. The scene of these endeavors was Goldfield's new courthouse, a structure with the solidity of a medieval fortress. Completed in 1908 from blocks of cut gray stone, it was made to endure an age at least, and it would outlast Goldfield by many years.

An extraordinary parade of cases would pass through the portals of the district attorney's office during George's tenure. An Egyptian tamale vendor had to be restrained from pressing his amorous attentions upon the ladies of Goldfield. A cool customer passed an 1862 Confederate bill in the tenderloin (no one even noticed it for quite some time). There was a robbery case, weakened somewhat by the regrettable disappearance of the evidence. Having captured the burglar red-handed with the stolen money and jewelry in his possession, the deputy sheriff stashed the evidence in the copious overcoat pockets of his wagon driver, and the three of them set off for the nearest town. The journey was long, the sun warm, and the rocking rhythm of the wagon rather soothing. Eventually the deputy and the driver awoke with a jolt from a pleasant doze to observe the prisoner some distance off in the sagebrush in the act of burying the money. The jewelry, apparently discarded somewhere along the way, was never recovered. In another notable larceny case, the evidence, was, at least, more difficult to conceal: the defendant was charged with stealing two houses.

Con artists appeared in rich variety. Young Mr. Fitler allowed it to be confidentially known that he was a man of great wealth and still greater expectations but found himself temporarily in need of cash, which his new friends would undoubtedly be happy to loan him. Dr. H. H. Muggsley, exquisitely tailored and flashing with diamond studs, arrived amply supplied with funds from credulous Philadelphia investors and with feminine companionship in the form of the voluptuous blonde who clung to one arm and the olive-skinned brunette who clasped the other. However, he departed for Los Angeles rather abruptly before the district attorney could inquire too closely into his affairs. In a classic case in which coals were not only brought to Newcastle but sold there for a tidy profit, the sheriff arrested two men posing as prospectors whose desperate financial circumstances compelled them to part most reluctantly with the treasured gold nuggets painstakingly gleaned over a lifetime of hardship in the cruel desert—nuggets they had actually manufactured by melting brass in a crucible and casting it in a bed of white quartz. Many Goldfielders who ought to have known better had eagerly purchased nuggets the size of pigeons' eggs at $5 or $10 apiece as pins and watch charms.

Misrepresentation came in many forms. My father made a determined attempt to secure payment for the miners working the Kewanas under a leaser who told them a large bank account had been set aside for their wages. When payday arrived, they learned no such account existed. In an age when labor legislation was still in its infancy, the only recourse for the worker cheated by his employer was a private civil suit or, more likely, a bitter shrug for a lost month of work. District attorneys rarely took an interest in these matters, in part because they had scant authority to act.

All the same, George listened to the story of these miners. Without question, they had been defrauded, and the man who had done it was scot-free. Surely the law must contain justice for them, but he could find no similar cases. It probably took hours of patient searching through the statute books before he came across the germ of an idea. It had never been tried, so far as he knew, but he thought he had hit upon a legal principle that could be stretched to cover these circumstances. This leaser was going to pay his men or face criminal charges.

George prosecuted under a statute obviously designed for con artists of the breed of Dr. H. H. Muggsley in their dealings with investors. It stated that "if any person by false representation of his own wealth" shall defraud others of "money, goods, chattels, wealth, or any other valuable thing, such offender shall be deemed a swindler." What had that to do with hard-rock miners who could scarcely claim the leaser had defrauded them of their possessions in wealth, goods, valuables, or chattels? George proceeded to demonstrate that it had a great deal to do with them. In a novel effort, which he was unable to buttress with any legal citations, he endeavored to prove that labor itself was a "valuable thing" within the meaning of the law and won his point.[3]

Misrepresentation of another sort came to light when two young ladies from Los Angeles arrived to take positions at the Turf "Cafe." They had been engaged by an agent, paid $35 for his labors in securing their services as entertainers at an establishment he described as similar to the elegant Los Angeles hotels where music of the cultivated variety was provided for the listening pleasure of patrons of the finer arts during the dinner hours. Indeed he had assured them that the rules of this exemplary establishment were so strict that even cigarette smoking was not permitted within its walls. Words could not convey the shock experienced when they crossed the threshold of the Turf and beheld not a hostelry of culture and refinement but a vulgar saloon with a long bar and gaming tables beneath which skulked mongrel dogs. They had glimpsed rear parlors, redolent of iniquity, where brutish looking men repaired to enjoy wine, women, and song. Needless to say, they had turned upon their heels and made an immediate exit. The press observed that many young women had been lured to Goldfield from Los Angeles with similar promises. And possibly not all had departed as hastily as these two.

Goldfield's most scandalous piece of con artistry, and the one that drew the largest crowd at the courthouse, was the Vortrees "badger game." Rumor had it that Jessie Vortrees was an old friend of George Wingfield and that Wingfield's intervention at the sheriff's office had secured him a commission as Goldfield deputy constable, despite a shady past that included more than one murder. But it was his wife the people wanted to see. When Jessie Vortrees's trial on an extortion charge began, the courtroom, the doorways, and the halls were crammed with Goldfielders eager for a glimpse of the luscious Annie May Vortrees, she of the pouting lips, the flashing brown eyes, the smooth hair combed low over her ears and knotted at the nape of her neck, and the buxom figure confined within a white embroidered shirtwaist and a black and red checked skirt. Over at the Hippodrome Theater, *Leah the Forsaken,* billed as "a powerful story of love, persecution, forgiveness, and death," was a poor second best to the real life drama of Annie May the Temptress. During the preliminary hearing, spectators unable to squeeze into the packed courtroom had clambered up on the windowsills to stare at the notorious lady in the peach-basket hat trimmed with yellow roses for whom Jessie Vortrees had fought and won a gun duel in Arizona.

The story of the badger game, laboriously extracted by Tilden from the very embarrassed young man who testified for the prosecution, had started at a dance in the town park. Meeting the toothsome Annie May, the young man had inquired if she would care to dance. The lady said she would. She was a sinuous dancer and clasped him tightly to her voluptuous bosom. Would she allow him to escort her home in his auto? The lady said she would. Would she consider a romantic interlude in the public bathhouse. Well, no—she might see someone she knew. Then perhaps at the Spencer rooming house, where lovers doomed to part must compress the sweet embraces of a lifetime within the span of a few brief hours? The lady said she would. Would she care to join him on the bed for a few moments of "earnest conversation?" The lady said she would.

But what was this? Her outraged husband burst into the room. He wore a tin star; he brandished a large revolver; he threatened to kill the man who would violate the sacred bonds of marriage. Ah, the tragedy of it all: the brief madness of a summer's evening, a waltz round the park, a little chug in the auto, a few moments of earnest conversation had led—alas—to this.

But wait—all was not yet lost for the hapless youth. Annie May was pleading for his life, and who could resist the tender entreaties of Annie May? Would the irate husband be persuaded to spare the young man's life? Yes, the irate husband said he might, and it would cost the young man a mere fifty bucks.

Goldfield roared. The first jury was unable to agree; the second found the irate husband guilty of extortion. But what of Annie May? Would twelve good men and true condemn those dancing eyes to durance vile, much less that delicately palpitating bosom? Tilden could not believe they would. The charges against Annie May were dismissed, and the lady undulated forth to console herself as best she could during the unavoidable absence of her husband.[4]

The granitic exteriors of those contentious, moralizing Goldfield juries often concealed rich deposits of sympathetic emotion which many lawyers delved industriously to uncover. A hung jury was not the exception but the rule, and the behavior of the jury itself was often more noteworthy than that of the defendants who trooped before them. Two carpenters appeared in court following a shooting in the railroad station during which one creased the scalp and drilled the shoulder of the "ingrate" who had run off with his wife. The jury, highly indignant, refused to indict the angry husband but administered a stern lecture to the "false friend" who showed his gratitude by wrecking the poor man's home. A man was tried for stealing two cows, and even this minor transgression raised issues of such complexity and of so grave and momentous a nature that the jury—as usual—found themselves unable to agree.

* * *

Not long after the jury pondered the matter of the two cows, another spring came to Goldfield. Burton's Blood Syrup, "an excellent spring tonic and blood purifier," was featured in the drugstores. Some debated whether the most stunning spring floral display belonged to the gentleman sporting three pots of azaleas on his front stoop or to his rival, whose carefully nurtured rosebush had actually produced a bona fide bud. Goldfield's first trees, fifty cottonwoods, were planted on Arbor Day, causing the editor of the *Tribune* to muse dreamily on a verdant future of lawns, flowers, and even songbirds. Striped awnings sprouted over Goldfield windows. Cows were turned loose from their winter confinement in backyards to graze among the oak shrubs on the Malapai. The ephemeral blooming of wild flowers tinted the eastern hills, and ladies with parasols set off on church picnics. Some planned outings to Stonewall Mountain to view the waterfall. Others went driving, shaded by huge hats, swathed in veils, and clad in what the fashion editors described as "the regulation one piece motoring suit of champagne rajah." My father, however, had no leisure to enjoy the season, for he was absorbed in the preparation of two major cases, the Rawhide graft trial and the bullion tax indictments.

Both sides stated the issues in the Rawhide graft trial in sweeping terms. The defense contended that the prosecution of County Commissioner Charles Worden and his co-defendants for conspiracy to defraud the county through fictitious drug and hospital bills was itself "the most damnable conspiracy ever enacted under the guise of justice anyplace under the sun"; indeed it was "a political trial of the county commissioners" manufactured by their political opponents. The courthouse was crowded with Republican politicians, watching and advising the defense at every turn, determined to protect their own. Probably Arthur Barnes, soon to be appointed justice of the peace, was there, and Ed Collins, postmaster and political agent of the Southern Pacific, and perhaps John Donnelley, occasional aide to Collins in political matters. It is certain that few local politicians of importance were missing and that Tilden and Springmeyer were emphatically persona non grata in the eyes of their own party.

This atmosphere failed to inhibit the prosecution. Tilden soon progressed to a sharp attack on the courthouse crowd. Not only had officials from the mining town of Rawhide presented fraudulent and vastly inflated hospital bills for payment in a conspiracy to defraud the county but also the statutory structure of county government had been subverted by the county commissioners when, instead of acting in concert, they informally divided the county into districts and allocated each commissioner carte blanche in his own bailiwick. All in all, bills for medications sufficient to treat half the population of Rawhide —which Tilden later declared to the jury he could visualize hobbling past "as an army of the sick, halt, lame, and blind," —had been submitted on behalf of about a dozen patients. Unfortunately, the only method by which these charges could be proven was a detailed and tedious accounting of the hospital bills from Rawhide.

Defense characterizations of various witnesses for the prosecution as "a piece of human putty," "a pitiable driveling idiot," "a damnable prostitution of womanhood," "venomous," and "frail in mind and frail in body," were lively enough, as was Tilden's gibe at defense attorney J. F. Douglas, manager of the Goldfield Hotel, for reverting to "the language of the bar room and the precincts of the roulette wheel, over which he daily presides." Equally lively was the sarcastic suggestion by the defense attorneys, made late in the afternoon, that a missing witness for the state should be sought in his bed "as he is not an early riser." Not least, the conduct of the Rawhide justice of the peace, who had admittedly sworn false affidavits, was sufficiently startling to prompt the presiding judge to remark after the verdict that he had "never known or heard of such careless and illegal methods."

Nonetheless, spring had turned to summer, the days were warm, and the jurors' attention was unmistakably wandering from the testimony on short deliveries of absorbent cotton and the price of Lysol. They leaned back in their large, wooden swivel chairs, their feet propped on the low, brass rails. The wooden ceiling fan with the elaborate iron scrollwork base turned slowly overhead. Outside horses clopped in the street and an occasional motorcycle zipped past on the sidewalk. A wind strong enough to rip bricks and stones from buildings and send tents skipping away tore through the streets.

Day by day, hour by hour, patient by patient, and almost pill by pill, the trial inched slowly forward. The flooding waters of the Bishop Creek left Goldfield without electricity for several days, and the night sessions proceeded by the flickering light of candles and kerosene lamps. The jury was allowed to go bowling, then swimming at the local bathhouse, and to play a game of box ball, but even these diversions did little to relieve the monotony. Many minds were obviously elsewhere, perhaps probing the night skies, where a mysterious airship with lights fore and aft had been seen sailing tranquilly over Rhyolite, and the presence of an eccentric inventor conducting secret experiments somewhere in the desert was suspected. It became extremely difficult for the prosecution to evoke any indignation among the jurors over those supplies of Lydia Pinkham's pills that the commissioner's wife had been in the habit of charging to the county.

Slowly the graft trials were swamped in an accumulating wave of minutiae, of thermometers, saline laxatives, quarts of whiskey (medicinal, of course), hot water bottles, and plaster of Paris bandages. After closing arguments were at last completed, the jury retired. Prolonged shouting echoed through the courthouse halls from the jury room. All favored acquittal save one, and he had resolved to cast his ballot for conviction "until doomsday" if necessary. He refused to change his mind. After members of the jury found themselves unable to agree, the indictments were dismissed.[5]

Tilden, then nearly forty, was a self-taught lawyer and a man of liberal sympathies. He had fought Boss Ruef within the San Francisco Republican party and, after his move to Nevada in 1904, had defended the WFM in the injunction suit instituted against it by the mine owners during the troubles of December 1907. Although he was a talented lawyer when sober, this was not always his condition. His benders often lasted a month at a time, and in his absence, George was left in charge of the district attorney's office. It was during one of his recurrent disappearances that George discovered that the Pittsburgh Silver Peak Mining Company and the Florence had not paid their bullion taxes, an assessment on mine produce based on the value of the ore. Further investigation revealed certain irregularities. The statement issued by Pittsburgh Silver Peak to its stockholders revealed a huge profit, while the report filed with the bullion tax collector showed no profit at all. Charges claimed for milling were inflated nearly four times over the amount listed in the company books. In the tax returns submitted by the Florence, losses sustained by unproductive leasers had been written off against profits, while lush royalties collected from the productive ones went unmentioned. This was dangerous ground for a young man planning to run for attorney general on the Republican ticket in the next election and in need of corporation support, and he would have been well advised to tread circumspectly—but that was not what George proceeded to do. He filed civil suits against the errant mining companies. More than that, he rocked the mining world by bringing criminal charges, on which company officials were indicted for conspiring to defraud the state of bullion tax.

The case was a sensation, not only because the financial practices of the big mining companies were rarely questioned, but also because several of the company directors under criminal indictment were men of national prominence, such as Pennsylvania Senator George Oliver, the millionaire newspaperman. The senator, of course, denied all knowledge of the machinations at Pittsburgh Silver Peak, and outrage was expressed in various quarters toward state officials who failed to approach those of rank and fortune with the customary deference. The *Goldfield Daily Tribune* blasted the prosecutors for treating men of "untold wealth" like "arch criminals,"[6] and George Wingfield darkly warned that "people in the East who have money" would be reluctant to invest in Goldfield securities because "the directors of two such big corporations have been classed as criminals."[7]

The concept that Pittsburgh Silver Peak should pay taxes as ordinary people did was a mutinous idea that company officials proceeded to resist by every means in their power, both legal and extralegal. The press reported a blatant effort to intimidate the judge when he refused to quash the indictments. In the lobby of the Goldfield Hotel, an attempt by the Silver Peak manager to find out what certain witnesses had said before the grand jury led to a heated exchange with my father and finally to a physical attack upon the bullion tax collector. A little more than a month later repeated threats against the lives of all officials connected with the suit had so unnerved the tax collector that he felt obliged to request police protection for himself and for the members of the district attorney's office.

When the cases were finally settled out of court, important legal principles that would substantially increase state revenues from the bullion tax had been established, and the presiding judge congratulated the grand jury and the prosecutor for their "fearless discharge of duty."[8] George's role in the matter was somewhat obliquely acknowledged by the mining companies when a representative from the Florence handed him a check for more than ten thousand dollars in bullion taxes—made out not to the state but to him.

The Fourth of July arrived and was celebrated with florid oratory and a barrage of dynamite canes. Terrified by the dynamite cartridges that small boys took such pleasure in exploding at their heels, Goldfield's floating population of stray dogs fled yelping to the hills. Meanwhile the county commissioners were preparing a dynamite cane of their own. The district attorney and his idealistic young assistant had persisted in prosecuting the Rawhide graft trial in the face of their displeasure. One of them had been indicted, and all of them had heard their methods of government scathingly condemned in the courtroom. Such temerity would not go unpunished.

The commissioners decided to raise the district attorney's bond. Usually this sum was fixed at roughly twice the total amount involved in current delinquent tax suits, but the board was permitted to set it at higher levels, and in the past, they had forced a Goldfield district attorney out of office by raising his bond to the exorbitant height, for those days, of $65,000. Tilden's bond had been fixed at $20,000 when he took office. George Wingfield, possibly displeased by the lack of reverence accorded to his views on bullion tax matters, now withdrew part of the sum he had earlier posted on Tilden's behalf, and the board, over my father's strenuously voiced objections, declared that Tilden would be compelled to post $95,000. If he failed, his office would be declared vacant and they would replace him. The board's attorney observed with evident satisfaction that the office of district attorney was now "in suspension."

Charging "fraud and oppression," Tilden secured a temporary writ against the board of county commissioners and set out on a frantic search for bondsmen. He would be obliged to comb the Nevada mining towns and the California coast before he was done. Goldfield watched and simmered through the hottest summer on record. Ice cream and soda water were in great demand. Even the thermometers could not tolerate the burning sun. The large model in front of Truitt's drugstore had been built to register temperatures as high as 130°; one day it rose to 104°; then, when the sun shone on it, the mercury skyrocketed and the instrument burst. That day, and every day, my father took care of the office in Tilden's absence, as he was by then accustomed to doing. Dogs could pant, lizards could stretch out in the shade, but people were expected to pursue their customary activities in the usual way. When George appeared in court without his jacket in the blistering heat, the judge sternly informed him that he would not be admitted unless he was "entirely clothed."

In September the heat, both climatic and official, abated. Tilden had miraculously scraped together most of the extraordinary sum demanded of him. More important, he had made it clear to the board that he would not allow himself to be forced out of office by this stratagem. They graciously accepted his bond, Tilden politely dropped his suit against them, and there were strained professions of harmony by all concerned.[9]

By this time my father had moved out of the rigors of the canvas-topped cabin into the luxuries of the new Goldfield Hotel. Not for nothing was it advertised as "the most elegantly equipped hotel between San Francisco and Denver." Its carpets were red; its dining room sported potted palms and white linen tablecloths; its floors had tiny black and white mosaic tiles set in the Greek key design at the borders; its beds were of brass and its hangings of velvet; its mahogany trimmed lobby was resplendent with gilded Greek columns, puffy black leather chairs, and globular chandeliers. The Goldfield Hotel was generally considered a shade more sumptuous than Versailles. Indeed it was a far cry from those six-hour shifts in the old Esmeralda. The opening of this $750,000 wonder, real brick and all of four stories high, had been toasted with three solid nights of champagne and dancing.

George's roommate in the Goldfield Hotel was a fellow law-yer named Michaelangelo Diskin (they called him Jack). George used to joke that he had "made a lawyer out of Jack"—who later became Nevada attorney general during the twenties—because during his sessions in court, he repeatedly had Jack appointed to the defense, then beat him in the case. Just a short time ago George himself had been too uncertain of his capabili-ties to take on a criminal case without bringing in an associate, but a lawyer learned quickly in Goldfield. Less than three years sufficed to turn a novice into an old pro. These educational workouts in the courtroom also enabled Jack to pay his half of the rent. Every Saturday night George helped him count out his weekly earnings in gold before he stashed them away in the hotel safe—confidence in the banks had faltered perceptibly since the panic of 1907.

After Jack's money was counted, if it was a bright moonlit night, George sometimes joined a group of young men and women for a ride of ten or fifteen miles across the desert to a grove of Joshua palms. By night the pale, bleached shades of the desert turned purple and the sand became silver when the moon rose. The Joshua palms, which resembled bundles of coarse grass tied loosely together by day, assumed the grotesque, mys-terious shapes of fanciful creatures. Listening to the Joshuas was the formal reason for these moonlight rides. When one of the branches was broken from a Joshua palm, it would "cry like a baby." Or like an investor in the Mountain Crown.

Because he neither gambled nor drank, George had little in-terest in the saloons, and many of his evenings were spent at the exclusive Montezuma Club joking with the Catholic priest, who was also a member. My father had a treasured collection of jokes, some fairly racy, and not a few concerned with priests and Irishmen. Father Dermody belonged to both categories. While the more frolicsome members of the Montezuma Club desported themselves at billiards, leapfrog, and pool, the jolly

Irish churchman would chuckle and tell a few stories of his own
—he must have known some good ones about atheists and
lawyers. My father used to say they stayed friends for a good
reason: the priest "never tried to talk me into being a Catholic
and I never tried to talk him out of being one."

One of the most sensitive cases George and Tilden undertook
was the prosecution of George's old friend Smith, who had once
again been arrested for high grading. Convictions for high grading had never been easily attained in Goldfield, where the public regarded the practice as a miner's perquisite and the recent
antagonism between miners and mine owners had kindled popular feeling on the issue. All told, the press was able to cite six
convictions. However, despite the unrelenting efforts of Wingfield's security men, no recent convictions had been secured in
cases involving Goldfield Con, a circumstance obviously nett-
lesome to Wingfield. In the fall of 1909 he charged that a million
dollars worth of ore had been stolen from the Consolidated and
processed by a cooperating confederacy of thirteen assayers. He
had instituted change rooms; smashed the union; hired a force
of detectives headed by his tough, brutal friend and sidekick,
Clarence Sage; secured legislation permitting the mine owners
to examine the assayer's books; and sued for a federal injunction to prevent the assayers from purchasing ore without his
permission, an injunction so supremely arrogant in its premises
that only Wingfield could have conceived it. But still the high
grading went on. Immediately preceding the Smith trial, Goldfield watched while another set of jurors remained closeted in
disagreement over their verdict in a separate case of high grading from Goldfield Con. Wingfield, angered by the probable
release of yet another high grader with a hung jury, moved
toward direct confrontation with the elusive enemy. When the
venire for the Smith case had been summoned and the jury was
about to be drawn, he issued a warning that, in effect, consti-
tuted blatant interference with the judicial process; his methods

were scarcely less direct than the day when he had forced the union men to buy newspapers at gunpoint.

He pointedly observed that as the largest taxpayer in Esmeralda County the Consolidated paid "more than half the salaries of county officials." The implication was unmistakable that they were therefore his employees and would do well to bestir themselves in his interests. The Consolidated, he noted, "can get along without Goldfield; as to whether Goldfield can get along without the Consolidated, I will leave to those gentlemen whose profession is politics to determine." Then he related a tale with an unmistakable moral concerning the decline of Titusville, Pennsylvania, when lack of local cooperation compelled the resident oil company to build a separate city of its own. "If the time shall come," Wingfield concluded threateningly, "that a man who steals from the company fails of conviction because of a sentiment in the community adverse to the company, it will be high time for the company to choose the community in which it shall do business."[10]

At first it appeared that the citizenry was prepared to enjoy a satisfying swig of the popular locally brewed product advertised as " 'High Grade,' Bottle Beer, an invigorating tonic" and ignore the expressed wishes of Goldfield Consolidated. The high grader before the court escaped with a hung jury, leading Tilden to observe with some dismay that the prosecution's case had been "absolutely conclusive" and the defendant had "made no explanation in his own behalf." The little scoop-shaped device attached at the point where the richest ore concentrates were gathering on the table in the Consolidated mill and the box of concentrates found in his possession seemed to require some explaining. For a time it seemed that the district attorney would be unable to produce a jury for the Smith trial because whenever he put the delicately phrased question, "Do you believe that a miner has a right to take a sample or specimen from a mine?" to a prospective jury man, the answer was more likely than not to be a resounding affirmative. He ran through nearly the complete venire of jury men before finding the necessary twelve. A new pool of jury men could be furnished only by the county commissioners, and had the venire been exhausted, all court proceedings might well have halted until the board's next scheduled meeting.

As the story unfolded, it appeared that Smith and a mill man working on the amalgamating plates at Goldfield Consolidated had worked out a scheme for stealing about $500 worth of metal from the plates each month under the justification that "as long as George Wingfield and the company were getting theirs, we might as well get ours." Smith would do the processing and the mill man would do the stealing, but it was necessary to fix the watchman at the mill. This task was assigned to Jake Hildebrandt, owner of the Turf Saloon. Hildebrandt, in turn, wanted to bring in Constable Bart Knight to "handle the jury" in case anything went wrong.

Everything would, no doubt, have proceeded according to plan if the watchman Hildebrandt was supposed to have fixed had not taken the story to Clarence Sage. While the watchman pretended to cooperate with the conspirators, Goldfield Con's security men built up an airtight case. The final piece of evidence was fitted into place when Constable Knight, in defiance of Hildebrandt's advice, went to the watchman's house to collect his cut and stayed to discuss the project in some detail while two witnesses concealed with flashlight and notebook behind a trapdoor took down his every word.

Emotions ran high in the packed courtroom. Public contempt for the stool pigeon watchman was so strong that even though the prosecution had carefully prepared the ground, rejecting all prospective jurors who admitted they would discount the evidence of "an accomplice" or they would disapprove of men who "turn state's evidence," defense attorney Harry Morehouse scored a telling point when he inquired whether the witness was "paid to get your friends into trouble." George was obliged to defend the man's credibility at some length. Although the press called Tilden's closing argument "the speech of his career," the oratorical laurels probably went to the eloquent and witty Morehouse, whose closing address culminated in a proposal for the formation of a lodge to be known as "The Grand Royal Order of High Graders," complete with signs and passwords. One admiring spectator afterwards remarked to Smith, "Well, [even] if you lose, you got your money's worth."

Mike Smith did lose, and despite his obvious guilt and the light sentence he had received out of judicial consideration for his wife and children, he walked out of the courtroom an embittered man. He probably would have said he suspected as much when the watchman received immunity for turning state's evidence, and Tilden, whose faith in his prospects for obtaining a jury, much less a conviction, was obviously faltering, explained some months later that Knight and Hildebrandt would not be tried because the principal witness against them had disappeared for parts unknown. Whatever Smith thought of this, the full weight of his bitterness fell upon my father, his friend, who had twice won his acquittal as a private attorney and had now refused to secure special treatment for him.[11]

The case was the first to demonstrate a crucial aspect of my father as a lawyer, one that would later cause a good deal of friction when he was United States attorney during the Prohibition era. Although he was not given to sanctimonious preachments on the subject, he harbored an inner ideal of justice without favoritism and never allowed friendship or anything else to interfere with a prosecution. This attitude was imperfectly understood by many of his friends and was incomprehensible to Smith, who never forgave him and always greeted him with a silent glare whenever the two passed each other on the street in future years.

Only once did he ever indicate he had disliked prosecuting a case, and the reason was not the ties of friendship that personally involved him with one of the principal figures. Prejudice ignored the rules to accommodate particular people, something my father never did, or even wanted to do; morality engendered an emotional necessity stronger than any personal relationship, something he now felt acutely when his legal role conflicted with his sense of fair play. Even so, he refrained from turning the case entirely over to Tilden, because this would have been a subtle dereliction of duty. Although the murdered man, Edward Baker, had been my father's friend ever since they were boys together in the Carson Valley before Baker abandoned the cowboy's life to become a gambler, my father could take no pleasure in prosecuting a man who had acted in self-defense, as he believed Slim Grimmett had. Honor bound to give the case his best effort regardless of his feelings, he was troubled less by his friend's death than by the innocence of the accused man before him.

The immediate issue at stake in the gun battle in which Grimmett had killed Baker was $7.50. Not exactly big money, even then. Grimmett had seen far greater sums change hands over the gambling tables as he worked Goldfield and Seven Troughs and other mining camps in the region. But it was almost two days wages in the mines, or the price of six union suits and one rocking chair, or two stetsons and one pair of Bull Dog suspenders, or five bottles of Black and White scotch with 20¢ left over in change for tickets to motion pictures and illustrated songs at Goldfield's Lyric Theater—and the tall, slim red-haired gambler meant to have it. When he encountered Baker in the bar of the Mina Hotel, he demanded the $7.50 that Baker owed him.

Considering the long-standing enmity between them and Baker's repeated threats to kill him, it was hardly the prudent thing to do. Baker was known for his hot temper and his fondness for gunplay. Considering that Baker believed Grimmett had cheated him out of $400 in a poker game, done him out of his share of the proceeds in the Mina Hotel bar, where both were professional gamblers, and stolen his shaving brush in the bargain, it might even have been thought a little unwise. But prudence was never a virtue much admired in those parts.

Baker flew into a violent rage. Calling Grimmett a "hophead" and a "son of a bitch," he flung his coat on a roulette wheel and went after Grimmett with a billiard cue. The boys at the bar wrested the billiard cue away. "So it's a gunfight you want," said Baker, noticing that Grimmett's hand had slipped under his coat. He dashed behind the bar and began rummaging through the drawers for a revolver. Grimmett's bullet whistled past; Baker returned his fire. Grimmett shot again, and this time Baker fell dead.

Although the prosecution was hampered somewhat by the appearance of their star witness in a condition too drunk to testify, George convinced the jury that the tall, lean red-haired gambler had fired the first shot while Baker's back was turned, and Grimmett was sentenced to six years for voluntary manslaughter. My father had succeeded altogether too well. Few of his cases were ever overturned on appeal, nor was it usually an occasion for gratification when they were, but never did he see a verdict reversed with less regret than when the state supreme court declared that a man in Grimmett's predicament "need not flee for safety but has the right to stand his ground and slay his adversary."[12]

Much of the milling for the Tonopah and Goldfield mines was done some distance to the north at Millers, a small community of educated young married couples. Many were mining engineers, regarded by those beneath them as a sort of aristocracy, "confident, smiling, strutting daytimes in high laced boots, trim riding breeches, well fitted flannel shirts, and at night often in tailored suits."[13] All in all, Millers was as close as the mining camps ever came to suburban domesticity. Yet the bloodiest crime my father was called upon to prosecute occurred not in the Northern or in the riotous brothels of Goldfield's northwest section, but in Millers.

And it occurred on no ordinary night. Nineteen-ten was the year of Halley's comet. Several Californians had already gone berserk in the belief that the heavenly wonder presaged the end of the world; others, of a more optimistic turn of mind, had built a tower in an effort to catch a piece of the comet's tail. Goldfielders were neither crazed by the comet nor anxious to seize it; they merely wanted a good view. On the first spring evenings when Halley's comet became visible in the night skies, many trooped out to the Malapai, and the mesa was lit up for half a mile with bonfires of sagebrush and Joshua trees. At the Turf Saloon in Millers, however, business went on as usual, undisturbed by the celestial spectacular. Some fifty men were lined up at the long bar drinking and quarreling as usual when an Italian immigrant named Antonini suddenly ran amok. He slashed five men with his big jackknife, and one of them later died from the ugly L-shaped gash in his abdomen. Although the officer who came to arrest Antonini was told he was not at home, he nonetheless uncovered the blood-spattered fugitive rolled up in a carpet.

When my father began Antonini's prosecution the following winter, the case seemed quite clearcut, but if any drop of sympathy for the defendant could be wrung from the evidence at hand, Antonini's attorney, John Sanders, was the man to do it, and he was exercising considerable ingenuity in the attempt. One evening the attorneys and several other men were waiting near the courtroom for the judge and jury to return from the supper recess. Standing near the large staircase with the carved wooden balustrade, my father watched the antics of the counsel for the defense with curiosity. Sanders, who would later serve as Nevada supreme court justice for nearly twenty years, was a tall, handsome Virginian of dignified bearing, but on this occasion, he was behaving most peculiarly. He had a huge, white handkerchief, which he repeatedly whipped out of his breast pocket, carefully folding and replacing it each time.

"Why do you keep doing that, John?" asked George.

"Oh," replied Sanders as casually as he could, "ah jes like to see how the handkerchief comes out."

Presently they filed back into the courtroom. The spectators seated themselves with obvious anticipation. The judge took his place between two lamps with twisted brass columns and red shades fringed with golden beads, which lent the courtroom something of the atmosphere of an ornate Victorian parlor. To Sanders, however, it was neither courtroom nor parlor but pure theater, and his histrionic effusions as he strode back and forth upon its boards were a marked contrast to my father's courtroom speeches, which, though forceful, were always logical, succinct, and unemotional. The romantic who read poetry and gazed fancifully at the desert sunsets was the private man; the professional George Springmeyer was a thoroughgoing rationalist and would have been embarrassed to emulate the beaters of breasts, whose courtroom antics offered him considerable private amusement.

There was much in the ensuing scene to amuse him. Sanders proceeded to make his case for the defense on the ground that his client had been drunk, "so dead drunk that it was suhprising he could stand." The plea became progressively more eloquent. "Ah mahself have been drunk in the guttah," declared Sanders, his eyes growing misty. "Ah have done things ah nevah would have done when ah was sobah!" At this point, he dramatically whipped out his immense handkerchief and burst into racking sobs. It was a flawless (and well-rehearsed) performance; the press described it as "a perfect oratorical gem"; no one could recall having seen anything so moving in years. All the same, Sanders's client was convicted.[14]

Throughout the trial, the prisoner had watched with smoldering hatred while the attorney explained the evidence against him so clearly and dispassionately. Finally, a pale and trembling Antonini was brought into the courtroom to receive the verdict. When he was pronounced guilty of second degree murder, he burst into tears and appeared about to collapse. Turning to George, he shouted, "You son of a bitch! Wait till I get out of prison. I'll kill you! You better watch out."

Some years later, George and Warden Ray Baker were walking at the prison farm when George recognized one of the trusties working nearby—it was Antonini. George walked over and talked to him for a while, finally remarking, "Are you still going to kill me when you get out?"

"No," said Antonini shamefacedly, "forget it. That's all over." But there was another man brooding in his cell in that prison who had forgiven and forgotten nothing, a man of whom the district attorney had once warned the jury, "This man is a dangerous man to be at large. Give him a pistol, a tin star and a few drinks of whiskey and he would go out and kill the best man in town."

His name was George Gibson. An Ohio-born former professional baseball player who had made his way to Montana and eventually to Goldfield, Gibson, at thirty-four, was no stranger to the courts. Indeed they had been occupied for more than two years with litigation concerning him. The sequence of events had started one summer night in the streets of the tenderloin, where Gibson, then a deputy sheriff, was walking two women home from Jake's Dance Hall. The popular lady known as Fighting Bill Hayden taunted him, much to the amusement of the crowd of young men who surrounded her. He arrested her for her remarks, but not without one of the fights she was famous for. She roughed him up and bloodied her white shirtwaist in the scuffle. Leaving his two female companions to await him in the Ajax Bar, Gibson marched her off to jail unsubdued; she defied him to bring charges against her. Later, while pausing for a few drinks in the Red Top Bar on his way back to the Ajax, Gibson allowed the young men, all greatly disappointed at being deprived of Fighting Bill's company, to persuade him to release her.

When Gibson finally rejoined the two women in the Ajax, his mood was even more disgruntled and truculent than usual. He had lost face in the episode with Fighting Bill and had been heard to remark that he would kill someone before morning. Three young mining engineers came in and asked one of Gibson's ladies the way to the nearest "hop joint." They were either oblivious to Gibson's badge or well aware that it signified no intention to uphold the laws against narcotics, only a license to kill. Gibson directed them "up the gulch," but they would never get that far. Within moments a brawl had started; Gibson grappled with one of the young men, then the engineer pitched out the door, fatally shot.

Hearing the shot as she passed by in the street, Fighting Bill hastened to cradle the dying man's head in her lap and tried to stanch the flowing blood. Someone said, "George, I think you have killed that man."

Gibson shrugged and turned his back on the fallen youth. "I don't care a damn if I did," he said.

After Gibson's first trial ended in a hung jury and before his second one began, Diamondfield Jack Davis undertook to intimidate Theodore Tobish, one of the murdered man's companions in the Ajax and the principal witness for the prosecution. Tobish swore in his affidavit that during an encounter on the street, Davis had declared, among other things, that he had a "notion to stamp his head in the ground" and a positive intention to "do him up" in the near future. Diamondfield Jack, while freely admitting his threats to "kick Tobish's head off" and a good deal more, denied that his remarks had anything to do with Tobish's forthcoming testimony. Gibson was nonetheless convicted on his second trial. The state supreme court then remanded the case on a technicality, and Tilden undertook a new prosecution, considerably hampered by the efforts of Clarence Sage and of Gibson's friends in the sheriff's office to conceal any evidence damaging to the defendant. Sage had declared he would "go down the line" for a friend, and George Wingfield was reportedly bankrolling Gibson's defense. Discouraged when the result was a hung jury, the district attorney announced that he could see no benefit in conducting yet another trial of George Gibson. The case would be dismissed. The judge gave the order but suggested that the defendant should take an oath of temperance. Gibson willingly swore "in the presence of Almighty God I will abstain from all intoxicating liquors for a period of three years."

The following summer, having beaten his common-law wife nearly insensible, Gibson was drinking in the Elite Bar. When Deputy Sheriff Mike Cahalan arrived with a warrant for his arrest on charges of assault and battery, Gibson shrugged his shoulders and suggested contemptuously that the deputy "cut out that stuff."

Describing what happened when he persisted in serving the warrant, Cahalan later said, "He sneered again and said he wouldn't go and commenced abusive talk. Then he put his hand on his gun. I pulled my gun from my holster, brought it to a half cock and told him that if he didn't go, I would have to take him anyway. Gibson continued to talk and finally pulled his gun out. I told him to drop it or I would kill him.

" 'Alright,' he said and put it back into his holster. 'I'll go with you.' Then I put my gun away and we were going to start for the sheriff's office when Gibson's companion bumped against me from the rear. I turned to see what was coming off in that direction and Gibson whipped out his gun again—a Colt's single action .45, shoved it against my body, and as he cocked it with his thumb, I made a grab for it. He pulled the trigger and the hammer caught the fleshy part of my hand between the thumb and forefinger.

"It was about as close a call as any man wants to get," Cahalan concluded.[15]

In December of 1910 my father began to prosecute Goldfield's fourth trial of George Gibson, this time for the attempted murder of Cahalan. Gibson, defended by Jack Diskin, denied all points in the indictment and secured the usual hung jury. "This is indeed a remarkable state of affairs, a sad commentary upon the judgment, and I might say the honesty, of at least one juror," my father declared to reporters with dismay and hinted at a forthcoming prosecution for perjury against the juror in question. Bribery, it appeared, was even more effective than stamping heads in the ground. The judge characterized this latest disagreement among jurors as "almost inconceivable." Meanwhile a brawl broke out in the Northern when some of the boys referred to the jury's conduct in even pithier terms and the friends and relatives of the jurors took exception to their remarks. In four trials, this was Gibson's third hung jury.

By the time my father commenced prosecuting the fifth trial of George Gibson, the prisoner was described in the press as confident, even "debonaire." He may have hoped that this latest hung jury, coupled with the fact that Springmeyer and Tilden would be out of office in less than three weeks when the next district attorney took over, would produce a dismissal without going through the motions of another trial, but he obviously had no qualms about the ultimate result. With gunmen like Diamondfield Jack and Clarence Sage behind him, he had every reason for complacency. When the new jury unexpectedly pronounced him guilty, Gibson leaped from his chair in surprise.

"The court believes you are not a brave man. No brave man habitually carries a gun," said the judge severely to Gibson at his final appearance. The maximum sentence was then imposed.

"Much obliged," snarled George Gibson. His cold, bitter eyes rested on my father. This was the man who had convicted him, and he would never forget it.

When the prisoner and a deputy sheriff subsequently set off on the train for the journey to the state penitentiary, Gibson had assumed a new role: George Gibson, model prisoner. He told the deputy that upon his release he intended to "go back East and never again touch liquor," a pledge he was always happy to take on appropriate occasions, and assured the man that he had "no hard feelings against anyone in Goldfield." With good behavior, the model prisoner could expect parole in about nine years, perhaps even less. Then he could do what he was planning.[16]

* * *

Although moral outrage had never rolled much farther in Goldfield than seven after snake eyes in a crap game, public concern over narcotics and prostitution was unmistakably increasing in 1909 and 1910. A Chinese gentleman named Tae Loy Jan was arrested as he alighted from the train with a straw suitcase containing eight cans of opium said to be worth $480 on the street. There was no lack of buyers. The Goldfield *Tribune* apprehensively reported the presence of "certain well guarded places in and about Goldfield where opium smokers may satisfy their desires," and also of numerous "cocaine fiends, morphine users and even eaters of 'yen-she' or ashes of opium." Unlike narcotics, the presence of prostitution was not considered alarming, provided it remained within certain clearly defined limits. But when the hurdy-gurdy houses in which the carousing went on all night and men and women were "allowed to mingle promiscuously," as the press rather stiffly described it, spilled out of the red-light district into Main and Columbia streets, the barriers that kept "the lower districts" conveniently out of sight had been breached, and the public demanded official action. Besides, the district attorney's office was besieged with complaints about the growing frequency of knife fights and the disorderly conduct of the prostitutes inside the district.[17]

One of the madams—let me call her Madam Sabrina—arrived at George's office to explain the state of affairs in the tenderloin. In later years George's work as a divorce attorney would bring him in contact with some of the most glamorous women of the period, but few would impress him as much as the perfectly poised lady who stood in his doorway that day. She was what my father always called "a real stunner," and that was an accolade he bestowed upon few women.

Real stunners were born and not made, or at least knew how to enhance their beauty so subtly that he could not recognize their artifices. His eyes rested on Madam Sabrina and found neither coarseness nor artifice. There was nothing hardened about her soft, brown eyes; her dark brown hair was charmingly arranged in billowing waves around her face and caught in a chignon; her lovely figure was discreetly molded in the full-bosomed, wasp-waisted silhouette of the period.

As they talked, he discovered that she was "clever and cultivated" as well as beautiful. Cultivated was another accolade George did not lightly bestow (and not on more than five people that I can recall). It meant she spoke so flawlessly that Professor Henry Higgins himself could not have improved upon her. It probably meant that her knowledge of Shakespeare exceeded his own and that she shared his literary taste for Swinburne and Shaw and the romantic novels of George Moore—and perhaps she even shared his enthusiasm for Wagnerian opera. The conversation must have wandered a bit from the subject of knifings in the tenderloin as they sat together in the office, and it appears that the impulse to race back to the dormitory George had experienced at the University of Nevada when he first found

GEORGE GIBSON
As he appeared in the court room yesterday.
—Sketched from life by Al. Dutton.

Goldfield gunman George Gibson as Al Dutton sketched him in a Goldfield court room, ten months before George Springmeyer won his conviction for the attempted murder of Mike Cahalan. *Goldfield Daily Tribune,* Feb. 3, 1910.

himself in the presence of a fallen woman was now well under control.

George dealt with the complaints about the red-light district as best he could by confining the prostitution to a restricted area of four or five square blocks, an innovation which is nowadays termed an adult entertainment zone. Nonetheless Madam Sabrina appeared in his doorway again and was received with the same gallant courtesy he accorded to every lady. These vexing problems in the bordellos suddenly seemed to require extensive discussion. Back she came, day after day, each time on a flimsier pretext than the last, until even George belatedly realized why she came. She waited outside. She made persistent attempts to "date" him, as he phrased it, in the evenings.

I see her as a fashion photograph from *Les Modes,* pacing with a rustle of silken petticoats in the courthouse hall under the fancy chandelier with curling brass leaves and fluted glass shades, her extravagant, broad-brimmed, high-crowned hat gliding past like a clipper ship under full sail. Or in front of the courthouse in the lamplight, waiting for the blue eyes, the warm smile, the polite tip of the hat, and the hand that will take her elbow to guide her courteously across the crowded street, but never, never any farther than that. She comes like Swinburne's Dolores to redeem from virtue, to turn the dusky lilies of poetry to life, yet he will not be redeemed. He has been raised by his parents' strict standards in the valley where a rancher's adulterous wife was ostracized for years after her lover's death; she has pursued a life he cannot contemplate without aversion. He is an officer of the law; she is a lady of the tenderloin. It is an impossible liaison. He walks away with resolution, though not entirely without regret.

In the lobby of the Goldfield Hotel she waits among the gilded columns, her youth and beauty the object of every passing eye. Not a few would know her already; even more would wish to make her acquaintance. Another bold, familiar pair of eyes stares down at hers, another greeting of assumed intimacy accosts her, another importunate male hand touches her sleeve. But she refuses, she is busy, she is waiting for someone. Soon all Goldfield knows for whom she waits and believes the young assistant district attorney is her lover. Could any man decline the favors of the beautiful Madam Sabrina? Goldfield cannot credit that. And if he is her lover, must he not also be involved in the lady's business? Goldfield is certain of it. The whole affair flames up in scandal. Finally he can no longer put off dealing with these rumors, so he tells her she must stop coming to see him. She turns away. Swinburne must have a verse for her in the well-thumbed book from the Harvard classics George has brought home from college, perhaps:

> If you were thrall to sorrow,
>   And I were page to joy,

We'd play for lives and seasons
With loving looks and treasons
And tears of night and morrow
    And laughs of maid and boy;
If you were thrall to sorrow,
    And I were page to joy.

But this is fantasy. They are what they are, and nothing can change it. I watch her elegant figure disappear in the hurly-burly crowds in the street. He will not see her again, yet I know, as she cannot, how much her unrequited passion will cost him. He will pay a higher price for Madam Sabrina than anyone has ever paid in the tenderloin.

Soon he knew it too, yet, speaking of her fifty years later, he still tipped his hat to her. He told me in a voice suddenly gentle that he thought she fell into her profession through youthful error. He remembered how beautiful she was, but that was not enough. I think he also wanted to believe that she was almost good.

The Unspiked Rail

"No CHARGE WAS TOO black for his tongue, no word too foul, no falsehood too shameful," wrote Morgan of my father in the pages of the *Reno Evening Gazette.* "Wherever he has gone, he has left his trail of mud, mud which was conceived in a black heart and issued by a depraved tongue."[1] It was a typical Morgan salvo in a campaign that may well have been the most savage in Nevada politics. "The great case of the People vs. the Southern Pacific," as my father later called it, was under way.

I do not know precisely when the election of 1910 began for him or when he decided to make Southern Pacific domination a central theme. Probably he had planned to make a second bid for the attorney generalship for quite some time and made no secret of his intention. In a scene of inescapable irony, in view of the large misunderstandings on both sides, Senator George Nixon offered him Nevada's one and only congressional nomination. Not unreasonably, the senator had supposed that an ambitious young politician who aspired to no more than a minor post in the roster of state officials could be tempted by the most desirable plum in the gift of the machine, a national office. He did not know my father well enough to realize that a seat in Congress, far from satisfying his ambition, would deprive him of the two things he loved above all else, Nevada and the law. George Springmeyer may have been the only young politician on the local scene in 1910 to whom Senator Nixon's plum was no plum at all.

When the nomination landed in my father's lap in 1906, he probably had only a hazy idea of what he might do with the attorney generalship. By 1910 we can surmise his intentions from his conduct in the district attorney's office: he would enforce the law. He would enforce it fairly, which sounds platitudinous enough, but the Pittsburgh Silver Peak indictments and the Rawhide graft trial had already taught him that the rub came with the prosecution of the powerful and the influential—Theodore Roosevelt's "malefactors of great wealth"; these he would not hesitate to pursue. He would enforce it against friend and foe alike, as he had done in the Smith case. And he would enforce it without regard to his personal belief in the guilt or innocence of the defendant. With this resolve, he had prosecuted Slim Grimmett. The vision of justice in blindfold was a mission to engage all the passionate idealism of his nature, but there was probably something else. The complex and important cases before the attorney general would give an outlet to this piercing intelligence that could swiftly render the gleanings from a tall stack of law books in a few succinct lines, this humming engine of energy that often rose at 5:30 and toiled till past midnight. Like one of his father's race horses, loosed from the rope and streaking in the wind through an open field, he would at last be free to make the kind of run that was in him.

He knew what he wanted. Yet the misunderstanding on his side was as great as Senator Nixon's, for he imagined he had the option to refuse and pursue his own aims without hindrance. No visible obstacle to his nomination as attorney general loomed on the horizon. Since the enactment of Nevada's first direct primary law the preceding year, convention maneuvering and support from powerful members of the party hierarchy were no longer the prerequisites to nomination. A candidate could appeal directly to the people, and George felt confident of their response. The machine had accepted his candidacy in 1906 and had made no demands upon him. He supposed 1910 would be no different. He did not realize a good deal had changed in the last four years and he was now a dangerous man in the eyes of the Southern Pacific.

* * *

For Ed Collins, the campaign of 1910 probably began late in July with the arrival of a letter from an unnamed San Francisco correspondent in the political bureau of the Southern Pacific directing him to "write me confidentially what your own views are in the matter and whether you can do anything with Springmeyer. If Springmeyer agrees, you must tie him down so he will remain tied after election."[2] He set off for the district attorney's office.

Ed Collins had been a well-known figure in Goldfield since 1903, when his oddly gnomic face—broad cheek bones, narrow eyes beneath overlapping folds of flesh, and flyaway ears—was first seen in the city. In 1904 the press was already referring to him as one of "the most popular old timers in Goldfield"—that meant he had been around for a solid year. He had served as justice of the peace, but at about the time that a drunken defendant, charged with disturbing the peace, disturbed it still more by flinging a large lamp at Collins's head, he concluded that his true vocation lay elsewhere. He rose to yet higher eminence as a saloon keeper, and later ascended to postmaster, the prized patronage plum with which the party rewarded its most favored sons. Somewhat later still, he would abruptly disappear, allegedly with several thousand dollars in postal funds. But in 1910 he was still the eminent postmaster, still "a strong political power" in Goldfield, and still the local contact for the political bureau of the Southern Pacific.[3]

Although the first generation of owners and agents had passed on to their reward and the ownership of the Southern Pacific had altered, the political aims and methods of the railroad had undergone little change or challenge. However, currents of reform dangerous to railroad ascendancy were beginning to stir. In California the Progressives, led by Hiram Johnson, were mounting a powerful campaign with the avowed objective of kicking the railroad out of politics. In Nevada a railroad commission with the power to regulate freight and passenger rates had been created by the legislature of 1907 and had not yet been neutralized by the railroad.

More disquieting still from the viewpoint of the railroad, the board of assessors created in 1901 had been roused from its slumberous state by the accession of Denver Dickerson to the governor's chair upon the death of Governor Sparks in 1908. Unlike his elderly predecessor, who had preferred contemplating the game park at his Alamo Ranch to thundering into the battles of political life with sword unsheathed, Denver Dickerson did not view the governorship as a decorative medal to complete the adornment of a successful rancher in the twilight of his years. At thirty-six he was the youngest governor in Nevada history, and he had the makings of a fiery reformer. The counties had long been separate fiefdoms in which the railroad was able to secure favorable tax assessments by exerting pressure upon the individual county assessors. When the assessors gathered in conclave with the governor and attorney general as a board of equalization, those friendly to the railroad continued to defend its interests. Now this cozy arrangement was in serious jeopardy. Dickerson had fought tenaciously in the board of assessors to raise railroad taxes and had even mounted a strong publicity campaign to bolster his position.

Once complacent during its long years of uninterrupted power, the political bureau of the railroad was now thoroughly aroused. Reformers were already ascendant in California; Nevada was slipping fast. If the old regime of railroad domination was to be salvaged, the attorney general was no less vital than the governor and the railroad commission. Together with the governor, he appointed the railroad commission and sat on the board of assessors. He was the official charged with bringing suit against the railroad under the railroad laws. As mineral land commissioner, he had the power to oppose—and the freedom not to oppose—applications for patents on the mineral lands within the railroad's vast domain. Springmeyer was no longer the unformed college boy they had known in the campaign of 1906. He had posed no apparent threat to the organization then, but now he was a public official with a reform record gained in the graft and the bullion tax cases, a man who had shown displeasing signs of sympathy for labor and scant respect for the high prerogatives of officials and corporations. To William Herrin, Boss Blakeslee, and the rest in the political bureau of the Southern Pacific, allowing the attorney generalship to fall into the hands of such a man was no trifling matter. Collins had his orders.

When he arrived at the district attorney's office, Collins attempted to dissuade George from entering the primary. Hugh Brown, the popular Tonopah attorney, would be a candidate, and his victory was a certainty. To oppose him would be a waste of time and money. So Collins said; privately he did not believe that Brown could be persuaded to run.[4] George nonetheless declared his candidacy.

Gentle persuasion had failed; it was clearly none too soon for Collins to resort to other methods. The postmaster again came calling at the district attorney's office and inquired amicably how George felt about the railroad commission. George said he favored the retention of the present members in office. If Hugh Brown and others could be assured that the commission was safe, said Collins, the Tonopah attorney would not enter the primary. "That sounds good to me," George replied.

However, Collins wanted his assurance in writing, so a letter was drafted to provide it. Later in public statements, my father claimed that was all the letter meant, but I find that hard to believe.[5] I think I understand why he never mentioned the name Ed Collins to me, and I had to piece the story of that July day together for myself. That was the day, the only day in all his blameless years, when I, who looked up to him all my life, could find him less than I thought, and he didn't want to talk about it.

Looking back through the stereopticon of history, as Ed Collins dictated and my father wrote out his promise to be guided by the machine in the choice of railroad commissioners in return for their support during the campaign, I cannot doubt that he believed he was making a deal. Perhaps he persuaded himself that it was a harmless deal because the machine was willing to pledge retention of the existing commission in the party platform and he had already resolved to push for a new law to make the commission an elective body, no longer subject to anyone's choice but the voters. Still, I cannot call that letter anything else.

I know he had no chance of success without the machine, and he must have known it even better. My professional education has taught me that the neophyte politician must accept his limitations, never forgetting that politics is the art of the possible. He must make certain compromises until his career is launched. Harry Truman would never have left Missouri without the Pendergast machine, and even the saintly Woodrow Wilson had to deal with the New Jersey bosses until he rose high enough to leave them behind him. This young man lacked the purse of a Francis Newlands and realized every major politician in Nevada from William Stewart on down had made his peace with the machine.

The political scientist in me has learned these things. Why then am I so disturbed by this conventional portrait of the turn-of-the-century politician as a young man? The Springmeyer in me wants to shout "No" to the man at the desk. "Don't deal with them, not for any price, not on any terms, not ever. Fight them, alone if you must. Cast aside your hopes, if this is the price of victory. Lose in a blaze of glory, if you cannot win, but make no promises to Ed Collins."

He must have thought so too, for in the end that was what he did. The letter was the only deal he ever made.

Within an hour of Collins's departure, a friend stopped George in the street to tell him that Brown had filed. George encountered Collins coming out of the post office and started to talk to him. Quickly, Collins drew him into his office. He did not intend to have this conversation overheard by the crowds outside. Closing the door, he turned to George and said, "Now we have got you just where we want you. You lay down or I'll publish that letter and kill you politically for all time."

My father, in his naiveté, had assumed the machine was dealing with him in good faith. Now he belatedly perceived the real intent of the letter. It was nothing less than blackmail, and blackmail was the wrong line to take with a man who had once watched his father face down Black Wallace and damn the consequences.

"You publish that letter," said George, "and I will tell how you got it. You have struck the wrong man. There is nothing in it but what I am willing to have published, and I defy you to publish it."

A good many angry words ensued, and before my father stalked out of Collins's office, he had sworn to "stay in and make that fight and publicly declare my stand on the railroad commission from every platform in the state." He did, and

would finally write the pledge to retain the present members of
the railroad commission in the Republican platform in September, along with a crucial plank granting the commission broader
authority and transforming it to an elective body. That law
could shatter the grip of the railroad. From that moment in Ed
Collins's office, the die was cast, the alien role of the smart
politician who figures which side his bread is buttered on was
set aside. He had not known how to deal, and never would. But
he knew how to fight.

Of course other options remained open, even after that interview with Collins. It was not too late to contact Senator Nixon.
The senator liked him, and quite probably the Nixon influence
could arrange an understanding with the Southern Pacific political bureau. If he capitalized on his contacts, his friendship with
George Wingfield could be turned to good account. Apparently
he made no such moves, nor did he consider abandoning his
candidacy. Asked by the press if he intended to withdraw in
view of the backing accorded to Brown by the party machine,
he said, "Surrender, hell. I haven't commenced fighting yet,"
loosely quoting John Paul Jones. The great case of the People
vs. the Southern Pacific would be tried before the court of
public opinion.[6]

My father began his canvass without powerful friends or
organized support. The *Ely Expositor* observed that he was
"waging one of the rarest singlehanded battles against en-
trenched interests ever undertaken in Nevada."[7] Democratic
cartoonists depicted him as "Nevada's first real twister," a human tornado sweeping across the countryside while Boss Blakeslee and Morgan raced for the cyclone cellars. Because the
Southern Pacific and the Republican organization were obviously working for Brown, George rapidly became known as
"the insurgent candidate." The Republican press refused to
print his advertisements. Some of these papers expressed judicious opposition to him; others reverberated with vilification;

all were implacably against him. He was undaunted. His friend Chester Lyman printed some posters proclaiming him "The Unspiked Rail in the Path of Railroad Domination," and my father set out alone.

Alone, that is, except for Mr. Jones, Brown's representative, who doggedly trailed him wherever he went. In the Jarbidge saloon, Jones's face could be glimpsed just inside the door; in Dayton his discreet figure was visible across the street. In Deeth, McGill, Aurora, Rhyolite, Mina, and all the other towns and mining camps to which my father made his way, Jones was never far behind, and there may have been some moments during those long, wearisome journeys across the lonely deserts when George was tempted to invite Jones to join up with him.

More than four years later George would learn that Brown had not actually been in league with Collins; however, in 1910 he was wholeheartedly angry with his opponent for his apparent role in Collins's machinations, and the contest between the two grew steadily more heated. Nevada, George said, had long been "ground under the heel of the railroad tyrant." The office of attorney general was vitally important to the railroad, never more so than now, when the Southern Pacific was planning to swindle the public out of 750,000 acres of mineral lands. Faced with a California reform movement more formidable than any of its predecessors, the Southern Pacific was becoming desperate and would "go to any length to defeat the will of the people." Brown was a "railroad protege," manifestly supported by Southern Pacific lobbyists and long in the employ of the railroads, with which his sympathies would undoubtedly remain. He had helped the railroads to acquire lands by fraudulent means in violation of the rights of settlers already living at Millers. He had advised his client, the Tonopah and Goldfield Railroad, that the strikebreakers they employed had the right to carry concealed weapons. There could be little doubt with which side he had aligned himself in labor-management dis-

George Nixon.

putes. Further, he had advocated a decrease in the bullion tax in the interest of the mining corporations. He had "the highest personal regard for Mr. Brown," George would conclude, but he objected to "the company he keeps."[8]

The campaign of his opponent, who had modestly styled himself "The Abraham Lincoln of Nevada Politics," was wholly defensive and not entirely free of invective. Relying on the organization's efforts on his behalf, Brown abstained from making a personal canvass. Important business, he said, prevented him from going forth to meet his "numerous friends." Nevertheless, the friendly Republican editors were always happy to print his public letters. In these he denied that he had been approached by the Southern Pacific, and if he had corporations among his clients, didn't every lawyer? Above all, George was a mudslinger who had slandered Brown's good name. The "Unspiked Rail" was a slogan that suited him, "for it is the habit of 'unspiked rails' and also of 'loose screws' to cause senseless, useless, and irreparable injury." George was not an insurgent but a "political renegade."[9]

The vengeful Morgan, the vitriolic Montrose of the *Carson City News,* and the editor of the *Goldfield Daily Tribune* went farther. Not only was George a mudslinger whose disbarment was clearly in order and a character assassin to be compared to John Wilkes Booth, but, at twenty-eight, he had not yet outgrown "the boyish years of unreliability." On top of that he had employed "advertising methods that would disgrace a traveling circus," observed the *Goldfield Daily Tribune* in a tone of prudish distaste that must have struck an odd note in a riproaring town like Goldfield, and his picture had actually been seen posted in *saloons* (Madam Sabrina, despite her well-known regard for him, had tactfully refrained from posting it in even more unsuitable places). Generally speaking, he had "struck deeper levels of depravity than were ever penetrated in the palmy days of juvenile statehood." Furthermore, asserted Montrose, who had publicly vowed never to endorse George even in the event of his nomination, he was so faithless to Republicanism that he had failed to pledge his support to Brown if Brown were the victor, and he should therefore be read out of the party. He had been seen consorting with known Democrats —a cartoon in the *Gazette* depicted them trundling him about in a baby carriage—and the friendly attitude of the Democratic press toward him revealed beyond a doubt that "birds of a feather flock together." Let all true Republicans reflect on that. Worst of all, "The Campaign Stinkpot" had written letters on stationery belonging to the district attorney's office (those letters, actually paid for by H.H., may have seemed a trifle picayune in comparison to a 750,000-acre mineral land swindle, but it was the best they could come up with under the circumstances).[10] When the tiny Douglas County *Record Courier* alone among the Republican papers endorsed George, the editor was roundly denounced by his peers as "a snake in the grass."

My father traveled on, past pale mountains—gray or lavender or mauve, mottled with indigo cloud shadows—through an occasional valley of green fields, poplar-lined lanes, and haystacks shaped in rounded humps, past mile after mile of gray sagebrush, brightened sometimes by the golden tips of rabbit brush in bloom and the red shadings of sand grass by the roadside. One mining town following the next. Another road stretched straight across another valley, like a fishing line hooked tight to another distant blue range of mountains. As he drew nearer, the ridges lightened, the blue retreated into rivulets of shadow, and the mountain silhouette resolved itself into the crumpled complications of peak and canyon. Then he arrived at the mining town, which was like a scattering of dice on the slope, unchanged in its essentials since J. Ross Browne sketched the simple cubicles of Virginia City on the treeless heights of Sun Peak in 1860. Another main street. Another bare, shabby saloon, furnished with no more than the functional necessities of table, chairs, and liquor—and these only in their most elemental forms. Somewhere in every town he always encountered a familiar face from the valley or from the university or, more often, from the streets of Goldfield.

He reached Ely, where Governor Dickerson's friends made the rounds with him, then on to Tonopah, and then Virginia City, where Gib Douglass campaigned with him. The investment of new capital had temporarily slowed the protracted decline of the Comstock, and the mountaintop city was once again bustling with activity. They went from saloon to saloon and store to store, with Gib introducing George to all the miners on the street. At one point, where a large crowd of miners had gathered, Gib presented him to the mine superintendent who served as Republican county chairman. The chairman glared at George, clasped his hands behind his back, and said, "I won't shake hands." By evening everyone in Virginia City had heard of the insult; they would later have occasion to recall it.

Although he could hardly have been unaware of the activities of the Storey County chairman, Collins, and the rest of the boys, Senator Nixon remained outwardly neutral during the primary. Less than impressive as a senator, less than involved as a Republican leader, Nixon's primary political talent lay in conciliation. He was also primarily concerned with a matter far more momentous to him than governors, attorneys general, or even the great case of People vs. the Southern Pacific: the reelection of Senator Nixon was at stake. Although the federal constitutional amendment on the direct election of U.S. senators was still three years in the future, Nevada had enacted a senatorial preference vote which the parties agreed to consider binding. Senators were therefore already selected by popular vote. The legislative maneuvers by which Black Wallace had secured Stewart's election in 1899 would no longer suffice. By hook or by crook, Nixon would have to produce a popular majority. He was unopposed in the primary, but a disquieting challenge from Key Pittman was looming up in the general election.

Beside Nixon stood his former partner, George Wingfield. No doubt to the surprise of no one, Wingfield announced that he would be "somewhat of a factor" in the campaign but not as an insurgent. Indeed Wingfield as an insurgent would have been an image only slightly more difficult to conjure up than Wingfield as an organizer for the IWW. He would actively oppose "certain people who are seeking office in this state before their feet have been callused by the burning desert sands" —probably a reference to Key Pittman and to Charles Sprague, a Democratic candidate for Congress who had resided in Nevada for an even shorter time than Wingfield himself and had lately aroused Wingfield's ire when his newspaper, the *Goldfield Daily News,* suggested that Wingfield was mortally ill, thereby causing considerable lapse of confidence in Wingfield securities. And this was not the worst of Sprague's offenses. Following the Smith high grade case, during which Sprague had served as foreman of the jury, the irreverent newspaperman had written a scathing editorial on Wingfield's attempts to intimidate the jury by threats both "boorish and brutal," when they were not "puerile and pusillanimous," and had further intimated that Wingfield had been bankrolling George Gibson's defense.[11]

Wingfield stood for the "men of capital," the Republicans, and Nixon against "the vampires, buzzards, and jackals of newspaperdom and politics," terms which may be taken to denote the socialists generally, Key Pittman probably, and Sprague particularly.[12] Although Wingfield would have been unlikely to acknowledge that he had anything in common with the detested socialists, he did, in fact, share with them a common perception of the nature of the coming political struggle: it was the men of capital versus the jackals. Him or them.

No knowledgeable observer of the local political scene entertained many doubts concerning the means that Wingfield and Nixon would use to accomplish their ends, and the only serious effort to check their influence at the source had about as much chance of success as an orange grove in the Malapai. All the same, my father tried it. A friend and he offered a novel resolution to the Esmeralda County central committee and the Goldfield Republican Campaign Club: candidates would take a "sacred pledge" not to serve as the agents of the Southern Pacific or any other corporation and not to accept financial aid from any source outside their personal funds. According to the Democratic press, this "preposterous" bit of foolishness was roundly denounced by the other members. The next speaker told the assembled candidates, "Not a man would refuse money from Nixon, the Goldfield Consolidated, or the Southern Pacific, and you all expect money from each one of these sources. Therefore, as I said; what is the use of trying to bull ourselves; save all this kind of buncombe for the dear public. They don't know any better." He sat down to tumultuous applause, and the offending resolution was resoundingly defeated.[13]

My father journeyed on alone, through hills tinted with the pale, flaxen sheen of dried range grass; past the blinding white of alkali flats; through valleys threaded by the winding ribbon of grass and cottonwood trees and silvery green willow bushes that marks the presence of a stream; across mountains pleated with canyons. He reached Deeth on the Southern Pacific line in eastern Nevada, then continued by stagecoach to Jarbidge, a new mining town of tents and wooden shacks strung out along the Jarbidge River 6,000 feet up in the barren, treeless mountain peaks near the Idaho border. In the mining towns he walked the streets talking with the men. In the tiny cow camps scattered over the rangeland, he rode with the cowboys, leaving Mr. Jones far behind. And he could feel that they were with him. Nevada is "ripe for reform," he declared jubilantly. "The state is neither Democratic nor Republican—it is insurgent."[14]

Insurgency was catching on. The other candidates took note and altered their positions accordingly. Comfortably ensconced on the fence that would ever provide his most favored political perch, Tasker Oddie paused in his campaign for the Republican gubernatorial nomination to cautiously announce that I "class myself with the insurgents but not with that class that are willing to disrupt and tear to pieces the whole Republican party." He also aligned himself with Brown and anxiously denied ever having suggested that Nixon was connected with the Southern Pacific.[15]

The preceding autumn an elderly Goldfield attorney known as "Lighthorse Harry" Morehouse had responded to reports in the Los Angeles papers that he would oppose Nixon with a statement that "Barkis is willin'." Southern born, a Confederate veteran wounded in the Battle of Mobile Bay, the old man with the hawk nose and the silver hair worn parted in the center could count on a wide audience in any political campaign he undertook because he was one of Nevada's most renowned orators. As the political risks of confronting Nixon became increasingly apparent, Barkis began to have second thoughts, but he still admired any man who had the courage to oppose railroad politics. He was the moving spirit behind the large meeting held in Goldfield late in August to form a Lincoln-Roosevelt League to back the Nevada insurgents in the same way that California's league of the same name was supporting Hiram Johnson in his drive to power outside the regular party organization. Although the new league endorsed various Progressive reform issues, notably the direct primary, recall, and popular election of United States senators, the overriding preoccupation of its members was unmistakably the Southern Pacific. Nevada, its constitution declared, was merely a "personal chattel to subserve the private ends of this vast corporation." The fundamental purpose of the league was "to overthrow this evil power in the Republican party."[16]

Morehouse had become well acquainted with railroad power in California. As a California legislator in 1899, he had seen the Southern Pacific in action using every political device, both fair and foul, to elect their man to the U.S. senate. He had also seen the antirailroad Republicans known as the "fifty-five stalwarts" hold the line against heavy pressure, even when it meant adjournment without electing a senator. It had been done in California: the fifty-five stalwarts had once halted the Southern Pacific; even now the reform movement was sweeping to victory with the California Progressives. Why couldn't it be done in Nevada? Though he abstained from the risks of candidacy, old Lighthorse Harry supported the effort. Unfortunately, Morehouse's political talents were more oratorical than organizational, and there is no evidence that the Nevada Lincoln-Roosevelt League was ever a viable organization. But his intentions were the best, and when George wound up his campaign in Reno, Lighthorse Harry gave one of those fine speeches for which he was famous.[17]

The campaign ended with a triumphant insurgent meeting in Reno's Grand Theater before a cheering, overflow crowd that included George Wingfield, a coterie of Republican machine leaders headed by Senator Nixon, and a number of prominent Democrats. That unlikely assemblage revealed a good deal about Nevada politics. Indeed it was an unlikely assemblage only to those who failed to grasp the curious intimacy of the Nevada political elite. They were men of diverse backgrounds, parties, goals, and beliefs who clashed with one another as they pursued their separate objectives; nonetheless they were bound by a certain camaraderie, most in evidence among the Goldfield crowd. That night the party leaders listened good humoredly while my father blasted the organization. Later, when they stood aside and left him to the tender mercies of the Southern Pacific, he would regard them with similar lack of rancor. Their battles were, in the last analysis, disagreements among friends.

Many of those in the audience that evening were there because they liked George, a few because they agreed with his ideas, and a sizable number had come because they wanted to hear the candidate the Democratic press called "the young man with the galvanic temperament" pour on "the red hot shot." They were not going to be disappointed.

At this point in the campaign, my father, who had been endowed with no small measure of the Springmeyer temper, was obviously blazing mad. He had already publicly suggested that Montrose might care to join him in the street and repeat some of the insults he had been printing in the *Carson City News,* an encounter which Montrose had assiduously avoided. He had challenged Brown to either produce the false allegations he claimed George had made against him in the course of a campaign during which George believed Brown had been treated "as courteously as the exigencies of a strenuous political war permit," or to desist from "cheap claptrap" about character assassination. Tonight he again stressed the importance of the attorney general to the Southern Pacific, criticized Brown for attempting to oust the settlers near Millers from their lands, and finally laced into Morgan, "the Bad Man from Bodie," for vilifying numerous candidates who had failed to pay him tribute. This "polecat of Nevada journalism," he said, was well paid by the Southern Pacific to wield his poisonous pen.

Then came Morehouse, with a speech that ranged from the fall of Rome through the well-remembered life and times of Black Wallace, "the finest political coyote that ever got into Nevada," and finally culminated with the dramatic question, "What I want to know about these candidates is whether, if I turn their collars down, I will find the S.P. brand on their necks?"[18]

The rally had been a smashing success, but as the day of the primary election dawned, not many men in Nevada would have slammed a $20 gold piece on the bar to bet for George. Possibly not even his father. In a statement widely commented upon in the newspaper headlines, H.H. humorously remarked to friends encountered in the street shortly before the election, "Douglas County is a Republican county, but after the primary election, I think it will be Democratic."[19] Collins and the dark, saturnine Blakeslee had been confident of the outcome from the start. Morgan and Montrose were already triumphant. "The better class of Republicans turn away from him in disgust," wrote Montrose in a rhapsodic editorial, "and flock to the standard of Brown as the flowers raise their heads to the warming rays of the sun after the visit of the storm."[20] The only one who really believed he would win was George himself.

Election night did not pass without incident. George was roused in the middle of the night by a telegram from a friend warning him that the organization would try to "count him out." A wire to H.H. sent the old man forth in the darkness to personally ensure that there was no crooked count in Douglas and Ormsby counties. All around the state, George's friends sprang into action to do the same.[21]

And miraculously, to the discomfiture of some and to the astonishment of all, he won, by a paper-thin margin of 34 votes out of nearly 6,000 cast. He had won ten of Nevada's fifteen counties, some by majorities over 70 percent, others by three or four votes. Brown had scored heavily in populous, conservative Reno, the stronghold of the machine, and in Tonopah, where he resided; but back home in Douglas County, on the cold mountain peaks of Jarbidge, on the rangeland near Deeth, in Millers, and in Goldfield, they had voted overwhelmingly for George.

A comparison with Tasker Oddie's victory in the same election further confirms the distinctions their separate campaigns had already suggested. Although both candidates, together with Ed Roberts, once George's rival in the convention of 1906 and now a congressional aspirant, were loosely dubbed "the insurgents" in the press, the sources of their electoral strength differed as much as their aims and their personal styles. Oddie's were similar to George's only in that both had won narrow victories and had lost decisively in Reno; apart from this the patterns of their electoral support were clearly disparate.[22] There was, in short, no "insurgent movement" as such; there were only George and Morehouse, and somewhere in the hazy nether distance two other candidates who had been termed "insurgents" primarily because they were not the organization's first choices.

* * *

And the Cyclone Cellars are Mighty Flimsy, at That!

In this cartoon drawn by Al Dutton during the 1910 primary campaign, George Springmeyer appears as a human cyclone whirling across the landscape while Tonopah attorney Hugh Brown (his opponent), editor Morgan of the *Reno Evening Gazette,* Lou Blakeslee (Southern Pacific political agent), and Judge Dennis head for the cyclone cellars. *Goldfield Daily News,* Sept. 3, 1910.

California had always been more wealthy, more populous, more opulent in resources, and better organized than Nevada, and nowhere were these pervasive differences more apparent than in the insurgent movements of the two states. In September 1910 the California Lincoln-Roosevelt League that provided the foundation for the Progressive movement in the state had been organized for three years. The foremost student of the movement would later write that "in practically every inhabited locality of the state, the league organization was at least equal in efficiency, if not superior to, the old Republican machine."[23] Several of the thirty-eight men who had attended its first convention had been editors, it enjoyed wide press support, and it had elected a vocal group of legislators. In Nevada the insurgent movement consisted of one candidate, one tiny weekly newspaper entitled the *Record Courier,* one aged orator of the Southern school, and one ephemeral Lincoln-Roosevelt League that had sprung full blown from the brain of Morehouse some two weeks previously.

The banner of insurgency fluttered forward toward the general election.

The Election Of 1910

T HE UNSPIKED RAIL HAD survived the primary, but he could not rest long upon his laurels. The organization had already been forced to accept an insurgent victory; they had no intention of accepting an insurgent platform. While Oddie stood aside "waiting to see which way the cat will jump," as one newspaper editor expressed it, the party leaders began heaping the "bull con" on Morehouse and laying plans to throttle George in the convention. However, one effective means of maintaining pressure on the organization remained—publicity. Morehouse warned in an interview that if the insurgent planks were not adopted he would support the Democrats.[1] In an unprecedented move, George issued a public statement just before the convention.

"Some may believe that the Southern Pacific is not in politics in Nevada. I happen to know from personal experience that it has been and is in politics," he wrote with a greater measure of graphic truth than his readers could possibly have guessed, "and if the full force of its sinister influence were known, the people would stand appalled, would rise in their wrath and destroy. Therefore, regardless of personal consequences, I am

determined to continue to the bitter end the battle I have commenced. To the people I say now that the struggle will not end
until the Southern Pacific, body, soul, and purse is kicked out
of Nevada politics." If the Republicans declined to accept his
platform, he threatened, he would issue it separately and make
his campaign alone.[2]

The organization capitulated. The popularity of George's
stand had been convincingly verified in the primary, and the
regulars had little taste for the prospect of battling the Unspiked Rail on the hustings as he attacked the symbiotic relationship between the Southern Pacific and the Republican
party. George received his place on the platform committee,
where he wrote the strongest reform program the Nevada Republican party had produced for a generation. Many issues
were included, from initiative, referendum, and recall through
free textbooks for schoolchildren and the pledge that the attorney general would protect prospectors' rights on mineral lands.
The key provision, however, was the one that began innocu-
ously by recognizing the "natural right" of the railroad to "con-
serve its just interests" but went on to "unhesitatingly condemn
the political activity of any corporation or railroad company
which seeks in any manner to influence the nomination and
election, or control of public officers"; pledged the retention of
the existing railroad commission in office; and demanded the
abolition of the board of assessors and the restructuring of the
railroad commission as an elective public service commission
with broad authority over taxation.[3]

Perhaps the elective feature was crude; modern scholarship
has not infrequently criticized the Progressives for their naive
faith in democracy. But the shortcomings of an appointive commission were already well known—Ed Collins had just provided George with a vivid demonstration of them. In addition,
the existing board of assessors had other obvious limitations.
Although the board had been an effective body under Dicker-

son's leadership, it was unlikely to remain so if Dickerson were replaced by a chief executive less committed to reform. It seemed that the best solution was to combine both the board and the railroad commission into a single, centralized, elective body and to delete the multiple pressure points that had often enabled the railroad to neutralize the board.

George was satisfied with the platform. He had made some compromises with the organization, softening the declaration that the "dominating influence" of the Southern Pacific was the paramount issue of the campaign and giving up his proposal for a platform commitment by all candidates to accept no financial aid from the Southern Pacific or any other corporation—that plank had fared no better at the convention than it had before the Goldfield Republican Campaign Club. But he had made no compromises on the public service commission or the plank designed to protect mineral lands from the encroaching tentacles of the railroad. The regular Republicans could hardly have been equally pleased, but they considered the alternatives and bolted the platform down in one unanimous gulp. For the moment, fence mending was the order of the day. Morehouse, for his part, declared that it was time to "fight against the common enemy."[4] Outwardly at least, the old party lines that had temporarily blurred during the primary, when the Democrats encouraged the insurgents, had been restored.

The Republican campaign party that set forth with this forceful reform platform in hand was not without its anomalies. At the head of the ticket was Senator Nixon, wealthy banker and corporation owner, with long-standing ties to the Southern Pacific. At the other extreme was my father, flanked by Morehouse, who was actively campaigning for the party. In between were Oddie and Roberts. Oddie was a New Jersey lawyer who had arrived in Nevada a decade before, made a fortune in the Tonopah boom, and lost it with astonishing rapidity. Lack of money was indeed the motive that had compelled him to seek

the governorship, yet some of the early luster of his involvement in the Tonopah boom still clung to him, and his principal
campaign asset was a degree of personal charm that even his
opponents were not immune to. In one of his more effusive
moments, Governor Dickerson described Oddie as "the most
lovable man I have ever met." Behind the charm, however, was
a dearth of ideas, goals, and commitments that led the opposition press to describe him, with some justice, as "Easy Oddie,"
a man both "weak and easily swayed." If he had not been the
organization's first choice, he was more than willing to be their
second. The essence of the man as a politician was summed up
well by the young Republican who helped to organize his campaign. "He always did what he was told," Thomas Miller later
recalled.[5]

The campaign party that took to the road under the Democratic label was, if anything, more anomalous than the Republican group. The Democratic platform contained many
significant reform planks, but on the railroad issue, the party
decided to settle for a blast of antirailroad rhetoric—"We declare that the Southern Pacific company has for years past been
perniciously active in the politics of Nevada and pledge the
Democratic party to the absolute destruction of the political
bureau of the Southern Pacific." This was combined with a
defense of the existing railroad commission and board of assessors.[6]

If the platform lacked meaningful proposals on the railroad
issue, Governor Dickerson's credentials as a reformer were
beyond reproach. He was not, however, a tactful man, and a
large faction of his party was bitterly opposed to him.[7] Somewhat to the right of Dickerson on the ideological spectrum
stood Pittman and Sprague, and at the farthest extreme from
the governor and his reform politics was a nominee for attorney
general with obvious familial connections to the Southern Pacific. At twenty-seven, Cleve Baker was a fortunate young man

—fortunate in his position as district attorney of Tonopah; fortunate in his brother Ray, an effective, if unscrupulous campaign manager; and more fortunate still in his father-in-law, George Perkins, U.S. senator from California and long-standing ally of the Southern Pacific. As George Mowry phrased it in his well-known study of the California Progressives, Perkins was "notoriously a servant of the railroad."[8]

From the very beginning, it was evident that the campaign of 1910 would be something rare, perhaps even unprecedented, in state politics: a debate upon the railroad issue. Other state elections had focused on the past, on the candidates' records, their personalities, and, often, their connections to the Southern Pacific. On the few occasions when significant innovations had been proposed in party platforms, as, for example, in the Democratic platform of 1890, discussion of these issues was muted, or even entirely omitted, during the campaign. Not infrequently, important measures like the railroad commission would suddenly appear in the legislature without public debate in the preceding election. To beard the Southern Pacific dragon in his lair had never been considered smart politics, although verbal denunciations of the railroad, sometimes termed "working on the railroad," had long been a campaign staple and the Southern Pacific was apparently willing to tolerate a certain amount of hostile rhetoric provided nothing substantive was at stake.[9] In short, serious proposals could be slipped into party platforms and introduced in the legislature, provided they were not mentioned on the hustings; conversely, antirailroad bombast was permissible, provided no serious proposals were made. The campaign of 1910, by contrast, was a debate upon just such a proposal.

The railroad plank in the Republican platform was the center of controversy. In speech after speech along the campaign trail, the Democrats charged that the Republican insurgents had surrendered "body and breeches to the enemy."[10] There would be a bonfire, perhaps a band concert, then a parade of Democrats through the streets, and the meeting would commence with a humorous speech by Sam Davis, the newspaper editor who was then seeking the office of state controller. After he heard More-house talk at the insurgent rally in Reno during the primary, said Davis, he was afraid to buy a Southern Pacific mileage ticket because when he got out to eastern Nevada, he might find the Southern Pacific had gone out of business and have to walk home. But after the convention, where the insurgents "first fell on Nixon's neck and then on his pocketbook," Davis concluded that it would be safe to buy a mileage ticket after all. Because the Democrats had resoundingly defended the existing railroad commission, the voters could plainly see that their platform contained all the principles of the Republican insurgents. Sprague would then attack the Republican platform as "a tissue of insincerity, evasion, compromise, and meaningless, high sounding rhetoric," after which Key Pittman would lash into it on the ground that the document contained no planks on na-tional railroad legislation or electoral reform.[11]

In the Democratic press as well, the insurgents and their platform were the major campaign issue. The insurgents were assailed for having betrayed the cause they stood for in a plat-form that would cast the railroad commission into the "mael-strom of politics" and deliver it over to the railroad, to whose agents the elected commissioners would undoubtedly become indebted for their success at the polls. When the platform was not being condemned as a misguided effort to dismember the railroad commission, it was dismissed as "wish-wash."[12]

Criticism of George seems to have been somewhat muted by editors who obviously retained considerable regard for him, even if they now felt obligated to support their party. Instead the bulk of the barrage was directed against Morehouse, who had rashly remarked in public that "a good old-fashioned Re-publican spanking" had been administered to him at the convention. Democratic editors seized upon this remark with glee. "What has become of the grandiloquent old man dragged from out his senile repose in the sere and yellow leaf to save the insurgents, the Republicans, the white man and the black man by the matchless sorcery of his babbling tongue?" inquired the editor of the *Journal*. [13] His betrayal of the voters' confidence was compared to larceny, and his speeches were invariably described as "a killing frost." Withdrawal of the support received from some of the Democratic papers during the primaries was a predictable part of the reversion to partisanship as usual, but it was a heavy blow to the insurgents because, unlike their California counterparts, they would receive little help from the Republican press. Having made their peace with the party, they were more alone than they had ever been.

If the criticism of George seems somewhat muted in retrospect, it was nonetheless more than sufficient to arouse the Springmeyer temper. He campaigned for the platform from one end of the state to the other, hotly challenging the critics to demonstrate how the platform differed from his views "in any material particular," declaring that "I stand where I have always stood," and inquiring why, if the Democrats were so anxious to oust the railroad from politics, they had neglected to do so during their decade in office. [14] Morehouse was by his side, unperturbed by this fusillade of insults from once friendly Democratic editors. While audiences shouted, "Go to it, old man," Lighthorse Harry declared that in his time he had been "roasted, boiled, pickled, broiled, scarified and cut into all sorts of figures and shapes," but all this had only strengthened "the wheels of the political chariot." [15]

Governor Dickerson made little criticism of the proposed public service commission; indeed he had presented a similar plan himself at an earlier date. Rather he stressed his personal fight for higher railroad assessments. "By heavens," he vowed, "I will make the railroads be fair to the people." [16] Oddie, by contrast, was not one to make rash statements concerning the Southern Pacific. He mildly remarked that he would strive for "closer harmony between the railroads and their patrons."[17] In fact, he was most comfortable when he could sidle away from the issues altogether. Nevada, he liked to say, was "one great family," where a man could walk into a strange town and always find a friend.[18] It was, in essence, the gubernatorial campaign of good fellowship by a popular figure identified with the southern mining boom that Mitchell had tried—and failed —to bring off in 1906.

George, usually in company with Morehouse, campaigned separately from Nixon and Oddie for the most part, but he appeared with the other candidates at a Virginia City rally before a large crowd of miners and their wives in Piper's Opera House. The candidates sat on the stage waiting to make their speeches after introductions by the county chairman, whom the occasion had inspired to flights of fulsome oratory.

"I now introduce to you the great—Sen-a-tor NIXON!" shouted the chairman and shook hands with that august personage. Oddie and Roberts, in turn, received no less flowery introductions and warm, manly handshakes.

What the devil will he say about me? thought George, remembering that scene in the street during the primary compaign less than two months before. Not a few in the audience who had been present that day were wondering the same thing. To George's surprise, the introductory speech praised him to the skies. When the chairman extended his hand, George said, "I won't shake hands with you." The crowd clapped, stomped, and cheered for ten minutes before he could begin his speech.

Although the railroad was the primary issue, the candidates were obviously bidding for the labor vote, an effort traditionally conducted by pointing with pride, scrambling for endorsements, and displaying their credentials as bona fide toilers of the earth—rarely by making policy commitments on forthcoming labor legislation. The Nevada State Labor League endorsed the Democratic ticket; the Republicans hastily secured an endorsement from the Reno Central Trades Council. Roberts would conspicuously display his miners' union card, which some union members were so unkind as to suggest did not represent labor in the mines but had, in fact, been hurriedly and fraudulently obtained for purely electoral purposes. (Rather embarrassingly, his own union rescinded its endorsement of him.) Although Nixon could hardly present himself to the voters as a simple miner, Republican campaigners would feelingly recall the days when their munificent patron had "cooked beans on the desert" twenty-nine years ago. Even the luxury of beans had been denied to *him,* candidate Oddie would touchingly confess, in the bygone days when he hungered, thirsted, and "perspired in the sun," a mere humble prospector like the "boys" in his audience.[19]

The Democrats went on in much the same vein, with the difference that Governor Dickerson's remarks had a certain ring of authenticity. "I am proud to state that I am a laboring man," the governor would tell his audiences with simple eloquence, "that I came from the ranks, that I worked with my hands." He would describe his experiences as a strike leader in Idaho and his confinement in the bull pens there. "I am a poor man," Sprague would declare, anxious not to be outdone, "and I belong to the plain people."[20] Cleve Baker would state that he favored a law to prevent strikebreakers from carrying concealed weapons, an issue George had popularized during the primary. Ironically, a broadside George was circulating presented evidence that Baker was himself an ex-strikebreaker, one of a group of university students who had taken summer jobs as scabs during the 1901 strike on the San Francisco docks when employer groups were conducting a successful effort to break the power of the waterfront unions. The Democrats quickly obtained a statement from a California trade unionist dismissing Baker's involvement in the affair—which had tied up the docks for two months, directly involved 15,000 men, and prompted an angry exchange between the presidents of the University of California and the San Francisco Labor Council on the role of student "scab stevedores"—as a mere "college lark."[21]

As the fall days turned colder, the Democratic campaign gave every outward sign of rolling along toward yet another triumph. A procession of hundreds of flag-waving, torch-bearing Democrats paraded through the streets of Goldfield led by Major Minnamascot, resplendent in his silver harness. The major was the Democrat mule himself, presented to Goldfield by William Jennings Bryan in recognition of the massive increase in the town's Democratic registration in 1908. Several miles outside Elko a cavalcade of horsemen and autos met the Democratic candidates for another triumphal procession through the streets. Yet beneath the surface bravado were increasing signs of trouble. The Democrats had Major Minnamascot and an outstanding record of achievement in state government, but the Republicans needed neither. They had Senator Nixon and the Southern Pacific.

No other candidate could begin to spend as lavishly as Nixon, who, if he was not the wealthiest man in the state, was unquestionably a close contender for that distinction. Headlines reported that Nixon was "Spending Money like Drunken Sailor in order to Buy his Election" and "Leaving Trail of Gold."[22] After every political meeting, Nixon's guards stood ready to buy booze for the audience. At Mina, a hamlet of 359 souls in the desert northwest of Goldfield, where the Soda Spring Valley passed near the Pilot Mountains, his nefarious methods were perceived at work. Republican agents spread false rumors that the scheduled Democratic rally had been canceled, then generously suggested that all should repair to the saloons for free drinks to assuage their disappointment. Few citizens appeared at the Democratic rally. At Schurz, on the Walker Indian Reservation, the senator produced attendance at the Republican meeting by promising all residents a ride in an auto. A real auto! Schurz had not seen such excitement since the great stagecoach robbery masterminded by one of the roving members of Butch Cassidy's gang some two years before. Nearly all its 144 inhabitants were waiting when the promised auto appeared to convey them along a road that had been lighted for the occasion with festive fusees thoughtfully provided by the Southern Pacific.[23]

At church fairs, no less than at saloons, Nixon's persistent generosity was taking its toll of Democratic hopes. Upon one such occasion, the senator chanced to observe that the church ceiling needed replastering and kindly volunteered to finance the needed repairs. The church fathers raised their eyes aloft to the crumbling plaster and reflected, we may well suppose, on the Grand Design of He who moves in mysterious ways His wonders to perform. None of His creatures does He create without a purpose. The politician had seemed a useless pest, no more to be restrained from droning out long speeches than a horsefly could be dissuaded from buzzing. Yet now the part that even this unlikely creature was destined to play in the Divine Plan had been miraculously revealed to them. The church fathers observed that it would be a great relief if accumulated church debts of some $200 could be settled. Senator Nixon replied that he would be much gratified if they would allow him to remove this burdensome anxiety from their minds.[24]

As the election drew nearer, reports of foul play began to appear. A legion of Southern Pacific employees was given two weeks' furlough to work for the ticket. In mounting frustration, Pittman asserted that "sneaking political tools" and "gumshoes" were hard at work all over the state insinuating and whispering Nixon's "miserable putrid political vilifications."[25] Nor did the Republican press lag behind when tangible inducements were at hand to inspire their efforts. Morgan was said to have been substantially rewarded for scatological reportage during the primary, and Montrose had been out touring the countryside in an expensive new auto. Democratic editors suspiciously observed that few others in the newspaper fraternity could "afford the price of gasoline." At first a few Republican papers began suggesting that the friends of Hugh Brown should throw their support to Cleve Baker. Then, on the eve of the election, the Republican *Yerington Times,* in which Nixon was reported to be financially interested, endorsed Democratic candidates for several state offices, including the attorney general. The *Journal* charged that Nixon was trading off the balance of the ticket in order to elect himself. Unquestionably, the split endorsement was an unusual development in an age even more partisan than ours, when the party press had been known to issue lukewarm endorsements of its candidates, even to pass over them in silence, but never to support the opposition. "Springmeyer is Forsaken Now That Heads are in Distress," read the *Journal* headline.[26] In truth, matters were a good deal worse than that.

On the day before the election, George finished his campaign in Reno, going from store to store and saloon to saloon as usual. He had planned to take the train back to Goldfield, but at five that afternoon, Senator Nixon invited him to his home. "We'll have dinner for two," he said. "I want to talk to you."

My father accepted and, at the appointed hour, walked briskly along the California Avenue bluff overlooking the Truckee River and the city. This was the tract of land H.H. had declined to develop in partnership with Francis Newlands because he had too much sagebrush land of his own. George arrived at an imposing stucco mansion, or at least one that would become imposing when the growth of trees and hedges caught up to it. He saw a curving sweep of drive, a red tiled roof, tall windows, gracious verandas, a gleaming expanse of parquet floors, and, at the end of them, the senator himself, a very small man in a very large house.

Later, after the two had dined well, Nixon began to tell my father what he wanted him to know, or perhaps to make a final veiled offer to a young man he was sorry to destroy. Even on that last night, it may not have been too late, if my father had been willing to give the assurances it never occurred to him to undertake.

"You'll never get anywhere in Nevada politics," said Senator Nixon, his pale, vague eyes resting on my father, "because you're too independent and you won't work with the party leaders and the machine. If you would, you would go far—to Congress and eventually to the Senate. George, you're going to be defeated."

"You said that before," said George, "but I beat the railroad, the machine, and everything else single-handed."

"This time you're going to be defeated," said Nixon. "We've turned loose a river of gold against you."

A river of gold, my father thought, as he rode the late train back to Goldfield through the silent, empty desert. It was a phrase he never forgot.

He lost the election, as he must by then have known he would. When the ballots were counted, Oddie had beaten Dickerson by a sizable majority, Nixon had downed Pittman by not much less, and George had been defeated by a heartbreakingly thin margin of sixty-five votes out of nearly twenty thousand cast. It had been a close election in virtually every county. Although he had won in a majority of counties, he had been badly hurt by losses in Tonopah and in populous Reno, where elections had been bought and sold ever since his college days. It was suggestive that Governor Dickerson had also suffered a serious defeat in Reno.

In the eastern Nevada ranching country, where George had ridden with the cowboys and walked with the miners, they had not forgotten him. He won in Jarbidge, despite the heavy preponderance of Democratic voters. He carried Goldfield, although there were two Democrats to every Republican registered there. The mystery was Millers. He had made a public issue of the rights of these settlers to their lands in their dispute with the Tonopah and Goldfield Railroad, and they had voted for him three to one in the primary. But in the general election they had turned against him. When he asked the young engineers what had happened, they told him that two nights before the election, Cleve Baker's brother Ray, formerly a good friend of George's at Stanford, had come out and told them that George was "living with a whore in Goldfield." At first they refused to believe it. They knew George wasn't that kind of man. But Ray said they must have heard those rumors about that woman, Madam Sabrina, who had been seen so often at the district attorney's office. They were forced to admit that they had. She was a real stunner too. They didn't suppose a woman like that waited around for nothing, did they? They had guessed not. If it wasn't true, Springmeyer would have scotched the rumors by saying so, wouldn't he?

"We couldn't support a man like that," said the respectable householders of Millers to George. "Why didn't you come out and deny it?"

"I never knew about it till now," said George, and for a rueful, bittersweet moment, he must have thought of Madam Sabrina. The smiles of a spring evening are not supposed to linger except in memory, Madam Sabrina. But you will not stay pressed in a leatherbound volume of poetry like a faded rose. In Millers, among these virtuous defenders of hearth and home, your elegant, hourglass silhouette fell across the case of the People vs. the Southern Pacific and the great debate on the public service commission grew illegible in your shadow. All those fine Progressive reforms, so staunchly fought for, were swept out of sight in the rustle of your silken petticoats. Millers reversed its vote, and the reason lay in you.

What had happened in railroad-controlled Reno was no mystery to George—or to the other candidates. Indeed much of Key Pittman's postmortem could be applied as well to the Republican candidate for attorney general. "Nixon personally expended over a quarter of a million dollars and the Southern Pacific expended about as much," Pittman wrote to a friend. "The Republicans had three daily newspapers furnished to each of the voters free of cost. . . . I was compelled to depend upon the support of my friends, while Nixon employed thousands of hired workers. I would have beaten him in spite of all this had it not been for the extensive bribery indulged in on election day."[27]

The Goldfield press reported "unusual conditions" during the tally. In Precinct 4, on the border of the tenderloin, two election officials casually altered their figures to suit whenever the calculations failed to agree. A number of Republican ballots were discarded on questionable grounds. In Precinct 3 the tally was conducted by allowing a Democratic poll watcher to read off the ballots at his discretion to an election official seated across the room.[28] Those were the only precincts in the city that George failed to carry.

Unfortunately, these conditions were not really unusual. George's friends reported crooked counting in a number of precincts, in addition to the many votes bought with the river of gold. George brought suit to win a recount, charging that election officials had unlawfully rejected more than two hundred ballots cast for him in Washoe, Esmeralda, and other counties. Baker's demurrer was overruled, but the litigation dragged on, while the term of office at stake dwindled away and the legal expenses mounted. Then, in the fall of 1911, the state supreme court ruled that the loser of the contested election must pay the entire cost of the proposed recount. J. W. Legate, the defeated candidate for clerk of the supreme court who had sued in conjunction with George, decided to drop the suit.

It was a painful decision for my father. He knew he was right and believed he could prove it, but he simply had no money left to do it. Two years of work for Esmeralda County had left him no better off than when he first packed his bag for Goldfield. H.H. had financed his son's campaign as best he could after the financial disaster he had suffered in the collapse of the Nye and Ormsby County Bank, and it was he who met the bills for these attenuated legal proceedings. It would later be said of George that he fought every battle to the last bullet. Although that was just what his pugnacious instincts strained to do in the fall of 1911, he had to acknowledge to himself that the risk of paying for a full recount was too much to ask of his father. So be it. He dropped the suit and allowed the decision to go against him.[29]

The platform George had fought for so hard fared little better than the antirailroad candidates. The public service commission foundered in the next legislature; the newly elected Democratic legislature of 1913 enacted it into law, but it was only a temporary achievement. Within five years the old system would be reconstituted in its essentials.[30]

In retrospect, 1910 was a kind of watershed, a transitional year that marked the beginning of some long, if not illustrious, political careers and the ending of others. Senator Nixon and Cleve Baker would be dead in less than three years, and George Wingfield's influence would expand to fill the vacuum created by the death of the Republican leader. Roberts would serve as congressman until 1918; later, defeated in his senatorial and gubernatorial ambitions, he would settle in as mayor of Reno. Oddie would be defeated in the next two gubernatorial elections; then, just when he was beginning to look like a perennial loser, he would be swept into the Senate, lagging well behind

You Can Lead a Horse to Water, But You Can't Make Him Drink.

Senator George Nixon and George Wingfield busy themselves at "The Corruption Sack" while postmaster Ed Collins (Southern Pacific agent and local Republican boss) carries off a pot of gold for distribution among the voters during the 1910 election. Attorney J. F. Douglas (at left with a scoop of coins) had defended County Commissioner Worden and his associates in the Rawhide graft case. *Goldfield Daily News,* Oct. 17, 1910; probably drawn by Boyd Moore.

the ticket, by the Harding landslide of 1920; and there he would repose until ejected by Pat McCarran, riding in on Franklin Roosevelt's coattails in 1932. Key Pittman would win his senatorial seat after Nixon's death in 1912 and would remain there, rising to ever higher positions of influence in the Senate even as he sank ever lower into the depths of chronic alcoholism, until his death in 1940, just after his sixth victorious campaign. Denver Dickerson and Charles Sprague would not seek high office in Nevada again. My father would campaign two more times, one of them only half seriously. But 1910 was the big one, the loss that hurt, the time he came so near to winning he could almost touch it.

I asked him once what his greatest disappointment had been, for he was not given to speaking of disappointments, much less to assigning them rank orders. He said it was *politics.* I am older now, have followed in his footsteps through page after page of newsprint, and understood at last, many years later, what that single word conveyed. If he were here today, I would no longer need to ask.

Battling at Armageddon

TWO MONTHS AFTER that campaign, my father left Gold-field for private practice in Carson City and Reno. Goldfield was still the second largest city in Nevada, but those unfailing signs of high prosperity in a mining region observed by Mark Twain were clearly in eclipse. No more were the jails and brothels overburdened with custom. The new sheriff announced that since Goldfield was "more orderly" he believed he could manage with a smaller force. Jake's Dance Hall, once the most famous in Goldfield, had been closed for a year. There had been a time when men had gladly paid a dollar for the pleasure of a two-minute dance on Jake's crowded floor; a popular lady from Alaska, collecting 50¢ corkage for every dollar pint of beer purchased by her customers, had earned $500 on corkage alone in a single night. A nearby dance hall named the People's Theater had been demolished, the lumber shipped away to Las Vegas. Vacant houses, robbed of doors and windows, stood abandoned on the ground where men had fought for tent space only four years before.

One after another they were leaving—George Wingfield, Kid Highley, and all the rest. Diamondfield Jack, pausing only to rescue a baroness in distress, was setting forth with an armada of 250 men and a thousand mules to "win a tremendous fortune" in the gold mines of eastern Brazil—or so he confidently anticipated. Even Major Minnamascot, once the pride of the Goldfield democracy, would be turned loose on the range to fend for himself after the brewery that employed him went out of business.[1]

Worse was still to come. Goldfield would be ravaged by fire and flood. Large-scale mining would cease when the mill closed down in 1919. But the city my father knew had really died when the exuberant spirit of the great boom drained away. Goldfield had always been, above all, a landscape of the imagination. In 1911 it was already time to go, though not time to forget. I remember the way he sometimes used to say the word *Goldfield,* the slight pause and the lowered timbre of his voice. That word seemed to echo inside him in a way no other ever did. George's new office was well located, not far from the massive, stone capitol on the quiet, shady streets of Carson City; but there would never be another like the first one across the street from the Northern when Goldfield was new, my father had just turned twenty-five, and all things were possible.

If the campaign of 1910 had demonstrated nothing else, it had surely indicated that the day of the reformer was not yet at hand in Nevada. Nonetheless, events would not allow George a prolonged respite from politics. Theodore Roosevelt's bid for the presidency was beginning to take shape in 1912, and Progressive Republicans everywhere were compelled to either stand up and fight for his candidacy or turn aside and let the victory go to Taft and the old guard. As early as 1907, Roosevelt's renomination had been a stated goal of the California Lincoln-Roosevelt League; in Nevada as well, his name was a symbol of liberal Republicanism. Nixon and Roberts predictably supported Taft, as did Wingfield and the party regulars. Oddie, also predictably, expressed himself in favor of Roosevelt, then hastily retreated when this position proved to be perilous. Whenever a pitched battle between Roosevelt's supporters and opponents was looming up, Oddie would characteristically absent himself from the scene. My father, no less predictably, chose to stand and fight.

The first battle occurred at the March 1912 meeting of the Republican state central committee. A plan by the regulars to select delegates instructed to Taft for the national convention without holding a state convention was successfully headed off. In an effort to democratize the state convention and capitalize on Roosevelt's popularity among the rank and file, George offered a resolution providing that the voters would be allowed to express their presidential preference in the delegate selection primaries, and he appealed to the committee to give him a "fair hearing." It was a vain appeal, based on concepts of party reform still many years ahead of their time and directed toward an establishment in no way inclined to relinquish control for the sake of democracy, especially when democracy meant Roosevelt.

After a debate that George called "perhaps the most stormy session in the history of Nevada politics during which very bitter accusations and recriminations were made," the resolution was lost by "devious parliamentary tactics."[2] The *Journal* noted that "Roll calls were dispensed with, parliamentary law was forgotten and when the chairman declared a measure carried or lost, it was carried or lost and that was an end on it." Because the Roosevelt supporters had substantial voting strength in the committee in the person of Charlie Reeves, chairman of the Progressive League of Nevada and the holder of twenty-four proxies, the regulars decided to bring the meeting to a speedy close without the election of new officers. As my father "grew eloquent in voicing the demands of the people," the chairman hastily interrupted his speech to announce adjournment.[3]

The process of selecting delegates for the state convention turned out to be a debacle for the liberal Republicans. Roosevelt's adherents "made the mistake of resting on their oars," George wrote with rueful hindsight when it was over, and were "out-generaled by the machine at every turn."[4] Reeves's leadership during this critical period proved as ineffectual as it had been at the March committee meeting. In three-quarters of the counties, no primaries were held at all, and delegates were instead selected by the county central committees. Collins and his cohorts were careful to ensure that no primaries should take place in Goldfield, where the voters were believed to be strongly in favor of Roosevelt. Of the three counties in which full primaries were held, two were long-standing strongholds of conservatism, where little popular support for Roosevelt could be anticipated. In the Carson City Republican meeting, the regulars, led by United States attorney Sam Platt, denied George's accusation that the meeting was packed and rejected his motion that the voters should choose between Taft and Roosevelt tickets. A Taft slate was named. Although the Roosevelt men submitted their own ticket, they were handily defeated in the primary.[5]

In Reno the regulars' victory was not accomplished without obvious chicanery. Their delegate slate was designated "uninstructed" and included the name of Pat Flanigan, the Republican senatorial candidate two years before and the most prominent figure on the Roosevelt slate. Although Reeves circulated cards on election day announcing that the "uninstructed ticket is a Taft ticket" and "the blue ticket is the People's ticket and not put out by the Southern Pacific," the organization's stratagems may well have bewildered voters. If so, they were probably no more confused than Flanigan himself. At the convention, he would announce that he was a Taft man; within a week he would be campaigning for Roosevelt in California; and not long afterward he would resign his post as

Republican national committeeman to assume a parallel position in the new Progressive party.[6]

Apart from Republicans who were perplexed and those who were committed conservatives, there was, as was usual in Reno, a sizable group who were neither bewildered, nor conservative, nor Republicans—nor even voters. In a reprise of 1910, railroad employees were furloughed, and George took note of the activities of "a well known railroad boss, whose fine hand had been shown at the Committee meeting, his petty henchmen and servitors." Because the ballots were of different colors, the bosses could readily see to it that their orders were obeyed. Again the Roosevelt slate was easily defeated.[7]

When the Republican convention assembled at Fallon in May, the only counties that sent strong Roosevelt delegations —most notably Lander, White Pine, and Douglas, where George's family had joined him in the campaign for Roosevelt— were those where Roosevelt men happened to be in control of the county organizations. It was clear that the Roosevelt supporters, with seventeen delegates to the organization's eighty, had no hope of victory. Taking cognizance of these overwhelming odds, the *Journal* observed: "It is highly unlikely that any strenuous protest will be made on the convention floor."[8] Being outnumbered more than four to one, however, was never sufficient to deter my father from strenuous protest. He was determined to "make things hum" as long as he could.

After caucusing separately, the Roosevelt men threatened that if they were not given "some consideration" they would make a "row" on the convention floor. The consideration they were seeking was an uninstructed delegation, or, failing that, the inclusion of Flanigan in the national delegation. The regulars were reportedly ready to accept Flanigan, but only as a Taft-instructed delegate, a position he was unwilling to take. There were contests before the credentials committee, as Roosevelt adherents from Goldfield and other districts objected

—in vain, of course—to the delegations appointed by the regulars.

Matters rapidly rolled to the inevitable conclusion. When the state platform was reported, George and Sardis Summerfield, an old friend since George was a child and Summerfield was H.H.'s attorney, submitted a minority report arguing that an instructed delegation was a departure from the traditions of the Nevada Republicans that would impair the delegation's usefulness and suggest distrust in their judgment. Morehouse, responding to a request from a top-hatted delegate to hear his "tragic tones," attacked Roosevelt on the third-term issue and the uninstructed delegation on the ground that "I do not want to stand around waiting for some grafter to buy me." Having observed the consequences of opposing the organization in 1910 and absorbed the lesson contained therein, Lighthorse Harry was now slated for a place on the national delegation. Reeves suggested shipping the delegation in a box to shield them from undue influences. George Wingfield, rising to thunderous applause, was clearly in no mood to listen to strenuous protest by the Roosevelt men; he moved that speeches be limited to three minutes.[9]

Then my father spoke. He complimented the organization on their "well-oiled machine." In a barb directed at the former leader of the Lincoln-Roosevelt League, he observed that, as he knew of no grafter waiting to buy the Nevada delegation, he had made no effort to join it. Since an uninstructed slate had won the primary vote, such as it was, a pledged delegation was clearly counter to the wishes of the voters. "If that is not betrayal of the people, I don't know what betrayal means." Abruptly, the regulars shouted that his time was up. To make it perfectly plain that Wingfield's three-minute rule was for Roosevelt supporters only, another delegate was then permitted to tell a long, rambling shaggy-dog story about a man named Casey.

At this point George Wingfield spoke, explaining why he "had no use for Theodore Roosevelt." Just how heavily personal were Wingfield's politics was well illustrated by this convention speech. When the president had visited Reno in 1908, said Wingfield, he had gone out of his way to mention Senator Newlands but had ignored Senator Nixon; furthermore Roosevelt was responsible for the 1907 panic that had cost Nixon and himself $5 million. Incidentally, Wingfield continued, he had never finished the trust prosecutions; indeed he never finished anything he started.[10] Wingfield might have added (although he did not) that had Roosevelt's war with the trusts been as decisively concluded as had his own disagreements with the IWW—those same disagreements on which Roosevelt had displayed such lamentable lack of understanding—the former president might have ranked a little higher in his estimation. Here in Fallon, northwest of the Dead Camel Mountains, where the fields of the Lahontan Valley were greening now, watered by the reclamation project that Roosevelt's support had made possible, the former president, who had captured the imagination of a generation of liberals, was as easily dimissed as a miner suspected of union sympathies at Goldfield Con. Roosevelt had slighted George Wingfield's partner and he had cost George Wingfield money—so much for the twenty-sixth president of the United States.

From the outset of the convention Governor Oddie had been in obvious disfavor with the regulars, although certainly not as a result of any propensity on his part to take an unequivocal stand for Roosevelt or anything else. The committee on resolutions had refused to present the resolution my father proposed commending the Oddie administration—a courtesy the convention that readily acclaimed Senator Nixon and Congressman Roberts would normally extend to the first governor the Republicans had succeeded in electing in twenty years. Oddie's retreat on Roosevelt, instead of ingratiating him with the regulars, appeared to arouse ridicule. The Democratic *Journal* reported that when the crucial roll call on the presidential issue came up on the convention floor, the Tonopah delegation, in a malicious attempt to compel the governor to declare himself, offered him a place to vote as one of their number. Oddie, however, had long since "taken to the woods" and was not to be found.[11]

As the roll call proceeded, the proponents of the uninstructed delegation were overwhelmingly defeated. The chairman of the convention, adding insult to injury, then referred to Roosevelt as an "outlaw." At that point, my father strode out of the convention hall in what the press called "high dudgeon."[12]

The regulars had retained their grip on the party organization and secured their Taft delegation, but their triumph would prove hollow. The outlaw from Oyster Bay would go on to seek the presidency under the banner of a new political party, and the men they had steam rollered at Fallon would found a Nevada Progressive party to back him up. Springmeyer, Summerfield, and Flanigan would rise cheering to their feet with the other delegates at the August convention in Chicago when Roosevelt issued his stirring summons to his followers, "We stand at Armageddon and we battle for the Lord." A Nevada victory for Taft would slip from their grasp. Taft had lost the state narrowly in 1908 to the West's own William Jennings Bryan, longtime champion of the silver cause so dear to the hearts of Nevadans, and could be expected to do far better against the cold, intellectual professor from New Jersey the Democrats had selected in 1912. Worse yet, Senator Nixon's sudden death in the summer of 1912 would unexpectedly compel them to fight for a position they had thought was safely nailed down until 1916, and to fight, moreover, without the advantages of Nixon's lavish purse and talents at conciliation.

In 1910 a split with the liberal wing of the party had threatened; in 1912 it became unforgettably clear just how disastrous the loss of the liberal Republicans could be.

If the Progressive revolt denoted a split in the Republican party, the ranks of the Roosevelt supporters themselves were by no means free of dissension. When the Nevada Progressive convention assembled in Reno in late July, a struggle for leadership between the Reeves faction on one hand and Summerfield and my father on the other was manifestly under way. The regulars were excoriated in rousing language in a Progressive manifesto: "We denounce as treason to our form and principles of government the larceny of the mock nomination of President Taft . . . and express the hope that not only the recipient of that pretended nomination but also all who either contrived, executed, or condone that brazen repudiation of the people's emphatically expressed choice will promptly be relegated to the wailing place of the politically unclean." But the denunciation of the regulars proved to be one of the few matters on which all Progressives could wholeheartedly agree.[13]

It seems probable that Summerfield and my father had no wish to entrust the Progressive cause to the ineffectual and disreputable Reeves, who had so disastrously botched the legal affairs of White Pine County when serving as district attorney that he had nearly been relieved of his duties by the attorney general. The immediate issue between the two factions, however, was the matter of delegate apportionment. Reeves, who favored dividing the delegates on the same basis as they had been divided in the regular Republican convention, grew increasingly restive as the credentials committee under George's leadership seated virtually every delegate who knocked on the door. Although this resulted in greater representation for the smaller counties, it was also thoroughly in keeping with the extraordinary openness that was one of the most notable features of the Nevada Progressive party. Further, it may have been the wisest policy for a new political party, organized within the span of two weeks. Being endowed with none of the loaves and fishes of patronage with which party organizations were generally nourished in that period, the Progressives could offer their adherents only the pleasure and honor of participation. When Reeves and others objected to this practice, George obligingly explained that the apportionment of the Republican convention had been rejected because the Progressives were creating something new that was not to be calculated on the same basis as the old Republican vote.

Before the day was through Reeves had denounced the convocation as a "Springmeyer-Summerfield convention" and declined to have anything further to do with it or to serve as state chairman. In September when Summerfield had received the Progressive nomination for United States Senator and George had accepted the nomination for Congress as a beau geste, secure in the belief that he could not possibly be elected and compelled to leave Nevada and his law practice for Washington, Reeves issued a sour statement declaring that he could "conceive of no greater calamity that could befall the state of Nevada" than the election of these two candidates and appended some additional remarks that even the scurrilous Morgan considered unprintable. Flanigan, who regarded Reeves as "a most despicable and disreputable libertine," accused the former leader of misuse of party funds and threatened a criminal suit and disbarment proceedings.[14]

One Bull Moose had bolted from the herd, but those who remained may well have been the most unlikely assemblage ever banded together in a common political cause, even in Nevada, where strange bedfellows abounded. Progressives prominent in party affairs varied in occupation from Episcopalian clerics and university professors to miners and ranchers; in age they varied from pioneer patriarchs to youths in their early twenties; in political background they varied from the old Yankee stock of the historians' Progressive prototype to foreign immigrants and their sons, including a substantial sprinkling of Italians, a sizable group in Nevada at that time, but one that was not yet appearing in positions of influence in the regular parties. In their future paths they would vary no less, for some would go on to distinguised political and professional careers and others would slide down into poverty and obscurity.

Despite this extraordinary variety, a common ideological strain could usually be detected among the Progressives. Interviews with descendants often yield little more than the observation that "I guess he just liked Theodore Roosevelt," but insofar as the shards of conviction can be pieced together so long after the fact, it appears that many were among the most liberal Republicans of their time and were, for one reason or another, at odds with the regular Republican organization. This was certainly true of my father. Several were former Populists, which in Nevada meant they had opposed the Southern Pacific. Pat Flanigan had staunchly resisted Black Wallace in the showdown of 1899, and his friends considered him ahead of his time in policy matters. According to his son, Flanigan believed the organization had not "treated him fairly" when he was refused a place in the national delegation on his own terms. Sardis Summerfield had an outstanding record as a reform legislator in the late nineties; his appointment as United States attorney on Senator Stewart's recommendation had been viewed as an effort to placate the liberal wing of the party; he had labored long in the service of the Republicans as an expert on platform committees and as a debater in the campaign of 1910 and may well have thought he deserved better of them than he had ever received.

Some of the Progressive candidates for lesser offices on the ticket also shared this strain of liberalism and dissidence. These included Walter Hastings, a Progressive candidate for the assembly, blocked in his previous efforts to win local office in

Washoe County because, according to his daughter, he refused to "kowtow to the big shots" and carry out their orders. Another was Judge William R. Thomas, candidate for state supreme court justice. Thomas had openly opposed Governor Oddie's recent dispatch of the state police to suppress labor unrest at Ely, a brave stance for a judicial candidate in that period; Nevada corporations, Thomas pointedly observed, should be "reduced to the basis of good citizenship."[15] Because of men like Thomas, and most of all, because of Roosevelt himself, my father envisaged the Progressives as "the idealistic soul" of the Republican party.

Others envisaged it differently. "At first we were regarded as a good joke," wrote one of the Goldfield activists to the chairman of the Progressive state committee. "We are now taken more seriously." Actually, though the Progressives were regarded as a threat to the victory of regular Republicans, they were not likely to be elected because their meager resources could support only the scantiest of campaigns. It was every man for himself. Summerfield managed a canvass of sorts, which he announced, in a futile effort to inspire the other candidates to declare their campaign expenses, had cost $408. This met with no response from his better-financed opponents: Key Pittman, determined to have what had been stolen from him in 1910; and Judge Massey, the regular Republican just appointed to Nixon's post after Wingfield declined the honor. The Progressive senatorial aspirant's challenge to a debate was rejected by Massey; this, Summerfield announced with notable lack of humility, was because the senator felt unable to cope with "the clear, cold logic and overpowering eloquence of the matchless Summerfield." In keeping with his modest financial circumstances and his belief that this campaign was a purely quixotic endeavor, George made no canvass and placed no advertisements, although he was often mentioned by the other candidates. Because of the party's lack of funds, declared one Progressive candidate for the legislature to the public, "the voters will not, in this campaign, be given the pleasure of hearing Nevada's first Progressive."[16]

With little press support or organization and less money, the Progressives' only real assets were the charismatic name of their leader; their strongly liberal platform, which they stressed at every opportunity; and their party label. The last of these was very nearly lost when Attorney General Baker attempted to have them designated as "Independents" on the ballot. This potentially disastrous maneuver was successfully foiled in the state supreme court with Summerfield effectively arguing that "the secretary of state can not assume the function of a high priest with the exclusive power of christening a new political party." In reaching their favorable decision, at least one of the justices had been much impressed by the petition filed by the Progressives to secure their place on the ballot. It contained nearly four thousand names, a number far in excess of legal requirements and equivalent to about a fifth of the voters who would cast presidential ballots in the forthcoming election.[17]

The high point of the campaign was, of course, the visit of the Rough Rider himself. When Roosevelt's special railroad car reached Wendover on the eastern Nevada border traveling westward from Utah, George, Summerfield, and Flanigan boarded the train and joined Roosevelt for breakfast in the observation area of the car. A messenger arrived with a telegram two or three pages long telling how the Republican orator Harlan, one of the spellbinders who was following Roosevelt on his tour, had just blasted the former president with a follow-up speech at the last stop. While his secretary read the wire to the group, Roosevelt glanced speculatively at the three Nevadans. There was Flanigan, even burlier and more thickly mustachioed than Roosevelt himself; Summerfield, who had been described in the press as "lean and brown as the ribbed sea sands", and my father, then almost thirty-one, young and handsome, with frank, open features, a commanding Roman nose, and the clear Springmeyer eyes under bushy, sandy eyebrows.

"Mr. Congressman," said Roosevelt with a bluff optimism that neither he nor George actually felt, "how would you answer that?"

If this was a litmus test of President Roosevelt's own devising, the answer undoubtedly pleased him. Ever since the campaign of 1906, George had been defending the president on the hustings with all the eloquence at his command. Roosevelt listened attentively, then turned to his secretary and said, "Have him repeat that, take it down, and put it on the wire to AP as my reply."

After innumerable whistle-stop pauses along the way, the train came to a halt in Reno, where the leaders were to appear in a parade. Progressives from all over the state had converged for the great occasion. Children, many of them clad in little Rough Rider suits, dipped their spoons into "Bull Moose Sundaes," advertised at the Bonboniere as "delightful combinations of fresh fruits, nuts, cherries, and ice cream," and played with the elaborate, colorful campaign buttons of that year. Roosevelt and the three Nevadans cruised slowly down the street in Flanigan's auto, preceded by a bagpipe band engaged by George. Perhaps because he loved the "wild and free" music of the bagpipes himself, my father harbored a lifelong conviction that the surefire way to attract the largest crowd to any political event was a bagpipe band. Beside the auto walked a young miner from the Black Hills, proud of being the one chosen to see that no harm should come to Roosevelt. As they proceeded, Reeves, who had always claimed he had fought at San Juan Hill, came up in a resplendent uniform shouting, "Hello, Teddy, how are you?" Roosevelt cupped his hand and muttered to his companions, "Who is that son of a bitch anyway?" When they told him, he cried jovially, "Hello, Charlie, you old bastard!"

Recalling this incident, which was repeated throughout the parade with many Nevadans who boasted acquaintance with Roosevelt, my father used to laugh heartily, which reveals a good deal more about politics in Nevada than it does about the former president. After all, we were the state where Key Pittman could say with no more than a pardonable degree of exaggeration that he knew all his constituents "personally," the state where no politician ever needed to pretend he remembered anyone because we were "one great family" of intimates.

When they arrived in Powning Park, Senator Newlands said a few words of greeting and Pat Flanigan's little son held out a Boy Scout flag and promptly forgot the speech he had carefully memorized for the occasion. Roosevelt laughed and sailed into a speech of his own, strongly emphasizing reclamation, boss rule, and special privilege—all topics he must have correctly surmised were of particular relevance in Nevada.[18] He was presented with eight late-summer cantaloupes from the Fallon fields, though he would no doubt have preferred a set of spring delegates from the Fallon convention. Children played at his feet, even swung from his coattails, and later remembered him as the kindliest of men.

After Roosevelt's train had rumbled away across the Sierra, the rest of the campaign seemed anticlimactic. The regulars, however, were troubled by a recurrent sense of impending disaster (notably, in this pre-opinion-poll period, politicians usually seemed to have a very accurate idea of the way the tide was running). Toward the end of the campaign, the chairman of the Republican state central committee, recognizing that Massey's defeat was imminent, sent letters to all signers of the Progressive petition urging them to vote for Massey because a vote for Summerfield would be, in effect, a vote for Key Pittman.[19] This did nothing to forestall the approaching donnybrook. Wilson won the state, the senatorial seat the Republicans had held since 1904 was snatched by Key Pittman, and the Republicans lost control of the assembly. Although Roosevelt trounced Taft and a few Progressive legislators were elected, the Progressive candidates for higher office were all dismally defeated.

No matter. They had demonstrated that the Nevada regulars could ignore the liberal wing of the party only at their peril; they had stood up and been counted. "Aggressive fighting for the right," read the motto beneath the bronze plaque of Theodore Roosevelt that always hung in my father's office, "is the noblest sport the world affords."

From Armageddon to Saint-Mihiel

FORMALLY MY FATHER remained a Progressive until the party disintegrated after Roosevelt's return to the Republicans in 1916; but by 1914 he was the only major politician still active in what was left of the Nevada Progressive party, and what was left was no more than a faint shadow of 1912. Nonetheless he filed as a Progressive candidate for attorney general. His Democratic opponent for the post would not be Cleve Baker, for death had brought the young attorney general's career to a premature close. Baker had fallen ill, and not long before the end came, he spoke of a deadly dream. In his dream "a prominent Nevadan" shot him in the stomach; within hours he hemorrhaged internally and died. The Democratic lieutenant governor first announced that no replacement would be made until Oddie returned from a governor's conference in the East; then, at the urging of Key Pittman, he rushed away from the funeral cortege to appoint George Thatcher, a Democrat, to the post.[1]

The regulars had probably hoped that the Progressives, suitably meek and chastened, would silently dissolve into the Republican ranks. Not the Progressives. They would sail back with flying colors and full prestige or not at all. When George filed as a Progressive candidate, the regulars were faced with a painful dilemma. A Progressive victory was no serious threat, but, as in 1912 and the primary of 1910, George's capacity for embarrassing them was great. Although he still had neither money nor press support nor an organization behind him, he was a fiery and popular campaign speaker whose galvanic temperament had mellowed not at all in the past four years and who was, moreover, as stubborn as the legendary dollar mule. Listening to the Progressives blast the organization during still another campaign was not a pleasing prospect. The Republicans had already accepted the nomination of Richard McKay for attorney general after legal efforts to enable the party to retract his candidacy during the primary and designate my father as their nominee in his place had failed.[2] During their postprimary convention, they argued long and heatedly into the night and finally reached a decision: McKay would withdraw; the Progressive and Republican parties would amalgamate; and the Republicans would endorse my father and other Progressive candidates for certain minor offices. Well aware that they could hope to accomplish little outside the Republican party, the last remnants of the Progressives found this compromise acceptable. The final benediction upon their reunion was pronounced by, of all people, Montrose. "Those who stepped out two years ago believing they were working for the greater benefit of their country," he wrote, "have now joined hands with their brothers."[3]

So it was, except for one small hitch. Despite legal efforts, which the party entrusted to Morehouse, it proved impossible to remove McKay's name from the ballot.[4] This, of course, ensured that even though McKay made no canvass and his withdrawal was widely publicized, the party label would draw enough votes to his name to split the Republican-Progressive vote, an outcome by no means unpleasing to the Democratic attorney general who had engineered it. It also occurs to me, although my father never suggested it, that the regulars may have been equally satisfied with the result. Attorney General Thatcher would later become (perhaps was already in the process of becoming) right-hand man to George Wingfield. A victory for Thatcher—a much more cooperative man, despite his Democratic affiliations, than my father—would be tolerable to the regulars for the price of tucking the Progressives safely back into the Republican fold.

This was, in fact, the way it turned out. The campaign was enlivened toward the end when the Democrats publicized the Collins letters, which had fallen into their possession after the hasty departure of the Goldfield boss. Some heated exchanges between my father and Thatcher ensued, but, as was so often the case, no real enmity was apparently involved. This had much to do with the underlying camaraderie of the Goldfield crowd, and perhaps something to do as well with my father's personality. "You could get mad at him," Federal Judge Bruce Thompson, his law partner of many years, told me once, "but you couldn't stay mad at him."

When the election results came in, the Democrats had swept all major state offices. It was my father's last campaign. Politics would be a passionate interest throughout his life, he would actively participate in party affairs on behalf of other men, but he would never seek an elective office again. He could have told himself with good cause that the vote for him combined with McKay's vote easily exceeded Thatcher's total, that his defeat was only a technical fluke resulting from their failure to remove McKay's name from the ballot, that it was worth going on—but he did not think in these terms. He had lost by a greater margin than in 1910; there was no more to be said. It was all behind him now: the cheering, stamping crowds of miners; the cowboys who stood with him; the hopes against all odds when the Unspiked Rail set forth in 1910; the river of gold that swept away the fragile craft of Nevada Progressivism. He turned his attention to other matters—to his bride and to the law.

Although no one ever told me much about my father's first wife, Tina, the little I have heard remains vividly in my mind. She was a beautiful Southern divorcee, dark-haired, as were all the women who most attracted him, golden-skinned, and seemingly endowed with a fine figure. But she was not, as it turned out after their hasty marriage, quite what my father had expected. Her bosom was created anew each morning by blowing into her inflatable brassiere; her mind was dilated each day by similar gaseous infusions of Christian Science. She began to press her atheistic husband to dedicate his life to missionary work for the Christian Scientists, and he reacted explosively to these suggestions.

They lived together for several years in their Reno home, less than joyously, it seems. Then one evening he took her out to dinner and noticed that she was wearing all her jewelry. She sat across the table from him like a gypsy or a barbaric Scythian queen, her fingers encrusted with rings, her arms stiff with bracelets, her inflated bosom dangerously laden with necklaces. When he asked her why, she said offhandedly that she "just felt like it," but he sensed correctly that this was a ceremonial occasion unrelated to Christian Science. That night she left him, took the train "back East," as they always say in Nevada, and he never saw her again.

His political campaigns were past and his marriage was over, but the law remained, and in it his professional reputation was growing steadily. In part his legal style was congruent with his political self—in politics he believed a man should speak his message and the people would follow him or not as they chose, better to lose than to win by manipulative devices that subverted their freedom of choice and denied their existence as reasoning men. In the law he felt little affinity for the sentimental courtroom sob sisters, common in those days, who strove to play lugubrious chords upon the heartstrings of the jurors. But more than that, these were another species of manipulative stratagems that vitiated the purpose of the legal process just as political trickery denied the assumptions of democracy. In law as in politics, he believed he should simply set forth the truth before the jury as he had done before the people, and let them decide.

In this he was consistent; however, during cross-examination, which soon became known as one of his finest legal accomplishments, the role he assumed in court was almost a reversal of the man. In ordinary life he was trusting, unsuspicious, even naive, and presumed only good of others until he was proven wrong beyond the shadow of a reasonable doubt. Forthright himself, disinterested in hidden motives, and disinclined to visualize clandestine plots within external events, he usually took the world at its word. But in the courtroom, this optimistic belief in the fundamental decency of all mankind and this indisposition to probe beneath surface realities were temporarily suspended, and my father became a keen hunter in pursuit of his quarry. As the hunter turns from the beaten track to find the real, the hidden, trail, so the trial lawyer must probe beneath testimony too smooth, too glib, too well rehearsed, until he finds the awkward, disjointed oddities of truth. As the hunter observes the faint, almost invisible imprint in the earth, so the lawyer reads the subtle shift in the witness's expression. As the hunter hears the rustle in the thicket, so too the lawyer perceives the brief hesitation, the minute change in the timbre of the voice. As the hunter peers at the displaced leaves and the broken twig, so too the lawyer marks the word just slightly out of place, the tiny fact that does not quite jibe with the rest. Finally, as the hunter knows without sight or sound that his quarry is hidden close at hand, so too must the trial lawyer's strange sixth sense lead him toward the spot where truth lies concealed, and there in the path he knows his quarry will take must he invisibly lay his carefully constructed trap.

Forty years later, when verbal bludgeoning in courtroom dramas had become a staple feature of popular entertainment, my father and I watched a movie in which a fictitious attorney was browbeating a witness. "No, no," said my father, shaking his head in disgust, "that could never happen in a court of law." Real cross-examination was a subtle affair, a lesson he himself had learned when he was defending a British mining company in a suit brought by a group of state officials over mining property in Copper Canyon worth half a million dollars. Not only was the property valuable in itself, but the case devolved upon an issue of much significance in the mining world up to the present day. A lode claim was invalid without the discovery of a vein. Should the opposition succeed in their contention that, even though the claim had been legitimately filed and development work had been done on the property over the years no vein had actually been found by the original locators, the law would sanction a modern form of claim jumping more insidious and ultimately more dangerous than the kind Pete Milich had faced when he dragged his shattered limbs to the cabin window sill and blasted away at the marauders. Witnesses scattered and died, claims were sold and resold, and the original discovery of a vein was often impossible to prove. If the title could be "broken by those claim jumpers," my father's client observed over a bottle of whiskey in a railway smoking car, then 95 percent of the claims in Nevada could be broken in the same way. The gentleman to whom he addressed his remarks, an expert witness for the opposition, took care to make no damaging admissions, but it was nonetheless an analysis with which few mining men would take serious issue.

When the trial began, the opposition was able to muster an impressive array of witnesses, the star of which was Nevada Governor Emmet Boyle, one of the most respected mining engineers in the state and, incidentally, the other occupant of the smoking car on that winter evening. The governor testified that he made a careful examination of the claim over a two-day period and had taken samples of rock, which he identified as "Weber quartzite." He then firmly stated his conclusion: he had seen nothing on the Copper Canyon claims "which I would consider a vein or lode," indeed nothing he thought worthy of development. His manner was brisk and businesslike, his hair straight and black, his gaze severe and authoritive from behind rimless spectacles. The jury was obviously much impressed.

That evening, while George and his associates were going over the transcript of the day's evidence, one of the mining engineers remarked that he had once read an engineering report very similar to that of the witness, though he could not remember where it was. The recurrent use of the term "quartzite" was odd and puzzling; geologists had long abandoned this identification for the rock in the Battle Mountain region. In the course of two hours' research that night, the engineer finally came upon an old report of a rough reconnaissance survey made in 1867 by Clarence King. The witness had used the language of this report, verbatim, in his testimony during the direct examination.

The possibilities this suggested must have come as a real shock to my father. He had known Boyle since their University of Nevada days more than fifteen years ago when he was a new arrival from the Carson Valley and Boyle was already a senior, brilliant enough to graduate at only twenty. Boyle had superintended the Esperanza mining operation in Mexico at an age when most young mining engineers were just beginning to work their way up, and his expert testimony was frequently requested in mining litigation throughout the Western states. My father had liked and admired him for years. Nonetheless, he had to pursue the track the discovery of the report had uncovered.

Why, George wondered, had the governor relied so heavily on the King report? Had his own examination been less thorough than he described? And if it needed bolstering, had he thought it wiser to use an old report, unfamiliar to modern engineers and unlikely to be recognized as another man's work? If George could prove that Boyle had only the scantiest knowledge of the mining property, then the governor's positive assertion that no vein had been uncovered prior to the arrival of the new claimants would quickly evaporate. The assertion was crucial to the case and devastating to my father's British client.

The cross-examination began promisingly but inconclusively. Under George's questioning, the governor admitted that the sample he had taken from the Copper Canyon dump could not fairly show the value of the vein; that claims assaying at $11.50, as did those of George's client, possessed commercial value; and that prospectors often located their claims on veins a mining engineer would turn down. Yet he continued to insist that the claim was "absolutely worthless," and at critical moments he was able to obscure what he was saying with the baffling technicalities and the knowledgeable generalities in which an expert witness tends to seek cover.

Still probing, my father turned to the matter of Weber quartzite—that was the term the governor had used to describe the prevailing formation on the claim, was it not? The governor confirmed it, and went on to casually mention that he was "indebted" to the old King survey for his ideas on the basic geology of the region. At that point my father must have permitted himself an interior smile; the full extent of the governor's debt to the King survey was a point he intended to explore in considerable detail.

Had the leading modern geologist who observed that the material described in the old reconnaissance survey was not quartzite at all made an error, he inquired? No, the geologist was probably right, but having examined a sample under a microscope, the governor believed it was quartzite. Inwardly my father wondered why the governor held so firmly to that telltale identification and concluded that he believed he was being questioned at random by an attorney who had no definite knowledge of the old report. My father continued to probe the subject of quartzite. The governor had used the term "altered quartzite"; could he cite any geologist who used that term? No? Well, perhaps he could explain what happened to quartzite when it altered? The changes were related to the aluminum in the Copper Canyon quartzite, said the governor, still exuding confidence and efficiency. My father inquired how the presence of aluminum was determined. The governor admitted he had taken it from someone else's report. When asked whether "you can not give that as a result of your own personal observations and experiments," he lamely replied that he could only do so in a general way because he knew Nevada quartzite contained a good deal of aluminum.

That was damaging enough to the witness, but my father meant to expose him beyond the shadow of a reasonable doubt. How had he determined the rock was Weber quartzite? The governor again cited the old report, an answer George emphasized with the pointed question: "When you say it is Weber quartzite, you simply say it was because King said so in his report?" To this the witness could only respond affirmatively. He found himself unable to recall any other geologist who had used the term.

My father now turned his attention to that microscope test. What had the governor seen when he put the sample under the microscope? He had seen "the almost microscopic angular structure of an altered sandstone, which is a quartzite." How could he distinguish the difference between quartz and aluminum in a microscope test? He confessed that it could not be done. How then did he positively know the rock was Weber quartzite?

"I didn't say that I did," said the witness, flushing scarlet. "I said that I think it is the Weber quartzite."

Still George pressed him further. "When you were examined on your direct," he said, moving in for the kill, "I understood you to say that it was positively Weber quartzite, but now you modify that and say that you think so because of Mr. King's observations and the slight test that you made?"

The governor turned pale, and the sweat burst out on his face. He stammered incoherently. At length he stuttered out the words George was waiting for, "Well, if I said positively at any time that any rock was a particular formation, I want it to be modified right now." With that tacit admission of perjury, the trap closed with a snap.

Although the governor's testimony was a shambles from this point forward, my father was not yet ready to dismiss him from the stand. Asked if he had found fossils in his samples, the governor displayed an embarrassing ignorance of the fact that fossils were characteristic of Weber quartzite. He found himself unable to say that volcanic intrusions from the east had not caused the Copper Canyon rock formations to dip westward and could frame no satisfactory reply to the question, "In fact, you have not made a careful enough geologic examination to determine these matters, have you?"

My father finally closed his cross-examination, satisfied that the expert witness's previous testimony had been razed to the ground. In this he was not wrong, but the human reality in the courtroom produced an unanticipated result. My father had gone too far, and he sensed it quickly. He had completely discredited the witness, but in the process, he had lost the jury—and the case. That day he learned something essential: never should an attorney press a witness too harshly, or the spectacle of his humiliation will arouse the jury's sympathies and none of the facts the attorney has labored to reveal will matter half so much as this.[5]

Although the governor's testimony was a minor scandal, it in no way interfered with his reelection three years later, for

Nevadans had never been prone to demand excessively high standards of conduct in their public officials. Nor did it alter the friendly feeling between the governor and my father. The British interests my father had represented eventually won their case on appeal. With the lesson of that disastrous day in court clearly in mind, George went on to become such a skillful cross-examiner that when other lawyers were involved in a difficult case they would often associate themselves with him for the sole purpose of having him conduct their cross-examinations. Although he was rather proud of that, he never exaggerated the importance of his courtroom skills in his professional life. He used to glance at the rows of well-worn law books that lined his office and tell me that 90 percent of a lawyer's time is spent with them.

* * *

He took just one prolonged leave of absence from his law books. As soon as America entered World War I, he was determined to be there and "see the excitement." When he began importuning every influential friend he had in Washington to secure an overseas commission in 1917, he was thirty-six, too old to be honor bound to serve; most of his friends thought his decision typically reckless. But he was the son of a proud hussar and the grandson of the shadowy Johann, who had fought his way homeward across the bloody snows of Russia; he could not stay home.

He told the army doctors who looked askance at his small, slight frame and asthmatically enlarged heart what were probably the only substantial lies of his life, lies having to do with cardiac hypertrophy, the effects of high altitude upon the size of the heart. A commission as a captain in the army and an overseas assignment were secured with the aid of two old Nevada acquaintances: Ray Baker, once the dirty trickster of the 1910 campaign and now the director of the United States

mint; and Tom Miller, who had returned to the East after his
sojourn in Nevada in 1910, when he managed Oddie's campaign, had just completed a term as congressman from Delaware, and was about to enlist himself.[6]

When he set forth as a courier carrying special messages from
Washington to General Pershing at Tours, George made the
journey on a German ocean liner that had been converted by
the American military. He made it his business to explore the
ship from top to bottom, and on the lower deck among stacks
of supplies, he discovered a large swimming pool left over from
the ship's more frivolous days. On the second or third night out,
George decided to take a swim. He was lightheartedly paddling
about in the nude when a German U-boat attack began and all
the lights abruptly went out. It was dark as a tomb, and the
depth charges the ship was dropping crashed like thunder. His
breath shortening, his arms turning leaden, George swam on
frantically in total darkness through a pool that suddenly
seemed as vast as the great ocean beyond. Surely, if he could
swim on only a little farther, he would strike the edge, but it
continued to elude him. He must have thrashed around and
around in panicky circles, punctuated by the ominous boom of
the explosives, like the tolling of a monstrous bell, until he was
certain his last moments had come. Instead of a kaleidoscope of
his past life, the one thought that entered his mind was, *at least
I'm going out of the world naked, the same way I came into it.* But
before his weakening arms gave way, the ship survived the
attack, the lights snapped on, the pool reverted to finite dimensions, and the swimmer belatedly reached the edge.

The voyage continued without incident until an American
ship burned at sea two nights later. Its troops, all blacks, were
transferred to George's ship. A strong wind was blowing that
night, and the swells rose to towering heights. George watched
the terrified men being "herded across the gangplank like
sheep," their eyes shining eerily in the darkness. Whenever one

panicked, lost his footing, and dropped into the black water, no attempt at rescue was made. Had the officers decided such efforts were useless, perhaps even dangerous, or were these men simply considered expendable? My father did not know the answer. Again, as when he had glimpsed the trampled miner in the Goldfield street, he found himself alone in an indifferent throng. Never before had he seen men die. That stormy night at sea he reached the war.

After delivering the messages from Washington to the American commander in France, George was stationed at Tours for two weeks. He spent every possible moment of that time with the lovely Marcelle Jumelon, a bilingual French secretary working at the army offices. She was "just like a doll," he used to say; she was petite, with dark hair, blue eyes, and a face that was perfect in every detail. On their last date, she confided that he was unique among the many American officers she had met because he was the only one who had failed to proposition her. "That," my mother used to interject with a touch of asperity when my father had taken to reminiscing about the lovely Marcelle, "was because she wondered what was wrong with you." My father would chuckle good-humoredly. After he was transferred to headquarters at Chaumont and from there to the ammunition service at the front lines, each mail delivery contained a stack of blue letters from Marcelle.

When my father reached the front in September, the Americans, nearly half a million strong, were preparing an assault on Saint-Mihiel, a position west of the Meuse River where the German sector cut sharply into the Allied lines. This first assignment for the American army as an independent unit was a quick success. Within two weeks of the victory at Saint-Mihiel, they would launch the massive Meuse-Argonne offensive. Against desperate German resistance from machine guns, artillery fortified in concrete, and deep lines of trenches behind barbed wire, they would fight their way through the thickly wooded hills, rocky slopes, and ravines of northwestern France to victory and the end of the war that had bled Europe for four years. The photographs in my father's album show glimpses of what he saw: a devastated landscape of rubble without a house or a tree left standing; the ruined French villages, thatch-roofed houses tumbled in, churches reduced to a wall or a few pillars of stone; the dead, crosses row after row, forlorn heaps of clothing, a white skull grinning from the tattered remnants of a German uniform.

On a beautiful moonlit night during the battle of Saint-Mihiel, George and some veterans from the first division were loading caissons in the ammunition dumps at the bottom of a narrow canyon. Hearing an airplane in the distance, they identified it as a German Fokker by its uneven rising and falling hum, which differed from the level murmur of the allied planes.

"Let's get in the dugouts!" yelled the veterans, running toward the sides of the canyon.

"No," said George, "I want to watch the son of a gun come over." Watch he did, and very soon he wished he had not. Shells whistled down and exploded all around him as the plane raked the ammunition dump. Some of the horses harnessed to the caissons just beside him were hit. He wanted to race for the dugouts, but his legs refused to obey. It seemed as though he too were harnessed where he stood. Glued, immobilized, rooted to the spot, he watched the plane wheel around to make a second pass over the dump. He could plainly see the pilot's face in the moonlight as he passed over no more than fifty feet above. When the Fokker droned away, the veterans scrambled out of the dugouts. Someone called to George, "You've got a lot of guts but no sense at all."

"It wasn't guts," said George a little shakily. "I was just too scared to move." He had only recently received a letter from his law partners announcing that he had been unceremoniously dropped from the firm because he was "such a rash damn fool" that they were certain he would be killed anyway. Just then in the canyon, he had to admit that their estimate of his character was not entirely in error.

Many long evenings were spent in the front-line dugouts, where the men used to pass the time by calculating how far behind them the American artillery was located by watching the flash of the guns, timing the number of seconds before the sound reached them, and figuring the speed of light and sound. Other nights were spent on the road, for as ordnance men it was their job to haul ammunition from the dumps by trucks and horse-drawn conveyances to the batteries and the infantry. There was something of the Conestoga wagon about these trucks, with their spoked wheels, their open, windowless cabs, and their arched, canvas-covered tops. In these, or in vehicles drawn by the mules my father labeled "comrades in service" in his photograph album, the ordnance men traveled, often under fire, usually by night, almost invariably in the rain, over roads churned into mud, camping where they could.

With George in charge, one of these ammunition convoys started forth from the canyon before sunrise in seven trucks. George told the drivers to stay fifty feet apart so all would not blow up if one was hit. As he jolted along in the first truck, he watched the shells exploding on the other wall of the canyon and wondered apprehensively how soon the German artillery would correct their range. Looking back, he was appalled to see the trucks crowded together bumper to bumper behind him. He jumped out and repeated his orders, but the panic-stricken drivers refused to separate. He had to raise his rifle and threaten to shoot them before they would space out their trucks.

George had been inexperienced that night when he stood out to watch the strafing of the ammunition dump, but new men were quickly turned into veterans under fire. As the armies moved on toward the plain of the Woevre, replacements arrived that were greener still. One day George was talking to some new men beside an ammunition dump of French seventy-fives. Suddenly an eight-inch German shell came sailing over and landed at their feet. Had it exploded, the ammunition dump would have blown up; instead it ploughed underground and came to the surface about seventy-five feet away. To George's horror, one of the new men came running proudly up to him a few minutes later with the shell "cradled in his arms like a baby." George instructed him to put it quickly and carefully down in the same position that he had found it because a change of position often caused the shells to explode. The group watched, breathless, intent, and frozen where they stood, while the recruit awkwardly lowered the shell safely to rest. My father no doubt had moments such as these in mind when he later wrote to a Nevada friend: "While no one ever told me I was frightened, I myself, deep inside, knew I was so badly scared that my hair lifted the helmet off my head. On such occasions, I covered by talking much and swearing more."

At Limey, George wandered across the now silent battlefield. There, at the beginning of the war, the French soldiers wearing their blue, red, and purple uniforms had marched into battle in neat lines a quarter mile apart as if they were going on parade. When the American forces reached Limey, fighting their way to Germany, the bodies of the French still lay unburied in their fancy uniforms. Hungry cats were still prowling over the battlefield. After the war my father was never able to look at a cat without a wave of revulsion, for he could not forget how often he had seen them prey upon the fallen soldiers.

The November armistice approached. My father wrote sadly home of the friends killed "in the last days and even hours of the war"; their sacrifice seemed "useless." For the last several days the offensive had gone on in "somewhat sporadic and desultory fashion," but during the final morning of the war came a "terrific barrage" that ended abruptly at 11:00.

The armies of the occupation moved forward toward Germany. Shivering in an open truck, George believed he had never been so cold in his life, not even on those Goldfield mornings when he used to waken under a snow-covered blanket. When the advancing forces crossed the border between France and Luxembourg and arrived at the city of Dudelange, he found to his pleasure that the few words of German he knew enabled him to talk a little with the pretty girls on the street. His superior officer, Colonel Prince, also noticed it.

"George," he said imperiously, "I see you speak German well. You talked to those girls. Go out and get me a good looking one."

"You go to hell," said George, so angry that his inferior rank no longer mattered. "Get your own women. I'm not a procurer for anyone." Remembering it more than forty years later, his blue eyes still blazed.

"Alright," said the colonel, "there will be no promotion for you." It was not the kind of promise the colonel was disposed to break. Many months would pass before George was promoted to major.

That rankled, but it was insignificant beside my father's pride in having been with the American army during an experience he later said he would not have missed for "anything in the world" and the pure pleasure of being out of the dugouts and still alive. "We can hardly realize the war is over. It is like a dream," he wrote his friend, like many a soldier before and since. "It is unreal that we do not hear the shells or bombs or machine guns. To think of it—no more will the rats crawl and scamper; no more filth and dirt; no more French itch; no more cooties. And when the other day, for the first time in four months, I slept in a real bed, between real sheets, instead of a dugout or a shell proof or in the open, I fancied I was home again."

It would be several months before he really was home again. Toward Christmas, they moved into Germany, where George was quartered for a time at Koblenz. The holidays brought a wistful awareness of the passing of time. The people "spend Christmas day here much the same as you used to spend yours when you were young and full of the joy of life and living," he wrote to his aging mother with no apparent sense that the similarities between her Westphalian ways and those of the Rhinelanders might be entirely unexpected. "The people here are very good—too good. We hardly know what to make of them and of the way they act toward us," he added with a note of surprise. They were supposed to be the enemy; this son of German immigrants, not yet one generation removed from the old country, had never thought of them in any other way.

Shortly after the war, when George had returned home, he was examining a witness in court and asked him the standard question, "Where were you born?"

"In Germany," the witness answered. There was a hostile murmur in the courtroom, for anti-German feeling was still very strong. The witness took note of this and added, with a crafty glance at the attorney, "Not far from vhere your own fadder vas born." Everyone, including my father, laughed heartily.

It was a connection that had to be pointed out by someone else. There was no hint during the war—or ever—that the German soldiers, whose burial mounds George had passed with "great satisfaction," thinking of his fallen American friends, were in any way his people; or that this land, where his cousins still worked the Westphalian earth not so many miles to the north, was in any way his own.

* * * * *

For Sallie Maria Ruperti, her own connection with Germany was clear enough. The difficulty lay in connecting the nice, young cousins with whom she had sung "Deutschland uber alles" among the rose trees at Eichenhof with the terrible Hun in spiked helmet on the posters at home in New York. When war was declared, her cousins had hastened home from Oxford to join the German army. They must be the Huns that horrified America. Still they bore no resemblance she could see to the poster's dark and monstrous silhouette, shown seizing a Belgian girl by her long, blonde hair before the flames of a burning city.

Sallie had been vacationing in Innsbruck with her family when the war broke out. At once her father began shepherding his flock toward Hamburg and the ship that would carry them back to America—but their progress was slow. They never knew in what remote wayside station their train would pause for the night, after being repeatedly shunted aside and halted each time the tracks were cleared for the military trains. Watching from the windows, the Ruperti girls lapsed into giggling fits from the excitement as the troop trains hurtled past with soldiers shouting and waving from the windows. Had they sensed their father's desperate haste to bring them safely out of Germany while there was still time, they would have wept instead of giggling at each successive delay, but he was calm and reserved as always. Years later Sallie would infer his urgency, though she never saw it in 1914.

When they passed through Munich, everyone was terrified that spies might have poisoned the water, and the Ruperti girls stared fearfully at the murky, green sediment swirling at the bottom of the water carafe on their table. They were forbidden to drink water, even after Munich was well behind them. Little by little, they made their way toward the sea and the sanctuary beyond—America. All the influence the merchant princes of Hamburg could muster had been used to secure something they would have scorned only two weeks before but was infinitely precious now: a set of cabins specially built next to the boiler room in the steerage section of a Dutch ship waiting in the harbor.

* * * * *

The new year 1919 brought George a warm dispute with Marcelle, who had turned against President Wilson because he opposed the destruction and enslavement of Germany that the embittered French were now demanding. She began to criticize the president severely in her letters. Although he realized that the French were becoming overwhelmingly anti-Wilson, George reprimanded her rather stiffly, writing that he did not "believe you should criticize the president of the United States or the government for their views" and adding that he "would never think of saying such things about Clemenceau." Their exchanges over this issue grew increasingly bitter. How like my father it was to quarrel with his sweetheart over political affairs. What mattered her blue eyes and perfect, doll-like face if she impugned the wisdom of President Wilson; what mattered his good humor and his gallant ways if his views on the peace treaty were hopelessly idealistic; what mattered youth, beauty, love, and the well-remembered summer evenings of 1918 if politics were not in accord. The day arrived when there were no more blue letters at mail call.

While they were stationed at Koblenz, my father wanted to hear the famous nightingales that sang in a forest not far away, so he and some friends organized a trip to the spot. After a party that had lasted throughout the night, they arrived at the place during the hour just before dawn when the nightingales were said to sing most beautifully. It was much as he had hoped it might be—the sky lightening and turning faintly rosy; the soft, leaf-scented earth; the little brown birds, invisible somewhere in the trees, pouring forth pure, silvery trills of unearthly loveliness. But it was ruined by his rowdy companions, shouting, joking, drinking, and screeching with laughter. My father was wholeheartedly angry with them. There would be many other parties, much laughter, many other women to caress, but he would never hear another nightingale.

* * *

From Koblenz George was transferred to a desolate area where only scrubby bushes grew, desolate enough for the job at hand—the destruction of German ammunition, much of which had been captured by the Germans from the French, British, and Russians. Photographs from my father's album show him and his friends posing with self-conscious bravado among 38 CM Russian shells not much smaller than themselves, or contemplating shells stacked in cordwood rows, or strolling like farmers in a melon patch among the globular shapes that litter the ground. Beyond lies a flat, barren, snow-encrusted plain; overhead, a clouded, sullen sky, broken only by the tall, black smokestack of the Espagit ammunition plant. My father thought it the most dismal place he had ever known and yearned to be done with it.

A concrete building three hundred feet long with an alley down the middle and small cells on each side had been constructed for the demolition work. Every hour it was George's duty to walk down the alley and check the cells, each of which contained a German bomb expert dismantling bombs and shells, some of them three feet high and over a foot in diameter. Every hour, every day, week after week he walked it, yet I doubt that those inspections ever became entirely routine. That same mathematically inclined corner of his mind that had figured the distance of the cannons by light and sound would also take note of the very small statistical probability that these stacks of deadly explosives could all be dismantled without incident. And they were not. One day George had just com-

George Springmeyer (right) stands beside Thomas Miller; photograph probably taken in Paris when they were helping to organize the American Legion.

pleted his tour and walked on some forty yards beyond the
building when one of the demolition men made a fatal error.
Three or four sections of the building blew out, and legs, arms,
heads, and bodies rained to the ground in one of the ghastliest
scenes George had witnessed during the entire war.

When the demolition work had been completed, Captain
Springmeyer was sent back to the states, over six months after
the war's end. He was more than ready to return. He had plain-
tively written "And when shall I get back?" across a copy of a
song he noted was "the most popular in the army of occupation." It ran in part:

Darling, I am coming back,
Silver threads among the black.
Now that peace in Europe nears,
I'll be back in seven years.
Once I thought by now I'd be
Sailing home across the sea,
Back to where you sit and pine,
But I am stuck here on the Rhine.
You can hear the gang all curse,
"War is hell but peace is worse."

Not long after George reached Nevada, a letter from Germany arrived, which he brought to his father to decipher. To
his surprise, H.H. glanced at the letter, then leaned back in his
chair and roared with laughter.

"This is from a German girl," he said. "She says you were
quartered at her father's house in Koblenz. She says she wants
to come and be your wife, or if that won't do, your mistress, or
as a last resort, your maid. You must," he added with a chuckle,
"have been a pretty lively young fellow."

In reality, George's relationship with the girl had been somewhat less intimate than his father supposed. She was a beauty,

but he had only seen her from a distance and never spoken to her. Though he might have preferred more flattering suppositions, he was forced to conclude that this was a form letter dispatched to every American soldier whose name she had been able to learn.

My father settled down in Reno without a bride, a mistress, or a maid but with various other memorabilia from the great war. There were his army knife and fork, with which he always ate his meals on Saturdays and Sundays; a certificate pronouncing him free of lice and venereal disease; a bronze star; a scrapbook his men had made for him with orders dated November 11 and marked "Secret: Hostile Situation at Beginning of Day"; maps of Germany with the positions of the American divisions marked in black and blue and brown and yellow inks; carefully hand ruled ammunition tables; large maps in intricate detail with wavering lines of tiny crosses and waves and dots on thick crackling beige paper (they had been found in the German trenches north of Limey); secret instructions to officers in which they are warned that military necessity "admits of deception but disclaims acts of perfidy"; and finally the big metal army trunk with the blue and white stripe that must have passed through all those bloody battlefields on the map before coming to rest at last, many years later, beside his bed in Long Valley.

Fast Mixing

"**G**.O.P. PRIMARY ELECTION Ends in Fist Fight. Platt and Springmeyer Settle Differences Before Large Crowd. Mayor Stops Battle. Former Army Captain Proves to Be Fast Mixer in Contest with Attorney," read the headlines.[1] My father was home from the war and once again in the midst of a political fray. However, the battle with Sam Platt in Reno's fanciest cafe was only the most widely publicized of several violent encounters in which he had been involved after his return. Ironically, he had emerged from the Argonne Forest without a scratch, but he would not be so fortunate in the streets of Reno.

The first encounter was a simple matter of revenge. George was walking down the east side of Center Street one afternoon after making a reservation at the railroad station for a trip he planned to make to California. Nothing was farther from his mind at that moment than George Gibson, whom he had prosecuted nearly a decade ago in Goldfield. When Gibson was released on parole several years before, the police had warned him to leave Reno; next he was dispatched from Tonopah by the police of that city after he pulled a knife in a saloon fight; finally, he was provided with a ticket to Tecopa and forcibly led to the train by the Goldfield sheriff.[2] But Nevada had not seen the last of him. Once, hoping for early parole, he had said he would set aside all hard feelings against the prosecutor and go back East after his release. He had done neither. Now the heat was off, and George Gibson was back in Nevada.

As my father strolled down the street toward his office, he encountered some friends from Goldfield. "For Christ's sake, George, look out!" they warned him. "George Gibson's out. He's looking for you, and he says he's going to get you. You'd better duck into a doorway. There he is now!"

George looked across the street. His eyes met the cold eyes of George Gibson, who was standing there watching him. Within a split second, he decided his only chance was to confront the man immediately. He walked briskly across the street to Gibson and said, "I hear you're looking for me. Here I am."

Gibson's eyes never wavered, the expression on his somewhat catlike features did not alter; still he was obviously nonplussed. He had probably expected hiding, cringing, a hasty dash, frantic pleas, perhaps abject terror, but not this.

"Yes, I've been looking for you," he said, "and I was going to shoot you the first chance I got, but I see you've got guts and here you are, so let's forget about it." He could kill a stranger in a drunken brawl, lie to a judge, break an oath, beat a quarrelsome woman, or pull the trigger at a sheriff, but he could not murder an unarmed man who had walked calmly across the street to confront him. In his own way, George Gibson had principles. The two shook hands.

* * *

There followed two tales of two anonymous gunmen, who briefly interjected themselves into my father's life while he was largely preoccupied with a legal-custody battle for a client. These episodes, each unrelated to the other, unrolled during a five-day period with all the confusion and jerky speed of the

Keystone cops in action. My father first appeared in newspaper headlines trailing an armed burglar who had broken into his office building on a chase that led through the streets of Reno, down the railroad tracks, and around the Southern Pacific depot while another lawyer summoned the police.

For most members of the bench and bar, that chase would provide sufficient excitement for the year 1920, and perhaps for the entire decade to come. Within days, however, an effort to bring the custody case to a quick and favorable conclusion sent him speeding across the Sierra in a car with his client and other parties, while their opponents followed close behind. The pursuer's car was temporarily delayed by an early snowfall, and by the time the two groups finally met in the streets of Auburn on the California side of the mountains in a grand brawl involving lawyers, clients and cab drivers, George had already returned to Reno, where he arrived in time to get shot.[3]

He had gone to a movie to relax awhile, then walked home to his apartment at the Colonial Hotel. As he passed the entrance of the building, a man stepped from behind a curtain, poked an automatic against his back, and said, "Put up your hands or I'll shoot." George—characteristically—refused and pushed him aside with his right arm. The man shot him in the leg and ran into the alley behind the hotel.

It was widely whispered throughout Reno that the bachelor lawyer had actually encountered an irate husband instead of the clean-shaven gunman neatly dressed in a dark suit that George had described to the police; indeed he was speedily compelled to issue a public denial that he was protecting his real assailant. "If I had any idea who shot me," he told the press, "I would do either one of two things. I would either kill him or report him immediately to the authorities."[4]

There was one person in Reno who believed him—and possibly not many more than one. Three months later, when the wound had healed, a waitress from the Grand Cafe came to see

George in his office and said in a rush, "I knew you weren't lying. I knew you were really held up by a stick up man because he was *my* man. He was a Chicago gangster on his way to California, where he was going to send for me. He came in that night, and he said, 'I've taught one damn fool a lesson. He'll know enough to stick up his hands the next time someone tells him to.' He was afraid he'd get caught, so I gave him what money I had, and he went. But all I ever heard from him was that he'd held up someone in a railroad underpass.

"He never sent for me," she concluded bitterly, "so I want you to get him." The woman also told her story to the chief of police, but efforts to arrest her man were fruitless.[5]

* * *

Like my father, George Wingfield had deserted Goldfield for Reno. If the description of Wingfield once penned by an enemy was too harsh when he was young, it had gained in applicability with the passage of the years. "Of stinted, meager frame, his was the extreme pallor that denoted ill health, years of hardship, or vicious habits," wrote George Graham Rice. "His eyes were watery, his look vacillating. Uncouth, cold of manner, and taciturn of disposition, he was the last man whom an observer would readily imagine to be the possessor of abilities of a superior order. In and around the camp, he was noted for secretiveness. He was rated a cool, calculating, selfish, surething gambler-man-of-affairs—the kind who uses the backstairs, never trusts anybody, is willing to wait a long time to accomplish a set purpose, keeps his mouth closed, and does not allow trifling scruples to stand in the way of final encompassment."[6]

In addition to these qualities of character and physique, Wingfield retained two persistent habits. While he sat thinking, his son informs us, he used to "shuffle silver dollars from stack to stack" so they always came out even.[7] Those ceaseless, effortless movements of his hands were the telltale habit of an

ex-gambler. More than that, however, they symbolized the
man, for silver dollars, and the getting and spending thereof,
were apparently Wingfield's major preoccupation. Although he
was less well armed these days than in Goldfield—Bernard
Baruch used to tell about a time during the troubles with the
IWW when he saw Wingfield carrying no less than five revolv-
ers[8]—he was still in the habit of wearing a six-shooter in his
belt on the left side. It was said that he needed it for self-
protection in the company he kept. Also he derived a curious
pleasure from pulling it on other men. Often, while he was
talking to a man, he would suddenly whip out the gun and jab
it in the other's stomach. He apparently did it to see the effect
—most people turned white. At the golf club after a few drinks,
he once shoved his gun in the midriff of a prominent divorce
seeker, and the man both turned white and fainted. (It occurs
to me that the "prominent Nevadan" Cleve Baker dreamed had
shot him in the stomach just before he hemorrhaged and died
was probably Wingfield.)

Two or three times a week Wingfield would pull this stunt
on George, evidently because it never produced the reaction he
expected. One day when he dug the gun into George's stomach,
George suddenly turned the muzzle and shoved it into Wingfield. "George, that thing might go off," he said to George
Wingfield, "and if it does, I'd rather have it poking in your belly
than in mine." Wingfield never jabbed his gun at George again.

When Wingfield really intended to get a man, he used more
subtle methods than the gun. During the developing power
struggle within the Nevada Republican party, he and George
would effectively suppress the challenge mounted by Sam Platt,
the former national committeeman and two-time senatorial
candidate. Why my father, who rarely disliked anyone, felt
such profound antipathy toward Platt is still unclear to me,
although I am familiar enough with the way he regarded most
of the politicians of the day.

At the top were the "crackerjacks" like Theodore Roosevelt and Denver Dickerson. If he called you a crackerjack, he admired you because he thought you were brilliant, honest, charismatic, humane, and a good deal more besides. Below the crackerjacks was a large area of in-between types, followed by the descending circles of a Dantean inferno. On the first level were "rogues" and "rascals"; that meant he knew you were unscrupulous but liked you anyway. George Wingfield was a rather special kind of rogue. Unscrupulous certainly, but one of the Goldfield crowd, and for this my father liked him. Then came "stuffed shirts," a category for individuals who were not very bright and took themselves much too seriously but had some redeeming features. Tasker Oddie was one of these.

Next came the "cranks." Pat McCarran was widely regarded as such, not only by my father and Wingfield, but also by most of the political elite of the period. There had always been something strange and repellent about McCarran; as one student who had attended the university with him remarked, "He was rather peculiar, and no one liked him much." Faced with the problem of how to dispose of this queer but persistent office seeker, the political leadership decided to get rid of him by sticking him on the state supreme court in 1912, a decision that reveals even more about their opinion of the court than it does about their estimate of McCarran. Their intent may have been evident even to McCarran himself. "There is no place on earth that constitutes so fine a political burying ground, as the bench," he wrote many years later. "That's where men are really buried politically."[9] But the leadership found itself unable to tolerate him even in this position. His bids for higher office were firmly quashed, and he was defeated in his campaign for reelection in 1918.

However, in 1932 the crank would emerge from his prolonged dormant state, affix himself to the United States Senate, produce such monumental legislative achievements as the

McCarran-Walter Immigration Act, and, in time, acquire luster from the persistent popular illusion that the occupants of great offices must also be great men. Hubris would set in. It had been a standard joke in Nevada that every time McCarran was scheduled to make a speech a crowd of bill collectors would gather at the bottom of the platform to await his arrival. In later years, the bill collectors would no longer dare to present their claims, for McCarran had come to regard Nevada as a sort of feudal domain in which the lesser gentry owed their liege lord not only homage and fealty but also service, whenever he was pleased to be entertained by them. My father would look on with some amazement when a Fallon hotel keeper who had the temerity to present the senator with a bill was greeted with a tempest of rage. This, then, was one of the better-known cranks.

On the lowest level of my father's Dantean inferno were the "sons of bitches," which referred to those who were in full possession of their faculties and had no redeeming features whatsoever. That rather summed up George's attitude toward Platt. Perhaps the source of his aversion lay in an unmentioned wound beneath the lighthearted image of Tina, George's first wife, as the gypsy queen wearing all her jewelry at once—Platt had been Tina's attorney in the divorce and also in the suit George had brought to be permitted to see their little daughter. When he was once allowed to visit the child just before shipping out with the army from the East Coast in World War I and she no longer knew him, the wound was visible enough. I don't think the scars of that meeting and the realization that his daughter was irretrievably lost to him ever entirely healed. But a man as scrupulously fair as my father would probably have bent over backward not to dislike Sam Platt for any reason connected with Tina and the divorce. Those who knew both men say it was simply a case of "I do not like thee, Dr. Fell, the reason why I can not tell."

The reasons why Wingfield detested Platt were a little easier to tell. If Wingfield had a political credo at all, it was his conviction that whatever was good for the Wingfield financial enterprises was good for Nevada. His prejudices, whenever they surfaced, were conservative (feminist hearts had fluttered apprehensively when he expressed opposition to woman suffrage during the 1914 referendum). Wealth and leadership had failed to enlarge his vision. He championed no leader; he cared for no cause; he retained to the end the narrow squint of the small-time gambler he had originally been, and that squint was unblinkingly affixed upon his accumulating stacks of silver dollars.

Aside from these paramount financial aims, Wingfield enjoyed making other men do his bidding. He saw politics as a means to secure his business empire, reward his friends, and punish his enemies; and if that is a poor synonym for ideology, it is a fairly good working definition of power. His friendship, insofar as his icy blood could be said to warm to that emotional level, was bestowed upon the men he had known in Goldfield, with whom he felt a kind of bond. Platt, although every bit as conservative as himself, was not one of his friends and stood in the way of his control of the Republican party.

When Platt was elected speaker of the state assembly in 1904, the first notable step in his political rise, Wingfield was still evolving from the Peely Kid to the Napoleon of Nevada finance. Wingfield's overriding concern at that time was making money, and the realization that protecting the prerogatives of his enterprises required political involvement remained several years in the future. Although Platt was only two years older than Wingfield, he was one of those men who always seemed old, even when young. He had attached himself to a group of stodgy old men, the diehards who served as the keepers of the emasculated remnants of the Republican party during the nineties while their less loyal brethren, George Nixon and William Stewart among them, temporarily deserted to the Silver party. These stalwarts, under whose tutelage Platt took his first political steps, lacked the panache of the Comstockers before them and of the Goldfield crowd that succeeded them. And Platt, their protégé, would forever seem one of this transitional group of dull graybeards. If the opportunism so evident in many of the Goldfield crowd was missing in Platt, so was their adventurousness, their rough-and-tumble good spirits, and their bonhomie. He had not shared their experience; he had not gone to Goldfield. Whom you knew and what crowd you belonged to had always been a matter of paramount importance in Nevada politics. Some say it still is.

Under the headline "An Impudent Campaign," the *Goldfield Daily Tribune* accused Platt of "thrusting personal ambition forward" and "attempting to build a personal or factional machine." His reported wish to be a delegate to the national convention was harmless enough. Even his senatorial ambitions were permissible, at least in those election years when he could not be expected to defeat Key Pittman. But his aspiration to be elected national committeeman with all the attendant powers within the party organization was unacceptable.[10] Although the Goldfield *Tribune* did not say so, there was an unannounced candidate for the post, who was engaged in building a personal or factional machine of his own—George Wingfield. On the eve of the Republican convention, Wingfield issued a statement to the press announcing that "it seems high time that the Republican party of this state be united," and adding in tones of judicious regret, "If it is necessary to eliminate Mr. Platt, he must be eliminated."[11]

That was what he said publicly. In private, he phrased it rather differently, and he had already taken steps during the preconvention period to ensure that Platt's elimination would be accomplished. On the evening of the Washoe County primary at which delegates were being chosen for the state convention, he hurriedly sought out George at Kane's Cafe, where he was having dinner with a lady friend.

"The Jews at city hall are counting us out," said Wingfield, whose crude prejudices were never far below the surface. "They're putting through a slate of delegates supporting Platt. You must go at once."

George was happy to oblige. He had already been quietly working with Frank Norcross against Platt, and he knew it was inappropriate for Wingfield to go himself, because he intended to be the next national committeeman. With a polite farewell to his pretty companion, George set off for city hall, where the delegates were being chosen by open ballot at a meeting in which both Republicans and Democrats were permitted to vote. The Platt group was attempting to pass out marked ballots. Shouldering his way through a large crowd that seemed to include all Platt's friends, George made certain that no more ballots cast in favor of the slate of delegates supporting General Leonard Wood, the contender he favored for the Republican presidential nomination, were counted in favor of Platt's slate.

Most of the delegates supported by George and Wingfield won;[12] when the slate had been certified by the election clerks, Platt said loudly, "It was only by Wingfield's side's crooked work, stuffing the ballot box, that they got chosen. Springmeyer was one of the crooks."

After listening to a good deal more of this, George finally said, "You're joking, aren't you?"

"Not by any means," said Platt. "You all did crooked work."

"If you mean that," George said, "let's have it out right here." Although Platt was considerably taller and heavier than George, he backed away so that George could not reach him. "Let's go outside where you have no women's skirts to hide behind," suggested George.

"I wouldn't dirty my hands on a dirty crook like you," said Platt, making washing motions with his hands.

"Alright," said George, as Platt edged away to a safer distance. "I'll catch you someday when you have no women's skirts to hide behind."

That day was not long in arriving. George was walking into Kane's Cafe for lunch when he ran into Platt and his partner. George took Platt by the shoulder and said, "Now you apologize for what you called me at that meeting the other night."

"It was all true," said Platt stubbornly. At that point, George landed a hard right to his face. Despite the fact that Platt's partner was swinging from his coattails and two other men had grabbed his arms, George succeeded in blackening both Platt's eyes and breaking his nose before Mayor Stewart and several volunteer peacemakers managed to restrain him. The mayor good-humoredly declared that no decision could be awarded because both lawyers were still on their feet at the finish, but a boxing promoter present at the scene remarked that he would much rather sign George than Platt.

There were no further encounters with Platt, but his Amazonian wife remained determined to avenge the family honor. An outstanding golfer, she would maneuver to a position one hole behind George on the golf course and aim her drives at him; on several occasions, she even attempted to run him down on street corners with her car.

Finally, after one too many of Mrs. Platt's powerful balls had whistled past, dangerously close to his ears, George remarked to a mutual friend, "You tell Sam Platt and his wife that the next time she tries to hit me with her car or her golf ball, I'll take it out of Sam's hide and give him another licking." This brought an immediate end to Mrs. Platt's persecutions.[13] When the Republican convention met, George Wingfield was elected national committeeman by acclamation.

From that vantage point, Wingfield addressed himself to the task of making one of the Goldfield crowd's favorite members, Tasker Oddie, a U.S. senator. Because 1920 was shaping up as a banner year for the Republicans, the winner of the primary could be fairly confident of victory in the general election. That the winner would be Oddie was far from certain; the ex-governor had lost the last two elections in which he had contended. Although my father never indicated to me that he had played an important part in the ensuing campaign, others believed his influence proved crucial. Not only was he still a power in the Republican party, but also many former Progressives and old opponents of the Southern Pacific still looked to him for leadership. These reform-minded Republicans were the natural constituency for Brewster Adams, the minister and civic leader who was Oddie's opponent in the primary. When my father's support swung the reform vote to his old friend Tasker Oddie, Adams blamed his defeat upon my father, and his resentment would smoulder for many years to come. Oddie, on the other hand, came out of the election owing a great deal to him, although my father would not have thought of it that way. He would have said he supported Oddie because he was the better man and there were no debts between friends.

In fact, his assistance in the race for senator was only a minor matter to him (though not to Oddie). His major efforts were exerted on behalf of General Wood's campaign for the presidency. He was chairman of the Nevada General Wood League, and although he was not a delegate, he attended the notorious national convention of 1920 as Nevada manager for Wood. Why he favored Wood he never said, beyond an offhanded remark that "all the veterans were for him." Yet it is easy to see that Wood was my father's kind of candidate. Since Theodore Roosevelt's death the year before, the general had emerged as the heir apparent for Roosevelt's supporters and as anathema to the old guard. He was a man of such uncompromising probity that he refused to make any deal with the regular politicians to secure the nomination. The bribery of delegates was summarily rejected; the emissary who offered fifty crucial Southwestern delegates in return for choosing the secretary of the interior and the ambassador to Mexico was cursed and ejected from his room; Boss Penrose's suggestion that his support was available at the price of three cabinet members would not even be discussed. In consequence, Warren Harding emerged from the now legendary "smoke-filled room" as the convention's nominee.[14]

In the meantime, my father was somewhat surprised to encounter George Sunday, son of the famous evangelist, in charge of distributing liquor on General Wood's behalf at the convention. For years the elder Sunday had been electrifying audiences with his famous Chautauqua lecture entitled "Booze, or get on the Water Wagon" and had been stomping up and down the length and breadth of the land declaring at revival meetings: "I have sworn eternal and everlasting enmity to the liquor traffic: as long as I have a foot, I'll kick it; as long as I have a fist, I'll hit it; as long as I have a tooth, I'll bite it; as long as I have a head, I'll butt it; and when I'm old, and gray and bootless, and toothless, I'll gum it till I go to heaven and it goes to hell."[15]

Young Sunday's views on demon rum were evidently more tolerant than those of his celebrated father, and George frequently had occasion to obtain bottled goods from him with which to ply the Nevada delegation, hoping they would desist from splitting their votes in ballot after ballot and cast a solid six for General Wood.

Finally, Sunday said to George in some exasperation, "What are these goddamn miners and ranchers? There's only a dozen of 'em, but I have to give you more liquor than I give the big delegations!"

My father laughed wholeheartedly. In 1920 he was still free to do so, but within a few years antagonistic Nevada newspaper editors would be featuring headlines like "Who Rustled Booze at Chicago Convention?" Although he would not be obliged to kick, bite, butt, and gum the bootleggers like Billy Sunday, he would nonetheless be an officer charged with the thankless task of enforcing the eighteenth amendment to the best of his ability.

The Storm Petrel

On a bitterly cold night in 1922 shortly before Christmas, Federal Prohibition Agents Nick Carter and Pete Dubois hid in the willows a short distance from the house on the Raine Ranch near Palisade in central Nevada. It was a dark and isolated spot, where low hills humped like sleeping beasts lay along the horizon and night blackened the winter ruddiness of the bushes around them. Above the sweet, herbal fragrance of willows another more significant redolence could be detected. The government trapper who tipped them off had made no mistake. They could smell the pungent odor of fermentation wafting from the dugout nearby.

Certain preparations had preceded their surreptitious arrival. They had arranged for Raine to receive a phone call warning him that Carlin Kitty had tipped off the feds, they would be at his ranch by daylight, and he better "dump that stuff in the willows." The agents did not have long to wait. Around midmight Raine and his sidekick arrived on horseback. As they proceeded to the dugout where the incriminating barrels were concealed, Carter and Dubois stepped out with their guns in hand and told Raine he was under arrest. Shots were fired, and

Nick Carter fell, mortally wounded. Dubois lifted him to his shoulders and carried him to the spot where the car was waiting half a mile away. On Christmas day he died.[1]

Nick was my father's friend. Ever since he became United States attorney, George had admired Nick as a "crack agent." In the beginning it was Nick who had shown him the ropes, Nick who had brought word that a raid was in order in Silver City and urged George to come along. George had agreed, and a search warrant was sworn out. Then George and Nick drove off together through the Virginia Range to their destination, a cluster of shacks crowded together at the foot of a steep canyon near the high, rocky parapet of Devil's Gate. Silver City was experiencing a brief mining boom and several hundred miners were working in the area. On this Saturday night three saloons were doing a roaring business. Nick selected the Combination Bar and cautioned George, "Now follow me and do exactly as I do."

The two entered and squeezed their way through the crowd of miners and women. George watched while Nick put his hands on the bar, leaped over with practiced grace, scuffled briefly with the bartenders, and seized some bottles before they disappeared. Rather more slowly and awkwardly, George also jumped over and began pasting stickers on bottles. To the gentlemen of the press, who were somewhat startled by a United States attorney who personally raided a bar, he observed that it had been an educational experience.[2] Nick had laughed about that.

Now he was dead. Whether Nick Carter believed in the misbegotten temperance law that occasioned his death, I cannot say, but I know my father did not. He thought Prohibition was a disaster. When requested in 1925 to give his views to a congressional committee investigating the liquor traffic, he told them "open and flagrant violations, disrespect of and contempt for the government, bribery and corruption of officials, favored and protected violators and offenders, and the desire by people in general and the rising generation in particular to experience the thrills of the forbidden jackass" would continue under the existing system. Prohibition should be changed "regardless of the shock it may entail to the virtuous and sanctimonious." The change he favored was government manufacture and sale of liquor, the so-called "Canadian plan" that was being much discussed in those days.

In the meantime, the law, be it "good or bad, popular or unpopular," should be enforced, not broken or ignored, least of all by those whose responsibility it was to uphold it. In no other way could American institutions be "respected, much less revered."[3] Enforcement could spur change; feeble laxity could only foster lawlessness. He stood for the law, as he always had. It was his way to make total commitments without exceptions or ambiguities. His devotion, once given, was complete; his loyalty, unswerving. He stood with Nick and the others, a handful of men who planned and strove and fought and sometimes died in the daily battle of wits against those who would subvert it, and could stand nowhere in between.

* * *

George was appointed United States attorney in the spring of 1922. He later said Wingfield "approved my request" for the position. Of course it could never have been granted without Wingfield's approval. George's predecessor in the office, Bill Woodburn, had been Wingfield's close associate of many years, and his successor would be handpicked by Wingfield for the job. Senator Tasker Oddie, George's nominal sponsor, called George's quest for the post a "hard battle" involving "severe strains and annoyances," among them, a personal call paid to President Harding by Sam Platt for the purpose of protesting against George's appointment.[4] But all this was inconsequential if Wingfield approved.

He did not do so immediately. Recollections of the Rawhide graft trial, the great case of the People versus the Southern Pacific, and the criminal indictments of the Pittsburgh Silver Peak officials in the face of his expressed displeasure may have aroused certain reservations. Tom Miller later recalled that Wingfield was originally unenthusiastic about the prospect of George Springmeyer as United States attorney, though he eventually allowed himself to be persuaded. Miller was then unquestionably at his most persuasive. He had directed the Republican national campaign in 1920, and he enjoyed both intimate acquaintance with the president and widespread popularity among the veterans, who connected him with the American Legion, of which he had been one of the original incorporators. (My father, another Legion activist, had prepared the congressional bill incorporating the organization, had assisted in drafting the War Service Education Act, and had helped found the Nevada post, but he later turned away from the organization in disillusionment with its ultraconservative political views.) Miller's recent appointment to the desirable bureaucratic position of Alien Property Custodian was another sign of the president's high regard.[5]

So Wingfield probably listened a little more than was his custom to this confidant of the high and the mighty, and to the other old friends from Goldfield who spoke up for George, and finally he came around. Although George Wingfield well knew that my father was neither as pliable as Oddie nor as closely in accord with him as Bill Woodburn, he accepted George as one of the "old Goldfield crowd." They had been friends for years, would remain so long after George left the United States attorney's office, and Wingfield had always enjoyed rewarding his friends. He was never in a better position to do so than in the twenties, when the shadowy bipartisan political machine he headed was at the height of its power and the old Goldfield crowd and their friends from Tonopah dominated the political scene.

It was ironic that Goldfield was mirrored so clearly in the politics of this period. The city was rapidly becoming a ghost town, and a decade or more had passed since the adventurous young men who flocked there in the boom days had abandoned her. Still, Goldfield had defined a political generation. Like the veterans of a great war, having been together set these men forever apart. The dominating figure in politics during the twenties was, of course, George Wingfield himself. Key Pittman and Tasker Oddie, both of Tonopah, were Nevada's United States senators. George's old roommate, Jack Diskin, became Nevada attorney general in 1922. Maurice Sullivan, once a Goldfield businessman, was lieutenant governor. John Sanders, he of the large white handkerchief, was a Nevada supreme court justice. The former sheriff of Tonopah, Ed Malley, was state treasurer, at least until shortages of more than half a million dollars in state funds were uncovered. Fred Balzar, the railroad conductor whose political fortunes George had pushed forward in the county convention of 1908, was elected governor in 1926. Jack Donnelley, once a storekeeper and deputy sheriff in Goldfield, was Nevada director of Prohibition. And my father was United States attorney.

Surveying his domain sometime after he took office, George noted wryly, "If Nevada is dry, then the Pacific Ocean is a desert." And the task of enforcing Prohibition grew more difficult with every passing year. Throughout the United States, the flood tide of fervent wartime morality that had swept the issue into the Constitution was rapidly ebbing, and speakeasies were sprouting up everywhere. By 1931 their number was estimated at 500,000, a figure well in excess of the number of saloons in the Bad Old Days. Nevada was believed to contain 750 bootleggers running liquor in about 150 autos—cars like Fritz Elges's powerful Hudson Super Six, for the former leader of the Uber lynch mob was now a prosperous bootlegger with a cigar perpetually tilted between his teeth. Seventy-five speakeasies, some of them advertised as "soft drink parlors," were said to be operating on two Reno streets alone. East Douglas Alley was lined with solid, dark, brick buildings devoid of names or numbers and known as "pillboxes." Everyone knew what was being served inside.[6]

It was the age when denatured alcohol was described as "America's new national beverage," and determined drinkers were recklessly consuming a variety of noxious brews that ranged in their effects from unsettling to fatal and were composed of ingredients that didn't bear thinking about. In Pittsburgh, they drank "administration booze," an evil-smelling beverage on which green scum often developed; Chicago swilled "yack yack bourbon," heavily laced with burned sugar and iodine; Alabama gulped "shinney," distilled from molasses and water and brewed in zinc garbage cans; Philadelphians sipped "happy Sally" and "soda pop moon," both packed with extremely toxic industrial alcohols; denizens of Oklahoma City desperately imbibed "jake," a medical preparation of Jamaica ginger formerly used in small quantities for stomachache, and 300 of them were paralyzed in consequence; Virginians downed "panther whiskey" loaded with fusel oil; Californians gulped "jackass" brandy compounded from rotten fruits, the fermentation of which was hastened with lye.

Not exactly the beer that made Milwaukee famous, but no one was particular anymore. Reported deaths from alcohol poisoning throughout the nation totaled 11,700 in 1927, and the following year more than 700 died in the Bowery alone, where the lower dives often served wood alcohol and men sometimes drank rubbing alcohol compounds.[7]

In Nevada they drank "jackass" or "moon" or "white mule," paid $80 a case wholesale for the stuff, and complained that it tasted like "liquid barbed wire." The more reckless drank canned heat, flavored with raspberry soda, or the cocktail popular among the Elko Indians, carbolic acid mixed with denatured alcohol. A suspiciously high number of fatalities were reported in White Pine County, and a Virginia City man expired, apparently as a result of drinking "fruit juice" in a "disorderly house" where 300 gallons of wine in barrels were subsequently discovered in the basement. Making fruit juice was permitted by the Volstead Act; of course the juice pressed from grapes, cherries, currants, dandelions, and all the rest had a way of evolving into wine. After contemplating the unfortunate gentleman's remains, the coroner's jury reported that "we shrink in horror" from the manner in which liquor is sold by those with government permits to manufacture "fruit juice."[8]

While most of the manufacturing was done in garages and cellars, one enterprising Carson Valley rancher constructed an elaborate subterranean distillery beneath a boulder in his feed corral. Once brewed, Nevada jackass had to be stored. It began turning up in the oddest places; in haystacks, in clothes baskets, or in barrels submerged in the river. And it sometimes had the oddest effects. After a jackass bender, one man became convinced he was a horse and altered his eating and living habits accordingly. He was not to be dissuaded from hitching himself to a wheelbarrow and setting off on a two-mile trot—the stuff was not called "jackass" for nothing.

At times this potent brew developed into a highly combustible mixture. The cork blew from a confiscated bottle in the Prohibition director's safe with a noise like a shotgun blast; fires believed to have originated in stills ravaged Goldfield; and in the Sierra west of Washoe Valley, a raging forest fire that started from an exploding still devastated Slide Mountain. Nonetheless, by the standards of the period, Nevada jackass was apparently pretty high-quality stuff.

Politicians and public officials were scarcely more enthusiastic about Prohibition than the determinedly drinking public. One crusader after another took office bristling with determination to bust the bootleggers only to give up shortly afterward in despair. One cocktail party followed another on the Wash-

ington social circuit. One bribery scandal after another involving bootleggers and Prohibition officers or police was reported
in the press. The attorney general was obliged to remove the
United States attorney in New Jersey from office as a result of
his failure to enforce the law. President Coolidge, appearing at
the governors' conference, found it necessary to remind those
present that "when laws have been made, there is and can be
no question as to the duty of executives to enforce them."

If official apathy and collusion were on the increase throughout the nation, they were rising even faster in Nevada, where
Prohibition had been a feeble and belated transplant from the
very beginning. Prior to the acceptance of a Prohibition initiative petition by a landslide vote in 1918 when the national
amendment was already pending, the liquor question had been
conspicuously absent. During earlier years, while the Midwest
was racked with titanic battles between the wets and drys, the
burning, emotional issue of the age was nearly invisible in
Nevada. A legislative novice who had introduced a Prohibition
measure in the 1911 session hurriedly attempted to withdraw
it, explaining apologetically that he hadn't realized the preceding session had informally agreed to restrict gambling and leave
Prohibition alone.[9] Nothing happened. The drys did not rise in
their wrath and destroy. Indeed no one seemed to notice. Then,
as before and after, it was extremely difficult for the boys at the
bar in the Northern to work up much sweat over this bizarre
and alien manifestation of Yankee morality. *The Moonshine
Trail,* a drama featuring Cynthia of the Hills, a Kentucky
maiden "stricken with tragedy because her father and brother
had paid the penalty of illicit liquor making" and her lover was
"tainted with a hereditary strain—the lust for moonshine in his
blood," was hopefully advertised by the Carson City Theater
in 1920 as "the photoplay of the hour." But the prospector who
the press reported had walked eighty miles for a drink of whis-

key when his supplies ran out prematurely was decidedly more Nevada's style.

By the time George took office in 1922, the retreat from the lofty pinnacles of morality and patriotism to which the voters had thoughtlessly clambered four years earlier was rapidly becoming a stampede. The first step in George's effort to stay the rout was a massive publicity blitz intended to win cooperation from the public and state and local officials. When the grand jury convened in October, George asked them to consider the problem of Prohibition enforcement in Nevada. Their report, made public with considerable fanfare in January, contained several specific recommendations and concluded that enforcement of Prohibition in Nevada was a "failure," indeed many had come to regard it as a "joke."[10]

It was an assessment with which few could disagree. Drys charged that there had been fewer than thirty arrests in three years under state Prohibition laws. Editors noted that Prohibition "is not being enforced in any city or town in the state that we know of"; juries were unwilling to convict, "even in the face of indisputable evidence"; and the people "don't care."[11]

So it seemed, and yet my father in his heart of hearts still retained the classic Progressive faith in the people. Surely they would neither condone systematic lawbreaking nor tolerate local politicians who flouted the Constitution itself. Rational men would choose the sensible course and obey a law, even though they opposed it, until it was repealed. Surely, if they only knew what was going on, they would do the right thing. He meant to see that they knew. Other Nevada U.S. attorneys had been quiet, unobtrusive figures; this one would be headline news.

Next came an all-out effort to secure better cooperation from local officials. George dispatched a public letter urging them to act in concert with federal authorities, to hire additional Prohibition officers, and to enact a "little Volstead Act" as a county ordinance in those counties where such regulations were not already on the books.[12] To Reno's Mayor Stewart, he wrote: "Bootleggers are becoming more and more cunning and resort to so many ruses in the battle of matching wits with officers that there should be a police force of adequate size." He noted pointedly that "sporadic arrests are so few as to result in unjust charges that certain persons and certain places are receiving protection." The chairman of the board of county commissioners in this locality, where no arrests under state Prohibition laws had been reported in recent memory, replied that such an undertaking would involve considerable expense.

In White Pine County the request provoked an observation from one of the county commissioners that "not one man in ten wants to see the saloons closed," a candid acknowledgement from the sheriff that closing the saloons would result in "forty or fifty bootleggers peddling from the hip, which would be a much more difficult situation to control." From the district attorney came an even more candid suggestion that "some should be controlled and unofficially allowed to run." No one bothered to deny that the saloons were in full swing.[13]

Such was the response to improved cooperation. Never disheartened, George turned to the next step in the drive for better enforcement, an effort to sharpen up every possible legal weapon within reach. Thus far, criminal prosecutions had failed to deter offenders, and "more drastic steps" were in order. A wave of civil abatement suits to close establishments where liquor was being sold would follow. This would relieve the crowded criminal docket, and the loss of rental income would provide landlords tempted by the high rents the bootleggers were willing to pay with a financial incentive to reject such tenants. When the places reopened, which would be none too soon, their windows must be "uncurtained and open to the public gaze." Some thirty-two abatement cases, bitterly contested by the offending parties, were set for trial in western

Nevada alone, and several early successes were hopefully announced.

In the legislative arena, George launched a major effort to alter state laws in accordance with the grand jury recommendations. The state's Prohibition law had frequently been criticized on the ground that it could not be enforced because it was too drastic, even more severe than the Volstead Act, which at least permitted liquor sales for medicinal and chemical purposes. Very well, if that was the problem—or the excuse—let the law be changed. George urged this course upon the governor in a public letter and took an active part in drafting new legislation repealing the old measures, substituting an adaption of the Volstead Act based upon California's Wright Law, and creating a state Prohibition agency with six agents and a total appropriation of about $54,000. He was roundly denounced in the press for his "unprecedented and extraordinary" demands and his attempts to "bulldoze state authorities"; what state and local authorities did or did not do, the editors declared, was "none of Mr. Springmeyer's business."[14]

Nullification of existing laws was the only aspect of this program that Nevada politicians seized upon with enthusiasm. Repeal legislation, unattached to any substitute Prohibition law, whipped through the legislature with dizzying speed and was enacted over the governor's veto by heavy majorities. The accompanying debate clearly suggested that the question uppermost in the legislators' minds was not the merits of various alternative Prohibition laws but the desirability of any law at all. This, however, was not openly stated; rather, it was obliquely suggested during the tangential exchanges on "economy," the banner beneath which the advancing legions of the wets were marching.

Editors, compelled to reply in kind, argued that Nevada owed much to the federal largesse she had received through reclamation, highway construction, and the Pittman Silver Act; Washington might look far less benevolently upon a state that was blatantly uncooperative in enforcing federal law. Friendly legislators protested that the eighteenth amendment was not an "economy question," nor one to be rejected because it was "unprofitable." But the horrifying descriptions of communities "debauched" by liquor, of drink sold to the young in alleys and "dark places," and the pleas to "do something for the children" that had roused the public to such a fever pitch in 1918 were suddenly dated and less moving than an exhortation to "Remember the Alamo."[15] The tone of the debate had been set by State Senator Scott, the author of the repeal bills. "The federal government owns 90 per cent of the lands in Nevada and it must do its just share of policing this empire. It is the logical agency for the major effort," he declared.[16] His meaning was plain enough: Washington had their constitutional amendment, albeit one that Nevada had readily ratified; let Washington try to enforce it.

The triumph of the wets was briefly modified when the law adopting the Volstead Act, stripped, of course, of that extravagant provision for a state enforcement agency with six agents, passed the legislature. Within months it had been declared unconstitutional. Although Prohibition legislation would again be introduced in the 1925 session—with the sponsor apologetically explaining that he was not a "reformer or uplifter" but felt obliged to point out that the only states in the entire union without Prohibition acts were Nevada and New York—the 1923 bill was the last Prohibition law that would ever be passed in Nevada.[17]

Henceforth the responsibility for enforcing the eighteenth amendment would rest upon a tiny force: the federal Prohibition department in Nevada consisted of six agents, occasionally assisted by "flying squads" of outside officers on special assignment. The beat of each of these six men was equivalent to

15,000 square miles of land containing 12,000 people.[18] The federal court, already clotted with cases, would be the only tribunal in which these offenses could be tried. In August 1922 George had announced that he and his lone assistant would be prosecuting 121 cases, most of them Prohibition violations, during the forthcoming session of the federal court; 85 more defendants were scheduled to arrive from outlying districts. And that was only the beginning.[19]

* * *

Although George was compelled to spend altogether too much time on Prohibition, other cases provided an occasional change of pace. Decidedly the most peculiar of these was the affair involving J. E. Sexton, the owner of the Eureka and Palisade narrow-gauge railroad known as "The Slim Princess." Sexton's one-man war against the government had started several years previously when the postmaster general ordered him to carry mail at a certain rate. He simply locked up the Slim Princess and went fishing until Washington agreed to his price. But the government was in no hurry to pay him, and Sexton, in common with most railroad operators, was compelled to carry mail under the deferred payment system. For years he sent in bills without receiving any payment. Finally Sexton grew fed up with waiting on those "detached warts" and "damned liars" in Washington. He wrote to the postmaster general threatening that unless he was paid by a certain date he would send the Japanese ambassador in Washington and the Japanese consul in San Francisco pictures of a boxcar upon which he had painted in large letters, "This car reserved for exclusive use dogs and Japanese." Copies would also be distributed in Japan. Believing that "the japs are very touchy" and that being classed with dogs was the greatest insult conceivable to the Japanese mind, Sexton confidently anticipated that "the Secretary of State is about the only bird in Washington who will trot through red tape like an elephant through a spider web." A small international incident might get him started.

The postmaster general wrote that no funds to pay the troublesome Sexton were available and asked George to prosecute the man. He did not, however, mention for what; George could find no statute applicable to boxcar graffiti. He replied that he must refuse to prosecute and suggested that Sexton should instead be promptly paid. He was.[20]

Another less comic problem involving railroads arose in the summer of 1922 when the national union of railroad shopmen refused to accept a second cut in wages recommended by the government Railroad Labor Board and went on strike. Because the locomotive engineers and the other railroad brotherhoods had not joined the striking shop workers, the trains continued to run. The railroads responded to the strike with a lockout and rejected President Harding's plea to reinstate the strikers on the terms proposed by the board. Sporadic violence ensued, and public opinion shifted against the strikers when a passenger train was stranded in the California desert for several days in 113-degree heat. The president was warmly applauded for a speech before Congress in which he declared his resolve to "use the power of the government to maintain transportation." On the first of September the attorney general secured a sweeping injunction against the strikers. The unions vainly protested that the closed-shop issue in which the attorney general perceived "the death knell of liberty" was outside the province of government.

While this drama was being played out to its inevitable conclusion, George was under heavy pressure from the railroads to prosecute strikers in Nevada. Nearly a month before the government injunction suit, railroad officials had written directly to Attorney General Daugherty, charging that federal officials in Nevada had refused to enforce the injunctions the railroads had

obtained against the strikers and demanding that the attorney
general should immediately direct them to discharge their "duties." George did not include union busting for the railroad
among his duties. He had a strong sense of his office as a public
one in the fullest sense of the word, dedicated to equality before
the law and intended to protect the rights of the silent and the
downtrodden as fully as those of the rich and the powerful. He
had been instructed to prosecute only violations of federal law,
and no amount of heavy-handed pressure from the railroads
could compel him to deviate from those instructions. He dispatched a wire to Daugherty advising him that railroad reports
of horrific events in Nevada were "hysterical" and "greatly
exaggerated." The federal marshal and the governor had ini-
tially been nervous and inclined to overreact. My father was
not. He knew the men. And knew the railroads.

After the September 1 injunction was issued, he announced
that his office would maintain a "hands off policy." The injunction had originated "from conditions east of the Mississippi and
Nevada will not be involved." He knew the situation was sensitive—a special assistant to the attorney general had been assigned to the West to investigate violations; the Southern
Pacific had hired 250 extra guards, most of them deployed at
bridges and water tanks; and eight men had just been convicted
in California for plotting to tie up the trains—but in Nevada
little violence had actually occurred, apart from a fist fight in the
Caliente post office. George reported to the attorney general's
special assistant that conditions within his jurisdiction were
entirely "satisfactory."

As the pressure mounted, George decided to make it absolutely clear that he had no intention of doing "police duty" for
the railroads. After a conference with union representatives, he
dispatched a public letter to the chairman of the Nevada Fed-
erated Shop Crafts assuring the strikers that "this office does
not enforce injunctions secured by railroads against strikers."

Suits against the railroads for violations of federal law would be prosecuted with "precisely the same spirit and vigor" as suits against strikers, and the unions were invited to present him with evidence of violations of federal laws by the railroads. He concluded by complimenting the men upon the "singular orderliness" with which the strike had been conducted.

This extraordinary declaration must have been received by the president of the Nevada local in Sparks with a measure of incredulity. The attorney general had accused the strikers of attempting to "dictate to the government" and had threatened that "the government will destroy the unions." The opening statement by the prosecution in the government injunction suit had described union violence and intimidation as "the filthiest record that ever stained a court." Down at union headquarters they were unaccustomed to evenhanded treatment from governmental authorities.

At the executive offices of the railroads, the United States attorney's public letter was probably read with mounting fury. This burst into the open in court some three weeks later when the Union Pacific attorney accused George of "favoring strikers by his attitude." During the prolonged and heated exchange that followed, George indignantly denied the charge. He believed he had done no more than accord the union the same legal rights the railroad had always presumed were theirs as a matter of course.

This explosive hearing was in reality an effort to compel George to file criminal proceedings against several strikers, a course of action he had been resisting for some time. The railroad attorneys could, if they chose, bring civil contempt proceedings to enforce the Union Pacific injunction and could initiate criminal suits in the state courts, but he was not going to harass the union for them. Under court order a limited number of prosecutions were started. However, George announced at the same time that he was filing several suits against the

Western Pacific for violations of the federal safety appliances act and had already requested the Interstate Commerce Commission (ICC) to investigate serious complaints against the railroads in Nevada.

Although the United States attorney for Nevada declined to assist them, the railroads had many other weapons to bring the strikers to their knees, and the full weight of the Harding administration was behind them. Railroad officials "introduced" tame unions to maintain "a mutually harmonious relationship" unsullied by troublesome demands from the workers. In the end, the union was totally defeated.[21]

* * * * *

In the same spring that George became United States attorney, Sallie Maria Ruperti was formally introduced to New York society at a coming-out party in the Rose Room of the Plaza Hotel. It was the next foreordained stage in the life of a young lady gently raised from her birth in the Rupertis' two conjoined brownstone houses on Manhattan's East Seventy-Second Street, cushioned in a domestic world replete with governesses, a tutor, and servants for everything—even a maid who had no other function than the laundering of the ladies' personal linen. I doubt that Sallie Maria's mother had ever ventured into the kitchen, or even had the vaguest idea what went on in that menial domain. She simply chose menus and, at intervals, decreed a soufflé as the test of a new cook. Most of her time was spent in entertaining and paying calls, the chief occupation of ladies in her social circle.

Their style of life had undergone little visible change since the war, though Justus Ruperti's business had been placed in receivership and his partner interned by the government. He showed no sign of anxiety or distress, but Sallie knew he must have lost a great deal of money. He had found it necessary to sell their beloved country place at Sterlington. Eichenhof had also been sold after the war, and their summers were no longer spent in Germany.

The photograph of Sallie's graduation in 1922 from Miss Chapin's exclusive school for young ladies shows a bevy of girls in white dresses, each wearing a single strand of pearls. She is still the dark swan, the one with hair arranged in smooth, black wings amidst all those blonde and curly heads, the one whose cool, sophisticated glance sets her apart from the naive and girlish faces around her. Seeing that dark beauty in the photograph, one does not need to be told why gentlemen callers knocked so frequently at the door of the Ruperti home.

* * * * *

In Nevada the effort to enforce Prohibition continued. A story about the preceding United States attorney was then going the rounds. That gentleman was said to have remarked at a luncheon that Nevada's largest still was being protected by a sheriff; immediately he had been deluged with letters from sheriffs all over the state inquiring, "Do you mean me?" Possibly an apocryphal tale, but by no means an implausible one. All the same, George kept trying to spur the local authorities into action.

Public letters were circulated to the sheriffs and district attorneys advising them of their powers to act, even in the absence of a state Prohibition law. Sheriffs could still arrest individuals for selling liquor without a license—if sheriffs were so disposed. District attorneys could still abate speakeasies as common nuisances—if district attorneys were so disposed. Should the legal work seem too burdensome, the United States attorney would undertake the prosecutions, if they would only secure the evidence and make the arrests. Local officials would not. As the press noted, the response to Springmeyer's appeals "has been anything but spontaneous."[22]

My father usually reacted to difficulties, however formidable, with a quotation from Napoleon: "Impossible is the adjective of fools." It was an adjective he was not yet ready to apply to the task before him. In a final effort to secure cooperation from these recalcitrant officials, he asked his old friend Governor Scrugham to call a law enforcement conference of district attorneys, sheriffs, and chiefs of police from all over the state. The conference was well attended, although when the possibility of sending the mayor to the conference at the state capital some 300 miles west was raised at an Ely city council meeting, the councilmen declared that the mayor would "find the walking fairly good." It was astonishing how economy-minded local officials suddenly became when Prohibition issues were raised.

An anonymous wag circulated a proposed program for the conference which included a lecture on "Monopolies Among Municipal Stills" by the White Pine County sheriff and a rendition of "Drink to Me Only with Thine Eyes" by the Reno police chief. It also featured a comic skit on "My Enforcement Program" by the Virginia City sheriff and a diatribe by "the storm petrel" (that is, the United States attorney), from which "no offense should be taken though some may be intended."

The actual conference would be about as lively and hardly more productive. It began platitudinously enough with vague statements by the governor on the need for cooperation with federal officials, although no suggestion was made that they should act under the legal authority still at their command or press for stronger statutory weapons. It dragged on in the same vein, as Prohibition Director Donnelley described the difficulties of policing so vast a territory with so small a staff of men. Then came the anticipated "fireworks." Before the conference convened, the press had been predicting that George was setting out "loaded for bear." As usual, they would not be disappointed.[23]

George charged several district attorneys with turning their backs on Prohibition. Some had even defended bootleggers in court. Names were named. He inquired "if it is any wonder that bootleggers are active when the district attorneys behave in that manner?" The district attorneys protested that they were being scolded, that they had been misquoted, and that the recent publication by the United States attorney of a letter from one of them requesting him to "lift the lid a little" was a violation of confidentiality. George replied rather sharply that his office was a public one with "nothing confidential about it."

The conference adjourned with no visible alteration in the apathy of most officials toward Prohibition. What had my father hoped to accomplish by excoriating them in public? It was, first of all, thoroughly in character. He had always believed in standing up vocally, publicly, and vehemently for what he thought was right, and ever since the campaign of 1910 he had been doing just that. Crushed by an overwhelming burden of cases and aided by a mere handful of federal agents, an appeal to public opinion and an effort to remind these recalcitrant officials of their duties to the law were his only options. That they did not take those duties as seriously as he did was a fact of life he probably found difficult to believe. Although he had always opposed Prohibition, he never questioned his duty to defend it.

As the dry conference adjourned in a round of vacuous compliments, my father once more turned his attention toward the press of legal business at his office and toward a misjudgment of his own that rankled a good deal more than the apathy of local officials. Using the evidence Nick Carter had given his life to obtain, George's assistants had just finished prosecuting Robert Raine, but the case was only an inconsequential sequel to the shooting in the willows on that winter's night. When Raine stood trial for Carter's murder seven months before in

Eureka County, George's assistant, Charles Cantwell, had begged to go in George's place to assist the Eureka County district attorney, and his argument was a persuasive one. Having formerly practiced in the area and served as district attorney of Lander County near Palisade, Cantwell believed that his many friends on the scene and his intimate knowledge of the region would be great assets in the trial. Although George knew Cantwell was not an outstanding lawyer, he thought local connections would probably weigh more heavily in Eureka County.

There was no sign that the case would be a difficult one. Apart from the officers and the unarmed government trapper, only two men had been present at the dugout—Raine and his sidekick, Brite. Dubois was prepared to testify that Nick had been shot by the man on horseback. This could only be Raine, since Brite had dismounted and entered the still before the gunfire began. Raine did not attempt to implicate Brite, and Brite had already charged Raine with the shooting in his confession. The evidence against Raine could hardly have been more conclusive. Besides, as the second attempt to shoot a Prohibition agent within the span of a year, the killing had aroused a storm of indignation in the press. The *Nevada State Journal*'s vehement attack on "cowardly criminals who would greedily grab bloodstained gold" was widely echoed by newspapers throughout the state. No one was prepared to condone murder, and it seemed as though, for once, the prosecutors would not need to contend with the popular prejudice on behalf of the bootleggers that made every jury trial a precarious undertaking.

George agreed to send Cantwell, but despite the best efforts of Cantwell and the local district attorney, Raine was found not guilty. It was a stinging defeat in an open-and-shut case, and as long as he lived my father would wonder if he might, somehow, have turned the tide where they had failed.

That November in Carson City George saw Raine convicted of manufacturing liquor, but it was a very small consolation to him and a very slight discomfiture to Raine. My father was not without vindictiveness—he liked winning, loved justice even more, and he had wanted to see the man he never doubted for a moment had murdered Nick receive his just desserts.[24] The decisions he made as United States attorney would bring him torrents of abuse from the press and threats of death from local gangsters, and would finally set him at odds with old friends, but turning the Raine case over to Cantwell was the only decision he ever regretted.

15

Cunning Ruses

PAST AGED, SAGGING cottonwood trees that grew on either side of the lane and mingled in a low and leafy arch above it, my father rode into Fallon, a small farming town in the Lahontan Valley sixty-five miles east of Reno. He was collecting evidence for the government suit to settle the water rights on the Carson and Walker rivers. The issues in the case were both technical and complex, and several days were required to obtain the records, question the projects engineer, and examine the channels and ditches. One evening George thought he would "take a walk around the town." In Fallon this was not an ambitious undertaking, and a brief stroll along the dusty, unpaved streets past stores with wooden front porches brought him to the little, white courthouse with the peak-roofed, colonnaded facade. The only oddity that had caught his eye along the way was a large assemblage of idlers lounging about by the street. Greeting the courthouse janitor, he pointed to a brick edifice across the street, and asked, "What is that building over there where all those men are sitting around?"

"That's Springmeyer's Sanitorium," said the janitor, unaware of the stranger's identity.

"Why is it called Springmeyer's Sanitorium?" asked George curiously.

"Well, you know George Springmeyer, the United States attorney?" said the janitor. George nodded. "He keeps the jails in Carson City and Reno and Minden full of Prohibitioners, so lately they've been sending the men down to the Fallon jail. Government pays us well for them, too. That's why we call it Springmeyer's Sanitorium."

"Is that right?" said George. It was true that it had been necessary to place federal prisoners in local jails to serve out their six months for Prohibition violations because there was no federal prison in Nevada. True too that the prison population was burgeoning during George's third year in office as total criminal convictions rose to nearly triple the number recorded during the last year of his predecessor's regime.

"Yep," chuckled the janitor, "it's a great joke on Springmeyer. He and the judge think the prisoners are being kept in jail, but they're just like free men. They sleep and eat on Uncle Sam, and the sheriff lets 'em out in the day time to do anything they like."

George laughed heartily. "Isn't that a good one on Springmeyer?" he said.

"By gosh," said the janitor, "it's the great joke of the town." The two laughed and joked together, and George refrained from spoiling the fun by telling the janitor who he was, though he later curtailed it considerably by bringing contempt proceedings against the sheriff.

In court Sheriff Crane admitted that he used to go to the movies with his charges and allow them to roam about the Fallon shops and pool halls by day, although he absolutely denied joining in their poker games, the stakes being entirely too high. He bore no grudge against George for bringing legal action against him, and whenever the two met on the streets of Reno, they had a good laugh about Springmeyer's Sanitorium.

Although the feds kept Springmeyer's Sanitorium solidly booked, their successes brought them no respite, for plenty of bootleggers remained at large. A bizarre assortment of devices figured in the ongoing struggle: disguises, medicines, lodge pins, button and flash mechanisms, secret cabinets in hotel walls that opened at a tap, hollow stairs with boards that tipped up when the supplies within were desired (and sometimes when they were not), specially constructed sinks with hollow legs in which bottles could be concealed, sob stories calculated to wring the most jaded heart, and, of course, every subterfuge, technicality, and delaying tactic the circuitous legal brains retained by the bootleggers could devise. But if the bootleggers were crafty, so were the feds. And sometimes more so.

A man in a brown suit, accompanied by a lady posing as his wife, registered in an Ely hotel. He allowed it to be known that he was an ex-preacher interested in purchasing a rooming house to provide a little income for his declining years and, as an ingenious crowning touch of authenticity, displayed an Elks pin to gain the confidence of the men he would shortly arrest. His credentials established, he proceeded to confide that he needed whiskey for his sick wife but could not go down to the red-light district to purchase it "on account of my family." His newfound friends appreciated the delicacy of his position, indeed they hastened to minister to his needs. The innocuous old gentleman did not quail in the resulting stampede of bootleggers. He only smiled and thanked them kindly and asked for more.

By the time the preacher and his ailing wife departed, they were prepared to testify against forty-five bootleggers. Although the evidence against thirty-seven of them proved insufficient because only a single purchase had been made from each, eight were arrested on federal indictments. The sheriff observed that it was "a hard proposition" to arrest his old friends. The distasteful deed was done as painlessly as possible at an affair described in the press as "a merry gathering, full of laughter and fun" in the sheriff's office.[1]

By the fall of 1922 certain "medicines," including a popular brand of bitters containing 50 percent alcohol, were so much in demand that they were being sold in soft-drink parlors and grocery stores as well as drugstores. One individual under surveillance was observed to purchase a bottle of medicine a day. Following a conference with the United States attorney, the manufacturer agreed that his potent patent remedy would henceforth be confined to drugstores, and George warned that grocers who rang it up with the flour and restauranteurs who served it with the coffee would henceforth be subject to prosecution.

If manufacturing bay rum and other medicines was profitable, not manufacturing them could be even more so. An eastern bootlegger named Pinkinson arrived in Reno for a divorce and, recognizing the land of opportunity when he saw it, remained to transform himself into the Malba Chemical Company and obtain a government permit allotting him 488 gallons of precious alcohol for the production of chemical compounds. The Malba Chemical Company? When federal agents went to inspect the plant, there was no Malba Chemical Company to be seen. Confronted with this embarrassing circumstance, Pinkinson explained that he had used the alcohol to concoct green soap and bay rum in his garage. Eventually, even Pinkinson admitted this tale was rather absurd. Perjury charges and a $300 fine ensued. Pinkinson had certain consolations nonetheless: it was estimated that he had cleared nearly $40,000 on the jackass brewed from his consignment of alcohol.

The bootleggers obligingly provided an impromptu demonstration of the button and flash for George's enlightenment one evening when he was returning home with several agents after trying some cases in the federal district court in Carson City. It was a more eventful journey then than now because cars generally proceeded through the Carson streets with a band of barking, snapping dogs in pursuit, and cattle were turned loose to graze on the Reno-Carson road. Numerous accidents had occurred, more to the detriment of cars than cows, and many sudden halts and sharp swerves were necessary to avoid the bovine shapes that loomed up suddenly out of the darkness. They had reached Reno and were driving past a Center Street hotel when one of the agents impulsively asked George, "Like to see how the button and flash work?"

George replied that he would, so the party started to enter the soft-drink bar in the hotel. So rapidly did the ensuing scene unfold that the man who blinked would miss the better part of it. Before you could say "jackass," the man behind the bar pressed a button, a light in the rear room flashed on, a face appeared at the small window, and the light went off. By the time they reached the room at the rear, water was running in the sink, a large pitcher was being flushed, and there was a distinct odor of corn whiskey.

After the "prohis" raided Tonopah's Big Casino Cabaret, the defense attorneys scouted around for a defect in the evidence and hit upon the issue of human fallibility. When the key witness for the prosecution testified that he had "several months experience" in testing beer and "knew the taste of it," the defense objected that his opinion was inconclusive because he had failed to test the beer with an ebullioscope. Does a man know when he's drinking a beer? Two years went by before this portentous matter had been fully weighed, examined, and explicated in all its aspects. Never mind the ebullioscope, the judges of the circuit court of appeals ultimately declared with firm finality: "The opinion of one who is long familiar with the taste of beer and who has had experience in testing it may be competent upon the question."[2] The Big Casino succumbed to the padlock.

Although the Ritter case presented a certain tactical variety, the defense was relying upon the human factor, not an absent ebullioscope. Even when George was in college, Ritter's "steam beer" had been a local specialty; by the twenties Ritter was operating a "soft-drink" saloon in Bowers's Mansion, a stolid relic of Comstock wealth and glory located in Washoe Valley south of Reno. On summer evenings flappers with their hair styled in the new King Tut bob would crowd to the outdoor dance platform with their dates, but in winter business was much slower. One chilly day in came the prohis, including agent Tom Scott, a towering hulk of a man whose innocent baby face invariably disarmed the suspicions of nervous bartenders. Shivering, shaking, and complaining of the cold, Tom and his companions said they needed some good stiff drinks to warm them up. After perfunctory denials that he was engaged in any such business, Ritter repaired to the second-story room where he kept two jugs and a funnel and produced the drinks. Later on, after the ice had been broken, so to speak, the agents returned and bought drinks without any preliminary rituals concerning the cold weather.[3] When the case came before the grand jury, George was surprised to hear Ritter's attorney ask permission for his client to testify.

Ritter took the stand and said tearfully, "Yes, gentlemen, I sold whiskey and I had whiskey in my possession, but please, please let me off and I'll never do it again!"

After this attempt to throw himself on the sympathy of the grand jury had failed, Ritter reversed his tactics. Before the trial jury, he denied his previous confession and produced a string of witnesses primed to provide sterling testimonials to his character. These George rather neatly discredited when they insisted Ritter had never conducted saloons on Sierra Street and in the Chophouse on Commercial Row; George then brought out the point that Ritter had conducted these saloons legitimately before Prohibition was enacted.

When this latest gambit also failed, Ritter appealed to a higher court on grounds of entrapment; Charlie Norcross, slated to become Donnelley's assistant director of Prohibition, appealed to George on grounds of friendship. Both appeals were denied, and Ritter became a trusty at the Reno jail. Whenever Ritter and George met on the street in later years, Ritter, grinding his dentures, would return George's jovial greeting with a wordless glare. Nearly a decade would pass before my father and Charlie Norcross were again on speaking terms.

In Elko on a chill November Monday local spirits were warmed by the appearance of a harbinger of good fortune—"Head Oil Driller McFadden" and his crew from the "Prairie Oil and Gas Company" had made their appearance in town. In joyous anticipation of the coming boom in the oil fields McFadden claimed were being discovered nearby, the doors of the Elko speakeasies swung open and their best brew was served up to entertain this important personage and his jovial band. Not until two days had passed did someone realize that head driller McFadden looked vaguely familiar. Alas, too late he was recognized as a member of the Prohibition squad that had recently raided Elko and made twenty-seven arrests.

McFadden and the old preacher were masters of disguise, but the same could not be said of the agent who tried to deck himself out in a false mustache as a rancher. Somehow he did not look like a rancher at all, only like an agent with a phoney mustache. Before he could buy a single glass of moon, every blind pig on Douglas Alley was wise to him. He trudged ineffectually from one club to another, followed by an uninvited audience of twenty curious onlookers, until finally he gave it up and ripped off his false mustache in disgust.

In these and other exploits, the agents well knew that the public was rooting for the bootleggers. And sometimes they did more than cheer. When the agents roared off in their car with several prisoners after a Virginia City raid, they did not roar far before the tires blew out. Horseshoe nails had been driven into them. At a Genoa dance they were compelled to fight a pitched battle with revelers wielding bottles and ax handles. Down among the willows by the river in Reno in the area known as "the jungle" because narcotics addicts habitually gathered there, a suspected informer for the prohis had to make a long dash from the spot where he had concealed himself to the comparative safety of his hotel with an angry mob at his heels. And when the annual order for the destruction of all the confiscated liquor on hand was pronounced in the courthouse, thirty mourners congregated in the adjacent alley and groaned.

It was as much as a man's life was worth to inquire whether a stranger at the bar in Silver City was a "Prohibition son of a bitch." Being called a "son of a bitch" might rile a man slightly, but a "*Prohibition* son of a bitch" was an insult no one worth a shot glass of genuine Nevada white mule could ignore. Talk like that could get a man killed—and at least once, it did.

The more practiced the feds became, the more clever were the bootleggers at caching their stores. The state was riddled with abandoned mines offering ideal concealment for stills. An elaborate operation had been uncovered in the old Wedekind near Reno, and another was spotted in a mine tunnel near Washoe Lake. Curiously, it might have passed unnoticed had the owner been less anxiety prone. He carefully transplanted some sagebrush to camouflage the mouth of the tunnel. Sagebrush, although ready enough to thrive when uninvited, prefers to advance at its own pace. It all died, and the incongruity of that pocket of dead brush in the sage-covered hills immediately attracted the attention of the prohis.

The feds won that round, and they won another when a large cache of liquor was unearthed (unrocked?) in a rock pile west of Huffakers. But it cannot have given them much satisfaction to consider just how many other stony outcroppings remained to be searched in the state of Nevada.

The more adept the agents became with ax and sledgehammer, the more impregnable grew the pillboxes. Indeed one was appropriately named The Fortress. A crack agent was not so called for nothing. He could demolish a massive door with two strokes of an ax, and he had to be quick because there were usually three or more doors to smash in before reaching the bar. Sometimes, of course, the ax at the door was in the nature of a diversion: while signal lights in Reno's Louvre Bar flashed and agents chopped at the door with something less than their usual vigor, another agent was making his entrance through the transom. Occasionally, there was a door it was foolhardy to handle too roughly. In the course of investigating the abundant supplies of wine stored in a Reno cellar, the agents found themselves face to face with a shotgun rigged up with pulleys and ropes and aimed toward the entrance. And sometimes they encountered a door they could not dent. When they knocked over the Log Cabin down in the jungle, the door refused to yield to their sledgehammers. So they bashed in the walls.

Such doings only served to impress the bootleggers with the necessity for sounder construction. Soon a "veritable fortress" with brick walls two feet thick and barred windows and doors was going up in a Reno alley, and agents wearily expressed the opinion that nothing short of a battering ram could breach it. Even this massive pillbox was less formidable than a well-known Sparks resort with stone walls eighteen inches thick, a ten-inch concrete roof, and steel-barred windows. Where aesthetics were concerned, it left something to be desired, but even the agents had to admit it was "stronger than any cell in the state."

* * *

Of bootleg jackass there was altogether too much, and of water there was never enough. In the twenties, as before and since, litigation over water rights remained a constant in Nevada courtrooms. George looked forward to the Washoe Lake and Galena Creek case as a welcome change from the unremitting pressure of Prohibition. However, his anticipation proved unfounded. The opposing attorney, Prince Hawkins, was Tennessee born, a pleasant Southern gentleman of much civility, who boasted that he had never accepted a criminal case. In keeping with the leisurely traditions of his youth, Hawkins's exposition crept forward, when it did not congeal entirely, at the slow, thick pace of southern molasses. This was a trait with which my father had little patience in the law or anywhere else; the composition of briefs that were really just that was one of the most valuable lessons his younger partners remembered learning from him.

The case dragged on, as it had done for two years past. The judge remarked rather tartly while winter waned that the attorneys "must show greater speed" if a decision was to be reached before the approaching irrigation season. He forbore from mentioning the Fourth of July or the next presidential election. Several days crawled past while Hawkins examined a single witness. When he finally declared that he expected to conclude this exercise in about fifteen minutes, the dozing attorneys at the bar revived. George sat up in his chair and exclaimed with an expression of jubilation on his face, "Gaudeamus igitur."

Hawkins whirled around with a spirited protest, apparently believing the well-known phrase from a medieval student drinking song was a profane expression. His motion to strike it from the record was granted. When the court reporter was asked if he had caught the remark, he calmly declared, "Mr. Springmeyer has just said, 'Gaudeamus igitur juvenus dum summus,' which is translated thus: 'Let us then rejoice while we are still young.'" Red-faced, Hawkins retired to his chair.

* * *

Nine months after my father took office Reno's most famous speakeasies—Rick's, Quinn's, and the Alpine Winery—were still running at full tilt. So was Tex Hall's notorious Reno Social Club on Mill Street, a private organization consisting mostly of lawyers. The club's membership restrictions were so stringent that no agent was ever able to obtain entry as a member. Persistent rumors that the club received protection probably had some foundation in fact, but protection was almost superfluous because private clubs with lengthy residence requirements inevitably presented an insoluble circular problem to the federal agents: to get evidence, they needed a search warrant; to get a search warrant, they needed evidence. Although George personally led a raid on the place, the case was subsequently killed in court because the search warrant was defective.

The three roadhouses proved to be less impregnable. Because the local agents were apparently well known to the canny roadhouse proprietors, unfamiliar outside agents were brought in, one posing as a Los Angeles movie director and another as a plumber. Pretending to be divorce seekers, the two agents consulted W. L. Hacker and another attorney, both well-known members of the Reno Social Club. These obliging gentlemen provided their clients with letters to the roadhouse managers vouching for their trustworthiness. Although the plumber and the movie director had shown their attorneys photographs and letters from the girls they intended to marry when their freedom had been won, the solicitous lawyers took pains to see that their clients should not lack feminine companionship while in Reno. The two men were introduced to young ladies not unused to spending an occasional evening in a roadhouse, the kind of girls who knew how to "fling a wicked shoe."

With such introductions and such gay company, the two jaunty young men in caps were able to pass scrutiny from the tiny window in the massive door constructed of tongue and groove flooring at the storm porch behind Quinn's. They were able to purchase liberal quantities of jackass and "Dewar's Scotch" at the Alpine Winery. At Rick's on the Verdi Road, they were seen refreshing themselves between dances, at least until Agent Cooper suddenly gave the prearranged signal to the other officers waiting outside and covered the astonished bartender with his guns while the reinforcements rushed in. Thirteen bootleggers were arrested.

That was disquieting to some, as were the abatement proceedings that had been initiated against the roadhouses. But few believed that anything would really come of it. As one Reno businessman wrote to George, "There were open bets offered and made, and on odds too, that these big fellows here would never be brought to trial; that there was not one single official in the State of Nevada who did not owe his election or appointment to the influence of the saloon ring; and that by resorting to technicalities and postponements they would never be brought to trial."[4]

Certainly this was also Hacker's assessment of the situation, as he explained to the group at the bar one night at Quinn's. A party of three men and two women had arrived at the small, one-story frame building in a taxi. They were admitted after ringing the bell, and Hacker, who was friendly with one of them, told the roadhouse manager it was alright for the group to buy drinks. They proceeded to buy ninety-one of them in the course of a merry evening that lasted until 2:30 in the morning. Hacker acknowledged to his newfound friends that the bogus plumber and the movie director had been "very clever" but he had advised Quinn's that they might as well keep right on operating because the feds already had as much on them as they could get.

As he consumed his share of drinks in this congenial company, Hacker grew even more voluble. He had the perfect plan for beating abatement, he confided to them. You bought two houses, and whenever one was abated, you just moved your club into the other one. No doubt such wise advice provoked general admiration.

In his office two days later, prior to another drinking party at Quinn's, Hacker expanded further upon these points. He told his sympathetic listeners, Mr. Hemphill and Mr. Kyle, that he had the plumber and the movie director scared stiff. They would never dare to testify because they knew he would "rip the pants off them if they ever come back." There were attorneys in Nevada, he explained with a complacent air, who knew how to "get things by."

Shortly afterward, Hacker was convicted on conspiracy charges, largely on the testimony of Agents Hemphill, Adams, and Kyle, the jovial gentlemen beside him at the bar that night at Quinn's. It was suggested in court that ninety-one drinks of whiskey sounded a trifle excessive for a single evening's entertainment, but the agents replied coolly that it was "the government's treat." The bootleggers arrested in the sweep stood trial, with the plumber and the movie director ready to risk their pants and testifying at some length. The roadhouses were abated. If you had laid one of those odds on bets against the United States attorney, you lost.[5]

All the same, it was no more than a beginning. My father believed Rick's and the Winery were run by a four-man ring that controlled the bootlegging industry and the narcotics trade in Reno. However, the link was kept carefully hidden, for business in the roadhouses was handled by a lower echelon of managers. The top men took care not to appear on the scene very often, and none of them were among those arrested. Somewhere in the background were Reno's most notorious gangsters, Jimmy McKay and Bill Graham. My father was just beginning to stir the murky depths of the Reno underworld, and the shadowy pattern had not assumed a definite shape. I do not believe he had yet realized what he began that February night in 1923 when they raided the roadhouses. Or in whose presence it would finally end.

A Walk on a Dark Street

MY FATHER HAD SOME belief in extrasensory perception and used to spend many pleasant evenings table tipping with friends at the former Nixon mansion, owned at that time by Senator Newlands's daughter and her husband. However, after a year of fireworks and unprecedented efforts at law enforcement, no psychic gifts were required to predict what lay ahead. When George was selected as United States attorney, the Democratic press had gleefully reported that the Republicans were deeply divided over placing the storm petrel in office. During his first full year in office, criminal convictions more than doubled and the number of civil suits, many of them abatement proceedings, increased twelve times.[1] It was an outstanding record from the viewpoint of the Justice Department, but the Democrats could safely anticipate that it would bring increasing pressure from two groups that often overlapped in the intimate, clubby atmosphere of Nevada politics: the bootleggers and certain politicians who found the enforcement of Prohibition uncomfortable at best and disastrous at worst.

My father's investigations brought him steadily closer to the knowledge that an unholy alliance existed between the politicians and the big ring. The roadhouse raids had been the first step. The second came in the spring of 1923 when he turned his attention to John Donnelley, the director of Nevada's Prohibition agency, and it was a step that would bring him into dangerous ground where Nevada United States attorneys usually found it safer to avert their eyes and retrace their paths. But that was not my father's way. As his successor on the college newspaper had written of him years ago: "When he was or believed he was right, fear of results was to him a thing unknown." The pertinence of those awkward and prescient phrases had only increased with the passage of more than twenty years. The stakes were far higher now than on the occasion of my father's expulsion from college, but even had he known in the beginning just how high they were, he would have done no differently. Fear of results was to him a thing unknown. Having taken the first steps, the rest would inexorably follow.

It was one of the supreme ironies of Prohibition that enforcement of this lofty moral reform nurtured a batch of the most corrupt public officials the nation ever produced. In the words of the president of the National Civic Reform League: "The posts of state director and enforcement agent were the most coveted of the patronage plums because bribery rendered them very profitable. Appointments were made on the behest of senators and representatives, who, in their turn, followed the demands of the state, county, and local political organizations, and the worst men with the strongest political backing secured the places."[2]

This situation was not likely to be any better in Nevada, where politics had never been precisely antiseptic, and, in fact, it was not. My father found "political influence is omnipresent in appointments and policy." Continued Prohibition enforcement under this "vicious and antiquated" system might "even result in the complete demoralization of our social and political customs and institutions."[3] The judge of the federal district of

Nevada took an equally dim view of matters. "Unless conditions improve, and improve speedily," he declared with unmistakable emphasis, "it will be necessary to . . . investigate the conduct and methods of every person employed by the government in Nevada."[4]

In the course of his work George encountered a number of agents of the variety Judge Farrington and the civic reformers were referring to, and whenever he could, he dispatched them to the reward they so richly deserved. Usually the agents had been paid off in advance, but on a few occasions they were even bribed while a case was in progress. When an agent made a raid, he had to paste a piece of paper on the confiscated bottles stating in his own handwriting what the bottle was, where it had been found, and by whom. He was also required to make a written report to the United States attorney. In the midst of trying a case hinging on one of these bottles, George was startled to hear the Prohibition agent testify that he had been unable to find any intoxicating liquor on the premises. He had apparently forgotten the report he had written and the bottles he had labeled after the raid eight months earlier. Questioned on the report, he denied writing it and claimed that one of the other officers had done it.

George said, "Will you please write these words." As he dictated, the officer wrote, seemingly unaware that these were the same words he had previously written and pasted on the bottle and certainly oblivious to the ultimate end of these standard and innocuous questions. "Now," said George, "you didn't make this report?"

"No."

"You didn't sign it?"

"No."

Then George produced the report and bottle and said, "Is this your handwriting?"

"Yes," admitted the officer, turning pale as he realized the words he had just written in an identical hand left him no possible avenue of escape. He pitched from his chair in a faint, and they had to carry him to a side room and summon a doctor. George later prosecuted him successfully for perjury.

* * *

As time went by George would realize that the corruption in Nevada's Prohibition agency extended all the way to the top. Director John Donnelley was an organization politician of exactly the type the civic reformers were criticizing. He had originally come to Nevada during the Goldfield boom from California, where he had served on the staff of Governor Gillett. It was noted in the press that no small measure of his early "political success" had been due to the influence of Gillett, the last of California's Republican railroad governors before the onslaught of Hiram Johnson. He had emerged in the company of Ed Collins during the political upheavals of 1910. As one of the Goldfield crowd, he had headed the state police when Oddie was governor and had aided Wingfield in the Republican preconvention battle with Platt in 1920. George had been on the same side that year and had enjoyed working with an old friend from Goldfield. So had Donnelley, indeed he would later claim he had been "among those who sponsored the appointment of Mr. Springmeyer against many party leaders who, with sounder judgment, opposed his appointment to an office of such power and prerogatives on the ground that he possessed an incurable propensity for sensationalism and inciting dissension."[5] If Donnelley had really sponsored George, he would quickly regret it. Goldfield was the bond between them, but not bond enough.

Soon after he settled in as United States attorney, my father began to notice some very peculiar things about Donnelley's administration. It had always been sluggish at best. George's open letters to the director advising him of the powers at the disposal of his agents had elicited nothing more than a feeble "no comment." Nearly every day the mail brought more complaints to George's office concerning bootlegging operations that Donnelley had neglected to deal with. Rumors that the director of Prohibition was raking in protection money grew so persistent that Donnelley's office was finally obliged to issue a public denial.[6] In early 1923 George came across indisputable evidence of wrongdoing.

It was during March of that year, shortly after the roadhouse raids, that Donnelley fired his two best agents. One was Percy Nash, a crack agent with whom George had been working closely since Nick Carter's death. Nash was often called upon to testify in Prohibition cases, and George used to tease him in court. Nash would seat himself in the witness chair, his bearing as dashing as that of the Canadian Mounties he so intensely admired. In the course of his examination, George would say, "Give your name."

"P. Nash," the handsome, young witness would answer in a ringing voice, straightening proudly in his chair.

George would pause, frowning at his papers in mock bewilderment. *"Percival* Nash?" he would inquire, as though this unfamiliar name required additional clarification.

"Percival Nash," the crestfallen witness would admit, slumping dejectedly in his seat. His dread secret was out again.

George was only joking; he knew a name like Percival was the only thing Nash had to hide. Ironically, in a service disgracefully riddled with corruption, the only charge that could be produced against Nash as the ostensible cause of his dismissal was "political activity." He had admittedly "boosted" Jack Diskin in his campaign for attorney general the preceding fall. A veteran Prohibition officer of three years' standing, Nash was as courageous, as direct in his methods, and as intent upon getting his man as the Mounties. He had been shot in the hand while bringing in a recalcitrant moonshiner from the Wadsworth hills; warrants had been sworn out for his arrest for arson when he burned a still in Mineral County two nights after Nick was shot down. Few major raids in the region had taken place without him, and upon receiving notice of his dismissal, he could say with grim pride, "Ask any of the local bootleggers if we have been active."

He may have been altogether too active. The press hinted that the removal of Nash and his partner, Henry Brown, was linked to a raid conducted while Donnelley was away on a trip. Never in the course of Donnelley's regime had Tex Hall's exclusive preserve, the Reno Social Club, been subject to invasion by the prohis. Might the director have preferred it if that raid had not taken place? So it seemed. Under questioning by federal officials, Donnelley subsequently admitted he had been extremely displeased when the United States attorney, accompanied by Nash and Brown, raided the club without his knowledge. Donnelley had warned the offending agents to do no more field work for the United States attorney without his permission. Their dismissal soon followed.

My father issued an angry statement aimed at Donnelley: "I did my utmost" to prevent the firing of Nash and Brown "because I felt that they were among the most efficient men on the force and that their removal would cripple the department; moreover, I had been informed that other men in the department had been just as active politically as Nash and Brown."[7]

Also during March a peculiar report came to George's attention. Ten barrels of liquor confiscated the previous September had been destroyed because there was "no case." Nash remembered the incident. In response to a phone call that September morning, he and other officers had gone out to examine a truck which had broken down on South Virginia Street on the outskirts of Reno. Finding ten barrels of beer in the truck, they brought it to city hall, where they unloaded, analyzed, and

labeled the beer before locking it in a government vault. Donnelley then arrived on the scene and, after a few words with the
truck driver, allowed him to depart with his truck. Somewhat
incredulous, Nash asked if he was releasing the man. Donnelley
casually replied that there was no case against him: "He said he
didn't know what was in the barrels," and "we can get him any
time." The truck had been plying its way back and forth between Quinn's and the residence of Jimmy McKay.

A few days later the same truck reappeared, newly fitted out
with a canvas cover and high-boarded sidings. The load of
barrels within was nonetheless clearly visible to the motorcycle
policeman who reported to Donnelley that he had followed the
truck from McKay's house to Rick's. On being asked what he
was going to do about "the truckload of booze," Donnelley
airily told the officer that he wasn't going to do anything.

Confronted with this, George arranged what appears to have
been a little test. An internal revenue agent would tell Donnelley he had information that a cache of liquor guarded by a
Chinese gunman was being stored in a garage in back of Rick's.
He would not, of course, reveal that his source was the United
States attorney. Curiously, on the very night that Donnelley
received the tip, the liquor supplies were moved.

When Donnelley came calling at George's office, any remain-
ing doubt that favored bootleggers enjoyed de facto immunity
was disspelled. The United States attorney, said the federal
director of Prohibition, "must help out the Republicans" by
dropping certain prosecutions or the party would suffer losses
at the next election. George shook his head and answered with
finality, "Everybody who is arrested—Republicans, Democrats,
or Socialists—will be prosecuted."

By the time of the dry conference, the gleeful Democratic
press was pointing to an open breach between Donnelley and
Springmeyer. George's vehement appeals at the conference for
better cooperation from local officials were obviously being

undercut by Donnelley. The rumors that the two had barely spoken since March may well have been true. Donnelley later acknowledged that they were at odds before George had been in office a year.[8]

At length, following one of Donnelley's frequent tours of the state (ostensibly undertaken to "study conditions" but allegedly a convenient means of collecting protection money), a group of private citizens began looking into the director's misuse of his office. The ingenious method Donnelley had devised for his collections was the organization of a mythical mine in Mexico, in which bootleggers who desired his protection were compelled to buy stock. According to the newspaper reporter who exposed the scheme several years later, one bootlegger admitted investing $5,000 in Donnelley's mine. Although such witnesses were understandably reluctant to come forward, a probe by Department of Justice and Internal Revenue agents, with such assistance from George as they requested, had produced additional evidence. The Winnemucca sheriff had arrested a man named Gabriel Scott for collecting protection money from the local bootleggers in the summer of 1922. These bootleggers apparently saw no reason to doubt Scott's claim that he was collecting on Donnelley's behalf, and the investigators had secured a letter definitely linking Scott to the federal director of Prohibition. "If I do not get on the payroll, I want to beg off," Scott had written to Donnelley. "That Winnemucca mess has taken all the heart out of me." Donnelley told the sheriff that Scott should be prosecuted if there was sufficient proof against him but the testimony of bootleggers would be worthless (unsurprisingly, no other kind of testimony was available).

My father obviously believed Scott had shown Donnelley his account book and had reported collecting hundreds of dollars in protection money. Donnelley had tried to shield Scott and would hardly have done so if Scott were not his man. All the same, it was doubtful that a strong case could be built around Scott. The man was too dull witted and easily confused to make an impressive witness. On each point that rested on his word against Donnelley's, he would probably come out the worse, and the opposition would not find it hard to undermine his credibility. Independent proof was lacking that Scott had, in fact, been collecting for Donnelley rather than himself.

Singly, the Scott affair probably would not have tumbled John Donnelley from office, but collectively, Scott, the hastily moved liquor cache at Quinn's, and the far more damaging evidence of the Curran beer truck proved sufficient. Percy Nash made a star witness, as everyone watching the case had no doubt realized he would. (Two months before the grand jury convened, Senator Tasker Oddie explained to George Wingfield that he had been unable to secure Nash's dismissal from his current job with the Biological Survey because Nash was a state, not a federal, employee. However, Oddie assured Wingfield that he had called on the Secretary of Agriculture personally and done his very best.) The apprehensions of these gentlemen proved well founded. The grand jury investigating Donnelley in the spring of 1924 recommended his "early removal" but abstained from indicting him in the belief that the loss of his position would be "sufficient punishment."[9]

Nonetheless, Donnelley refused to resign. In his first statement to the press, he announced that the patience and forbearance that had led him to maintain a gentlemanly silence while Springmeyer confided his "suspicions, feelings, and emotions" to the press with "copious regularity" were now ended. "Mr. Springmeyer," he charged, "has used the power of his office to accomplish my ruin and disgrace." Questioned before the grand jury concerning that broken-down truck, he angrily told George, "It's none of your business whether it was part of the McKay supply of liquor or not" and "I'll run my own office." My father had sometimes been charged in the press with "fighting every battle to the last bullet." This time the attorney general had directed him to prosecute Donnelley if necessary, and that was just what he would have to do.[10]

Within the next three months, Donnelley resigned, was indicted and arraigned, with Wingfield standing bond for him, and was suspended in apparent anticipation of his next move, an unavailing attempt to rescind his resignation. The accompanying legal moves and countermoves fairly ignite the paper on which they are recorded. In an unsuccessful motion to quash his indictment, Donnelley charged George with misconduct "impelled by malice." In his affidavit, he declared that the United States attorney "is a man of such mental characteristics as to be unable normally to withstand criticism whether just or unjust affecting . . . his official conduct, and of such moral character as to be willing and desirous, either for his own augmentation or to relieve himself from criticism, to wrongfully accuse others of misconduct and to prostitute the powers of his office to the accomplishment of such ends." However, the United States attorney's record provided little support for these allegations. The only scrap of public criticism Donnelley could cite arose from George's failure to bring the Reno Social Club case to a successful conclusion.

My father's blue eyes must have been blazing as he dashed his strong, angular signature across the demurrer, but he confined himself to describing Donnelley's motion as "frivolous and sham, scandalous and scurrilous, offensive and in contempt of this honorable court, and filed herein for publicity and propaganda purposes."

During the first legal round of 1925, a verbal conflict erupted before the evidence against Donnelley had even been presented. With the jury temporarily excluded from the courtroom, Donnelley's attorneys requested the judge to instruct the jury that the United States attorney cannot ask any witness to give hearsay or secondary evidence and that he has no right to express an opinion on questions of fact, weight of evidence, or credibility of witnesses, or to influence the jury in its findings. Assistant U.S. Attorney Cantwell, speaking for the prosecution, charged that instructions intimating that Springmeyer would violate his oath of office would be an "insult" and would lead the jury to view the United States attorney's statements with suspicion. The judge ended the controversy by refusing to give the disputed instructions, sharply reminding Donnelley's attorney, former Nevada Supreme Court Justice Frank Norcross, that if he had knowledge of any wrongdoing on the part of the U.S. attorney, it was his duty to file charges. Some five years earlier Norcross had been George's principal ally in the 1920 battle against Platt on behalf of Wingfield.[11]

In order to dispel rumors that "the prosecution is personal on my part" and to quell any doubts that Donnelley would receive a fair trial, George asked the attorney general to appoint a special prosecutor.[12] The attorney general, however, refused, and George's assistants handled the case; the U.S. attorney himself served as one of the principal witnesses for the prosecution. Late in 1925 Donnelley was convicted of "willful failure" to report a Prohibition violation. Ironically, it was the beer truck that had broken down on the way from McKay's to Quinn's that finally proved to be the instrument of his undoing.

When Donnelley's appeals reached the Supreme Court more than two years later, the prosecutor assigned to the case was Mabel Walker Willebrandt, the assistant attorney general in charge of Prohibition, the idol of the temperance groups and club women of her day, and an attorney well known to George because she had been his immediate superior in the Justice Department and he used to travel to Washington regularly to report to her. To George's astonishment, the Justice Department filed a paper confessing error and consenting that the case be dismissed. George concluded they must be under pressure from the interests involved, but the file was not yet closed on the

Donnelley case. In a surprise development, Chief Justice Taft ordered government lawyers to present a brief and prosecute the case, a highly unusual move because the court rarely told the Justice Department how to proceed. When, metaphorically at least, that troublesome beer truck came clanking into the Supreme Court nearly six years after it had broken down on South Virginia Street, Donnelley's conviction was upheld.

In her memoirs Mrs. Willebrandt cheerfully and somewhat defensively explained that this curious affair was the product of disagreement within the Justice Department over "a nice legal point"; there had been much "friendly bantering" between herself and the solicitor general, who believed the Prohibition law was not intended to punish failure to report crime. When the Supreme Court held otherwise, the decision had a "noticeably wholesome effect on agents and United States attorneys alike."[13] As for herself, Mrs. Willebrandt would eventually exit from the Justice Department for private practice (one of her more important clients was the California Grape Growers Association, which was a painful disenchantment to the zealots of temperance). Donnelley, fined but not imprisoned, would move on to greener pastures outside Nevada. Although he had been a useful figure to the chieftains of Reno's underworld, in fact one whose diligence in their behalf had provoked his own downfall, they survived his departure. More than that, they prospered and grew fat, for they had friends in still higher places.

* * *

Even before the Donnelley affair unwound before the public gaze, my father was an issue in his own right. Handbills urging the citizens to "vote for Coolidge and keep George Springmeyer the crusading United States attorney in office" were circulated during the 1924 election. His desk became cluttered with letters of approbation. "It is good to believe that we still have a few officers who are fearless enough to buck the very active and loud mouthed minority who so openly flout the laws of our land," wrote one Reno businessman. An Ely copper corporation, irritated because "the bootleggers deliver the stuff at the mine and of course the force indulges more or less and as a consequence are generally demoralized," was behind him.[14]

Although prudence might have suggested that a United States attorney whose enemies were proliferating would do well to rally these corporate officials and any other supporters he could find around him, George continued to see himself as an impartial officer of the law, personally opposed to Prohibition, and to abstain from association with the forces of temperance. All the same, crusading clerics like the Reverend Pendleton were eager to embrace him as one of their own. Now that Ed Roberts had been elected mayor on a platform ambiguously stated but well understood by all, Reno was known as a "wide open city," and the Reverend Pendleton had taken to lecturing on "The Trend towards Lawlessness in Reno," by which he largely meant the red-light district. The prostitutes had grown so bold that invitations were mailed to fraternity houses, said Pendleton, and worse yet, so fascinating that a group of high-school girls had cut classes to go down to the district to "look around and see what was going on." Pendleton's dire warnings upon "the pestilence in our city" also touched upon bootlegging, a crime on which he declared "George Springmeyer alone stood flat-footed for law and order."[15]

However, there were those who did not admire that flat-footed stance as warmly as the good reverend, those who considered my father not only flat-footed but bullheaded. Pressure to cease and desist from his campaign against the bootleggers, or at least to show a due regard for influential people with influential friends, began to mount. A public utility corporation, irate at the loss of some of its most valuable customers, threatened broad financial retaliation, which Nevada consumers were likely to blame on George's policies. "In case of abatement proceedings and the closing up of these business places," the corporation informed the United States attorney, "the deficiency of revenue will have to be made up by an increase in rates or otherwise to the public."[16] George showed the letter to the press. In another episode a district judge tried to intercede on behalf of a White Pine County bootlegger George was prosecuting, coyly explaining that he would disclose his reasons "at a future date." When George revealed the bootlegger's attempt to bribe him and the judge's letter in court, it was a sensation.[17]

* * *

The United States attorney had made it clear again and again that he was unwilling to see reason, and the bootleggers had their own methods of dealing with those who opposed them. Those methods were often ugly. Circling hawks at Frazier's Wells near Tonopah had led to the discovery of a murdered man, the loser in the latest bootlegger war—the alleged murderers were later arrested at "Devil's Den," the headquarters for bootlegging operations near Bakersfield, California. A man suspected of acting as a stool pigeon for the feds had been ambushed and badly beaten in Reno; Percy had been wounded and removed from his job; Nick was dead. It was time, even past time, to bring the bloodhound who pursued them so relentlessly to heel.

The subtlest of means to tumble a crusading United States attorney from power would be to compromise him by entrapment, and everyone knew George Springmeyer had an eye for the ladies. Someone, somewhere, must have figured his appreciative eye could easily linger on a woman like the good-looking young wife of Bill McKnight, former deputy Nevada attorney general and chairman of the Democratic state central committee (later to become a district judge). When George was

walking home late at night from his office to his room at the
Colonial Hotel, Mrs. McKnight would cruise up in her car and
offer him a ride. Despite her sweet pleadings ("Come on,
George, we've always been good friends"), the fact that the lady
had never shown such an interest in him before he took office
made George wary. He conjectured that it might be very convenient for the bootleggers if he were caught in a car that contained liquor. Although he was not usually one to reject an
invitation from a pretty woman, he resisted the temptations of
Mrs. McKnight.

Where guile had failed, strong-arm tactics might succeed, and
the infamous, foulmouthed Blackie Bassett, proprietor of the
Ranch 101 on Douglas Alley and later of the Question Mark
Resort, had no compunction about using his gun. He had already been publicly charged with assault: standing in the darkness of a lady friend's yard, he had cursed her for the company
she kept, then called her to the bedroom window and shot her.
During Bassett's trial for liquor law violations in 1924, the
prosecution was held up because the principal witness for the
government had mysteriously disappeared.

A similar and more serious incident involving a witness occurred in the late summer of 1925 when Bassett and Agent
Turner were arrested on bribery charges. Bassett had successfully avoided some $15,000 in fines by bribing Turner to tip him
off with the telephone message "a checkered cab will call tonight" whenever a raid was at hand. So successful was the
scheme that Bassett laid plans to expand and include other
clubs; an unidentified figure known only as "the boss" lurked
somewhere in the background.

As the Secret Service wound up their investigation, much
depended on the testimony of Turner's partner, Agent Byrne,
whom Bassett and Turner had attempted to co-opt. After the
arrests a transparent attempt to frame Byrne on robbery charges
was launched. Having failed to appear at the preliminary hear-

ing for the accused pair, the beleaguered agent was reported in the press to be "under terrific mental strain." He then disappeared. A few days later a badly frightened man walked into my father's office—Byrne. The bootleggers had been trying to intimidate him, said Byrne, and he had been drinking heavily. He expressed a desire for a transfer to the relative tranquility of the narcotics squad. Thanks to an ironclad alibi and the transparent clumsiness of the frameup, the robbery charges against Byrne were dismissed, and he summoned sufficient fortitude to testify against Turner. Whether he could survive mentally and physically intact until Bassett's trial remained an open question.[18]

If Bassett did not scruple to bully and shoot these others who angered him, he could hardly do less for the United States attorney who was the principal obstacle to his schemes; the attempt would come at the Moana Dance Hall. George and Carlyle Robinson, Charlie Chaplin's former manager, had taken two girls dancing there in order to find out if liquor was being served. As soon as they came in the door, bottles began to disappear. Shortly afterward, when the foursome returned to their table after dancing, a collection of bottles had been ostentatiously thrown under it. Bassett and one of his sidekicks sat down at the next table, laid their guns out before them, and began to abuse George with vile language. George quickly understood what Blackie was trying to do. The volatile Springmeyer temper was well known throughout the length and breadth of Nevada, and Blackie was obviously hoping to provoke him into starting something in order to create an excuse to kill him. George was smoldering, but he forced himself to ignore Blackie.

The gangster pushed him farther. While George was dancing, Blackie followed him around the floor, thrusting his gun roughly into George's back. As George and Carlyle took the terrified girls home, Blackie's auto was following close behind.

In connection with the Turner affair, Bassett was charged
with conspiracy, bribery, and Prohibition violations, forty-one
counts in all. The bootlegger, under $15,000 bond, would flee
to Canada, where he would successfully elude the efforts of the
Justice and State departments to extradite him. Nonetheless he
had already paid a penalty of sorts. The day after the unpleas-
antness at the Moana Dance Hall George saw Blackie on the
courthouse steps. Although George was unarmed as always, he
stuck his hand in his pocket as if he had a gun and proceeded
to abuse the bootlegger in what he later called "the foulest
language I ever heard the mule skinners use back on the ranch."
Blackie was carrying his gun, but he thought George had the
drop on him, so he stood there and meekly accepted a well-
deserved tongue-lashing.

The damn fool the Chicago gangster once shot in the leg had
not learned his lesson after all. The lesson that mattered was the
one many years before when a small, asthmatic child was left
home to die and willed himself to live. From that time forward,
impossible was the adjective of fools. If flesh was only flesh and
all could not be conquered by sheer force of will, my father
would never learn it. Nor would many of his contemporaries
really understand his powerful will and the fierce sense of
honor behind it. The lawyers who coldly dropped him from the
firm during the war saw only recklessness, the kind of recklessness they had no doubt would kill him; others saw courage, the
kind George Wingfield was always probing for when he tested
men with his gun to see if they would quail. Perhaps it was for
this that Wingfield respected George Springmeyer, since most
of his other qualities were not the kind the boss of the bipartisan machine would have valued or understood. My father was
not entirely foolhardy: he had bided his time at the Moana
Dance Hall. Still there was a large element of risk in what he
did, more risk than Wingfield, who made sure the odds were
heavily in his own favor at all times, would care to take. Wing-

field always carried one gun, and when he believed himself in mortal danger, he strapped on four more and surrounded himself with bodyguards. Yet even he may have found something to admire in the man who stood on the courthouse steps with his hand in an empty pocket, blistering the gunman before him with curses.

* * *

George's pocket stayed empty, even when the attempts at intimidation began. Someone, somewhere, must have figured no man was too strong to be worn down slowly and steadily by threats that came, then ceased for a time, yet always recurred, in an unremitting war of nerves. Often when George sat bent over his desk working late at his office, a woman would call around ten o'clock. The voice was different every time; the message was always the same. She would tell him she admired him but she was connected with "the bootlegging ring." Then she would warn him that if he walked home that night without police protection "someone will pick you off."

My father would glance at his watch and say, "Well, I'll be going home at 12:30 tonight alone, and I'll be ready for anyone."

At 12:30 sharp, unarmed, he would close the door of the empty building behind him and walk to the right, down the dark street. Though he dismissed these nighttime warnings as mere threats, he could never be entirely certain. Whatever awaited him on that deserted street, he walked to meet it, and knowing him, I am certain he never hesitated a moment nor glanced over his shoulder. No one tried to shoot him.

In the face of these menacing calls, wearing a gun would seem like a wise precaution, but he had always considered it an affectation, a swaggering declaration of toughness, unnecessary unless a man felt the need to proclaim his courage. He felt no such need. Everyone knew he had never worn one, even in

Goldfield when the men connected with the Pittsburgh Silver Peak indictments had been placed under police protection, and to do it now would suggest that the bootleggers had succeeded in frightening him. He had an even more compelling reason: by slipping a pistol in his pocket, he would tacitly agree to settle his differences with the chieftains of the big ring in a blaze of gunfire by the river. There was no rule of law, no right reason, and no justice in that. So he walked alone and unarmed through the dark streets and spoke to no one, as far as I can tell, of the threats against his life.

The Big Ring

FROM THE VERY BEGINNING, crime in Nevada had been sporadic, disorganized, and individualistic, as it continued to be in the little hamlets scattered over the great deserts and the isolated valleys beyond the Truckee Meadows. Nevada had drawn ruffians and bad men, sometimes men whose business was crime, but never before that period of transformation in the twenties, when the floodtide of bootlegging money and the new chieftains conjoined, had she nurtured men who set about making crime a systematic business, as well organized as any other, and far more profitable. Nor did her past, riddled though it was with venality and corruption, reveal a comparable interlocking of crime and politics.

In retrospect it is evident that the leaders of the big ring had made a discovery as filled with portents as the mysterious "blue stuff" on the Comstock or Tom Fisherman's gold, and certainly one of far greater significance to future economic development. Moreover, this newly discovered vein could not dwindle away to a thread or break off at a fault in the capricious earth; it would only widen to yield, in time, even greater profit from prostitution and gambling than from bootlegging and narcotics.

The market in vice would never fall as the market in silver did, and unlike the more frugal bounties of the rocky hills, vice was inexhaustible. It would last as long as human folly itself, in other words, forever. A great bonanza, the richest El Dorado of them all, yawned at their feet. The first assays were in, and the early indications were highly promising. The day of the prospectors, the pioneer ranchers, and the kings of the Comstock was past. Their dreams were fading into irrelevancy, their work into redundancy, as they dissolved away from living presences into ghosts. A modern order of a kind Bill Stewart and John Mackay and Old Dutch Fred Dangberg would not have recognized was rising in the land. Though no one realized it at the time, the new Nevada was in the making.

My father, like the rest, was not prophet enough to foresee these things, though he must have realized the fragile equilibrium of Nevada's bare-bones economy was changing. These thinly populated deserts bred no diversity of interests substantial enough to counterbalance the new El Dorado. Industry was virtually nonexistent; mining, episodic; ranching, severely limited by the scarcity of water. Of the scanty resources Nevada possessed, many were in the hands of absentee owners uninterested in local politics, and none were sufficient to provide an alternative power base for the dissident. Thus the scales tipped toward the chieftains of the big ring. Money not only spoke but commanded. Those who took their places in the new order would rise to wealth and power; those who resisted would be cast aside. The man who walked alone on the dark road by the river would follow his path to an inevitable conclusion.

"You're too independent," Senator Nixon had told George in 1910, "and you won't work with the party leaders and the machine." Nor had the years changed him. Once again signs of friction with the Republican elite began to appear, this time over the issue of equal justice. One cartoonist depicted Senator Oddie with his head in his hands, sweating profusely, while the word *Springmeyer* hovered in the atmosphere above his bald dome and George pranced about with Carrie Nation's hatchet; it was a dilemma that had troubled the senator for nearly three years. Democratic editors noted with satisfaction in November 1923 that the breach among Republicans was widening and offered a helpful suggestion: Oddie should take Springmeyer "to one side when he next visits Nevada and tell the federal district attorney that he is losing more friends for the senator than any other individual or collection under the Republican administration in Nevada."[1]

In fact the senator probably had already done so. The exact date is unknown but there is nothing uncertain about the confrontation that occurred when Oddie appeared in the United States attorney's office. It was one that still burned in my father's consciousness as he related it to me nearly forty years later. Noting with surprise that several party stalwarts had recently been arrested, Oddie told him bluntly, "This has got to stop." Unless the party could keep the support of Republican bootleggers and other political friends in the Tonopah area, such as the Crumley brothers, it would be impossible to win the next election. Furthermore, he wanted the Donnelly investigation halted.

Goldfield had burned during the summer of 1923 in a conflagration believed to have started in a moonshiner's still. The local citizens had—significantly—preferred not to confide their suspicions to Donnelley's office. Instead they hired private detectives. As a result of these investigations and an earlier series of major raids on Tonopah by a flying squad from Los Angeles, numerous cases were being prosecuted. Included were abatement proceedings against the Goldfield Hotel, recently sold to Newton Crumley by George Wingfield, and charges against Crumley's partner in the Bonanza Hotel Company. Grant Crumley, Wingfield's partner in the Storm Cloud and other mining enterprises, had been awarded the ceremonial honor of nominating the boss of the bipartisan machine for Republican national committeeman in the 1920 convention three years earlier.

My father knew these things. And knew also that before his appointment he had "no understanding with anyone" to go "easy on the Republicans." He told Oddie, "No favorites will be played by me. When Republicans are arrested, they will be prosecuted like Democrats."[2]

Again the voice of the political scientist in me counsels caution to my father. Speak more softly. Refuse more gently. Though Wingfield is the final arbiter, the senator's favor could be useful to you when you seek reappointment. Vacillate. Procrastinate. Say you will see what you can do. Suggest that your superiors might be suspicious. Tell him that dropping the prosecutions at this stage might create a scandal that could harm him in the next election. Speak to him of self-interest, of avarice, and of fear. These things he can understand. But do not speak to him of justice.

Still I acknowledge that the ending is inevitable. My father is incapable of these calculations and dissimulations. Even if I stood at his elbow instead of years away in his future, I could no more alter his course than I could dissuade Oedipus the king from striking the man at the crossroads or from listening to the shepherd's tale. As the Greek tragedians knew, your character is your fate.

George and Oddie had been friends ever since the campaign of 1910, but this meeting permanently ended that friendship. George offered his resignation. Oddie, mindful of how that would look to the world at large, declined to accept it. Once Oddie had described himself to my father as "one who is your friend and who admires your splendid ability and loyalty, with no desire to do anything but be of the utmost assistance and help to you at all times."[3] By 1925, as Oddie's letters reveal, that warm regard had curdled into poisonous resentment. Oddie would privately characterize his former friend, the man who had helped to put him where he was, as "yellow, ungrateful, and dirty in the extreme in his treatment of me."[4] My father's own anger would not soon be set aside, for it was tinged with disillusionment and a sense of betrayal. Oddie was not only a friend of many years' standing, even if he was a bit of a stuffed shirt, but also a senator in whom many voters had placed their trust. When the gangsters and their crowd tried to pressure my father, he was unsurprised and only briefly incensed. Rascals were rascals, and were presumed to brandish the low weapons of their kind, just as cougars were presumed to rely upon their teeth and claws. But from the man who held the highest office in the gift of the people of Nevada, my father had expected something rather different.

On visits to Washington, he neglected his courtesy calls on the senator, less, I suspect, out of anger than embarrassment. Having found the senator corrupt, he was no longer at ease in his presence. So the informal contact between old friends that might have healed the breach was cut off. Oddie's letters obliquely suggest an awareness of how much he had fallen in George's estimation. Oddie would hardly have been so slighted by the United States attorney's failure to pay a call unless he had wanted George to come to him in the old, easy way. George did not come, and knowing why fueled the senator's increasing spite.

Rumors began circulating in the press that "efforts have been made recently in Washington to get the federal prosecutor's scalp." Headlines read "Too Active to Suit Booze Men," and editors noted that George's "political enemies" were "boldly predicting an early end to his tenure."[5] Oddie bitterly observed that "I should have had Springmeyer fired long ago." This, however, was more easily said than done in the absence of any misconduct on the part of the United States attorney, and was politically dangerous in the bargain. Over a year earlier my father had warned Oddie that he would tell his story to the press if the senator tried to force him to resign. In the flurry of letters that passed between Reno and Washington, D.C., in the first two months of 1924, unknown to my father, George Wingfield's expressed wishes concerning the resignation can be readily inferred from Tasker Oddie's replies. Oddie assured Wingfield that he had written Springmeyer a letter indicating his willingness to accept the United States attorney's resignation, a copy of which he enclosed for his superior's approval, but he expressed fears that an attempt to force the issue would send Springmeyer to the press and arouse "all kinds of fireworks." A subsequent letter, protesting to Wingfield that "to insist on the resignation now would mean a contest," could only come from a very worried senator, a senator who had his marching orders and sought a reprieve so he could "lay low for the present." He apparently got it when George Wingfield himself at length reached the same conclusion and turned to more subtle means. A tempting position in Washington, engineered at Wingfield's suggestion by the ever-obliging Tom Miller, was offered to George—he refused it.[6]

The United States attorney remained in office, and in a separate controversy he would again appear as an unyielding obstacle to the senator's wishes. As the first ripples of opposition to the proposed suit by the federal government to settle the water rights on the Carson River began to emerge in 1924, my father wrote Oddie to "lay the whole matter before you for such action as you may deem proper." Although some state officials favored halting the case, George believed the suit was "the only way of taking this matter out of the political sphere."[7] Parallel litigation was already under way on the Walker River. When the attorney general ordered George to file the Carson River suit in 1925, the question of legal or political action was closed, at least as far as George was concerned. These legal undertakings aroused a furor in Douglas County—indeed some of the Dang-

George Springmeyer as Boyd Moore drew him in the 1920s.

bergs, now increasingly paranoid on the subject of the Spring-meyers, regarded the matter as a personal vendetta. George was clearly stung by the reaction among the ranchers he had grown up with in the valley, but, being under orders from the attorney general, he had no choice but to proceed. Further, he believed the suits were a necessary step to establish water rights and provide for impartial distribution so that "waterhogs" with large landholdings upstream would no longer be able to en-croach upon the rights of small holders and Indians. "The greedy whites may gnash their teeth and curse the red man," he later wrote in a public letter on the water rights issue. "But let them not forget that the process of extermination wreaked upon the American Indian is a blot upon the United States of which we should be ashamed."[8]

Shame did not appear among the dominant emotions of Tasker Oddie and the large landholders when contemplating the low estate of the Indians. Wretched these Indians certainly were, and it naturally followed that they were also stupid and contemptible. Rights were not for such as these; they wouldn't know what to do with them. My father knew Indians. He had grown up beside their campoodies on a ranch that employed more Indians than most others in the valley, and he was encum-bered with none of these prejudices and assumptions of superi-ority. If their estate was low, the white man who decimated them, destroyed their hunting grounds, and took the best of their lands had brought them to it, and by his deeds had for-feited the right to despise them. It was George's conviction that these Indians belonged beside other men in the common realm of humanity and also of the law. In the twenties that was still a revolutionary idea.

He went to talk with the chiefs at Pyramid Lake and liked them at once. Perhaps he had seen more to despise in the ap-plauded occupants of high offices than he saw here. These men were not stupid or contemptible; he found them intelligent, dignified, and worthy of anyone's respect. And they, responding to an esteem they did not often encounter, pressed him with the only gifts they had to give. He tried to refuse, and soon saw that he could not without giving offense. So he took the things they held out to him: the baskets for winnowing pine nuts; the beaded necklaces; the beaded cylinders for gun powder; the intricate, beaded ornaments to be hung on the breast of a horse; the gloves of soft, white leather decorated with a design of blue butterflies; and the papoose basket of woven willow and of leather beaded with red, white, and black triple-petalled flowers.

Beads and baskets, given in thanks that he had listened or in hope that he would not forget. Even he, believing as he did in law as the source of impartial justice, must have seen how slight was their chance against the landed wealth and political power ranged against them. The large landholders would be laying offerings of another kind before their chosen advocates. Campaign donations, votes, publicity, influence—those were the coin of the political realm, and no man knew better how heavily they weighed. How often, with the fair-minded decency that never wavered, had he upheld the weak, denying that law could become servant to the strong, and roused a storm of affronted outrage. Often enough, some might say, to learn the lessons of expediency; but when these turning points arrived, my father did not turn. The attorney general had ordered him to take up the cause of these Indians, so no power on earth could force him to put it down.

All the same, the powers would try, using both the threat of his removal from office if he persisted and the hint that he might, in spite of everything, win reappointment if he cooperated. They were wasting their time. Indignant over an article in the *Reno Evening Gazette* portraying him as an insidious enemy of the farmers and suggesting that his reappointment hinged upon "proper consideration" for the upstream interests, he fired off a series of angry questions to the editor: "What a spectacle if a United States Attorney should neglect the interests of the government and its reservation and project farmers! Do you expect a United States Attorney to act for the defendants? Since when have defendants who are being sued arrogated to themselves or been given the privilege of dictating who shall be United States attorney? Am I to be misrepresented and put out for doing my duty? Do you want in my place and stead a lawyer who represents defendants in these water suits?" A copy of the letter was dispatched to Senator Oddie in the hope that "it clarifies the situation in your mind."[9]

No further clarification was needed, either at the end of my father's term when that letter was written, or during the prolonged period of conflict that preceded it. There was nothing the senator would like better than a lawyer who represented the defendants, not only in these suits but also in others of particular interest to him. The rights of small holders and Indians were of no concern to Oddie, especially when his local contacts advised that "the suit will hurt you some politically."[10] Predictably he favored the large landholders, euphemistically referred to in his correspondence as "the best people in the state." Far from removing the controversy from the political sphere to the courts as my father advised, he was anxious to nudge it into the arena in which his influence would be most effective. He pressed the Departments of Justice and the Interior to discontinue, or at least postpone, the suits. One of his primary methods in this campaign was an effort to discredit my father. In a typical letter to the secretary of the interior, Oddie observed that the United States attorney "is not a fit man at all to have anything to do with this matter, and his judgment on it is not to be relied upon."[11]

George was called to Washington early in 1925 amid rumors that he was "slated to lose his official head." Returning to Nevada, he acknowledged to the press that his enemies had fired off a "barrage of birdshot" and suggested that "heavier ammunition" would be needed to penetrate his "tough old hide." Oddie's barrage had failed to shake his superiors, and in July the attorney general replied to Oddie's latest letter with an assessment that had been conveyed to the senator in various forms on several previous occasions: "In all respects those here who have been in touch with this litigation are unanimous in the opinion that so far as their knowledge goes no fault is to be found with the acts of Mr. Springmeyer."[12] The suit was irrevocably launched, though my father would not remain in office long enough to see the end of it.

Needless to say, my father was no more inclined to support Oddie in the next senatorial primary than Oddie was inclined to entreat George Wingfield for permission to reappoint the United States attorney. George suddenly became aware of virtues he had never previously noticed in Ed Roberts, mayor of wide-open Reno, Oddie's opponent in the Republican senatorial primary, and, in 1906, George's own rival for the nomination for attorney general. From my father's point of view, one thing could be said in Roberts's favor: he was not a hypocrite. A minor virtue, perhaps, but one that raised him considerably above the level of Tasker Oddie. George wrote a letter backing Roberts, who was nevertheless resoundingly defeated by the incumbent senator in the primary.

The final footnote to the Oddie affair appeared when my father left office and revealed to the press Oddie's attempts to influence him in the bootlegger suits. No one was more infuriated by this breach of party etiquette than rheumy, old Bill Booth, editor of the *Tonopah Bonanza* and a reliable Republican war-horse for more than twenty years. He launched an editorial attack against George charging that the United States attorney was a traitor "worse than Benedict Arnold" because he had repaid his Republican benefactor by exposure. A more temperate man might have shrugged it off as the trivial maundering of a very unimportant newspaper editor in a very small town, as indeed it was; but to a man with my father's touchy sense of honor, it was the flick of a duelist's glove. When he read Booth's remarks, the Springmeyer temper was sufficiently aroused for him to dash off a public letter to Booth saying, "No one, certainly not you, indecent liar . . . can say that I am worse than Benedict Arnold, traitor of traitors, without being called to account. If you were a man, I would lick the hell out of you. But as your decrepit and whiskey-soaked carcass would fall to pieces at a blow, I shall merely pull your bulbous, red nose on the first opportunity, and I will sue you for libel."[13]

Booth was enraged, and as the libel suit approached, he grew more so. Possibly he had not been so irate since he shot his wife's lover some thirty-five years before. If he could not have a fight with Springmeyer, at least not yet, he meant to have a fight with one of Springmeyer's friends. On the occasion of a Democratic rally in Tonopah, he popped out of his miniscule newspaper office like an agitated jackrabbit from its burrow. The Democratic speakers in the auditorium set him to ruminating, then to muttering in the street, and finally to pacing up and down the lobby of the Mizpah Hotel and ranting about the Democrats and other nefarious beings. Seeing Governor Scrugham enter the lobby, Booth dashed up and charged him with sending "carbon copies of that Springmeyer letter all over the state."

"You are a liar," said the governor tersely. Booth made a lunge for Scrugham. The governor dodged a blow aimed at his face and squared off facing his assailant. "I'd smash your face in if it wasn't for your age," he told Booth.

"Never mind my age," shrieked Booth. At that point, bystanders rushed up and separated the two.

"I'll see you when you sober up," said the governor, without pausing to consider the unlikelihood of that eventuality. Gradually the large crowd around the two men dispersed.[14]

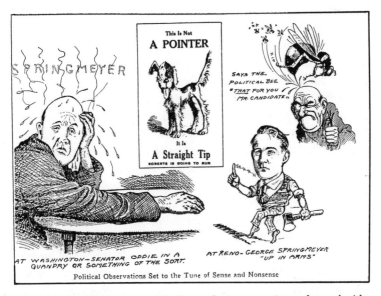

Senator Tasker Oddie sweats while George Springmeyer tiptoes forward with Carrie Nation's hatchet. Probably drawn by Boyd Moore prior to the 1926 senatorial primary.

Unfortunately for George, a libel suit must be brought in the county where the defendant resides. That meant Tonopah, and Tonopah knew whose side it was on. George's lawyer was Sardis Summerfield and Booth's was Jim Boyd, a florid Irishman, with wisps of white hair flying in various directions, whom George had lately bested in the Ritter trial. Because the evidence was hardly disputable, Boyd resorted to an emotional appeal to the jury not to convict "this poor old man who has lost his son in the war." The fact that young Booth had not been killed in combat, as Boyd mournfully implied, but had met his end while careening about in a sidecar after a drunken party, added an extra dash of irony to the occasion—at least in the mind of George, who had witnessed the unfortunate accident.

As the black clad, beetle-like figure of Boyd scuttled up and down, introducing more and more irrelevant material into evidence, George, bursting with impatience, vainly strove to persuade Summerfield to object. Although the "clear, cold logic and overpowering eloquence" of which Summerfield had once boasted were obviously fading since the days of Armageddon, George was unwilling to dismiss his old Progressive comrade in arms in the middle of the case. He could only take lean comfort from the fact that the stony, set faces of the jurors suggested that Tonopah's own Bill Booth was in no danger of an adverse judgment from his friends and neighbors no matter how the case was conducted.

This suspicion proved correct. Although charging a man with a felony is *ipso facto* libel and the judge instructed the jury that libel had been committed, they returned a verdict of "not guilty." It took a while, but in later years, my father would chuckle about that. He used to say he was "probably the only man in the United States to be convicted, in effect, of treason worse than Benedict Arnold."

* * *

If the pressures Senator Oddie had attempted to exert on behalf of the bootleggers had any discernible effect on the United States attorney, they only served to enhance his resolve. In mid-December of 1923 George issued a public statement: "Apparently we are getting nowhere on enforcement." Bootleggers had begun barricading themselves behind "heavily barred doors and windows," which allowed them more time to destroy incriminating evidence. Henceforth maximum sentences would be sought and conspiracy charges, which involved heavier penalties than simple Prohibition violations, would be filed whenever possible. Perhaps the announcement was an oblique reminder to Senator Oddie and his friends.[15]

That year the number convicted in criminal cases in the federal district court rose by 26 percent; the amount of fines imposed increased by more than 80 percent. The following year George's report to the attorney general would record 324 criminal convictions, 148 civil convictions, many of them in abatement suits, and more than $89,000 in fines imposed. Each figure was a record for Nevada during the decade from 1920 to 1930. Average sentences were nearly twice the national norm. Six of every thousand adults in Nevada stood trial in the federal court during that single year; in Idaho less than two adults in every thousand were tried; in Colorado and Montana the figures were less than one. And my father remained determined to crack the big ring. A few days after he announced his new and tougher enforcement policies, they raided Jimmy McKay.[16]

No doubt McKay figured prominently in those odds on bets the men in the street were laying against my father. Around his notorious name swirled an aura of danger and rumor. The press tactfully referred to him as a "Nevada sportsman," which was probably as close as they could come to saying what McKay did for a living this side of libel. The "McKay supply of liquor" figured prominently in the Donnelley case. The profits realized at the central source of liquor for most of the Reno roadhouses were allegedly enormous, and the rake-off from the earnings of the lesser bootleggers was once estimated as high as 50 percent. Together with his partner, Bill Graham, McKay was said to be financially interested in the impregnable Reno Social Club, the Bank Club, and the red-light district. The pair also were believed to run the illegal gambling concession for Wingfield in the Golden Hotel.

All this was not accomplished without occasional resort to those methods by which differences of opinion were resolved in the world of Jimmy McKay. When McKay was still a Tonopah cafe owner in 1920 before his momentous move to Reno, few believed he had really suffered a little mishap with his own revolver when he turned up with a gunshot wound in his leg. Roughly a decade later in a Reno dive known as the Haymarket, Bill Graham would shoot professional gambler William McCracken, and the coroner, citing self-defense, would quickly exonerate him of murder charges. A few years later when the two were indicted for running an international swindling ring, a key witness permanently disappeared.[17]

Much was said, more was suspected, but very little was ever proven, because Jimmy McKay was shrewder and more careful than others of his kind who came to early and spectacular ends. He was short legged with the heavy torso of a fighter; otherwise his appearance was unremarkable and unobtrusive. Dressed like any other Reno businessman, he seemed indistinguishable in speech and manner from the others in the crowd into which he so easily disappeared. Yet my father knew what he was, and who his friends were, for McKay too was part of the "old Goldfield crowd."

Because Donnelley had not yet been unseated, Washington sent the chief of the Pacific Coast division of Internal Revenue and his men on special assignment to do the job. On the day they selected for the raid, McKay, in his capacity as Nevada sportsman, was at the Tijuana track in Mexico with a string of his racehorses. Four truckloads of liquor, including champagne, Gordon's gin, and good whiskey from Canada and Mexico, as well as ten-gallon kegs of moonshine, were found hidden behind secret panels in his house. A narcotics officer began searching for drugs, but confronted with vehement protests from Mrs. McKay, he desisted, fearful that the lack of a specific narcotics warrant might nullify the operation. Whatever else may have remained secreted in that house, the seizure was the largest in the history of Nevada Prohibition.[18]

At the outset the McKay attorneys, Thatcher and Woodburn, gave every sign of confidence. Thatcher was the former Nevada attorney general and my father's opponent in 1914; Woodburn had been my father's predecessor as United States attorney; both were best known for their close relationship with George Wingfield. An arrogant statement was issued declaring that Thatcher expected to secure the return of the confiscated liquor to its rightful owners.

In order to force the woman witness whose affidavit was the basis of the McKay search warrant to appear in court for interrogation, Thatcher brought out a writ of traverse. At the first hearing, his prolonged and clever efforts to extract more information about this witness from the United States commissioner in charge finally brought Springmeyer to his feet, expostulating, "Wait a minute! I do not think the commissioner is subject to an inquisition here!" The United States attorney himself, well aware of the probable consequences of exposure for the witness, refused to supply additional information, and suggestions that the mystery woman was fictitious were advanced by Thatcher. Handwriting experts and detectives would eventually be engaged to decipher the real identity beneath the undercover agent's nom de guerre. It was a matter of some interest to the bootleggers: if the witness did not exist, the warrant was defective and the case would crumble; if the government could be forced to disclose her identity, they would deal with her in their own way.[19]

In March, when the grand jury was considering Donnelley's misconduct and other matters, persons described in the press as "some of the higher ups in the bootlegging and narcotics rings" threatened to murder two female witnesses if they did not remain silent. The frightened women begged George not to call them to the stand. George promised armed protection, and finally they agreed to come forth. The McKays,

Bill Graham, Tex Hall, and others were indicted on conspiracy charges.[20]

Thatcher and Woodburn left no legal stone unturned. Motions were filed for a writ of review, for annulment of the United States commissioner's action, and for the invalidation of the indictment. Still my father pressed forward, patiently and inexorably. And it began to seem as though the unthinkable possibility, the one event that no one in Nevada had seriously believed could ever happen, might really come to pass: the McKays were going to be tried.

It was then that George Wingfield invited the United States attorney to dinner. Again dinner. My father seats himself at the table across from the boss of his party, as he once did in the mansion of a small man with pale, gray eyes in 1910. We have been here before. I find a ceremonial quality in these dinners, like the wedding feast or the funeral wake. This too is an occasion of a kind, the beginning or the ending of a political life, a feast or a wake.

It began as a pleasant meal, with conversation of no particular consequence. Then McKay, flanked by Graham and several henchmen, walked in, and the conversation that ensued was one my father would never forget. "You must dismiss that case," said one of the bootleggers, "because if you don't you will be prosecuted for violation of the Mann Act, and your father and mother, who, as you know, are very old, will be disgraced to such an extent that your disgrace will result in their early death." He went on to say that they knew George had taken a beautiful, red-haired divorcee on a ten-day auto trip to Yosemite and the Del Monte Hotel near San Francisco, traveling as man and wife.

"That's not true," said George, incredulous at this crude threat. "I never slept with her in California. What's the matter with you men? Do you think a man has to take a divorcee to another state to sleep with her? You know better than that."

"We have photocopies of the registers of all those places showing you registered as husband and wife."

"You have no such thing," said George angrily. "If you have anything to that effect, it is a forgery and won't stand up in court."

"The attorney general has been informed of what you've done. He's going to dismiss you as United States attorney, and you will receive terrible publicity unless you dismiss those charges. Remember what effect this would have on your mother and father."

Again my father countered with the observation that a doctored hotel register was perjured evidence, certain to be discredited in court. But the response was swift and threatening.

"Oh, no, we have that all fixed up. You'd better think of your mother and father."

Although McKay and his cohorts made few false moves, those repeated efforts to conjure up George's parents were ill-suited to their aims. It was true that where the old couple lived out their retirement on the quiet, shady back streets of Carson City in the little, turreted Jacobean house, painted charcoal gray with white trim, the most scandalous object in view was the etching of the wood nymph gazing soulfully over her shoulder that hung on the parlor wall above the tiny, stiff chairs and settees. Carson was not far in miles from the Reno roadhouses and the brothels and saloons of the mining towns, yet Carson remained somehow a separate world, simple, rural, Victorian, and as far removed from these other racier Nevada cities as from New York or Chicago. It was true, too, that in this tightly corseted milieu the violators of the Mann Act, those lecherous men who transported a woman across a state line for "immoral purposes," were a shame and a disgrace.

The bootleggers knew the place, but not the man. H.H. was then nearing the eightieth year of his life. His face had furrowed, his body had shrunken, and his clothes hung loosely on his tall, thin frame. But he still had the thick, dark hair of a young man, the eyes that glinted ice blue in anger, and the same tough fiber. A bold spirit like my father rarely required support, but if there was ever a moment when reinforcements were needed, a vision of what the old hussar would have said if he had been present in that room was more than enough.

"Well," my father told them, "you can neither bluff nor scare me that way because I know my father and mother, as well as the public, would have no trouble seeing the forgery, and experts would have no trouble finding it and clearing me. You ought to know by this time, after the many threats that have been made against my life, that I don't scare easily. And I'm too old to learn how to run away. So to hell with your threats. Do your damndest, but I'm going through with those cases."

Throughout this heavy-handed attempt to blackmail the United States attorney, George Wingfield sat silent in the shadows. That, in fact, was his usual method during this period. Although his name had been briefly glimpsed from time to time as Crumley's intimate, as Donnelley's bondsman, or as Oddie's mentor, it had as quickly vanished from public view. The boss of the bipartisan machine occupied no public office apart from the nominal position of Republican national committeeman and preferred to pursue his private ends without the encumbrance of public responsibility or the inconvenience of public scrutiny. His place was in the shadows, and his methods were usually oblique. When questioned in the course of a legal trial some years later on the directions he customarily gave his two right-hand men, Thatcher and Woodburn, Wingfield's answer had the solid ring of truth. "I do not know that I gave them any instructions," he said. "They knew what I wanted."[21] My father also knew well enough what George Wingfield wanted. But he was paying no mind.

Nonetheless Wingfield would have his way in the end, as he nearly always did. Though he had abandoned his initial plan to

have Oddie demand Springmeyer's resignation immediately after the McKay raid, though the offer of a federal sinecure had
failed to tempt as he had hoped it might, though even blackmail
carefully calibrated to George Springmeyer's love for his parents and his consciousness of their pride in him had failed,
Wingfield still had other strategies, less swift, less economical,
less certain perhaps—for the United States attorney rarely
failed to convict his man—yet far more discreet. Now, as always, Thatcher and Woodburn knew what George Wingfield
wanted. By the end of the summer the judge had denied their
motions to quash the McKay search warrants, but the following
spring he consented to take motions for a rehearing under ad-
visement. My father's term of office had less than a year to run.
These motions remained under consideration during the summer of 1925. In November demurrers alleging that the indictments had been too vaguely drawn were filed by the
defendants. Only five months to go. After Christmas the demurrers were denied, but the McKays had until mid-January to
file their bill of exceptions. Less than three months remained.
And it was not enough. Thatcher and Woodburn succeeded in
delaying the case until George's term of office had expired.[22]

"It is a cinch that Springmeyer will not be reappointed,"
Senator Oddie assured George Wingfield. Noting the "necessity
for keeping the people there in line," Oddie himself favored a
new United States attorney from the Fallon region as a sort of
geographic consolation prize to soften the resentment his stance
on the water rights controversy had aroused among the small
holders on the Newlands project. However, he dutifully obeyed
his instructions. George's successor, Harry H. Atkinson, personally summoned to the position by Wingfield, did not see fit
to prosecute McKay.[23]

In a more congenial climate, the big ring would rapidly recover from the damage inflicted by Donnelley's conviction and
the roadhouse suits. The percentage of liquor cases discontin-

George Wingfield at the Weepah mining boom in 1927.

ued by an order of nolle prosequi declaring the prosecutor does not intend to proceed further had more than doubled in Nevada four years after 1924–1925 (abuses of this nature finally became so notorious throughout the nation that United States attorneys were required to obtain permission from the Justice Department in "nolle prossing" cases). Four years after my father's last full year in office (1924–1925), total criminal convictions had plummeted by 42 percent, fines imposed had dropped by 58 percent, and favorable decisions were secured in only 44 percent of the civil suits tried by the government, a figure dramatically below the 84 percent rate George had achieved.[24]

So my father returned to private life, his tough old hide still miraculously unscathed, still flat-footed for law and order, still unspiked, with only one mistake he regretted: he had not gone to Eureka, and Nick Carter's murderer would never see justice.

Divorce Attorney

MY FATHER RETURNED to his old offices at the First National Bank Building, this time for good. At Jimmy McKay's glamorous supper club, "The Willows," the door swung wide to receive the former United States attorney as a frequent and honored guest, and the coveted privilege of admission was readily extended to anyone who had his name for an introduction. One had won, the other had lost. Now the game was over, and there was no enmity on either side. Emancipated from his former duties to the eighteenth amendment, George was now free to unwind in the relaxed atmosphere of a wide-ranging law practice with clients everywhere in western Nevada. He did corporation work, carried on water-rights litigation—having been initiated at his father's knee into the intricate world of marls, declivities, tile lands, evaporation, percolation, scapage, head gates, tail ditches, channels, and flumes, he had a rare understanding of it—and accepted cases of several other varieties. Part of the time, though, he began to concern himself with one of Reno's major industries in that period—divorce.

Divorce had long been easily obtained in Nevada, and although the residence period was temporarily lengthened while moral legislation was at its height during the Progressive period, Nevada legislators were not disposed to suppress a vital sector of the local economy for long. In 1927 the six-month residence period was cut to three; not long afterward it dwindled to six weeks. In many states the legal grounds on which a divorce might be obtained were prohibitively restrictive, but in Nevada they were broad enough for any unhappy couple to comfortably stroll thereon. That divorce was in reality an infant industry was obvious enough. From time to time the press would observe that "Reno Divorces Show Strong During Month," much as the *Wall Street Journal* might have commented on corn futures.

A few spectacular out-of-staters had obtained Nevada divorces after the turn of the century; many prominent Nevadans were themselves divorced—Oddie, Summerfield, Wingfield, and my father, to mention only a few—a fact that did not seem to scandalize their contemporaries. By the twenties the highly publicized divorces of socialite Olga Bayne in 1918 and Mary Pickford in 1919 had been news throughout the nation. Increasingly Reno became the place where divorce seekers from all over the land converged for a brief time to sever the ties that bind and cast their wedding rings into the shallow, babbling waters of the Truckee. (Such, at least, was the tradition, though none of the enterprising boys I knew who used to splash around among the rocks looking for rings ever succeeded in finding any.)

In an earlier day Nevada's emergence as a divorce center had aroused some moralistic criticism. "Free and easy toleration of the whims and caprices of women who find affinities after marriage or who consider the yoke of matrimony too irksome is used as a vehicle for dirty flings and taunts throughout the East," wrote a censorious local editor in 1911. "The name of Nevada is coupled with the erotic intimation that this is the land of free love."[1] That was a fairly accurate assessment of the racy reputation Nevada was acquiring in the East and would retain for nearly half a century. By the twenties, however, most Nevadans had accepted "the divorce business," as it was commonly referred to, and local criticism had died away to be replaced by a standard body of Reno witticisms: Reno was the only city in America where lawyers met all the trains. Reno was known as the "Great Divide" because after the judge divides the wife and husband, she divides the husband's dough with her lawyer. It was better to have loved and lost than to win and pay alimony. Reno restaurants were right in keeping with the times—they served split pea soup, halved peaches, and separator cream. If a wife had the same husband longer than two years she was considered old-fashioned—if she had him more than three, she was considered selfish. Matches, it was said, were made in heaven, lighted on earth, and put out in Reno.[2]

Over the years a long procession of judges presided over the divorce ritual in court. One of the more memorable was Barney Moran, who adorned the bench for over a quarter century and was better remembered not for his legal learning but for his Irish brogue, his rapid volte-faces, and his Gaelic prejudices, with which the attorneys learned to steer a careful course, like sea captains taking advantage of the prevailing winds. On his first day as district judge in 1910, Moran granted nine divorces. Within two weeks he had set a divorce record.[3] More than a decade later divorces were still being churned out at a rapid pace in the Moran court, but once in a while the judge behaved contrarily and rejected a divorce plea. On one of these occasions the judicial gavel had descended, the judicial voice had pronounced the evidence insufficient and the divorce denied, and a heavy gloom had settled over the counselor's bench. The lady divorce seeker was pallid and crushed; her attorney bent dejectedly to pack his papers into his briefcase. Suddenly, seized with a last-minute inspiration, he hurried up to the judge. His client's husband, he said hopefully, was English and—he got no farther.

"What? Hehr uzband was *English?*" roared Judge Moran, frowning sympathetically down from the heights. "Bluidy Englishman niver knew how to treat a woman. Divorhrce grhranted." Again the judicial gavel descended with a resounding bang.

People connected with the new moving-picture industry were a small but highly visible proportion of the divorce colony, and, then as now, their marital mishaps were meat and drink to the press—never more so than when Two Gun Bill Hart and Winifred Westover parted company. Hart, with his "new realism," was the director-star who had rescued the languishing Western from a slough of unpopularity. By the twenties, millions were familiar with his intent gaze, his rounded, high-crowned hat, and his famous crouching stance, guns at the ready, in such silent films as *Hell's Hinges, Sand*, and *Wagon Tracks*.

In keeping, no doubt, with the new realism, Hart repeatedly fell in love with his leading ladies, and finally he married one of them, the flower-faced starlet with tousled, blonde curls named Winifred Westover, who co-starred with him in *John Petticoats*. It was what would later become known as a "typical Hollywood marriage"—by the time Hollywood had been around long enough for people to decide what was typical there. The marital troubles of the Harts were soon making lurid headlines, and Winifred arrived at my father's office. After the divorce proceedings, she dissolved into tears on the courthouse steps declaring that "I always and still am unalterably opposed to divorce." It was a scene as moving as any she had ever played on the screen, but her audience of newspaper reporters unaccountably failed to sympathize with a woman's deepest feelings on such a sad occasion, especially a young and pretty woman with a very large financial settlement in hand. Not long afterward the aggrieved starlet appeared clinging to my father's arm and vowing that she intended to sue certain New York papers for libel.[4]

Lovely she was, but another less glamorous divorce seeker nearly a decade earlier had impressed my father far more vividly. This lady was Olga Roosevelt Bayne, Washington socialite, cousin of Theodore Roosevelt, and heiress to a $10 million fortune. Gossip columnists noted that "smart Washington" had gasped again and again at Olga's "mad impetuosity." Wherever she went, whatever she did, and most of all, whatever she *might* do were matters for breathless commentary and feverish speculation on the society page. Her divorce in 1918 was probably the most sensational in Nevada during the wartime period. By the time she had parted company with one war hero and married another, the whole affair had titillated gossips in the capital city for quite some time.[5] There was evidently an interlude of romance with my father during her sojourn in Nevada. The large number of Olga's photographs in my father's album would attest to it, if nothing else did. In a photograph George labeled "Olga shows poise (and beautiful legs)," she is in a black turban, a black four-tiered dress ending above the knee, and black stockings, balancing precariously on the rocks at the Lake Tahoe shore. In another, where he wrote "Olga at her loveliest," she wears a boldly striped dress and broad-brimmed, white hat and carries a parasol. Many other pictures follow before the last, Olga and her second husband, across the edge of which my father wrote ruefully "Wherefore, finis." Certainly Olga was not easily forgotten, but when he spoke of her, it was not the romance he dwelled upon. It was the snakes.

Olga was an outstanding sportswoman, and my father often took her golfing. As they proceeded around the course, she would find snakes in the grass and pick them up. Seeing George's unmistakable distaste for the slimy, fork-tongued reptiles, she would teasingly hold them out to him and say, "Oh, look at him, George! Isn't he sweet? Wouldn't you like to hold him?"

Decidedly he would not, but he was thoroughly ashamed of being afraid to handle snakes when a woman was doing it. He forced himself to snatch the wriggling reptiles as Olga did. Thenceforth they made their way around the golf course swinging at balls and picking up snakes together.

* * *

One day a drunken and persistent Indian insisted on seeing George despite the secretary's repeated efforts to repulse him. When at length she wearily admitted him, he said to my father "Aw, George, don't look so rough," and asked the attorney if he could recover the fifty dollars forfeited from his unwelcome client the night before when he was locked up in the cooler. George answered curtly that he didn't "fool around with the police courts."

"Hold on a minute, George," said the Indian, his black eyes fixed on my father. "You wouldn't treat me that way. One time just like brothers and sisters, don't you remember? When we little fellows so high, we play together. Have many good times. Don't you remember big ditch at barn? One day you fall in and I take you out. And we fish and run races and ride. Then you grow up and go school and I go away Stewart Indian school and learn read and write just like you. Now I not see you for long, long time, but I read about you and talk about you. Don't you remember now?"

"Fiddlesticks no, I've forgotten all that," said George, studying the middle-aged man across the desk intently. "Who are you anyway?"

"Dick Springmeyer."

"The devil you say," my father said laughing. Dick was the one who had saved his sister Clare from the wild parsnip nearly forty years before. He told his secretary the other clients would have to wait because he had important business to attend to. They set out together in high good humor, George's arm around Dick's shoulders to steer his wavering course. The judge in police court did not trouble to conceal his amazement when one of Nevada's most famous attorneys appeared to secure bond for a drunken vagrant and furthermore proceeded to introduce the Indian who stood somewhat unsteadily at his side as "my brother Dick Springmeyer."

* * *

A succession of pretty, feminine clients appeared in my father's office—Noras, Amys, Junes, and Rebas. While their legal affairs awaited Judge Moran's pounding gavel, it was always a pleasure to entertain them. He took them fishing, golfing, and horseback riding, or sleighing and skiing in winter. They appear in his old photo album wearing wide picture hats and carefully arranged in languorous three-quarter poses; some perch on rounded boulders at Lake Tahoe or display large fish caught at Pyramid Lake. My father, sometimes mugging, sometimes looking rather dashing in knee-high riding boots or a golfing cap, appears in these photos too.

But sooner or later a lady was bound to come who was more than another photo in the album, someone special and different from all the rest. And one evening in 1930, she did. At last, owing to the restrictive divorce laws of New York and the permissive ones of Nevada, the paths of those two vastly different families, the merchant princes of Hamburg and the peasant farmers of Westphalia, would cross. The chasm, unbridgeable in Germany, would close. Though East was East and West was West and never the twain should meet, the world of New York society was about to touch the American West. Sallie Maria Ruperti was coming to Nevada.

Her coming-out party in the Rose Room had been followed by cruises, balls, Vassar, and in due time, marriage to a charming young man who squandered her dowry on Florida real estate and showed himself keenly aware of something Sallie had never particularly noticed: that she knew everyone worth knowing. He was himself a Southerner in the social sense of the word, which meant his mother wore a black velvet ribbon around her neck and he never lost sight of the only two things that really mattered in his milieu—who your family was and where your money came from. The trouble with Sallie, as he explained it, was that she had never "used her connections properly." She had grown up with the cream of New York, and if that fortunate asset were assiduously exploited, she could be invited to all the best places—accompanied, of course, by her delightful husband. Enchanting vistas of parties, bridge, and country weekends loomed before them, theirs simply for the asking.

But Sallie remained inexplicably indifferent to using her connections. Soon she was on the train to Reno, cautioned by numerous admonitions from her anxious mother. Although many of Mrs. Ruperti's acquaintances had traveled widely in Europe, few had ever ventured west of Philadelphia, and she was unshakably convinced that Nevada was a wild, uncivilized, and vaguely dangerous place. Indeed she was not entirely certain that hostile Indians were not on the loose in that trackless wilderness beyond the limits of the known world. Bravely, Sallie steeled herself for the ordeal ahead.

When she stepped down from the train in Reno, she must have looked unbelievably beautiful, with her wide, brown eyes, her classic profile, and her long, black hair, parted in the middle and twisted in a chignon at the nape of her graceful neck. As she moved through a crowd of women with curls and fashionable hairstyles, every eye always turned toward that smooth, dark head. Her natural beauty, heightened by no more than a shading of lipstick and a slight buffing of the nails, made the rouge, the painted nails, and all the little allurements of others appear hopelessly artificial; her simple, severe suits made other women in ruffles, ribbons, and flowery prints seem fluffy and faintly ridiculous. Beside her, the Amys, the Junes, and the Rebas could only fade into insignificance. The attorney her

New York lawyer had engaged for her, a Mr. George Springmeyer, was waiting on the station platform. His eyes lit on this
loveliest of all the dark ladies, and he took her dancing immediately.

Sallie's mother had not been entirely wrong. One did not go
dancing from the train in New York; and if Reno was not
exactly dangerous, there certainly was something a bit racy and
impetuous about it. Sallie thought her attorney was a "terrible
person." But apparently not so terrible that she would reject his
attentions entirely.

Presently she took an apartment in a building owned by
Charlie Norcross, once the assistant director of Prohibition under Donnelley. Norcross and George had not been on speaking
terms since my father refused Norcross's request to call off the
Ritter prosecution, but in the disarming presence of this lovely
lady, loud men suddenly spoke softly, rude men grew civil,
stern men smiled, shy men bloomed, and angry men forgot
what it was they had quarreled about. So it was, at last, with
Charlie Norcross and George Springmeyer when my mother
arrived in Reno.

My father always said he fell in love with her the day they
went horseback riding, he on the fine, black stallion he kept
stabled in Reno and she on a slower steed. Although she had
been listening with lively interest to his discourse on political
affairs, her horse lagged behind. He turned and saw she had
soundlessly fallen from her horse. Was he charmed by the way
she perched in the dirt with the same unruffled aplomb with
which she would seat herself on a Louis Quinze chair? Or did
the lady in the dust seem a shade more vulnerable than before?
On horseback she was beautiful, but unseated, she totally en-
chanted him, and from that moment he loved her.

Yet, the thought that this princess from back East, this para-
gon of beauty twenty-two years younger than himself, could
possibly care for him did not enter his mind. He might never

have spoken to her of love had it not been for the fortuitous presence of another client. He was then handling the divorce of an heiress to one of America's great railroad fortunes. With the heiress in Reno was the man she would soon marry, an English aristocrat. The foursome saw a good deal of each other, and Sallie and George found the Englishman very charming, although it was never clear exactly what he did—for a living, that is. But however nebulous his career, he understood women very well indeed, far better than my father. He must have watched the attorney's humorous, blue eyes and strong, commanding features, handsomer than ever at forty-nine, now that the years had wiped away the boyish look that clung to him so long. And he must have watched the way Sallie's own glance rested on that face. He must have seen, as only a stranger could, the magnetic appeal of that crystalline purity of spirit for more complex and subtle beings. It was he who took George privately aside and urged him to press his suit ("she likes you, you know"). Thus encouraged, George did, and to his astonishment, the beautiful Sallie consented to marry him.

When he took her to see H.H., the old man looked at her long, slender hands. That was a thing he had always admired in a woman, he said. Wilhelmine, now dead these two years past, had hands like that when he first brought her to the ship at Bremerhaven more than sixty years ago. Then came the cabin on the frontier and the ten children. He had watched her hands roughen and gnarl and wither during all those years of hard work. But he saw her still as she had been in the beginning, a shy girl sitting in the Westphalian meadow so long ago. Such beautiful hands she had then. The old man nodded; he approved of Sallie Maria Ruperti.

Still my father could not entirely believe his good fortune, nor was he the sort of man to press his advantage. It was agreed that Sallie would go home for six months to "think it over" and to consider whether she was really prepared to abandon New

York for the wilderness west of Philadelphia. When he knew her even better, he would learn she was totally devoid of fluttery vacillations and rarely reconsidered anything. In her fashion, she was almost as irrevocable as the Springmeyers. He would later tease her about her impatience, her way of wanting a thing immediately after she had decided to have it, and I sometimes wonder if she had not decided upon him with just that kind of swiftness and certainty. All the same, she went back to New York as planned. Like one of the soufflés with which Sallie's mother tested the skill of her cooks, this new romance would either remain crisply aloft when removed from the heat or settle limply back in the pan.

At home she was now a wicked divorcee and something of a pariah in the eyes of society. It was not quite the scarlet letter, but almost. When she received a dinner invitation, her mother remarked with some surprise, "It was very kind of them to ask you, dear—*considering*." At another affair, Sallie and a divorced man, both feeling like the carriers of a contagious disease, were seated at a separate table for two at a safe distance from the other guests. Though New York hostesses tended to be glacial, the reception she received from her Eastern suitors was considerably warmer. Yet she did not waver in her decision. She loved the man, and, eccentric as it seemed to her family, the life he offered appealed to her.

As a girl her summers in the country had been her happiest times. Her mother had thought her odd; her father had seemed sympathetic, though he was so shy and reticent that one could not be certain. She knew he had wanted to farm before he was ordered to take his place in the family business, and only on the country estate had he ever seemed purely happy. She hoped that now he also understood, for she found it hard to explain, while seated in a Manhattan drawing room, what the world was like out in the West. It was difficult to describe this pioneer son of the frontier she intended to marry, this man so unlike anyone her parents had ever met. It was impossible to convey a sense of the gay, little city at the foot of the Sierra, of the piercing blue days, the smell of sage after rain, the clean, sun-washed emptiness of Western space. How could she make them believe that she wanted this and not a future of unending bridge parties and dinners and dancing? She tried.

At the end of April 1931, my father set out on the train for New York. Although he did not know it, he was preceded by a sort of letter of recommendation from Tom Miller, which made a great impression on Sallie's father—ironically, had Justus Ruperti realized that his correspondent was the former Alien Property Custodian, an instrument in the financial ruin of the Ruperti mercantile empire, and a recent parolee from the federal prison where he had been dispatched for his alleged misdeeds in office, Ruperti might have been less favorably impressed.[6] Upon George's arrival, Sallie's choice became far more comprehensible to her family and her friends. My father always said he felt he received the final seal of approval at a large dinner given in honor of the engaged couple when, during a brief lull in the conversation, Sallie's aged godfather was overheard to loudly declare, "At least he's a damn sight better than the last one."

They were married at a small town in Connecticut by a minister so embarrassed and nonplussed by the necessity for presiding over the union of two divorced persons that he concocted an original and peculiar ceremony especially to suit the occasion. They honeymooned on the coast of Maine, feasting on shellfish and taking long walks on the cold, rocky beaches, and finally returned to Reno. The iris were blooming along the driveway bordered with great Dutch elms as they drove up to the house he had bought for her, a white house with a red-tiled roof and acres of gardens and apple orchards set on a hill outside of town overlooking a vista of mountains and meadow-lands. Taking the first letters of their two names, they called it Sage.

* * *

By now Reno was the acknowledged divorce capital of America, and divorce cases were consuming an increasing proportion of my father's time. On several occasions he rejected offers of judicial appointments because he said he lacked the impartial judicial temperament, that he was born to take sides. To some other lawyers, especially the younger ones who admired him, this concentration upon divorce seemed a waste of an extraordinary legal talent. My mother did not think of it that way. At this particular stage in his life, she told me, he was "not averse to making money," by no means an inconsequential consideration during the depression. Along with many others, he had lost virtually everything in the failure of the Wingfield banks (Wingfield himself was rumored to have prudently withdrawn his personal funds before the collapse). He did make it, but corporation work would probably have been equally lucrative. The most intriguing feature of divorce work from his point of view was the unending human interest it provided. An extraordinary parade of people would pass through his office during the next thirty years.

They ranged from the Nobel prize-winning scientist with whom my father played ping pong to the Indianapolis correspondent who wrote, "Dear Sir: Having hear of Andy Jackson Brown gon to Nevadow to get a divorce of his sweet little wife he left hear with a nother woman. He is a thief a ornery man just send back to court to get his petigree." From Madam Soong, a relative of Madam Chiang Kai-shek and a lady of quiet elegance and infinite refinement, to the bouncy little nightclub singer who billed herself "the cheerful little earful" and married Jack Dempsey. From the former madam (from Goldfield?), now a lady of property and a respected club woman in a social milieu where her friends had no inkling of her origins, and the men who did never told, to the New York society woman who marched into his office in a huff, slammed her girdle down on his desk, and ordered him to return it to a New York department store for her immediately.

From renowned writers, including John Gunther and Kay Boyle, to the Florida lady who titled herself "Musician and Authoress" and declared that although she was "versatile and familiar with many things and friends seers and sages" she had made an "unfortunate mistake" and married a "stock owner" who subsequently proved to be a waiter, "treacherous as they come . . . shrewd, diplomatic clever and knows *ALL* tricks." From the famed artist whose caretaker was continually obliged to retrieve him from police court in an inebriated condition to the local artist who appeared in the doorway and declared in a portentous bark, "I am Hans von Mayer Kassel"—an announcement which was obviously expected to elicit a bit of bowing and scraping, if not a ten-gun salute. A long pause ensued. My father, who never put his feet on his desk, made an exception on this occasion, leaned back in his chair, eyed the man quizzically for a few moments, and finally said casually, "The hell you are."

From Rockefellers and Du Ponts to penniless domestics to whom my father charged nothing at all for his legal work so the bar association could not accuse him of cutting fees. From the British military gentleman who strode up to the office building and announced to the elevator man that he wanted to engage the attorney who habitually came to work at the earliest hour (that, of course, was my father, who always arrived at 8:30), to the Jewish client who had selected my father in the mistaken belief that our German name was Jewish and leaned over the secretary's desk to inquire breathily, "Are you *one of us* too?" From a client who somewhat surprised my father with revela-

Sage, the Springmeyer's Reno home, as it appeared on a winter day in the 1930s.

tions concerning Kay Summersby and not entirely in keeping with the public image of General Eisenhower that prevailed in that era of homage, to the Delaware man who wrote that his wife had "kept house for A Widdower and tried to Mary him up by reporting I was dead" and he now suspected she was "hatching up a Corospondance so she might get Alamoney."[7]

From the famous and fearless aviatrix, Ruth Elder, to the Canadian politician my parents endeavored to entertain with an excursion to Lake Tahoe over Kingsbury Grade. It proved to be a memorable ride. Sallie, as always, was at the wheel, for George had not driven in years. His mind was prone to wander to other matters when driving, and he had shown a recurrent tendency to end up in the ditch. In those days Kingsbury Grade rose from the Carson Valley in a series of precipitate hairpin turns shallowly carved on the steep slope of the Sierra Nevada. So narrow were these serpentine curvatures that two cars could not be accommodated at the same time and each bend had to be approached with honks to forewarn motorists advancing on the other side. More than one careless driver had plunged to his doom in the abyss, but the view was marvelous, and my parents thought the drive was great fun. Not the Canadian. As the valley receded beneath them and the chasm a few feet outside the car window yawned deeper at every curve, he progressed from nervousness to terror. Finally Sallie yielded to his piteous entreaties to turn back. Turn, however, was not quite the word, for no space on that narrow road was wide enough to turn around in. Consequently, she was compelled to back the car all the way down the hairpin turns of Kingsbury Grade, honking as she went, while the Canadian lapsed into helpless hysteria.

* * *

The most important clients, those whose presence in Reno was a dark secret, stayed in rented houses and apartments. Many others sojourned at dude ranches outside the city at Washoe Valley or Pyramid Lake. The gayer set whiled away the time in the downtown hotels. And many divorce seekers gravitated to Ruth Shaw's inn down Arlington Avenue from our house. Because she saw it as a "haven for the distressed," Ruth had christened the big, white house with the dark green trim "Shangri-la"; in the popular James Hilton novel of the period, that was the name of the idyllic, lost kingdom in the Himalayas where everyone is wise and serene and no one ever grows old.

Later Ruth Shaw would say those days at the inn were "like life on a boat," and indeed that is the way it must have been: a group of people, previously unknown to one another, cast together in isolated and intimate circumstances for a brief period. Although "houseguests" arrived from all over the United States, most were from the Northeast; many, like Sallie's mother, had only the vaguest idea what lay west of Philadelphia in that blank region delimited on the outer rim by San Francisco, the Pacific Ocean, and Japan. It had been necessary to locate this place called Reno on the map before starting out. When they embarked on the good ship Shangri-la, Ruth provided genteel games of croquet on the lawn bordered with evergreens and roses, bridge and "musical evenings" in the gracious rooms decorated with hand-carved mahogany furniture, luncheons in a verdant sunroom, and at intervals, festive "hang dinners" for which the divorcee who had just received a decree could choose the menu. Weekly picnics were held in the countryside, and Ruth would even gamely arise at five in the morning to go fishing with the sportsmen among her guests.

Although Ruth Shaw was careful to see that the time should pass pleasantly, many of the male divorce seekers who came to her inn were deeply troubled. Often they would drop by in the evening to talk things over at the cottage where Ruth lived adjoining Shangri-la. The story often was: He had fallen in love with another woman, but he couldn't bear to hurt his wife. It was an old story, and within the secluded walls of her living room, Ruth listened to it many, many times. The women rarely came. They seem to have been more self-contained, more single-minded—or perhaps only more fatalistic.[8]

Sitting in his small, book-lined office at the desk beside the curtains patterned with St. George and the dragon that my mother had teasingly chosen for her unbelieving husband, my father listened to even more intimate stories. One of the primary reasons for "going to Reno" was not only the speed and certainty of the result but also the comfortable discretion with which it was accomplished. There was no need for painful and embarrassing revelations in court; one was only required to murmur something rather vague about "mental cruelty," nothing more. But there in the office beneath the big photograph of two rearing stallions fighting over a herd of mares (an appropriate decorative motif, as it turned out, in view of the numerous tales of sexual combat that were related within those walls), where the clients found themselves talking to this kind, sympathetic man so wholeheartedly on their side—a father confessor and a knight-errant in one—everything came tumbling out. Their privacy was respected. My father spoke to no one, not even to my mother or to me, about his clients. He carried their secrets with him, quite literally, to the grave. I know only his general conclusion: sexual incompatibility was the most common cause of divorce among his clients, and this was not merely symptomatic of other forms of estrangement but was in itself the fundamental cause for parting.

Publicity was often a problem for the better-known clients. Whenever one of these appeared at the Reno courthouse, a welcoming party of reporters from the *Police Gazette*, the New York *Daily News*, and other papers would inevitably be waiting on the steps. A few sought publicity and even wrote the press of their impending arrival. Others tolerated it. When Mrs. Ely Culbertson, wife of the noted bridge expert appeared, my father declared that "we might as well get it over with" and astonished the reporters by inviting them in right away.

The difficulties developed with the most prominent clients, who were invariably anxious to avoid publicity altogether, and the reporters who relentlessly pursued them. My father's particular nemesis among these news hounds was Lulu Bell, a stout, gray-haired woman addicted to miniscule hats, who had no scruples about invading the rooms of divorce seekers and going through their personal belongings in search of a scandalous tidbit with which to titillate her readers. There were occasions, however, when even the indefatigable Lulu Bell was foiled. The Portuguese Princess Briganza, pregnant, blonde, azure-eyed, and altogether the most beautiful woman my father had ever seen, was hidden away so secretly that no one even knew she was there.

My father's favorite stratagem in such cases was to file the divorce suit in one of the small towns outside Reno. Word seldom leaked out, the local residents were generally unaware that anything unusual was going on, and the reporters hanging around the courthouse steps in Reno learned too late that they had missed a scoop. But this device was only a qualified success on the day when Mrs. Franklin D. Roosevelt, Jr., the former Ethel Du Pont, went clambering out the window of the Minden courthouse while my father distracted the reporters in the hallway with animated conversation—"Mrs. Roosevelt and Attorney Stage Fox and Hounds Chase with Wire Service Reporters" read the headlines.

It also went awry, through no fault of my father's, on the day of the Hartford affair. The middle-aged heiress to the A & P fortune was seeking a divorce, after which she and the Italian Prince Pignatelli intended to be married. Both the lady and the prince impressed upon my father the absolutely vital importance of complete secrecy. Publicity would be the gravest calamity. Their privacy must be preserved at any cost.

My father, in his usual way, managed it rather well. He decided on Yerington, a little town nestled among the fertile hay fields of the Mason Valley some eighty miles southeast of Reno, and not a word leaked out—at least, not until the day arrived. As my father awaited his clients, the prince and the heiress came roaring down from the skies in a private airplane. It was an immediate sensation. A real private airplane had rarely been seen at Yerington in those days. People came running from every direction to stare at the extraordinary machine and its occupants. In no time at all, the great secret was out.

* * *

These were years of gaiety and laughter for my parents; of dancing in the intimate darkness of The Willows; of "clients' teas," when the current crop of divorcees congregated in our sunlit dining room; and of Eddie Cantor movies, to which George took his wife for the pure pleasure of watching that lovely, poised face, which sometimes smiled but rarely laughed, crinkle into uncontrollable giggles. While she watched the movies, he watched her. The busy little suite of offices in the First National Bank Building had none of the dull and pretentious atmosphere of many of its modern counterparts because, as my father's partner put it, "George was so damn much fun to be around." But these were also years of much hard work. My father was still imbued with the "German work complex," and my mother was as energetic as she was beautiful. They decided that she too would become a lawyer and share his work. So, while my father reverted to bachelor life in the company of Tom Miller and a Chinese cook, my mother went away to law school at Stanford and the University of Southern California. He would visit her; there were romantic weekends at the old Spanish inn near Los Angeles where the fountain played in the patio and reunions in the Stanford quad, while the faculty and the other law students, a straitlaced lot in those days, gaped with scandalized expressions at their passionate kisses and embraces. That, at least, is the way their friends describe the scene —my parents were oblivious to everyone but each other.

When H.H. died and his lands were divided among his children, there was a choice to be made between Lake Tahoe and Long Valley. My father had been given a large portion of Crystal Bay on the north shore of the lake as a legal fee, and in those days that steep, unspoiled slope of pale granite boulders among tall pines above the clear, blue water was even more glorious than it is now. All the same, my father was uninterested. There was "really nothing to do up there" he said and, of course, from his point of view, there was not. He was congenitally incapable of lying in a lounge chair at Lake Tahoe. So they kept only a token slice of Crystal Bay for the sake of the two spectacular boulders poised upon its slope and went camping under the juniper tree by Indian Creek in Long Valley.

At dawn a luminous golden glow began to shine just north of Horseshoe Bend where the dark, blue Pine Nut Hills dipped low. The water birds wheeling high above the reservoir glinted white as snowflakes when the first beams caught the rocky tips of the sage-furred hills beside the lake. They sifted down to a light on the glassy water or the sanded shore, dotted with clumps of willow bushes, then rose again with a joyous cacophony. White, water-smoothened boulders lay scattered like a herd of sheep on the grassy slope where the stream gurgled cheerfully past the flank of Springmeyer Peak; the west wind swept down from the Sierra; eagles soared above the rocky mesa to the west. My father knew where they nested, had known since he was a boy. The valley was still much the same as in the days when Pete Milich rode up from the Comstock, still the same wild, romantic place.

They decided they would develop Long Valley in their leisure hours; it was "more creative" than lying in the sun, more satisfying than speculating in real estate. And that is what they did. The blanket under the juniper tree was replaced by a small ranch house of brick and cement blocks, solid as the rocky peaks around it, set near the reservoir on the knoll overlooking Long Valley and the swaying layers of the Pine Nut Hills. For many of the years since Leo and Charlie had refused to make their lives here, these lands had been rented out as pasturage and eaten down by sheep, a species of animal which my father, like any true son of a cattleman, thoroughly detested. Still he thought H.H. had been right when he said this was good cropland. When it came to land and what could be done with it, he had never known the old man to go wrong. The pastures, the cropland, and the forage in the hills could support a good-sized herd of cattle. He wanted to start with Herefords, a breed whose merits he had seen when H.H. brought in those first rambunctious bulls more than thirty years before. A few years later George would introduce the Carson Valley's first Angus cattle, and Angus we have raised ever since. Not, of course, without the recurrent natural disasters that inevitably accompany the rural life: the flood that destroyed our new dam on Indian Creek, the drought, the fire that burned our ranch buildings, the star thistle, and the plague of mice that made the fields ripple and seethe with their scurrying and nibbling and tunneling. But my mother and father were not easily discouraged. Adversity meant working, and working was living. In time, they made Long Valley one of the more valuable ranches in Douglas County.

My father had a Westphalian peasant's feeling for the land, and I think he had always loved this particular portion of earth, ever since he used to ride up with his father to watch the Indian crews clear the sagebrush. As a teenager he had been sent there in the summers to cook for the men while they built the fences —fences that still stand today. But more than these remembrances, he had, like his father before him, the pioneer's relish for new beginnings, for making something out of nothing. Land was not to contemplate for its beauty or to buy and sell for profit. It was to work, changing it as it changes you, until you have made it your own. There was no pleasure in buying a valuable ranch, already developed, and maintaining it—at least, that was the sort of enterprise that neither my father nor my grandfather ever undertook. The pleasure was in a piece of land, unfinished, even barren, but with possibilities. Land to ride and plan for, until finally its smell is in your nostrils, you feel the color of its light, you know the shape of its slopes and canyons better than the contours of your own face; the wind that lashes its mountains stings your back; the sun that shines on its pastures warms your skin, until it becomes a part of you. Or you are part of it, no more to be ripped asunder than the mountain from the valley. Perhaps, as the sixtieth year of his life drew nearer, my father was turning back toward his own beginnings.

* * *

Weekdays were spent in Reno at Sage, a miniature farm in itself, with a large vegetable garden, chickens, rabbits, and a few cattle. When one of these heifers sickened, she was brought in to recuperate in our dining room, where she stood, bleary-eyed and miserable, under the gold-framed portraits of my mother's aristocratic ancestors. Weekends were spent on the ranch, where my mother coped under rather primitive conditions with a cheerful capability no pioneer could have improved upon—and apparently with never a passing thought of the servants in her parents' household. She cooked our meals on an old, iron wood-burning stove; simmered jelly from the tiny, bitter chokecherries gathered in the mountains; made apple cider in a wooden press; and drove my father in a jolting truck along a road that was scarcely more than a faint rut to our summer pastures on the mountaintops, where fields of wild iris bloomed and the horses shied sometimes, sensing the unseen presence of bears in the pines.

And I, their only child, born six years after their marriage, sometimes played dress up with the beautiful clothes my mother had brought from New York: the black and golden sandals; the shawls, red lace, or black chiffon, delicate as smoke, beaded in flower patterns, and fringed with dull gold beads; the orange evening gown with the black ostrich-feather trim in which she had tangoed under a Caribbean moon; and the little jacket so cleverly fashioned of strings of rhinestones in spider-web patterns. There was not much call for these things in Nevada.

Yet, although her lovely clothes were packed away, every-thing she did retained an ineradicable touch of breeding. After the flickering kerosene lamps had been lit and our supper had been cooked on the wood stove, she always dressed for dinner. Later my father bought some land for summer pasturage near the mountain hamlet of Markleeville and built a tiny cabin there, which we occasionally shared with Klaus Ehlers, the stooped, misanthropic, old herdsman who looked after our cat-tle; even in those mountains, where we had to carry our water up the hill from the river in buckets and Klaus Ehlers grunted and applied Absorbine Junior to his grimy toes during meals, mother's dinners were always stylishly served—in courses.

* * *

After World War II began, George agreed to serve on Neva-da's Alien Enemy Hearing Board, one of many local groups organized throughout the United States by the Justice Depart-ment to determine which enemy aliens should be interned be-cause they were potentially dangerous to national security. Although the Nevada board's concern was the selective confinement of individuals—Germans and Italians, as well as Japanese—it had to operate in a climate of virulent public an-tagonism against the Japanese. Wartime hysteria among the alarmed residents of the Pacific Coast and their congressional representatives, coupled with the contingency planning of ner-vous American commanders who feared a fifth column in the coastal region, resulted in a presidential decision to evacuate California's entire Japanese population and incarcerate them in detention camps. Not only were the constitutional rights of American-born citizens of Japanese ancestry cast aside, but a host of lesser cruelties were inflicted upon them during their miserable exodus from the coast. Under California's an-tievacuee laws, the Japanese were not permitted to engage a hotel room or purchase a meal without publishing their intent three times; in Nevada it was equally difficult because many shopkeepers declined to "trade with the enemy." Officials observed that Reno was "the weakest spot in our national relocations operation." Japanese women with small children had been forced to camp for as long as three days in the Reno railroad station because they were unable to buy food or rent a room in the hostile city outside.[9] In this atmosphere, the local Alien Enemy Hearing Board commenced their deliberations.

In addition to my father, the board included Brewster Adams, minister and civic leader, and Reuben Thompson, the gentle, sagacious professor of philosophy best known to me as my godfather. It should, in theory, have been an ideal tribunal combining the logic, detachment, and wisdom of philosophy (Thompson) with the morality and compassion of Christianity (Adams) and the impartiality and concern for individual rights of law (my father). However, its performance sometimes failed to reflect the three great ethical and intellectual currents of the western world so fortuitously represented by its membership. Although these were men who had known each other long and well, there was an undercurrent of resentment among them that would do nothing to assuage the sharp disagreements that would presently break out within the confines of the board. Adams had been nursing secret animosities against George since 1920, the year when he believed George's support of Oddie had cost him the Republican senatorial primary. My father, for his part, was not one of Adams's numerous admirers. If he had any prejudice at all, it was against ministers, whom he thought were hypocrites more often than not.

The board's proceedings did nothing to disabuse him of that notion. The boards were supposed to operate quickly and informally with greater emphasis on common sense than on legal procedure. The United States attorney presented the facts, any fair evidence was admissible, and the aliens defended them-

George Springmeyer, in his seventies, riding his bay horse Andy at the Long Valley ranch in the 1950s.

selves as best they could, since they were not permitted to have lawyers. A question arose concerning a Japanese who had been turned in by his suspicious and envenomed neighbors: What should be done when there was no real evidence against the man except his ancestry and the hearsay testimony collected by FBI agents? The FBI representative in the room argued that such testimony was acceptable under his instructions. Adams, too, was anxious to dispatch the Japanese to the concentration camps without a hearing, but my father insisted that the man had the right to confront his accusers. Privately he wondered at the rapidity with which this man discarded the charity, the compassion, the belief in the brotherhood of man, and the tender regard for the beatitudes that were supposed to be the hallmark of the Christian ministry. He would not let the Constitution be cast so lightly aside.

Nearly twenty years before as United States attorney he had upheld the impartiality of the law at the cost of his office and the risk of his life, and time had not blunted his lance. Tempers grew shorter; my father's blazing eyes and burning face betrayed his rising anger. As Adams demanded more and more vociferously that the hapless Japanese should be interned without further delay, my father said with finality, "We can't do that under the Constitution of the United States."

He insisted on writing for an opinion from Attorney General Francis Biddle, and his position was upheld. No Japanese under the jurisdiction of the board would be interned without a hearing in which he could confront his accusers. A dry, legalistic axiom lacking in eloquent sonorities. It would ring poorly in a pulpit. Yet it contained something definite and precise that a man could take hold of. It would not evaporate in his hand. It was concerned not with multitudes but with individual men, and it sustained and protected the weak as surely as the strong. This was something worth fighting for.

Long after my father's death, Judge Bruce Thompson, the son of Reuben Thompson and my father's law partner for many years, was remembering these events. "Your father had a very fine perception of the law," the judge told me reflectively. "He understood the Constitution of the United States in an era when most people didn't think about the Constitution."[10] A very fine perception of the law. The judge described it well and saw the legal issues much as my father himself had seen them, but I doubt that the quiet Japanese gentleman who brought flowers to my father each year for many years afterward thought of it in exactly those terms.

* * *

After the campaign of 1920 my father rarely took an active part in political affairs, but he still retained a lively interest in politics. In 1928 he decided to leave the Republican party, in which all his family had been leading members ever since H.H. and Old Dutch Fred Dangberg had quarreled in 1886, and vote for Al Smith, an intention he expressed to his older brother Leo as the two were driving along in Leo's car. Leo was so outraged that he put George out of the car in the middle of the desert and left him there to make his own way home.

Recalling the heated political arguments that used to swirl above my childish head, I do not find this difficult to believe. My Aunt Emma, when in need of a little excitement, would place a photograph of General MacArthur in a prominent position on her sideboard, a maneuver which never failed of its intended effect. Within moments of his arrival my father would be flushed and furious. The mere thought of the monumental egoist who could say "I shall return" without mentioning the American soldiers who would do the actual fighting never failed to arouse his ire.

His arguments with his brothers-in-law were even more tempestuous. My father was always liberal and forward looking; my conservative uncles had not advanced beyond the point when they were all Progressives together in 1912, if they had not come to rather regret that moment of youthful folly. This early atmosphere of heated debate no doubt had something to do with the career I finally settled upon. I was helplessly propelled by an irresistible blast of rhetoric issuing from the living rooms and barns of my youth into the vineyards of political science, where I have labored ever since.

Apart from these animated family discussions, my father's last active involvement in politics was the Wallace party episode in 1948. In that year former vice president Henry Wallace had broken away from the Democrats to form a new Progressive party and seek the presidency. My father was attracted by Wallace's liberal ideas and repelled by the "raw deal" Wallace had received at the hands of the party when he was ousted from the vice presidency four years earlier. As the most prominent Nevadan to align himself with Wallace, George was looked upon as the natural leader of the local party that was beginning to take shape. However, others were scheming to seize control, for in Nevada—as elsewhere—Communists were rapidly infiltrating the Progressive party. I can remember being told one day that the arrival of "Communists from California" was presently anticipated.

Communists from California! I could not have been more intrigued if my father had said the Loch Ness monster would presently undulate its serpentine coils between the wrought iron gates of our driveway. I am not certain what I envisaged, perhaps bearded old men, heavy set, with no ties, who stomped and talked of the "victory of the masses," attended by fanatical women with long, straight, black hair and flat shoes and cold-eyed young men in rimless spectacles who said things like "dialectical materialism." I am afraid I must have stared shamelessly at the thoroughly mundane group of people who eventually materialized on our lawn. I know I listened in vain for "the victory of the masses" or "dialectical materialism" or any hint at all of revolutionary fervor and was thoroughly bored by all I heard. Afterward I could only recall a high-pitched, oddly petulant tone of voice, a kind of plaintive whine, belonging to a sharp-nosed gentleman with thin, gray hair, who sat in the shade of our elm trees and talked at interminable length for most of the afternoon. Some years would pass before I ceased to see Communism in his image, indissolubly associated with complaint.

Sallie and George Springmeyer with their daughter Sally in a donkey cart at the Long Valley ranch about 1940.

Although my father received these people with courtesy, he was actually preparing for a showdown. He had recently taken a drive out to the Long Valley ranch with a good friend. That friend was Bill Bailey, a raw-boned black man, fully six feet six inches tall, the operator of Reno's famous Club Harlem, and a leader in the black community. Together they planned a preamble to the state platform specifically declaring the Progressive party's opposition to Communism, Nazism, and fascism.

The Communists, for their part, had prepared much more than a preamble. Efforts were made to win over Bailey and other black leaders during all-night "discussion sessions" in the dormitory bedrooms of the university with pretty, young women, recently arrived from California for "special seminars." Pleasant as this may have been, the humorous, cynical Bailey

was not so easily seduced, at least not ideologically. He was in
no way deceived concerning their intent.

Although they failed to co-opt Bailey, the Communists had
slight cause to complain, for they succeeded in taking over the
party with very little effort. None of the traditional safeguards
of delegate apportionment or voting criteria were in force at the
big, informal, chaotic meeting intended to organize the Nevada
branch of the Progressive party and simultaneously to serve as
the state convention. Everyone present was automatically a
member with full voting rights—1912, all over again, but this
time the opposition was more formidable than poor Charlie
Reeves. The Communists took care to pack the convention with
enough loyal followers from California to ensure that the vote
would go their way when they needed it.

After the convention had elected him state chairman, my
father promptly introduced the anti-Communist preamble Bailey and he had planned. This met with an enthusiastic reception
from many of the Nevada members, some of whom noted that
it was "time to take a stand" and they were "tired of being
called Communists." Others believed their jobs were already in
jeopardy as a result of the Wallace party's ambiguous relationship to Communism.

The Californians moved quickly to reverse this trend. Elinor
Kahn, one of the leaders in the group and an officer in the
California longshoreman's union, gave a lengthy oration on
"phoney red baiting." As the Californians spoke on, warmly
applauded by their own contingent, while no one else was
permitted to rise and make a point, the Nevadans realized a
filibuster was in progress. In its essentials, this scene foreshad-
owed the Progressive national convention one month later, of
which H. L. Mencken, whose acerb wit often amused my father,
would write: "A plank disclaiming any intention to support the
Russian assassins in every eventuality . . . was first given a hard
parliamentary squeeze by the Moscow fuglemen on the plat-

form, and then bawled to death on the floor. No one who has followed the proceedings can have any doubt that the Communists have come out on top."[11] So too in Nevada.

By evening my father could see well enough what the outcome would be, and the Springmeyer temper was blazing. He was no man to lend his name and reputation to a Communist front organization. He warned the convention that by refusing to deny the party's Communist leanings "we are tacitly accepting the charge." Then, just four hours after his election, he resigned the chairmanship. "I will refuse to head a group which does not have the courage to state its position," he said. "I am not a Communist and am determined to so declare myself."[12]

It was fifty years since he had listened quietly in the ranch living room, a wide-eyed teenager, and watched his father damn Black Wallace and destroy his own political career. He had traveled a long way since then, had fought the great case of the People versus the Southern Pacific, championed the doomed cause of Theodore Roosevelt, and upheld the embattled standard of equal justice during the twenties. Lost causes, one and all, but worth fighting for all the same. He had outlived the Southern Pacific, or at least seen it dwindle to inconsequentiality. He had watched Progressivism metamorphose from Roosevelt's movement to Wallace's. He too had changed, for he was always open to new ideas, independent, moving with the liberal thinkers of his time. Yet some things he had never cared to learn in all those years: he was still no organizer or manipulator, no hand at convention infighting. And that, perhaps, was his undoing, and always had been. More than forty years before, a very young man, just home from college, had started forth on his first campaign; on a June night in 1948, moments before the vote on the disputed preamble was taken and lost, the Unspiked Rail, now nearly seventy years old, picked up his white straw hat and walked out for the last time.

Sallie Maria Ruperti around the time that she met George Springmeyer.

19

Endings

I T ENDED FINALLY. Or perhaps it did not end but only circled in a mysterious way. Confronted on a ride to Horseshoe Bend with a particularly witless horse that had stretched himself over a fallen tree and was too frightened to back away, it was permissible under the Springmeyer code for my father to call him "the brute" but not to curse him more harshly than that nor to strike him, for H.H. had taught his sons from the very beginning never to mistreat a horse. At length my father lifted the animal's forequarters over the tree. Was it prudent, at almost seventy, to lift a horse? Such questions do not occur to a man who believes impossible is the adjective of fools. A few hours later he suffered his first heart attack.

He had aged well, and at first he seemed very little changed. His hair was only a little thinner and still more brown than gray. He had kept the lean, hard Springmeyer face, though the roman nose was now more prominent and hawklike than ever. Only later, when he could no longer ride on the ranch each weekend as he had done for so many years, did the ruddy tan I had always supposed was his natural color begin to recede from his face. The Springmeyers did not run to corpulence, and his slight body had never thickened. But in enforced idleness he began to lose his muscular athleticism. His quick steps grew careful. The hand that held the evening paper began to shake a little. He began to speak sometimes of the friends who had fallen on the battlefields of France nearly forty years before. They had suffered no protracted ministrations to prolong life, no humiliating decline into infirmity, no struggle to live on as the ruined shell of a man. "In the army," he said, "they knew enough to leave a dying man alone." It had been a good way to die.

Although he moved more slowly, he still liked to walk a few blocks along the river on the way to his office. One day on that street he encountered a man he used to know, now grown heavy and ponderous in old age, the sometime friend and some-time nemesis, his polar opposite, who had stalked the fringes of his life for almost half a century. "You know, George," said George Wingfield to my father, "we're the last of the old Gold-field crowd left alive." Even God Almighty had waited on George Wingfield: the bells of Trinity Church down the hill from his bedroom window were never rung on Sunday morn-ings for fear of disturbing his slumbers. But God Almighty does not wait forever. Soon George Wingfield too was gone, and then my father. The prophecy he had confounded as a child was fulfilled nearly eighty years late when his fierce will could no longer command his failing body: in the end he did stay home to die.

The last act of his my mother can remember was laughter, and that is surely as it should be. For the last five years of his life he was partially bedridden at home following a stroke. His speech had slurred a little, but his mind was keen as ever, his interest in politics had never wavered, and one of the larger events in his constricting world was the arrival of the morning newspaper. On that last May morning at Sage, he was sitting up in bed reading the paper in the pretty, yellow bedroom with

French doors that opened out onto a rose garden not yet in bloom. My mother looked in from her morning chores and found him reading a laudatory item about Norman Biltz, the financier and successor to George Wingfield's title as the "King of Nevada." My father still thought of Biltz not as royalty but as the rascal he had known many years ago when he loaned Biltz $30 to get married and Jimmy McKay advanced him the rest. So my father spoke of it and chuckled, and my mother smiled too. I do not think she ever heard him speak again before the heart attack struck him and he died.

Just short of a century from the year Herman and Wilhelmine had set out from Westphalia, my mother climbed through the pine nut trees to the rocky crest of Springmeyer Peak carrying his ashes. That is where he had said he wanted to be. On the mountain in Long Valley overlooking the lands he had loved like the bone of his bone and the flesh of his flesh. And that is where he is. Every time I look at the mountain I feel his presence. Sometimes seeing it is almost like talking to him.

Most of us are there too, or not far away. On a May morning when the iris were blooming, just as they had forty-five years before when my father first brought his bride home, my mother walked down the driveway of Sage for the last time. She said she wanted to end in Long Valley. Where he is. So she lives there still, in the shadow of the mountain. And my cousins and second cousins and third cousins are scattered in Carson City and Reno and the Carson Valley. We are still cast in the Springmeyer mold, although the clear, blue eyes of the first generation rarely turn up anymore. Our eyes are gray or brown or hazel. Perhaps we are also more darkened and clouded within. The moral certainties and the raw courage of the pioneers are shadowed by the ambiguities of our age. We are sadder too; there is less laughter, less warmth, than in those we remember.

And yet, though we have lost much, we are still identifiably Springmeyers. The "Springmeyer temper" remains an expression that requires no explanation in the Carson Valley. We are still vaguely ill at ease in lounge chairs, spurred to ceaseless activity by the ancestral abhorrence of "letting things go" and the unreasoning and ulcer-provoking certainty that everything we do matters a great deal. We are still loners, mulishly stubborn and transparently honest. We retain our taste for those who stand up and are counted and our disdain for pretensions and social distinctions. If the race is not to the swift, if men do not receive as they deserve, and surely we should know by now that they do not, we still find it hard to speak more softly to those we might use with advantage or to buy a victory at the going price. Every battle is still fought the way the old hussar fought them—to the last bullet.

Are we also identifiably German, we who are only a scant two generations removed from the Westphalian earth? I am not certain, but I think we are Lutheran in a bone-deep sense beyond hymn or ritual. We walked out of the church, cast it aside, and no amount of beating could force that obstinate child, my grandfather, to repeat its cant. Yet I think we can understand that supremely stubborn priest rebel who started it all, Martin Luther. Not Luther as he ended, the ally of princes against the mutinous peasantry, but Luther as he began. The Luther who said, when all the powers of his time were ranged against him, "Here I stand. I can do no other, so help me God." As it turned out, dynasties crumbled before him and the medieval universe tilted, never to be the same again. But had it been otherwise, had he failed and been burned at the stake an obscure heretic, he would have done no differently.

My people came from Lutheran country, and though the church that cast its bladed shadow over their lives had changed from Catholic to Lutheran, the old, rebellious Lutheran response to authority endured. For my father and my grandfather, it was only a short step beyond Martin Luther into the godless void where they would venture entirely alone and say,

Springmeyer Peak.

"Here I stand. I can do no other," and ask no help from God or anyone, and damn the consequences. Perhaps in that lonely independence, that indomitable stubbornness, that fierce moral pride, that unyielding conviction that there are certain things a man must do even though his fondest hopes are destroyed in the doing, they were, after all, the unknowing heirs of Martin Luther.

Perhaps we are still peasants too, at least in the consuming preoccupation with the weather that is ineradicably embedded inside us. Even the ones who left have never lost it. In the valley everything depended on the weather; in the towns with air-conditioned buildings where some of us now live and work, it hardly matters if the rain falls or the sun shines. Yet we raise our eyes anxiously to the sky. A Greek chorus of voices murmurs perpetually on in the inner recesses of our minds: late spring frost, few apples will mature; little snow this winter, no melt will trickle down to water the second crop; raging August wind, the windrows of hay will scatter before they are stacked; early fall, the cattle should be driven down from the high country. We raise no apples, we mow no hay, we are far from the high country, yet the valley still tingles in our nerve centers like the hand of an amputated arm.

* * *

As we of the later generations have changed, so has the valley. My cousin Duane Mack, on the home ranch in the shade of the old apple trees, has been troubled by vandals who burn the haystacks. The juniper and pine nut fence posts, now pock-marked with nail holes, still stand as they have stood these hundred years, and the alfalfa my grandfather once tried to root out still grows tall and fine, but it has been necessary to sell some land; a border of boxy, little houses with tiny yards now fringes the ranch. Many years have come and gone since the roving bands of Civil War veterans walked up the lane for the summer harvest and the Indians swung their mattocks under the glass eye of Lyman Frisbie. Now there are only high school boys in search of summer jobs and, for a while, an Indian who consented to work provided he was chauffeured back and forth from his residence some ten miles away. He was chauffeured, for ranch labor is hard to come by these days.

The Dangberg lands have been sold for a price that would have strained the imagination of Old Dutch Fred. Men shake their heads. Whatever you might say about the Dangbergs—and there is plenty you might—at least they knew the water rights, and that you have to grow up with to really understand. It will be hard, they say, having someone new in the valley.

Many new people are already in the valley. The ranchers are there still, but they no longer control county affairs, nor are the old towns of Gardnerville and Genoa the centers. The hub of Douglas County is now the big casinos at the south shore of

Lake Tahoe. The walls of the ranch houses near the highway vibrate as the huge, orange garbage truck rumbles past carrying Tahoe's refuse to the valley. New houses have been built in the mountains. A development, referred to by the older residents in a tone of voice that used to be reserved for the gophers as "those ranchos over there," sits on a treeless, sagebush flat on the eastern side. These are skimpy houses—you feel that several could fit inside an old Carson Valley barn—and they are cramped together as though there were not room enough in this vast sweep of space for a garden or an orchard. But the old dream of the blossoming desert has failed to take hold in the ranchos. The planters of orchards and gardens were buried long ago, and the new people look to other things. The venerable Kingsbury Grade Road, with its precipitous hairpin turns, had been converted to a superhighway, the more quickly to transport pleasure seekers driving in from the north and casino workers, who know nothing of horses or Poland Chinas or getting in the third crop, from their ranchos to Tahoe beyond the rim of the mountains.

I had been told these things, yet did not fully grasp them until we were driving into the valley late at night from an unfamiliar direction, from the east. My husband said we had reached the valley. I denied it. I had thought by all reckoning we should be there, but this could not be our valley. I knew our mountains, not only by their height and their jagged outline but also by their impenetrable black stillness. I had seen them thus so many times when it grew dark and we lit the kerosene lamps in Long Valley. In memory, I saw them still. And these could not be our mountains: they glittered with lights.

My husband was right, of course. The new houses on the mountain and the cars traveling on the superhighway made the lights. And I felt a sense of betrayal. It was as though I had walked past my mother in the street without recognizing her. I had not known our own valley.

Most of the Springmeyers never left. I did. And only came back far too late, not to live but to listen and to recapture what I could of the irredeemably precious heritage I once cast so carelessly aside. When I remember the first time I saw Goldfield, it seems almost like an allegory of what was to come.

I was disappointed. My father, pleased to be walking those streets again, was pointing places out to me, mostly places that no longer existed, for they had been dismantled for lumber or burned in the fire. Nothing remained but a few landmarks—the Goldfield Hotel, the courthouse, the bottle house—and a scattering of forlorn, neglected shacks, a windmill, a dooryard grown ferny with tamarisk. The air shimmered with heat and dust, and I couldn't wait to see Vegas. I said impatiently to my father that there was nothing there. We went on, to Las Vegas and beyond.

Thirty years have passed since then, and Goldfield has not changed much. It is I who have altered beyond recognition; instead of hastening on, I want to look back. Now when I stand on the bare, stony earth of a hill south of Goldfield and look toward Columbia Mountain, it is all there.

Notes

Chapter 1

1. On the invasion of Russia, see Eugene Tarle, *Napoleon's Invasion of Russia, 1812* (New York: Oxford University Press, 1942), esp. pp. 94–97, 357–404.

2. Springer, the closest counterpart to this name in the dictionary of surnames, may be derived from an ancestral farmer in the dell but may also denote an agile forebear or a tumbler at county fairs. "Sprinkmeyer" appears to have been one of the agile variety. See Elsdon C. Smith, *New Dictionary of American Family Names* (New York: Harper & Row, 1973), p. 484.

3. The order has been reversed since Twain was traveling in the other direction. Quoted in Oscar Lewis, *Sea Routes to the Gold Fields* (New York: Alfred A. Knopf, 1949), p. 221. Also see pp. 201–23 on the Nicaragua route.

Chapter 2

1. J. Ross Browne, *A Peep at Washoe and Washoe Revisited* (Balboa Island, California: Paisano Press, 1959), p. 53.

2. Owen E. Jones, "Recollections," *Record Courier*, Sept. 4, 1925.

3. George Springmeyer, "Douglas County," in Sam P. Davis, ed., *The History of Nevada*, Vol. 2 (Los Angeles: Elms Publishing Company, 1913), pp. 806–17.

4. Springmeyer, op. cit., pp. 810–11; also see Jones, loc. cit.

5. *Nevada State Journal,* Sept. 1, 1901.

6. *Genoa Journal,* Oct. 20, 1880.

7. On the term "Dutchman," see Peter Watts, *A Dictionary of the Old West, 1850–1900* (New York: Alfred A. Knopf, 1977), p. 123.

8. Sam P. Davis, "Letter," *San Francisco Daily Examiner,* Feb. 10, 1889, p. 19.

9. On Arbor Day and the Forest Commission, see Legislature, *Journal of the Assembly,* 1887, pp. 87, 94.

Chapter 3

1. "Wild parsnip" was the local term for the deadly water hemlock; on Indian use of the root for suicide, also see Ella M. Cain, *The Story of Early Mono County* (San Francisco: Fearon Publishers, 1961), p. 100.

Chapter 4

1. On the Indian battle in Long Valley, see Jones, loc. cit.

2. On Milich, also see Adam S. Eterovich, *Yugoslavs in Nevada, 1859–1900* (San Francisco: R and E Research Associates, 1973), pp. 73, 90, 130, 179, 196, 232. Lacking the date of Milich's alleged fight with the claim jumpers, I have tentatively placed it before his ride to Long Valley.

3. On Newlands's reclamation plans, see William Lilley, III, "The Early Career of Francis G. Newlands, 1848–1897." (Ph.D. dissertation, Yale University, 1965.)

4. The projected reservoir in Long Valley would contain water diverted through Dutch Valley from a small reservoir to be constructed at Hope Valley on the West Fork of the Carson River and channeled in from the East Fork through a tunnel to be built at Horseshoe Bend. Water from the receiving reservoir would then be distributed by two canals, one to the head of the Carson Valley and the other to the east side to irrigate that region and supply the Empire Mills. See "Statement of Lyman Bridges," *United States Senate Reports,* No. 928, Part 3, Vol. 5, 51 cong., 1st sess., 1889–1890, pp. 498–502.

5. "Report of the Nevada State Board of Reclamation and Internal Improvement," *United States Senate Reports,* No. 928, Part 3, Vol. 5, 51 cong., 1st sess., 1889–1890, pp. 129–45.

6. Mark Twain, *Roughing It* (New York: New American Library, 1962), p. 236.

7. On the Ferris wheel, see the collection at the Carson Valley Historical Society Museum, Genoa, Nevada.

Chapter 5

1. *Genoa Courier*, Dec. 3, 1897.

2. Ibid., Jan. 14, 1898.

3. Alf Chartz, who had been engaged as Uber's attorney, customarily wrote the "Carson Letter" column signed by "Quelquefois." See the *Genoa Courier*, Jan. 7 and 14, 1898.

4. Ibid., Dec. 31, 1897, and Jan. 7, 1898.

5. Ibid., Dec. 17, 1897. A letter, reportedly by Uber, detailing his escape plans, was found in jail. However, this does not foreclose the obvious possibility that the letter was a forgery intended to justify the lynching on the ground that Uber was likely to elude the formal legal process.

6. Ibid., Jan. 14, 1898.

7. Ibid., Jan. 21, 1898.

8. In addition to the last two incidents and the Elges beating recounted by my father, I have included some of the tragedies described in Phillip I. Earl, "Adam Uber, the Murderer Lynched by a Mob," *Nevada Historical Society Quarterly* (Spring 1973), pp. 1–19; and Kenneth Miller, "The Lynching of Adam Uber," (unpublished research paper, 1973, The Henry Van Sickle Library of Materials for the History of the Carson Valley, Minden, Nevada), pp. 8–9.

9. Davis, *The History of Nevada*, Vol. 1, p. 441.

10. On Wallace's role in the campaign to reelect Senator William Stewart in 1898–1899, see Mary E. Glass, *Silver and Politics in Nevada: 1892–1902* (Reno: University of Nevada Press, 1969), pp. 131–60; and Russell R. Elliott, *History of Nevada* (Lincoln: University of Nebraska Press, 1973), pp. 202–8. Wallace's intensive effort in this campaign probably explains why he approached H.H. in 1898—he had not done so in H.H.'s previous legislative contests in 1886, 1888, and 1892. His reasons for selecting H.H. when his own Silver party had an incumbent legislative candidate on the scene are less readily explained, unless he was already laying the groundwork for the eventual return of the Silverites to the Republican party. Martin's substantial victory in the

election suggests that he was a popular candidate who might well have won without any assistance from the Southern Pacific.

Chapter 6

1. *Student Record,* Feb. 1, 1899; on falling asleep in the Carson street, see Browne, op. cit., p. 57.

2. *Student Record,* Feb. 1, 1899, and Sept. 15, 1901.

3. Ibid., Oct. 15, 1901.

4. On Stubbs's views on coeducation, see the *Appendix to the Journals of the Senate and Assembly, 1903,* Report No. 21, p. 19.

5. *Student Record,* Dec. 1, 1899.

6. Ibid., Oct. 1 and Oct. 15, 1901.

7. Ibid., Dec. 15, 1901, and Feb. 1, 1902.

8. *Nevada State Journal,* Feb. 9, 1902.

9. Ibid., Feb. 16, 1902.

10. Statement by the "Committee from the Lincoln Hall Students," published in the *Nevada State Journal,* Feb. 15, 1902.

11. *Nevada State Journal,* Feb. 16, 1902.

12. *Student Record,* Mar. 1, 1902.

13. *Nevada State Journal,* June 5, 1902.

14. Telegram from H. H. Atkinson, quoted in the *Carson City News,* Aug. 26, 1910.

15. *Fallon Eagle,* Oct. 22, 1910.

16. Orrin L. Elliott, *Stanford University* (Stanford, California: Stanford University Press, 1937), p. 385; also see pp. 379–86, and Edith R. Mirrielees, *Stanford* (New York: G. P. Putnam's Sons, 1959), p. 64.

17. On Frankfurter, see Liva Baker, *Felix Frankfurter* (New York: Coward–McCann, 1969), p. 15.

18. *Record Courier,* Aug. 17, 1906.

19. The incumbent attorney general, James Sweeney, was reported to have been the youngest attorney general in the history of the United States when he was elected to the office in 1902 at age twenty-five; see Davis, *The History of Nevada,* Vol. 2, p. 1210. Woodbury was probably the mill owner and one-time county commissioner of Ormsby County.

20. *Carson Appeal,* Aug. 31, 1910.

21. On the subsidized partisan press, see Gilman M. Ostrander, *Nevada: The Great Rotten Borough, 1859–1964* (New York: Alfred A. Knopf, 1966), pp. 125–31.

22. *Record Courier,* Oct. 26, 1906; *Nevada State Journal,* Oct. 25 and Nov. 1, 1906, *Goldfield Daily Tribune,* Oct. 9, 1906.

23. On this incident, also see the *Reno Evening Gazette,* Oct. 3, 1906. Brown was the judge of the fourth judicial district, composed of the counties on Nevada's eastern border.

Chapter 7

1. *Goldfield Daily Tribune,* Jan. 9, 1909. Also see Nov. 27, 1906.

2. On Davis in Idaho, see David H. Grover, "Diamondfield Jack: A Range War in Court," *Idaho Yesterdays,* Vol. 7 (Summer, 1963), pp. 8–14.

3. *Goldfield Daily Tribune,* Jan. 28, 1910. On the Peely Kid, see the April 26, 1909, issue.

4. George G. Rice, *My Adventures with Your Money* (New York: Bookfinger, 1974), p. 149. On Wingfield's business methods, see *Mining and Scientific Press,* Vol. 98 (1909), pp. 430, 499, 514.

5. This incident may be tentatively placed around Mar. 29, 1907, when union difficulties involving the newspapers were reported in the *Reno Evening Gazette.* A similar incident involving Wingfield at a different date is recounted in Carl B. Glasscock, *Gold in Them Hills* (Indianapolis: Bobbs-Merrill Company, 1932), pp. 301–2. On Wingfield's precautionary measures, see the *Reno Evening Gazette,* Mar. 13, 1907.

6. Rice, op. cit., p. 147.

7. Twain, op. cit., p. 168.

8. Clarence Eddy, "John Skinum Binks," *Goldfield Daily Tribune,* Dec. 14, 1910.

9. Twain, op. cit., p. 152.

10. Huntington to Hopkins, April 28, 1869, quoted in Ostrander, op. cit., p. 93. Huntington also noted that Stewart was "peculiar but thoroughly honest and will bear no dictation." On Stewart, also see David A. Johnson, "A Case of Mistaken Identity: William M. Stewart and the Rejection of Nevada's First Constitution," *Nevada Historical Society Quarterly,* Vol. 22 (Fall, 1979), pp. 186–98.

11. Reprinted in the *Nevada State Journal,* Aug. 27, 1902.

12. I am unable to date this encounter; my father told me only that it took place not long before Stewart's death in his Washington, D.C., home on April 23, 1909. An additional source on Stewart is C. C.

Goodwin, *As I Remember Them* (Salt Lake City: Salt Lake Commercial Club, 1913), pp. 140–45.

13. On Fisherman, see the *Carson City Daily Appeal,* Jan. 25, 1923.

14. The number of illegal assayers has been variously estimated at 50 (see Russell R. Elliott, "Labor Troubles in the Mining Camp at Goldfield, Nevada, 1906–1908," *Pacific Historical Review,* Vol. 19 [1950] p. 375), or 60 (see Carl Glasscock, *Gold in Them Hills* [Indianapolis: Bobbs-Merrill Company, 1932], p. 115), or even 106 (see the *Goldfield Daily Tribune,* Oct. 14, 1909). However, Guy L. Rocha finds that estimates of high grading in Goldfield were considerably exaggerated ("Radical Labor Struggles in the Tonopah-Goldfield Mining District, 1901–1922," *Nevada Historical Society Quarterly,* Vol. 20 [Spring, 1977], pp. 15–16). My father believed the number of illegal assayers was small.

15. 60th Cong., 1st sess., *House Exec. Doc.* No. 607, p. 23. On these events, also see Elliott, "Labor Troubles in the Mining Camp at Goldfield, Nevada, 1906–1908," pp. 369–84, and Rocha, op. cit., pp. 3–45.

Chapter 8

1. Twain, op. cit., p. 271.

2. Myron Angel, ed., *History of Nevada* (Oakland: Thompson and West, 1881), p. 340.

3. *Goldfield Daily Tribune,* April 14, 1910.

4. Ibid., Aug. 6 and Oct. 21, 1909.

5. Ibid., June 20–July 3, 1909; also see the *Goldfield Daily News,* June 17–29, 1909.

6. *Goldfield Daily Tribune,* July 18, 1909.

7. Ibid., July 7, 1909.

8. Ibid., June 5, 6, 19, and 26, 1909; also see the *Goldfield Daily News,* May 14, June 4 and 16, and July 19 and 20, 1909, and *Mining and Scientific Press,* Vol. 98, p. 816.

9. *Goldfield Daily News,* July 5, 7, 9, 17, and 19, and Sept. 4 and 10, 1909.

10. *Goldfield Daily Tribune,* May 25, 1910; on Wingfield's injunction suit, see the *Goldfield Daily News,* Nov. 5 and 9, 1909.

11. On the Smith case and other high-grading cases, see the *Goldfield Daily Tribune,* Feb. 15, May 18, May 25–June 15, Oct. 4, and Dec. 9, 1910; also see the *Goldfield Daily News,* June 1 and 4, 1910.

12. *Pacific Reporter,* Vol. 112, p. 273; also see the *Goldfield Daily Tribune,* May 27–29, 1910.

13. Emmett L. Arnold, *Goldcamp Drifter, 1906-1910* (Reno: University of Nevada Press, 1973), p. 144.

14. On the Antonini case, see the *Goldfield Daily Tribune,* May 24, June 1, and Dec. 1–10, 1910.

15. *Goldfield Daily Tribune,* Aug. 25, 1910.

16. On Gibson, see the *Goldfield Daily Tribune,* Jan 29–Feb. 4, Aug. 25, and Dec. 6-20, 1910, and the *Goldfield Daily News,* Dec. 6, 1910.

17. On narcotics, see the *Goldfield Daily Tribune,* Nov. 19 and Dec. 17, 1910; on prostitution, see the *Goldfield Daily News,* May 5, 1910.

Chapter 9

1. *Reno Evening Gazette,* Sept. 3, 1910.

2. Reprinted in the Elko *Weekly Independent,* Nov. 6, 1914.

3. On Collins, see Glasscock, op. cit., pp. 168–169.

4. See Springmeyer's statement in the *Fallon Eagle,* Oct. 31, 1914.

5. Ibid.; also see the letters reprinted in the *Weekly Independent,* Nov. 6, 1914.

6. Ibid.

7. *Ely Expositor,* Aug. 16, 1910.

8. See the public letters from Springmeyer reprinted in the *Carson City News,* Aug. 4, 1910; the *Carson Appeal,* Aug. 31, 1910; and the *Nevada State Journal,* Aug. 31, 1910. See also the report on a speech at an insurgent meeting in Reno in the *Nevada State Journal,* Sept. 1, 1910.

9. See Brown's statements in the *Reese River Reveille,* Aug. 13, 1910, and the *Carson City News,* Aug. 24, 1910.

10. See the *Carson City News,* Aug. 25 and 31 and Sept. 4, 1910, the *Goldfield Daily Tribune,* Aug. 25, 1910, and the *Reno Evening Gazette,* Sept. 3, 1910.

11. *Goldfield Daily News,* June 9, 1910.

12. See the interview in the *Reese River Reveille,* Sept. 3, 1910.

13. *Goldfield Daily News,* July 18, 1910.

14. *Nevada State Journal,* Aug. 27, 1910.

15. *White Pine News,* Sept. 4, 1910; *Reno Evening Gazette,* Aug. 22, 1910.

16. *Goldfield Daily News,* Aug. 26, 1910.

17. On Morehouse, see Boyd Moore, *Persons in the Foreground* (n.p.: 1915), and the *Goldfield Daily Tribune,* Sept. 16, 1909.

18. *Nevada State Journal,* Sept. 1, 1910.

19. *Carson Appeal,* Sept. 1, 1910; *Reno Evening Gazette,* Sept. 3, 1910.

20. *Carson City News,* Sept. 4, 1910.

21. Ibid., Sept. (n.d.), 1910.

22. These statistics appear in Report No. 32, "Official Returns of the Direct Primary Election of 1910," *Appendix to the Journals of the Senate and Assembly, 1911,* Vol. 2, pp. 12–13.

23. George Mowry, *The California Progressives* (Berkeley: University of California Press, 1951), p. 123. On the California Progressives, also see, Spencer C. Olin, *California's Prodigal Sons* (Berkeley: University of California Press, 1968), pp. 11–19.

Chapter 10

1. *Nevada State Journal,* Oct. 4, 1910.

2. *Carson Appeal,* Sept. 23, 1910.

3. Reprinted in the *Carson City News,* Sept. 28, 1910. The first portion of the plank, dealing with the "natural right" of the railroad and the retention of the membership of the existing railroad commission, had been Senator Nixon's suggestion; see the *Goldfield Daily Tribune,* Sept. 7, 1910.

4. *Carson City News,* Sept. 23, 1910. On the platform, also see the editorial in the *Goldfield Daily News,* Sept. 29, 1910; another plank in George's proposed platform, favoring the downward revision of the Payne-Aldrich tariff, was also deleted; however, all specific objectives of the Nevada Lincoln-Roosevelt League—i.e., recall, direct election of United States senators, and the maintenance of the direct primary law —were incorporated in the Republican platform.

5. Oral interview, Reno, Nevada, June 29, 1972.

6. Reprinted in the *Nevada State Journal,* Sept. 29 and 30, 1910.

7. *Nevada State Journal,* Nov. 7, 1910.

8. Mowry, op. cit., p. 16.

9. On "working on the railroad," see Ostrander, op. cit., pp. 75–96.

10. For example, see Sam Davis's speech at a Democratic rally at Rawhide reported in the *Nevada State Journal,* Oct. 13, 1910.

11. See the report on a Democratic rally at Carson City in the *Nevada State Journal,* Sept. 30, 1910.

12. See the editorials in the *Nevada State Journal,* Oct. 7 and 16, 1910.

13. Ibid., Oct. 14, 1910.

14. See the *White Pine News,* Oct. 9, 1910, the report in the *Elko Free Press,* Oct. 13, 1910, on a speech by Springmeyer in Elko, and the report on a Republican rally in Goldfield in the *Goldfield Daily Tribune,* Oct. 25, 1910.

15. See the report on a Republican rally in Goldfield in the *Goldfield Daily Tribune,* Oct. 25, 1910.

16. See the report on Dickerson's speech in Carson City in the *Nevada State Journal,* Oct. 3, 1910.

17. *Carson City News,* Oct. 25, 1910.

18. *White Pine News,* Oct. 3, 1910.

19. On Nixon, see the *Goldfield Daily Tribune,* Nov. 4, 1910; on Oddie, see the Oct. 7, 1910 issue.

20. See the reports in the *Nevada State Journal,* Oct. 17, 1910, on Dickerson's speech in McGill and Sprague's speech in Winnemucca.

21. The unionist also contended that Baker had been present on the docks only in an effort to persuade other students to go home; see the *Nevada State Journal,* Oct. 27, 1910. For a copy of the Springmeyer broadside, see the Newlands Collection, Yale University; on the dock strike, see Walton Bean, *Boss Ruef's San Francisco* (Berkeley: University of California Press, 1952), pp. 11–16.

22. *Nevada State Journal,* Oct. 28, 1910.

23. Ibid., Oct. 16, 1910 (Mina), and Nov. 1, 1910 (Schurz).

24. Ibid., Oct. 28, 1910.

25. Ibid., Nov. 4 and 6, 1910.

26. Ibid., Nov. 8, 1910. On Morgan and Montrose, see the *Goldfield Daily News,* Sept. 19 and Oct. 3, 1910.

27. Pittman to R. J. Mapes, Nov. 18, 1910, quoted in Fred L. Israel, *Nevada's Key Pittman* (Lincoln: University of Nebraska Press, 1963), p. 24.

28. *Goldfield Daily Tribune,* Nov. 9, 1910.

29. *Springmeyer* v. *Baker,* Supreme Court of Nevada, 1911. Also see the *Nevada State Journal,* Oct. 7 and 10, 1911.

30. On the tortuous history of the tax commission, see Romanzo Adams, *Taxation in Nevada* (Reno: Nevada Historical Society, 1918), pp. 61–70.

Chapter 11

1. On the decline of Goldfield, see the *Goldfield Daily Tribune,* Sept. 15 and Nov. 20, 1910, and Jan. 3, 1911.

2. George Springmeyer, "History of the Progressive Party in Nevada," in Davis, ed., *The History of Nevada,* Vol. 1, p. 454.

3. *Nevada State Journal,* Mar. 3, 1912; on Reeves, also see Eric N. Moody, "Nevada's Bull Moose Progressives: The Formation and Function of a State Political Party in 1912," *Nevada Historical Society Quarterly* (Fall, 1973), p. 160.

4. Springmeyer, "History of the Progressive Party in Nevada," p. 454.

5. *Nevada State Journal,* Apr. 6, 1912; in addition to the three primaries mentioned, Moody notes that a partial primary was held in Elko County; see Moody, op. cit., p. 162.

6. *Nevada State Journal,* Apr. 7, 1912.

7. Springmeyer, "History of the Progressive Party in Nevada," p. 454.

8. *Nevada State Journal,* Apr. 9, 1912.

9. Ibid., May 7, 1912.

10. Ibid.

11. Ibid. On Oddie, also see Loren B. Chan, *Sagebrush Statesman: Tasker L. Oddie of Nevada* (Reno: University of Nevada Press, 1973), pp. 60–68.

12. *Nevada State Journal,* May 7, 1912.

13. Ibid., July 24, 1912.

14. Moody, op. cit., pp. 168–170; also see the *Fallon Eagle,* Sept. 14, 1912, and the *Nevada State Journal,* July 24, 1912. On Reeves's near removal from office in White Pine County, see the *Goldfield Daily Tribune,* Apr. 3, 1910.

15. See Judge Thomas's advertisement in the *Nevada State Journal,* Oct. 20, 1912; Paul Flanigan (Oral interview, Reno, Aug. 17, 1974); and Marion Lamb, daughter of Progressive legislative candidate Walter Hastings (Oral interview, Aug. 11–12, 1974).

16. See Isidor Wood's advertisement in the *Nevada State Journal,* Oct. 15, 1912. The letter from Goldfield activist M. B. Aston to Progressive state committee chairman H. B. Lind is quoted in the same advertisement. Also see Summerfield's advertisements in the same newspaper on Oct. 25 and 28, 1912.

17. State ex rel. *Springmeyer* v. *Brodigan,* Supreme Court of Nevada, 1912. *Pacific Reporter,* Vol. 126, pp. 680–88.

18. *Nevada State Journal,* Sept. 15, 1912.

19. See Summerfield's advertisement in the *Nevada State Journal,* Oct. 28, 1912.

Chapter 12

1. On Thatcher's appointment, see the *Goldfield Daily Tribune,* Dec. 8 and 10, 1912. Thatcher had been one of Baker's opponents in the Democratic primary of 1910.

2. State ex. rel. *Thatcher* v. *Brodigan, Pacific Reporter,* Vol. 142, pp. 520–3.

3. *Carson City News,* Sept. 24, 1914; on the Republican convention, also see the *Nevada State Journal,* Sept. 23–25, 1914.

4. State ex. rel. *Maxson* v. *Brodigan, Pacific Reporter,* Vol. 143, pp. 306–7.

5. Testimony of Emmet D. Boyle, *Cole* v. *Ralph,* District Court of the United States, Nevada, 1915, pp. 149–85; *Ralph* v. *Cole, Federal Reporter,* Vol. 249, pp. 81–97.

6. Also see Thomas W. Miller, "Memoirs of Thomas Woodnut Miller, a Public Spirited Citizen of Delaware and Nevada" (Oral History Project: University of Nevada, Reno, 1965), pp. 217–18.

Chapter 13

1. Clipping dated March 29, 1920, in the Springmeyer Collection; also see the *San Francisco Chronicle,* March 31, 1920.

2. *Carson City Daily Appeal,* Nov. 6, 1913.

3. Clipping dated Sept. 21, 1920, Springmeyer Collection; *Reno Evening Gazette,* Sept. 26, 1920.

4. *Reno Evening Gazette,* Sept. 25, 1920.

5. Undated clipping, Springmeyer Collection.

6. Rice, op. cit., p. 149.

7. *Nevada State Journal,* Aug. 14, 1976.

8. John Hersey, "The Old Man," *The New Yorker,* Vol. 23 (Jan. 3, 1948), p. 28.

9. McCarran to Pete Petersen, Apr. 9, 1947, quoted in Jerome E. Edwards, "Patrick A. McCarran: His years on the Nevada Supreme Court, 1913–1918," *Nevada Historical Society Quarterly* (Winter 1975), p. 185.

10. *Goldfield Daily Tribune,* Apr. 14, 1920.

11. Undated clipping, Springmeyer Collection.

12. Not all delegates on the so-called Springmeyer-Norcross Ticket won; a subsequent effort by Springmeyer, Wingfield, and others to secure a recount was rejected by Platt, who had gained control of the county central committee by using proxies from the outlying districts. See the *Nevada State Journal,* March 28–31, 1920.

13. Miller, op. cit., p. 221.

14. On Wood and the 1920 convention, see Francis Russell, *The Shadow of Blooming Grove* (New York: McGraw-Hill Book Company, 1968), pp. 355–96.

15. William G. McLoughlin, Jr., *Billy Sunday Was His Real Name* (Chicago: University of Chicago Press, 1955), pp. 175–76; also see pp. 156, 181–83, and 284.

Chapter 14

1. *Raine* v. *United States,* United States Circuit Court of Appeals, Ninth Circuit, 1924. *Federal Reporter,* Vol. 299, pp. 407–11. Also see the *Carson City Daily Appeal,* Dec. 21, 1922.

2. Undated clipping, Springmeyer Collection.

3. Undated clipping, Springmeyer Collection.

4. Oddie to Springmeyer, Apr. 21, 1922; also see Oddie to Springmeyer, Apr. 11, 1922 (Oddie Collection, Nevada Historical Society).

5. Undated clipping, Springmeyer Collection; also see Miller, op. cit., p. 220.

6. *Carson City Daily Appeal,* May 8, 1924.

7. John Kobler, *Ardent Spirits* (New York: G. P. Putnam's Sons, 1973), esp. pp. 309–314; and Henry Lee, *How Dry We Were* (Englewood Cliffs: Prentice-Hall, 1963), pp. 67–68.

8. Undated clipping, Springmeyer Collection.

9. *Carson City Daily Appeal,* Feb. 10, 1911.

10. *Silver State,* Jan. 18, 1923.

11. *Nevada State Journal,* Jan. 23, 1923; undated clippings, Springmeyer Collection.

12. Four additional officers were requested in populous counties, two in small counties, three in cities, and two in small towns, clipping dated Jan. 18, 1923, Springmeyer Collection.

13. *Ely Record,* Jan. 26, 1923.

14. Clipping dated Jan. 28, 1923, Springmeyer Collection; on the abatement suits, see various undated clippings in the Springmeyer Collection.

15. Undated clipping reporting a speech by State Senator Charles Sprague on Jan. 30, 1923, in the Springmeyer Collection; also see the *Carson City News,* Jan. 31, 1923.

16. Clipping dated Feb. 1, 1923, Springmeyer Collection.

17. Public letter by State Senator Charles Sprague dated Feb. 23, 1925, Springmeyer Collection.

18. See the statement by Assistant Prohibition Director Charles Norcross, *Reno Evening Gazette,* Dec. 15, 1923.

19. *Sacramento Bee,* Aug. 5, 1922. A second assistant was added at the end of 1923.

20. J. E. Sexton to H. C. New, postmaster general, with railroad car photos, Oct. 2, 1924, Springmeyer Collection.

21. *San Francisco Chronicle,* Sept. 2, 1922; *Carson City Daily Appeal,* Nov. 14, 1922; *Nevada State Journal,* Sept. 15, 1922; *Reno Evening Gazette,* Sept. 11, 1922; and other undated clippings in the Springmeyer Collection. Also see Report No. 9, "Biennial Report of the Commissioner of Labor for the Years 1923–1924," *Appendix to the Journals of the Nevada Senate and Assembly, 1925,* pp. 11–12. On the strike and the Harding Administration, see Russell, op. cit., pp. 545–49, and United States Attorney General, *Appendix to the Annual Report, 1922. Lawless Disorders and Their Suppression* (Washington: GPO, 1924), pp. 408–18.

22. Clipping dated 1923, Springmeyer Collection.

23. *Reno Evening Gazette,* Nov. 13, 1923, and other undated clippings in the Springmeyer Collection.

24. Raine was acquitted of murder charges in the Eureka County District Court in April 1923; in November 1923, in the Federal District Court, he was found guilty of manufacturing liquor, and his conviction was subsequently upheld on appeal. See *Raine* v. *United States,* United States Circuit Court of Appeals, Ninth Circuit, 1924. *Federal Reporter,* Vol. 299, pp. 407–11. Also see the *Carson City Daily Appeal,* Dec. 21, 1922, Apr. 21, 1923, and Nov. 9, 1923.

Chapter 15

1. *White Pine News,* Jan. 28, 1923, and undated clippings in the Springmeyer Collection.

2. *Kennedy* v. *United States,* United States Circuit Court of Appeals, Ninth Circuit, 1925. *Federal Reporter,* Vol. 5, 2nd series, pp. 132–33. *Kennedy et al.* v. *United States,* United States Circuit Court of Appeals, Ninth Circuit, 1925. *Federal Reporter,* Vol. 4, 2nd series, pp. 488–90.

3. *Ritter* v. *United States,* United States Circuit Court of Appeals, Ninth Circuit, 1923. *Federal Reporter,* Vol. 293, pp. 187–89.

4. *Reno Evening Gazette,* Sept. 22, 1923; on the raids, also see the Feb. 28 issue.

5. *Hacker* v. *United States,* United States Circuit Court of Appeals, Ninth Circuit, 1925. *Federal Reporter,* Vol. 5, 2nd series, pp. 132–33; also see the *Carson City Daily Appeal,* May 1, 1924; the *Nevada State Journal,* Dec. 1, 1925; and the testimony of F. F. English in *United States* v. *Rickman et al.,* District Court of the United States, Nevada, 1924.

Chapter 16

1. U.S. Attorney General, *Annual Report, 1923,* p. 169; *Annual Report,* 1922, p. 164.

2. Speech by William D. Foulke in Washington, D.C., Nov. 7, 1923, Springmeyer Collection.

3. *Nevada State Journal,* Jan. 15, 1925.

4. Judge Farrington's remarks were made upon publication of the grand jury report investigating Prohibition enforcement in Nevada. See *Silver State,* Jan. 18, 1923.

5. Clipping marked "*News,* 4/29/24," Springmeyer Collection.

6. Undated clipping, Springmeyer Collection; on the letters, see the *Carson City Daily Appeal,* Sept. 29, 1923.

7. *Nevada State Journal,* Mar. 20, 1923, also see an undated clipping from the *Reno Evening Gazette* in the Springmeyer Collection, and the interrogation of Donnelley by Special Agent Alf Oftedal and others on Nov. 13, 1925, in the file of *United States* v. *Donnelley,* District Court of the United States, Nevada, 1924, in the Federal Archives, San Bruno, California.

8. *Carson City Daily Appeal,* Nov. 17, 1923, and undated clippings in the Springmeyer Collection.

9. See the *Reno Evening Gazette,* Mar. 23, 1925, and the *Carson City Daily Appeal,* Apr. 26, 1924. Also see G. Scott to J. P. Donnelley, July 8, 1922, and the affidavit of John P. Donnelley in *United States* v. *Donnelley,* and Tasker L. Oddie to George Wingfield, Jan. 18, 1924, Oddie Collection.

10. Undated clipping, Springmeyer Collection.

11. Norcross was then a partner of Wingfield's lieutenants, Thatcher and Woodburn. See a clipping dated Jan. 15, Springmeyer Collection; Donnelley affidavit; Motion to Set Aside and Quash Indictment; and Demurrer and Motion to Strike Motion to Quash and Set Aside Indictment, *United States* v. *Donnelley.*

12. *Reno Evening Gazette,* Mar. 23, 1925.

13. Mabel W. Willebrandt, *The Inside of Prohibition* (Indianapolis: Bobbs-Merrill Company, 1929), pp. 242–43; *Supreme Court Reporter,* Vol. 48, Oct. term, 1927, pp. 400–3; *U.S. Reports,* Vol. 276, pp. 505–18; and the briefs filed for Donnelley's appeal.

14. *Reno Evening Gazette,* Sept. 22, 1923.

15. *Nevada State Journal,* Nov. 19, 1923. On Mayor Roberts's orientation, see the *Carson City Daily Appeal,* May 9 and Dec. 3, 1923. Springmeyer had allegedly favored Harry Stewart, Roberts's opponent, in the mayoral election; see Fred J. Siebert to Tasker L. Oddie, Apr. 20, 1923, Oddie Collection, Nevada Historical Society.

16. *Reno Evening Gazette,* Sept. 22, 1923.

17. Undated clipping, Springmeyer Collection.

18. On the bedroom window shooting, see the *Carson City Daily Appeal,* Sept. 20, 1922; on Bassett's 1924 trial, see the Apr. 29, 1924 issue. On Bassett, Turner, and Byrne, see the issues of Aug. 15, 21, 28, and 29, 1925; Sept. 3 and 9, 1925; Oct. 10, 1925; Dec. 17–23, 1925; Jan. 14–18, 1926; and Mar. 21, 1926. Also see the *Reno Evening Gazette,* Sept. 9 and 12, Aug. 25, and Dec. 17, 19, and 22, 1925. Bassett's "Ranch 101" was probably named after the famed Harlem nightclub of the period.

Chapter 17

1. *Carson City Daily Appeal,* Nov. 17, 1923.

2. Although the date of this interview is unknown, I would place it during August-September 1923, when Oddie was in Nevada, the Tonopah raids had recently occurred, and the proceedings against the Goldfield Hotel, which was abated in late November 1923, were under

way. On Newton Crumley's purchase of the Goldfield Hotel, see the *Carson City Daily Appeal,* July 17, 1923; its abatement and the guilty pleas filed by Crumley's partner, George Holstein, are reported in the Nov. 23 and 26 issues; on the Tonopah-Goldfield raids, see the June 21 and Sept. 7 issues; on Grant Crumley's partnership with Wingfield in the Tonopah Mining Company, see the Oct. 29, 1924 issue. Wingfield's nomination by Grant Crumley is reported in the *Carson City News,* Apr. 25, 1920; on the purchase of all Bonanza Hotel Company stock from Wingfield by Newton Crumley and Holstein, see the *Goldfield Daily Tribune,* Sept. 7, 1923.

3. Tasker L. Oddie to George Springmeyer, Apr. 11, 1922, Oddie Collection.

4. Tasker L. Oddie to Clarence Oddie, Feb. 17, 1925, Oddie Collection.

5. Undated clipping, Springmeyer Collection.

6. Miller interview; Tasker L. Oddie to Clarence Oddie, Feb. 17, 1925, and to George Wingfield on Jan. 10, 1924, Feb. 2, 1924, and Feb. 24, 1924, Oddie Collection. In the last of these letters, Oddie reported Springmeyer had agreed to resign if he was not handling his office properly.

7. George Springmeyer to Tasker L. Oddie, Sept. 15, 1924, Oddie Collection.

8. *Nevada State Journal,* July 27, 1927; on the Dangbergs, see the discussion of *U.S.* v. *Alpine Land and Reservoir Company* in Grace Dangberg, *Conflict on the Carson* (Minden: Carson Valley Historical Society, 1975), pp. 190–92, esp. the footnote on p. 192.

9. George Springmeyer to the editor of the *Reno Evening Gazette,* Mar. 8, 1926, Oddie Collection; George Springmeyer to Tasker L. Oddie, Mar. 8, 1926, Oddie Collection.

10. Graham Sanford to Tasker L. Oddie, Mar. 14, 1925, Oddie Collection.

11. Tasker L. Oddie to E. C. Finney, Mar. 20, 1925, Oddie Collection; also see Oddie's letters to John Sargent, the attorney general (July 26, 1925, and Jan. 9, 1926), and the letter of Harlan Stone, attorney general, to Oddie on Dec. 23, 1924, also in the Oddie Collection.

12. John Sargent, attorney general, to Tasker L. Oddie, July 31, 1925, Oddie Collection.

13. *Tonopah Daily Bonanza,* June 14, 1926.

14. *Carson City Daily Appeal,* Oct. 18, 1926.

15. *Nevada State Journal,* Dec. 13, 1923.

16. U.S. Attorney General, *Annual Report,* 1923, p. 169; *Annual Report*, 1924, p. 170; *Annual Report,* 1925, pp. 154, 163, 185, 187. Figures on the number tried on criminal charges in every thousand of the adult population were based on the total convicted and acquitted and the census department figures for the population twenty years of age and over in 1920 and twenty-one years of age and over in 1930. Population changes were calculated as though they were evenly dispersed over the intercensal decade.

17. On McKay and Graham, see Barbara C. Thornton, "George Wingfield in Nevada from 1896 to 1932," (master's thesis, University of Nevada, 1967), p. 61. Also see Laura Vitray series, 1931, George Wingfield vertical file, Nevada Historical Society.

18. *Carson City Daily Appeal,* Dec. 17 and 27, 1923.

19. *Carson City Daily Appeal,* Dec. 31, 1923, and Jan. 17, 1924; also see the transcript of the testimony on the search warrant before the United States commissioner on Jan. 4, 1924, in the Federal Archives, San Bruno, California, and *United States* v. *McKay et al.* District Court of the United States, Nevada, 1924, *Federal Reporter,* Vol. 2, 2nd series, pp. 257–60.

20. *Carson City Daily Appeal,* Mar. 17, 1924, and the *Nevada State Journal,* Mar. 18, 1924.

21. *State* v. *Malley et al.*, District Court of Ormsby County, Nevada, 1927, George Wingfield testimony, pp. 1062–64. Although my father did not say who the speaker was during the scene of attempted blackmail recounted here, it is probable that McKay, whom my father seemed to regard as the leader of the bootlegger group, was also the primary spokesman.

22. On these events, see the *Carson City Daily Appeal,* May 18, July 16, Nov. 10, and Dec. 29, 1925. Although my father's term expired in April, his successor's confirmation was delayed until June.

23. The McKay case was finally dismissed in 1937. On the appointment of Springmeyer's successor, see Harry H. Atkinson, "Tonopah and Reno Memories of a Nevada Attorney," (Oral History Project: University of Nevada, Reno, 1967), pp. 65–66, and Tasker L. Oddie to George Wingfield, Mar. 12, 1926, Oddie Collection. Also see Oddie's letters to Wingfield of Feb. 6 and Feb. 10, 1926.

24. United States Attorney General, *Annual Report,* 1925, p. 181; *Annual Report,* 1929, p. 145. The percentage of nol pros and discontinued cases was determined as the portion such cases comprise of total

cases terminated; on nol pros as a national abuse, see Willebrandt, op. cit., p. 138.

Chapter 18

1. *Goldfield Daily Tribune,* Jan. 11, 1911.

2. Newspaper essay by John P. Medbury dated 1921, Springmeyer Collection.

3. On Moran, see the *Goldfield Daily News,* Dec. 10, 1910, and an undated clipping in the Springmeyer Collection.

4. New York *Daily News,* Feb. 12, 1927. Also see undated clippings in the Springmeyer Collection and George N. Fenin and William K. Everson, *The Western,* revised ed. (New York: Grossman Publishers, 1973), pp. 74–105.

5. Undated clipping in the Springmeyer Collection from the *Washington Post.*

6. For a kindly but inaccurate version of these events, see Miller, op. cit., p. 220.

7. The letters quoted in these paragraphs are from a file entitled "Samples of letters received by Reno lawyers" in the Springmeyer Collection; there are no notations to indicate which attorneys received the letters.

8. Ruth Shaw (Interview, August 1976).

9. Undated letter from Ralph P. Merritt to Robert B. Cozzens, quoted in Michi Weglyn, *Years of Infamy* (New York: William Morrow and Company, 1976), p. 100. Also see U.S. Attorney General, *Annual Report,* 1943, pp. 6–11; *Annual Report,* 1944, pp. 8–9.

10. Bruce Thompson (Interview, August 1975). On the Alien Enemy Hearing Boards, also see Francis Biddle, *In Brief Authority* (New York: Doubleday & Company, 1962), pp. 205–26.

11. *Baltimore Evening Sun,* July 26, 1948.

12. See the *Reno Evening Gazette,* June 25, 1948, and the *Nevada State Journal* of the same date. Bailey was elected a delegate to the national convention but refused to attend. On these and other aspects of the Wallace Progressives, I am indebted to William Bailey (Interview, Feb. 25, 1977), and to my mother.

Bibliography

Articles

Brown, Hugh. "Letter." *Reese River Reveille,* Aug. 13, 1910.

———. "Letter." *Carson City News,* Aug. 24, 1910.

Davis, Sam P. "Letter." *San Francisco Examiner,* Feb. 10, 1889, 19.

Earl, Phillip I. "Adam Uber, the Murderer Lynched by a Mob." *Nevada Historical Society Quarterly* 16 (Spring 1973): 1–19.

Eddy, Clarence. "John Skinum Binks," poem. *Goldfield Daily Tribune,* Dec. 14, 1910.

Edwards, Jerome E. "Patrick A. McCarran: His Years on the Nevada Supreme Court, 1913–1918." *Nevada Historical Society Quarterly* 18 (Winter 1975), 185–205.

Elliott, Russell R. "Labor Troubles in the Mining Camp at Goldfield, Nevada, 1906–1908." *Pacific Historical Review* 19 (1950), 369–84.

Grover, David H. "Diamondfield Jack: A Range War in Court." *Idaho Yesterdays* 7 (Summer 1963), 8–14.

Hersey, John. "The Old Man." *The New Yorker* 23 (Jan. 3, 1948), 28–37.

Johnson, David A. "A Case of Mistaken Identity: William M. Stewart and the Rejection of Nevada's First Constitution." *Nevada Historical Society Quarterly* 22 (Fall 1979), 186–98.

Jones, Owen E. "Recollections." Gardnerville *Record Courier,* Sept. 4, 1925.

Lincoln Hall Students. "Statement from the Committee." *Nevada State Journal,* Feb. 15, 1902.

Medbury, John P. "Essay." 1921, Springmeyer Collection.

Moody, Eric N. "Nevada's Bull Moose Progressives: The Formation and Function of a State Political Party in 1912." *Nevada Historical Society Quarterly* 16 (Fall 1973), 157–79.

Rocha, Guy L. "Radical Labor Struggles in the Tonopah-Goldfield Mining District, 1901–1922." *Nevada Historical Society Quarterly.* 20 (Spring 1977), 3–45.

Sprague, Charles. "Letter." Springmeyer Collection, Feb. 1, 1923.

Springmeyer, George. "Douglas County," in *The History of Nevada,* Vol. 1, Edited by Sam P. Davis. (Reno and Los Angeles: Elms Publishing Company, 1913) pp. 806–7.

———. "History of the Progressive Party in Nevada," in *The History of Nevada,* Vol. 1, Edited by Sam P. Davis (Reno and Los Angeles: Elms Publishing Company, 1913), pp. 453–57.

———. "Letter." *Carson City News,* Aug. 4, 1910.

———. "Letter." *Carson Appeal,* Aug. 31, 1910.

Books

Adams, Romanzo. *Taxation in Nevada.* Reno: Nevada Historical Society, 1918.

Angel, Myron, ed. *History of Nevada.* Oakland: Thompson and West, 1881.

Arnold, Emmett L. *Goldcamp Drifter, 1906–1910.* Reno: University of Nevada Press, 1973.

Baker, Liva. *Felix Frankfurter.* New York: Coward-McCann, 1969.

Bean, Walton. *Boss Ruef's San Francisco.* Berkeley: University of California Press, 1952.

Biddle, Francis. *In Brief Authority.* New York: Doubleday & Company, 1962.

Browne, J. Ross. *A Peep at Washoe and Washoe Revisited.* Balboa Island, California: Paisano Press, 1959.

Cain, Ella M. *The Story of Early Mono County.* San Francisco: Fearon Publishers, 1961.

Chan, Loren B. *Sagebrush Statesman: Tasker L. Oddie of Nevada.* Reno: University of Nevada Press, 1973.

Dangberg, Grace. *Conflict on the Carson.* Minden, Nevada: Carson Valley Historical Society, 1975.

Davis, Sam P. *The History of Nevada.* 2 vols. Reno and Los Angeles: Elms Publishing Company, 1913.

Elliott, Orrin L. *Stanford University.* Stanford, California: Stanford University Press, 1937.

Elliott, Russell R. *History of Nevada.* Lincoln: University of Nebraska Press, 1973.

Eterovich, Adam S. *Yugoslavs in Nevada, 1859–1900.* San Francisco: R and E Research Associates, 1973.

Fenin, George N., and Everson, William K. *The Western.* Revised ed. New York: Grossman Publishers, 1973.

Glass, Mary E. *Silver and Politics in Nevada.* Reno: University of Nevada Press, 1969.

Glasscock, Carl B. *Gold in Them Hills.* Indianapolis: Bobbs-Merrill Company, 1932.

Goodwin, C. C. *As I Remember Them.* Salt Lake City: Salt Lake Commercial Club, 1913.

Israel, Fred L. *Nevada's Key Pittman.* Lincoln: University of Nebraska Press, 1963.

Kobler, John. *Ardent Spirits.* New York: G. P. Putnam's Sons, 1973.

Lee, Henry. *How Dry We Were.* Englewood Cliffs: Prentice-Hall, 1963.

Lewis, Oscar. *Sea Routes to the Gold Fields.* New York: Alfred A. Knopf, 1949.

McLoughlin, William G. *Billy Sunday Was His Real Name.* Chicago: University of Chicago Press, 1955.

Mirrielees, Edith R. *Stanford.* New York: G. P. Putnam's Sons, 1959.

Moore, Boyd. *Persons in the Foreground.* n.p., 1915.

Mowry, George. *The California Progressives.* Berkeley: University of California Press, 1951.

Olin, Spencer C. *California's Prodigal Sons.* Berkeley: University of California Press, 1968.

Ostrander, Gilman M. *Nevada: The Great Rotten Borough, 1859–1964.* New York: Alfred A. Knopf, 1966.

Rice, George G. *My Adventures with Your Money.* New York: Bookfinger, 1974.

Russell, Francis. *The Shadow of Blooming Grove.* New York: McGraw-Hill Book Company, 1968.

Smith, Elsdon C. *New Dictionary of American Family Names.* New York: Harper & Row, 1973.

Tarle, Eugene. *Napoleon's Invasion of Russia, 1812.* New York: Oxford University Press, 1942.

Twain, Mark. *Roughing It.* New York: New American Library, 1962.

Watts, Peter. *A Dictionary of the Old West, 1850–1900.* New York: Alfred A. Knopf, 1977.

Weglyn, Michi. *Years of Infamy.* New York: William Morrow and Company, 1976.

Willebrandt, Mabel W. *The Inside of Prohibition.* Indianapolis: Bobbs-Merrill Company, 1929.

Court Cases

Cole v. *Ralph.* District Court of the United States, Nevada, 1915.

Donnelley v. *United States.* Supreme Court of the United States, 1927–28. *Supreme Court Reporter,* 48, 400–3; *United States Reports,* 276, 505–518.

Hacker v. *United States.* United States Circuit Court of Appeals, Ninth Circuit, 1925. *Federal Reporter,* 5, 2nd series, 132–33.

Kennedy v. *United States.* United States Circuit Court of Appeals, Ninth Circuit, 1925. *Federal Reporter,* 4, 2nd series, 486–88.

Kennedy et al. v. *United States.* United States Circuit Court of Appeals, Ninth Circuit, 1925. *Federal Reporter,* 4, 2nd series, 488–90.

Raine v. *United States.* United States Circuit Court of Appeals, Ninth Circuit, 1924. *Federal Reporter,* 299, 407–11.

Ralph v. *Cole.* United States Circuit Court of Appeals, Ninth Circuit, 1918. *Federal Reporter,* 249, 81–97.

Ritter v. *United States.* United States Circuit Court of Appeals, Ninth Circuit, 1923. *Federal Reporter,* 293, 187–89.

Springmeyer v. *Baker.* Supreme Court of Nevada, 1911.

State v. *Grimmett.* Supreme Court of Nevada, 1910. *Pacific Reporter,* 112, 273.

State v. *Malley et al.* District Court of Ormsby County, Nevada, 1927.

State ex rel. Maxson v. *Brodigan.* Supreme Court of Nevada, 1914. *Pacific Reporter,* 143, 306–7.

State ex rel. Springmeyer v. *Brodigan.* Supreme Court of Nevada, 1912. *Pacific Reporter,* 126, 680–88.

State ex rel. Thatcher v. *Brodigan.* Supreme Court of Nevada, 1914. *Pacific Reporter,* 142, 520–23.

United States v. *Donnelley,* District Court of the United States, Nevada, 1924.

United States v. *McKay et al.,* District Court of the United States, Nevada, 1924.

United States v. *Rickman et al.* District Court of the United States, Nevada, 1924.

Government Documents

Congress. House. 60th Cong., 1st sess., House Exec. Doc. No. 607.
———. Senate. *United States Senate Reports,* No. 928, Part 3, Vol 5, 51st Cong., 1st sess., 1889–90.
Legislature. *Appendix to the Journals of the Senate and Assembly,* 1903–11.
———. *Journal of the Assembly,* 1887.
State Labor Commissioner. "Biennial Report of the Commissioner of Labor for the Years 1923–1924." *Appendix to the Journals of the Senate and Assembly,* 1925.
United States Attorney General. *Annual Report,* 1922, 1923, 1924, 1925, 1926, 1929, 1943, 1944.
———. *Appendix to the Annual Report. Lawless Disorders and Their Suppression,* 1922.

Interviews

Bailey, William. Edgemont, South Dakota. Feb. 25, 1977.
Flanigan, Paul. Reno, Nevada. Aug. 17, 1974.
Lamb, Marion. Carson City, Nevada. Aug. 11–12, 1974.
Miller, Thomas W. Reno, Nevada. June 29, 1972.
Shaw, Ruth. Minden, Nevada. Aug. 1976.
Thompson, Bruce. Reno, Nevada. Aug. 1975.

Newspapers and Periodicals

Baltimore Evening Sun
Carson City Daily Appeal
Carson City News
Daily News (New York)

Elko Free Press
Ely Expositor
Ely Record
Fallon Eagle
Genoa Courier
Genoa Journal
Goldfield Daily News
Goldfield Daily Tribune
Mining and Scientific Press
Morning Appeal (Carson City)
Nevada State Journal
Record Courier (Gardnerville)

Reese River Reveille (Austin)
Reno Evening Gazette
Sacramento Bee
San Francisco Chronicle
San Francisco Examiner
Silver State (Winnemucca)
Student Record (University of
    Nevada, Reno)
Tonopah Daily Bonanza
Washington Post
Weekly Independent (Elko)
White Pine News

Oral Histories, Manuscript Collections, and Other Unpublished Materials

Atkinson, Harry H. "Tonopah and Reno Memories of a Nevada Attorney." Oral History Project, University of Nevada, Reno, 1967.

Lilley III, William. "The Early Career of Francis G. Newlands, 1848–1897." Ph.D. Dissertation, Yale University, 1965.

Miller, Kenneth. "The Lynching of Adam Uber." Research paper, Henry Van Sickle Library Collection, Minden, Nevada, 1973.

Miller, Thomas W. "Memoirs of Thomas Woodnut Miller, a Public Spirited Citizen of Delaware and Nevada." Oral History Project, University of Nevada, Reno, 1965.

Newlands Collection, Yale University.

Oddie Collection, Nevada Historical Society, Reno, Nevada.

Springmeyer Collection, private.

Thornton, Barbara C. "George Wingfield in Nevada from 1896 to 1932." Master's thesis, University of Nevada, Reno, 1967.

Wingfield, George, vertical file, Nevada Historical Society.